OXFORD STUDIES IN EUROPEAN LAW

Coherence in EU Competition Law

OXFORD STUDIES IN EUROPEAN LAW

Series Editors
Paul Craig, Professor of English Law at St John's College, Oxford and
Gráinne de Búrca, Professor of Law at New York University School of Law

The aim of this series is to publish important and original research on EU law. The focus is on scholarly monographs, with a particular emphasis on those which are interdisciplinary in nature. Edited collections of essays will also be included where they are appropriate. The series is wide in scope and aims to cover studies of particular areas of substantive and of institutional law, historical works, theoretical studies, and analyses of current debates, as well as questions of perennial interest such as the relationship between national and EU law and the novel forms of governance emerging in and beyond Europe. The fact that many of the works are interdisciplinary will make the series of interest to all those concerned with the governance and operation of the EU.

OTHER TITLES IN THIS SERIES

Foreign Policy Objectives in European Constitutional Law
Joris Larik

Economic Governance in Europe
Comparative Paradoxes and Constitutional Challenges
Federico Fabbrini

Private Regulation and the Internal Market
Sports, Legal Services, and Standard Setting in EU Economic Law
Mislav Mataija

The EU Deep Trade Agenda
Law and Policy
Billy A. Melo Araujo

The Human Rights of Migrants and Refugees in European Law
Cathryn Costello

An Ever More Powerful Court?
The Political Constraints of Legal Integration in the European Union
Dorte Sindbjerg Martinsen

The Concept of State Aid under EU Law
From internal market to competition and beyond
Juan Jorge Piernas López

Justice in the EU
The Emergence of Transnational Solidarity
Floris de Witte

The Euro Area Crisis in Constitutional Perspective
Alicia Hinarejos

The European Fundamental Freedoms
A Contextual Approach
Pedro Caro de Sousa

National Identity in EU Law
Elke Cloots

The Constitutional Foundations of European Contract Law
A Comparative Analysis
Kathleen Gutman

The Criminalization of European Cartel Enforcement
Theoretical, Legal, and Practical Challenges
Peter Whelan

Fundamental Rights in Europe
Challenges and Transformations in Comparative Perspective
Federico Fabbrini

The Principle of Loyalty in EU Law
Marcus Klamert

Constitutional Pluralism in the EU
Klemen Jaklic

EU Consumer Law and Human Rights
Iris Benöhr

The Principle of Mutual Recognition in EU Law
Christine Janssens

Coherence in EU Competition Law

WOLF SAUTER
Professor of Economic Law, Tilburg University

OXFORD
UNIVERSITY PRESS

OXFORD
UNIVERSITY PRESS

Great Clarendon Street, Oxford, OX2 6DP,
United Kingdom

Oxford University Press is a department of the University of Oxford. It furthers the University's objective of excellence in research, scholarship, and education by publishing worldwide. Oxford is a registered trade mark of Oxford University Press in the UK and in certain other countries

First Edition published in 2016

Published in the United States of America by Oxford University Press
198 Madison Avenue, New York, NY 10016, United States of America

British Library Cataloguing in Publication Data
Data available

Library of Congress Control Number: 2016936070

ISBN 978–0–19–874915–8

Series Editors' Preface

Competition law has been a central feature of substantive EU law from the very inception of the Community. The ECJ laid the juridical foundations for the law in this area in seminal judgments delivered in the 1960s and 1970s and the jurisprudence has developed since then, with the Court of First Instance (as it then was) playing a leading role in the years after the Single European Act. The development of the courts' case law has been matched by increased academic scholarship, the range and variety of which bears testimony to the intellectual and pragmatic interest generated by this body of law. This scholarship examines competition law from a plethora of perspectives, including doctrinal, historical, theoretical and functional. This is unsurprising given the various roles played by competition law in relation to European integration. The foundational precepts now found in Articles 101 and 102 TFEU serve, inter alia, to promote economic efficiency, and at the same time protect the single market against partition by private actors through the instrumentality of cartel agreements and the like.

Wolf Sauter's study is a valuable addition to this rich literature. It analyses competition law from a perspective that has not been considered in depth thus far, which is that of coherence, asking what degree of coherence exists in EU competition law, how this coherence can be explained, and how it contributes to the legitimacy and effectiveness of EU competition law. The study focuses on competition law in the immediate sense of the prohibitions on cartels and abuse of dominant position, and also covers a broader range of material, including mergers, state aid and the sectoral competition regimes for electronic communications and energy.

The book draws on conceptions of coherence developed in the philosophical literature. Sauter distinguishes between two types of coherence. External coherence locates EU competition law within the overall system of EU law and the process of European integration, exploring the objectives of competition law and the way in which it safeguards the internal market. Internal coherence addresses the system of EU competition law itself, distinguishing between EU competition law as a whole, its individual norms and its enforcement and judicial review by the Commission and the European Courts, as well as by national competition authorities and national courts.

The search for coherence is set against the decentralized regime for competition enforcement that was established at the turn of the new millennium, and the author examines the principal sources and mechanisms to ensure coherent application of EU competition law, asking whether they suffice to ensure its legitimacy and effectiveness. He explores how the substantive and institutional complexity of competition law can be managed in various ways, including through common norms, procedures and remedies, institutions, coordination and hierarchy, thereby controlling complexity, reducing divergence and promoting coherence.

The book will be of interest to all those with a specialist interest in competition law, and also to those who wish to reflect more generally on the tensions between coherence and diversity within a specific area of EU law.

Paul Craig and Gráinne de Búrca

Acknowledgements

This book started as a research project that I kept in reserve for five years after first formulating it in the context of a job application that was unsuccessful (probably justifiably so, but not, I believe, on account of the proposal). I picked it up again when (i) the topic gained in significance, (ii) there was a ten-year anniversary of EU competition law modernization in the wings, and (iii) I saw a window of opportunity to write it up. Coincidentally, since then my non-academic career has also swung back in the direction of general competition policy, at least provisionally, after having focused on sector specific competition policy (albeit both in relation to healthcare) over much of the past decade.

This book could not have been completed without the generous help of others, who I would like to briefly acknowledge here.

First of all I would like to thank the series editors, Paul Craig and Gráinne de Búrca, for supporting this project, and the OUP's anonymous referees for their critical comments on the proposal.

I am grateful for the thoughtful comments and criticism received at various stages of the research as well as on individual chapters by Pieter van Cleynenbreugel, Kevin Coates, Juliette Enser, Leigh Hancher, Christian Joerges, Pierre Larouche, Giorgio Monti, Harm Schepel, Heike Schweitzer, and Rein Wesseling. I owe a particular debt of gratitude to Erik Kloosterhuis who read and commented on the manuscript as a whole.

The Tilburg Law and Economics Centre (TILEC) at Tilburg University funded invaluable research assistance provided there by Charlotte Aardoom. It also forms a stimulating research community from which I have benefitted immensely over the past eight years. This book may serve in paying back a small part of this intellectual debt. Among TILEC members not already referred to above I would like to mention especially Cédric Argenton, Panos Delimatsis, and Ilse Streng for their backing.

At the strategy and legal affairs directorate of the Dutch Healthcare Authority I would like to thank foremost Misja Mikkers and Annemiek van der Laan for encouraging my research activities. The same more recently holds true for Bart Broers of the healthcare taskforce at the Dutch competition authority (ACM). However, please note that all opinions expressed in this book are the author's.

The staff at OUP, Alex Flach, Natasha Flemming, Gemma Parsons, and Elinor Shields have been unfailingly helpful and professional throughout the process of producing this book.

Finally I would like to acknowledge the support from my family, especially my children Zachary, Aäron, and Zoë. This book is dedicated to them.

Contents

Table of Cases

CASE LAW CJEU

CASE LAW GENERAL COURT

COMPETITION CASES COMMISSION

AMICUS CURIAE (CHRONOLOGICAL)

NATIONAL CASES (CHRONOLOGICAL)

COMPETITION CASES NCAS

OTHER DOCUMENTS

Table of Legislation

TREATIES

REGULATIONS

DIRECTIVES

PROPOSALS

COMMISSION DECISIONS

COMMISSION NOTICES

COMMISSION COMMUNICATION

COMMISSION WORKING GROUP

COMMISSION STAFF WORKING DOCUMENT/PAPER

COMMISSION INTERPRETATIVE COMMISSIONS

Guidelines

GREEN PAPERS

White papers

COUNCIL RESOLUTIONS

European Parliament Resolutions

RECOMMENDATIONS

STATEMENTS/REST CATEGORIE?

I

Introduction, Concepts, and Questions

1. Introduction

European Union (EU) competition law is an area of exclusive competence of the Union (where there is an effect on trade) that is managed by the European Commission. Following modernization ten years ago, however, the enforcement of its antitrust dimension (cartels and dominance abuse) has been decentralized in large part to national competition authorities (NCAs) and courts and is, to a certain extent, coordinated by the Commission. As a result, the Commission claims that 'the EU competition rules have to a large extent become the "law of the land" for the whole of the EU'.[1] EU competition law plays a central role in the process of European integration both as a multifaceted tool for creating and policing the internal market as well as in organizing national markets, yet as a consequence of this role it is also subject to increasingly complex demands, a proliferation of (sectoral) regimes, and multiple objectives at both EU and national level. This profligacy entails risks of fragmentation and divergence which could jeopardize the proper functioning of the internal market.

In terms of antitrust matters, this risk was first addressed in 1969 in *Walt Wilhelm* with regard to a potential discrepancy between the application of the established German national competition rules by the national competition authority (the Bundeskartellamt) and the fledgling EU regime. The Court stated:

> National authorities may take action against an agreement in accordance with their national law, even when an examination of the agreement from the point of view of its compatibility with Community law is pending before the Commission, subject however to the condition that the application of national law may not prejudice the full and uniform application of Community law or the effects of measures taken or to be taken to implement it.[2]

[1] Communication from the Commission to the European Parliament and the Council, Ten years of antitrust enforcement under Regulation 1/2003: achievement and future perspectives, COM(2014) 453, para 23; and Commission staff working document, Enhancing competition enforcement by the Member States' competition authorities: institutional and procedural issues, SWD(2014) 231, para 5.

[2] Case 14/68 *Walt Wilhelm et al. v Bundeskartellamt* [1969] ECR 1, para 9.

Thirty years later in *Masterfoods* the parallel application of EU competition law by a national court in Ireland and by the European Commission was at issue. Here, the Court of Justice of the European Union (CJEU) held:

> When the outcome of the dispute before the national court depends on the validity of the Commission decision, it follows from the obligation of sincere cooperation that the national court should, in order to avoid reaching a decision that runs counter to that of the Commission, stay its proceedings pending final judgment in the action for annulment by the Community Courts, unless it considers that, in the circumstances of the case, a reference to the Court of Justice for a preliminary ruling on the validity of the Commission decision is warranted.[3]

Both issues—the role of national competition law applied by national authorities and that of national courts applying EU law—were raised in the context of securing the uniformity and effectiveness of EU law. They have been addressed in de modernization Regulation 1/2003 codifying and extending this case law for antitrust (in particular Articles 3, 11(6), and 16).[4] The result is the combination of hierarchy and cooperation within a network of authorities (and to a lesser extent courts) guided by the Commission and the European courts. The situation for competition law beyond antitrust is more varied.

2. Outline

This forms the background to the following three issues that I intend to examine in this book: (i) the degree of coherence that exists in EU competition law; (ii) how this coherence can be explained (including in the broader context of integration by EU law); and (iii) how it contributes to the legitimacy and effectiveness of EU competition law. My emphasis will be on the decentralized application of competition law in the narrow sense as antitrust: the prohibitions on cartels and abuse of dominant position (or Articles 101 and 102 of the Treaty on the Functioning of the European Union (TFEU): antitrust). To obtain a full picture, however, I also intend to look at competition law in the broad sense of mergers and state aid. Moreover, for comparative purposes I will examine the sectoral competition regimes for electronic communications and energy as well.

This broad scope is required because competition policy is increasingly relevant not just in policing already functioning markets but also in the context of liberalization and setting up more or less permanent sector-specific regulatory regimes in the context of market creation. At the same time, many claims concerning the benefits of liberalized markets depend on the success of competition policy as a governance device, including in terms of accommodating

[3] Case C-344/98 *Masterfoods Ltd v HB Ice Cream Ltd* [2000] ECR I-11369, para 57.

[4] Council Regulation (EC) No 1/2003 of 16 December 2002 on the implementation of the rules on competition laid down in Articles 81 and 82 of the Treaty, OJ 2003 L1/1.

alternative objectives of public policy. In both respects, competition law serves to protect the functioning of the internal market. Thus, in my view the internal (competition law as such) and external (as part of EU law more broadly) coherence of competition law may well be important not only to the success of the particular economic projects involved but to European integration at large.

In the following chapters I will primarily investigate the objectives (notably the consumer interest) and the various instruments of competition law (rules and exceptions) in order to examine the socially relevant question of whether they achieve a degree of uniformity that promotes their effectiveness and if they can provide a source of legitimacy based on concrete results (or output legitimacy). More generally, I will also look at the question of whether decentralization leads to the formation of a broader enforcement community and common competition-based norms permeating the Member States (possibly promoting input legitimacy). In the remainder of this chapter, I will consider comprehensively the object and the method chosen for this book. Next I will analyse the concept of coherence (in contrast with fragmentation) in order to provide a working definition that will serve as a framework for the text as a whole. For this purpose I will draw on the debate in legal philosophy on the argument regarding coherence which involves both coherence in terms of integrity of argumentation in individual cases and the coherence of rules and their application.

I will also make use of the existing work on coherence in free movement and other areas of EU law. Working models for legal standards for legitimacy and effectiveness will be identified and related to competition law. I will then set out the key research questions regarding coherence and competition law and develop the methodology applied, including its comparative elements. Finally I link the research questions and methodological approach to their respective chapters. Readers less interested in examining the full theoretical framework of this book may wish to skip sections 4 to 6.

3. Background

Coherence in a context of decentralization

Article 3(1)b TFEU states that the Union shall have exclusive competence in establishing the competition rules necessary for the functioning of the internal market.[5] Promoting and enforcing competition has become one of the key ways in which EU law affects the economies of the Member States, reforming national legal systems in the process.

[5] In addition, Protocol 27 of the TEU and TFEU states that 'the internal market as set out in Article 3 of the Treaty on European Union includes a system ensuring that competition is not distorted'.

Phases of competition law and policy

The development of general EU competition law and policy can be seen as a continuum starting with the Rome Treaty in 1957 (and at sectoral level with the European Coal and Steel Community six years earlier) that can be divided into a number of distinct phases.[6] An initial establishment phase, setting out basic principles starting from *Consten-Gründig*[7] and *United Brands*,[8] was followed by the 'public turn' of competition law associated with the *Van Eycke* judgment that tackled Member States' facilitating or imposing anticompetitive practices.[9] This was followed by retrenching after the *Meng*, *Reiff*, and *Ohra* judgments.[10] In 1989 merger control was centralized at EU level and quickly became an important branch of competition policy. More recently, the Leniency Notice enhanced cartel enforcement spectacularly, while the previously centralized exemption system for antitrust was replaced by a decentralized legal exception system, freeing up enforcement capacity at EU level.[11] Finally, with key investigations involving *Microsoft*,[12] *Intel*,[13] *Google*,[14] and recently *Amazon*,[15] the Commission is making its mark on enforcement in the information age. The investigation in *Gazprom* shows that the heat is on in energy markets as well.[16]

A hallmark of the present phase appears to be the proliferation of nominally similar but (formally and/or factually) distinct competition rules. With the success and expansion of competition law comes a multiplicity of competition policy regimes, both in terms of the classic 'general' competition policy (ie of Articles 101 and 102 TFEU and the Merger Control Regulation; as well as Articles 107 and 108 (State Aid) and 106(1) and 106(2) TFEU (special and exclusive rights

[6] Cf. D.J. Gerber, *Law and Competition in Twentieth Century Europe: Protecting Prometheus* (Oxford: Oxford University Press, 1998); K.K. Patel and H. Schweitzer (eds), *The Historical Foundations of EU Competition Law* (Oxford: Oxford University Press, 2013).

[7] Joined cases 56 and 58–64 *Établissements Consten S.à.R.L. and Grundig-Verkaufs-GmbH v Commission* [1966] ECR 429.

[8] Case 27/76 *United Brands Company and United Brands Continentaal BV v Commission* [1978] ECR 207.

[9] Case 267/86 *Pascal Van Eycke v ASPA NV* [1988] ECR 4769.

[10] Case C-2/91 *Criminal proceedings against Wolf W. Meng* [1993] ECR I-5751; Case C-185/91 *Bundesanstalt für den Güterfernverkehr v Gebrüder Reiff GmbH & Co. KG.* [1993] Page I-5801; Case C-245/91 *Criminal proceedings against Ohra Schadeverzekeringen NV* [1993] ECR I-5851. N. Reich, 'The "November revolution" of the European Court of Justice: *Keck, Meng* and *Audi* revisited', *Common Market Law Review* 31 (1994) 459–92.

[11] Commission Notice on the non-imposition or reduction of fines in cartel cases OJ 1996 C 207/4 (Now Commission Notice on immunity from fines and reduction of fines in cartel cases, OJ 2006, C298/17).

[12] Commission Decision of 24 May 2004 relating to a proceeding pursuant to Article 82 EC against Microsoft Corporation (Case COMP/C-3/37.792 *Microsoft*) OJ 2007 L 32/23; Case T-201/04 *Microsoft Corp. v Commission* [2007] II-3601.

[13] Confirmed in Case T-286/09 *Intel Corp. v Commission*, Judgment of 12 June 2014.

[14] Case COMP/39740 *Google Search*, statement of objections of 15 April 2015.

[15] Case COMP/40153 *E-book MFNs and related matters*, opened on 11 June 2015.

[16] Case COMP/39816 *Upstream gas supplies in Central and Eastern Europe*, statement of objections of 22 April 2015.

respectively services of general economic interest)), and the EU's sector-specific competition rules, notably for electronic communications and energy.

At the same time, the system of EU antitrust law itself has been developed and modernized. Arguably, one of the main benefits of the centralized system of individual exemptions from the cartel prohibition in the hands of the European Commission until 2004 was that it safeguarded the coherence of EU competition law; however, centralization also handicapped the widespread effective application of these rules. Thus, ten years ago this system was replaced by a decentralized structure relying on national competition authorities and courts applying the substantive rules of EU antitrust, coordinated to some extent by the European Commission as *primus inter pares*. Because the rules on procedures and remedies have not been harmonized, there are however twenty-eight national regimes in place in addition to that of the EU. Arguably it is the interplay between institutional, normative, and substantive factors that accounts for the transformational force of EU competition law. In my analysis I intend to combine all three, with an emphasis on the first two.

Other areas of competition law display contrasting features. Most notably, State aid remains largely centralized whereas the sectoral regimes for electronic communications and energy were from the outset decentralized, albeit while imposing coordination structures on national regulatory authorities. With the proliferation of rules, authorities, and structures, the challenges to coherence also multiply. There thus seems to be strong centrifugal and centripetal tendencies in competition law that can at the same time be expressed in EU law terms (eg uniformity versus subsidiarity), or in terms of analytical concepts such as expansion and contraction, divergence and convergence, hierarchy and coordination.

The role of competition law in EU integration

This suggests a process of competition policy expansion and integration within the framework of the development of European integration at large.[17] From the constitutional function claimed by the German law and economics school of Ordoliberalism, through the primacy of the integration objective, to the focus on the consumer associated with Chicago School neo-liberalism, theoretical readings of the role of competition policy form the backdrop to this study.[18] This involves three notable trends:

- Increasing reliance on economic concepts and economic logic: this so-called new economic approach feeds the rationalization of EU competition law in

[17] Cf. W. Sauter and H. Schepel, *State and Market in European Union Law: The Public and Private Spheres of the Internal Market before the EU Courts* (Cambridge: Cambridge University Press, 2009); J. Baquero Cruz, *Between Competition and Free Movement: The Economic Constitutional Law of the European Community* (Oxford: Hart Publishing, 2002).

[18] Cf. Gerber (n 6); W. Sauter, 'The economic constitution of the European Union', *Columbia Journal of European Law* 27 (1998) 27–68.

the broad sense.[19] The resulting effects-based approach can be contrasted with the benefits of per se rules in terms of effective deterrence and enforcement.[20]

- The decentralization of EU antitrust to NCAs and national courts based on Regulation 1/2003 paired with spontaneous substantive harmonization of national competition law (but in the absence of procedural harmonization).[21]
- The emergence of networks of specialized, national sector-specific regulatory authorities (NRAs) based on EU law, and the coordination mechanism between them and the Commission.[22]

All of this is happening in a Community that now numbers twenty-eight Member States (compared to the six originally subject to EU competition law) with a broader range of economic development and market conditions (including regulation) than ever before in the history of the EU. At the same time, general competition policy tends to be reactive ('policing working markets') and based on *ex post* enforcement, whereas sector specific competition policy is intended to be proactive ('making markets work') and based on *ex ante* regulation. As a result of this difference in approach, the regimes for regulation intensive network sectors have been 'hived off' and are applied in parallel to the general competition rules.

There appear to be various methods for managing the resulting complexity, including utilizing: (i) common norms (objectives, boundaries, rules, and exceptions); (ii) procedures and remedies; (iii) institutions; (iv) coordination; and (v) hierarchy. By controlling complexity these methods are each likely to reduce divergence and promote coherence. In the following I provide an overview of how such methods might apply more specifically to competition law.

1. Focusing on a common objective, such as the general consumer interest, including formal categories such as consumer welfare, promotes coherence.[23] By contrast, might choosing multiple objectives, such as protecting the competitive process and the market structure, or European integration, automatically lead to divergence?[24]

[19] Cf. eg M. Motta, *Competition Policy: Theory and Practice* (Cambridge: Cambridge University Press, 2004); R. O'Donohue and J. Padilla, *The Law and Economics of Article 102 TFEU* (Oxford: Hart Publishing, 2013).

[20] R.A. Epstein, *Simple rules for a complex world*, rev. edn. (Harvard, CT: Harvard University Press, 1997). This contrast can also be linked to substantive 'output legitimacy' versus procedural 'input legitimacy'. See F.W. Scharpf, *Community and Autonomy: Institutions, Policies and Legitimacy in Multilevel Europe* (Berlin: Campus, 2010).

[21] Council Regulation 1/2003 (n 1); see Commission staff working paper, Report on the functioning of Regulation 1/2003, COM(2009) 206 final, especially paras 248–268. See H. Vedder, 'Spontaneous harmonisation of national (competition) laws in the wake of the modernisation of EC competition law', *Competition Law Review* 1 (2004) 5–21.

[22] S.A.C.M. Lavrijssen and L. Hancher 'Networks of regulatory agencies in Europe', in P. Larouche and P. Cserne (eds), *National Legal Systems and Globalization: New Role, Continuing Relevance* (The Hague: TMC Asser Press/Springer, 2013) 183; M. De Visser, *Network-Based Governance in EC Law* (Oxford: Hart Publishing, 2009).

[23] Cf. K.J. Cseres, *Competition Law and Consumer Protection* (The Hague: Kluwer Law International, 2005).

[24] Joined Cases C-501/06 P, C-513/06 P, C-515/06 P and C-519/06 P *GlaxoSmithKline Services Unlimited v Commission (C-501/06 P)* and *Commission v GlaxoSmithKline Services Unlimited*

2. Streamlining competition law by assigning a central role to specific economic concepts—notably market power, and consequently market definition, but also market (and government) failure.
3. Focusing on exclusion/foreclosure and on selling power rather than exploitation and buyer power,[25] and on horizontal instead of vertical restraints.
4. Filtering out complex cases where public interests are involved as falling outside the scope of Article 101(1) TFEU altogether, such as *Wouters* and *Mecca-Medina*,[26] or outside the concept of undertaking as in *Van der Woude* and *Kattner*,[27] or in *FENIN*.[28] A comparable role is played by the exception that is provided by services of general economic interest (SGEIs), especially in the context of the State aid rules.[29]
5. Developing procedural requirements, including a uniform procedural framework (found in electronic communications but not antitrust).[30] There has also been a harmonization of remedies in the field of private damages claims.[31]
6. Adjusting the standard required for meeting EU rules—for example, the standard applied under the proportionality principle and the role of harmonization and pre-emption in this context.
7. Creating, alongside the European Competition Network (ECN) of NCAs, EU 'network' agencies for the coordination of national regulatory authorities (NRAs), notably in electronic communications (BEREC), and the energy sector (ACER).

(C-513/06 P) and European Association of Euro Pharmaceutical Companies (EAEPC) v Commission (C-515/06 P) and *Asociación de exportadores españoles de productos farmacéuticos (Aseprofar) v Commission (C-519/06 P)* [2009] ECR I-9291; Case C-8/08 *T-Mobile Netherlands BV, KPN Mobile NV, Orange Nederland NV and Vodafone Libertel NV v Raad van bestuur van de Nederlandse Mededingingsautoriteit* [2009] ECR I-4529.

[25] Communication from the Commission, Guidance on the Commission's enforcement priorities in applying Article 82 of the EC Treaty to abusive exclusionary conduct by dominant undertakings, OJ 2009, C45/7.

[26] Case C-67/96 *Albany International BV v Stichting Bedrijfspensioenfonds Textielindustrie* [1999] ECR I-5751; Case C-309/99 *J.C.J. Wouters, J.W. Savelbergh and Price Waterhouse Belastingadviseurs BV v Algemene Raad van de Nederlandse Orde van Advocaten* [2002] ECR I-1577; Case C-519/04P *David Meca-Medina and Igor Majcen v Commission* [2006] ECR I-6991.

[27] Case 222-/98 *Hendrik van der Woude v Stichting Beatrixoord* [2000] ECR I-7111; Case C-350/07 *Kattner Stahlbau GmbH v Maschinenbau- und Metall- Berufsgenossenschaft*, Judgment of 5 May 2009.

[28] Case C-205/03 P *Federación Española de Empresas de Tecnología Sanitaria (FENIN) v Commission* [2006] ECR I-6295.

[29] Case T-289/03 *British United Provident Association Ltd (BUPA), BUPA Insurance Ltd and BUPA Ireland Ltd v Commission* [2008] ECR II-81.

[30] Case C-439/08 *Vlaamse federatie van verenigingen van Brood- en Banketbakkers, Ijsbereiders en Chocoladebewerkers (VEBIC) VZW* [2010] I-12471. Cf. also M.J. Frese, *Sanctions in EU competition law: principles and practice* (Oxford: Hart Publishing, 2014).

[31] Directive 2014/104/EU of the European Parliament and of the Council of 26 November 2014 on certain rules governing actions for damages under national law for infringements of the competition law provisions of the Member States and of the European Union, OJ 2014, L349/1.

8. Applying principles of hierarchy and coordination within the networks of (sector-specific) competition authorities (eg for general competition policy in terms of Regulation 1/2003).[32]
9. Implementing -re-emption and control as coordination mechanisms, with a Commission monopoly on certain types of decision.[33] This includes notably a finding of inapplicability with regard to Articles 101(1) and 102 TFEU based on Article 10 of Regulation 1/2003 and of compatibility with the internal market under Article 107(3) TFEU in the context of State aid control.
10. Applying a single standard of legal review by the Community Courts, or in any event a centralized system of legal review, supported by the system of prejudicial references to coordinate the approach of national courts.

A further factor might be reliance on a rule of reason approach (and balancing of pro- and anticompetitive effects) instead of per se rules with exceptions.[34] Its impact on coherence is likely to be unpredictable because this approach seems less structured than one based on a legal exception, such as Article 101(3) TFEU. Also, the practical role played by the rule of reason (at least in antitrust), although well-publicized, appears to be minimal. By contrast, reliance on a legal exception regime versus a regime based on individual notifications and exemption is of course the central theme of modernization and will be discussed as such. Nevertheless, balancing is at the heart of the process of establishing compatibility with the internal market in State aid law.

These factors and their respective impact on the coherence of EU competition law will be addressed in the following chapters. First, I will set out the theoretical framework.

4. Definitions and Research Questions

Defining coherence

The term coherence pops up from time to time in EU documents regarding competition law. Thus, in its evaluation of the first ten years of Regulation 1/2003 the Commission claims that 'enforcement by the NCAs has developed in a broadly coherent manner' and that the work of the ECN 'has become increasingly important to ensure coherent enforcement'.[35] Article 15(3) of Regulation 1/2003 provides that the Commission may act as *amicus curiae* before national courts

[32] Commission Notice on cooperation within the Network of Competition Authorities, OJ 2004, C101/43.

[33] Case C-375/09 *Prezes Urzędu Ochrony Konkurencji i Konsumentów v Tele2 Polska sp. z o.o., now Netia SA* [2011] ECR I-3055.

[34] R. Wesseling, *The Modernisation of EC Antitrust Law* (Oxford: Hart Publishing, 2000). Per se rules, however, continue to exist: Case C-8/08 *T-Mobile* (n 24).

[35] COM(2014) 453 (n 1), paras 8 and 23.

where necessary for the coherent application of Articles 1010 and 102 TFEU. The primary objective of this book is to study whether, and if so how, competition law maintains its coherence in a context where it is subject to centrifugal as well as centripetal forces and comprises an increasing number of regimes, norms, and objectives.

Coherence as such is not a legal term of art or a principle of EU law, even if it may well eventually emerge as such in the free movement context.[36] However, it already captures aspects of several such principles, such as the unity and effectiveness of EU law, and is more flexible because it can also encapsulate the way the enforcement of EU competition law is organized. Hence, the use of objectives and instruments and substantive and institutional variables can be taken into account. We must first define what constitutes coherence and what constitutes an effective degree of coherence.

Provisionally (based on the *Oxford English Dictionary*) I define coherence as (i) logically consistent, and (ii) part of, or itself constituting a unified, systemic (or in other words, functional) whole.[37] To this I add the important third dimension (iii) that the former two factors should serve a clearly identifiable objective and/or set of principles (see the discussion under section 5 regarding the argument about coherence in legal philosophy). Thus coherence seems compatible with the goal-oriented or teleological approach that the EU courts have frequently adopted at the boundaries of EU law (as is postulated by legal theorists working on the argument regarding coherence). Thus, separate from the rules, the goals of EU competition law are essential. Coherence and uniformity are similar but not identical: in my view coherence is more dynamic and flexible, requiring consistency in terms of rules and principles, and uniformity is more monolithic and deterministic in terms of outcomes. Of course, uniformity of EU law is in the final instance guaranteed by the fact that the Court of Justice alone can provide a final authoritative interpretation of EU law—an authority which comes paired with the constitutional responsibility of the Court to provide coherent precedents for EU lawyers (including the national judiciary) to observe.[38]

Three levels of coherence

I now want to develop the definition one step further by distinguishing two types and three related levels of coherence: (1) external coherence, the level which locates EU competition law within the context of the system of EU law and of the process of European integration; and internal coherence, which can be distinguished

36 Case C-500/06 *Corporación Dermoestética SA v To Me Group Advertising Media* [2008] ECR I-5785 Case C-169/07 *Hartlauer Handelsgesellschaft mbH v Wiener Landesregierung and Oberösterreichische Landesregierung* [2009] ECR I-1721.

37 In psychology coherence has also been defined as the characteristic of a set of events where 'each element is connected, and each supports and strengthens the other'. D. Kahneman, *Thinking Fast and Slow* (London: Penguin Books, 2011) at 51.

38 N. Nic Shuibhne, *The Coherence of EU Free Movement Law: Constitutional Responsibility and the Court of Justice* (Oxford: Oxford University Press, 2013).

Table 1.1 Three levels of coherence

Level of analysis	Types of coherence	Type of analysis/method
EU law as a whole	External coherence	Contextual
System of EU competition law	Internal coherence type 'A'	Focus of analysis
Components of EU competition law	Internal coherence type 'B'	Examples for analysis

between the levels of the system of EU competition law as a (2a) whole, and that of its components—(2b) individual rules and rulings. The way in which this will be applied is summarized in Table 1.1.

First, examining the external or contextual approach to coherence I will look primarily at the manner in which competition law is anchored within EU law, for instance by means of its objectives and by way of its connection with safeguarding the internal market. Second, coherence can be applied at the level of competition law as a system of legal norms, and third, at the level of its enforcement and judicial review by the Commission and the European Courts as well as by NCAs and national courts. We will examine here to what extent internal coherence is compatible with a degree of freedom at national level.[39] In both cases of internal coherence there is a substantive and a procedural dimension although substance is likely to matter more in the former setting (the system of legal norms) and procedure more in the latter (the system of enforcement and judicial review).

Adding legitimacy and effectiveness

Coherence is not to be equated with the kind of monochromatic consistency that has been criticized variously as 'the hobgoblin of little minds' and as 'the last refuge of the unimaginative'.[40] It is my view that studying the substantive and procedural coherence of EU competition law is ultimately relevant not because it is a valuable activity per se but especially because this coherence has a material impact.[41] This is so in relation to the explicit objectives of EU competition law which will be examined in the following chapters. However, it can also be expressed in terms of the legitimacy and effectiveness of EU competition law, where predictability is a virtue and not a source of *ennui*. I will therefore add these two categories to the concept of coherence as requirements that must be satisfied to a sufficient degree in order for meaningful coherence to exist.

[39] See C. Townley, 'Co-ordinated diversity: revolutionary suggestions for EU competition law (and for EU law too)', *Yearbook of European Law* 33 (2014) 1–51.

[40] Ralph Waldo Emerson, *Self Reliance* (1841) respectively Oscar Wilde, 'The Relation of Dress to Art' in the *Pall Mall Gazette* 28 February 1885.

[41] A difference in degree with Giorgio Monti who believes that the better way (to judge the success of Regulation 1/2003) is to look at results rather than at (constitutional) coherence. G. Monti, 'A plea for "extraterritorial" antitrust enforcement by national competition authorities', unpublished paper, EUI 2014.

This can also be seen as a specific expression on these two variables of overall coherence within the legal system of which EU competition law forms a part—hence of external coherence. The demands of legitimacy and effectiveness, however, come into play at all levels and not just at that of the overarching system. The relationship between coherence, effectiveness, and legitimacy will be described in some more detail in the next section.

Research questions

Given these reflections on the concept of coherence and its underlying material norms I propose to study coherence:

- As a legal construct, both at the level of the rules concerned and at that of the system of EU competition law, in the context of EU law as a whole, starting from objectives and boundaries
- In terms of its own objectives and structure
- In terms of legitimacy and effectiveness of EU law, taking into account the contrasting claims of uniformity and subsidiarity
- Over time and between settings (instruments and sectors)
- With an emphasis on antitrust following the decentralization of antitrust

In conclusion, I would like to situate this topic in the broader EU integration context, albeit evidently with a light touch. Using the benchmark set out earlier I will examine to what extent EU competition law is coherent and what factors explain the degree of coherence that it has attained. My aim is to identify those strategies aimed at coherence that have been successful, those that have not, and to explain these features. Given time and spatial constraints, I will focus largely on EU competition policy in the narrow sense as antitrust but I will bring in EU competition in the broad sense for comparative purposes: this includes chapters on mergers and State aid as well as the sector-specific competition rules for electronic communications and energy.

This leads to the following set of research questions:

(i) Which are the main sources and mechanisms that ensure coherent application of EU competition law?

(ii) What are their effects more specifically in the context of EU law; at the systemic level of EU competition law; and at the level of individual rules (including exceptions) and rulings?

(iii) Are they at present sufficient to ensure the legitimacy and the effectiveness of EU competition law (and if not, how can they be strengthened)?

These questions will be elaborated in more detail as necessary for the individual chapters. The main challenge will be how to formulate concrete tests in order to be able to address the third question.

I will now turn to consider the existing literature and where this book intends to contribute to its development.

5. Coherence, Legal Principles, and Categories

Let me now give some more depth to my understanding of coherence as a legal concept, referring to the relevant accounts in legal philosophy, to the adjacent or subsidiary principles of legitimacy and effectiveness, and to the literature on coherence and EU law.

The argument from coherence in legal philosophy

There exists significant philosophical literature on the issue of coherence.[42] Some of the main elements that appear to be pertinent to my inquiry are as follows.

One of the main theorists of coherence is the late Scottish legal philosopher Neil MacCormick who distinguishes between normative and narrative coherence. In his view 'the coherence of norms is a matter of their "making sense" by being rationally related as a set, instrumentally or intrinsically, *either* to the realization of some common value or values; *or* to the fulfilment of some common principle or principles'.[43] Consequently, normative coherence relies on a mutually consistent set of higher-order principles and/or objectives that can direct and justify lower-order decisions. In my view this is the key dimension that distinguishes coherence from mere consistency. Narrative coherence, on the other hand, is 'a test of truth or probability in questions of fact and evidence upon which direct proof by immediate observation is unavoidable'.[44] Because it is concerned with the truthfulness of conclusions with regard to facts this dimension of coherence is less important here.

Both types of coherence can be used to evaluate the justification of individual legal decisions.[45] In this context an individual ruling can both be decided based on its coherence with the preceding body of law and it can itself bolster this coherence by adding a new element of reasoning or ramification.[46] An argument from coherence can be either backward looking (towards the precedents and rules of a legal system) or forward looking (towards the objectives and principles of a legal system). It can also be used either to select a preferred solution or to reject a proposed solution.[47] All these dimensions appear to be pertinent. On the assumption that the moral dimension of competition law is limited however (although an

[42] Eg N. MacCormick, 'Coherence in legal justification', in W. Kravietz *et al.* (eds), *Theorie der Normen* (Berlin: Duncker & Humblot, 1984) 37–53; N. MacCormick, *Rhetoric and the Rule of Law: A Theory of Legal Reasoning* (Oxford: Oxford University Press, 2005); and R. Dworkin, *Law's Empire* (London: Fontana, 1984) on integrity.

[43] MacCormick (1984), (n 42) 41–2.

[44] Ibid, 48.

[45] S. Bertea, 'The arguments from coherence: analysis and evaluation', *Oxford Journal of Legal Studies* 25 (2005) 369–91, at 372.

[46] MacCormick (2005) (n 42), at 189. See L. Moral Soriano, 'A modest notion of coherence in legal reasoning: a model for the European Court of Justice', *Ratio Juris* 16 (2003) 296–323.

[47] S. Bertea, 'Does arguing from coherence make sense?', *Argumentation* 19 (2005) 433–46, 438–49.

argument could be made here for consumer welfare), a dimension that does not concern me here is what to do about cases which are more coherent but morally less preferable.[48]

Most significant from the perspective of an analysis under EU law is that, according to MacCormick (with reference to the work on integrity by Ronald Dworkin), the ideal of overall coherence enables the view of a legal system as a system and justifies various types of systemic argument (such as contextual arguments, arguments based on precedent, analogy, logical conceptual arguments, arguments from history and from general principles of law). Moreover, he maintains that the argument from coherence is a necessary supplement to teleological (and deontological) arguments.[49] This is also consistent with a broader view of coherence as something that subjects the legal issue at hand to a contextual approach.

Sometimes legal theorists have used the categories of coherence and teleology interchangeably, however treating coherence and teleology as distinct variables appears to provide a better fit with standard accounts and terminology of EU law where teleology is evidently a more familiar concept.[50] That is so because teleological argumentation is favoured by the Court of Justice in those cases where EU legal instruments do not contain direct and/or unequivocal interpretative guidance. The symbiosis of coherence and teleology as interpretive instruments in EU law is relevant to my research on coherence in competition law at several levels:

i. to justify its relevance, which is assumed to exist regarding teleology;
ii. to indicate a way in which the degree of coherence in EU law may be tested—that is as the realization of common principles or objectives which, however, remain to be established; and
iii. how it may contribute to integration through law—by providing its justification through consistency and thereby legitimacy and by means of allowing a forward-looking approach, thereby promoting effectiveness.

Finally, it is worth mentioning that these elements can be related to the rule of law, as McCormick has linked coherence with the rule of law in his work, identifying legal certainty, the protection of legitimate expectations, and protection from arbitrary intervention as its most important aspects.[51] This brings to mind Hayek's emphasis on predictability as the main virtue of the rule of law which

[48] See J. Dickson, 'Interpretation and coherence in legal reasoning', in *Stanford Encyclopedia of Philosophy*, (revised 10 February 2010). Available at: <http://plato.stanford.edu/entries/legal-reas-interpret/> para 3.3. Another dimension examined by Dickson is local (to one area of law) versus global (the law as a whole, presumably at the level of a legal system) coherence. Cf. Moral Soriano (n 46).

[49] N. MacCormick, 'Argumentation and interpretation in law', in *Ratio Juris* 3 (1993) 16–29, at 22–4.

[50] In legal theory the terminology is mixed. Bertea (n 45) 378 and 382: 'There are several types of context-establishing argument…Among these, the argument from coherence can be described as a teleo-systemic canon. By teleo-systemic canon is meant a combination of teleological and systemic arguments.'

[51] McCormick (2005) (n 42) 16.

would allow undertakings to work around imperfect rules as necessary while enabling the economic process to proceed.[52] More recently but apparently in the same vein, the president of the General Court has stated '[c]oherence, consistency and certainty are essential elements of case law in a healthy State governed by the rule of law'.[53] Here, these authors focus on (formal) consistency again rather than on the guiding principle, although there are also accounts that require a moral (substantive) component.[54]

Centralization, decentralization, and principles of EU law

Having looked at the theoretical underpinnings of coherence as a legal concept, I now turn to the organization of EU law. The variable of centralization versus decentralization is an important dimension helping to determine the degree of coherence. Uniformity and primacy (supremacy) are principles of EU law that enhance coherence and favour hierarchy and centralization at EU level. Both in a formal and a practical sense unity or uniformity of EU law is in the final instance guaranteed by the rule that the Court of Justice provides the final authoritative interpretation of EU law as the most extreme example of centralized control. This also applies to competition law. The Commission remains the central (or even single) arbiter of merger control and State aid (the CJEU—General Court and Court of Justice—excepted), and even following modernization can trump national authorities as well as national courts in antitrust—see inter alia *Masterfoods*[55] as well as Articles 3, 11(6), and 16 of Regulation 1/2003.[56] Tension between practical and formal claims can exist if the logical consistency of the individual judgments with regard to the norms involved (such as goals and boundaries, or rules and exceptions) is sketchy and thus incoherent.

Subsidiarity, moreover, may enhance legitimacy while favouring decentralization at Member State level. The same holds for proportionality, using the least intrusive effective means. As will be discussed further below, legitimacy in turn can be understood in terms of procedure and form-based legality (input legitimacy), which includes broad participation and deliberation and substantive support for effective outcomes (output legitimacy). This means that whereas when the conditions of uniformity and effectiveness are met coherence may promote the legitimacy of EU law, there are also forms of legitimacy that are potentially at cross-purposes with it. Coordination and cooperation mechanisms may bridge

[52] F.A. Hayek, *The Road to Serfdom* (London: Routledge, 2001) chapter 6.

[53] M. Jaeger, 'Standard of review in competition cases: can the General Court increase coherence in the European Union judicial system', in T Baumé *et al.* (eds), *Today's Multilayered Legal Order: Current Issues and Perspectives. Liber amicorum in Honour of Arjen W.H. Meij* (Zutphen: Paris Publishers, 2011) 115–40, at 138.

[54] See T. Bingham, *The Rule of Law* (London: Penguin Books, 2010). By contrast see J. Raz, 'The rule of law and its virtue', in *The Authority of Law: Essays on Law and Morality* (Oxford: Clarendon Press, 1979) 210. An overview in P. Craig, 'Formal and substantive conceptions of the rule of law: an analytical framework', *Public Law* (1997) 467–87.

[55] Case C-344/98 *Masterfoods* (n 3).

[56] Council Regulation 1/2003 (n 1).

Table 1.2 Spatial organization

Spatial organization	Centralization: more control	Decentralization: more reach
EU legal principles	Uniformity, primacy	Subsidiarity, proportionality
Type of legitimacy	Output legitimacy	Input legitimacy

these variables while simultaneously respecting them. Finally, it may well be that there are various stable equilibria of coherence at different levels of centralization (such as existed before and after modernization, if we abstract for the time being from the respective drawbacks and advantages of these systems), and for different aspects of EU competition law. Given their significance, I will return to centralization and decentralization, as well as the principles of uniformity, primacy, and subsidiarity in subsequent chapters.

Table 1.2 sets out the different dimensions of the spatial organization of coherence and relates them to legitimacy. I will now move on to discuss legitimacy and effectiveness in more detail.

Coherence as promoting legitimacy and effectiveness

Achieving coherence can be seen a central factor underpinning the legitimacy and effectiveness of EU competition law. The success (or otherwise) of the legitimacy and efficacy of this same law will co-determine successful coherence.[57] In the context of external coherence within the legal system as a whole (which is obviously much broader in scope), scales of legitimacy and efficacy can be seen as yardsticks or touchstones that may be used to assess whether a meaningful form of coherence has been achieved or not.[58] At the same time, the demands of effectiveness and legitimacy apply at other levels: EU competition law as a whole and its separate instruments. Pieter van Cleynenbreugel has suggested what appears to be a similar structuring of these three variables (coherence, effectiveness, and legitimacy), albeit not focused on coherence but on legitimacy: 'In order to be perceived as legitimate, competition law itself requires principles of institutional organization that enable efficiency and justice to be balanced in a constitutionally coherent fashion.'[59]

This line of thought broadly supports a reading of coherence as connected with legitimacy and effectiveness.

[57] F. Snyder, 'The effectiveness of European Community law: institutions, processes, tools and techniques', *Modern Law Review* 56 (1993) 19–54.

[58] M. Marquis, P. Lowe, and G. Monti (eds), *Effective and Legitimate Enforcement of Competition Law* (Oxford: Hart Publishing, forthcoming 2016); G. Monti, 'Independence, interdependence and legitimacy: the EU Commission, national competition authorities and the European Competition Network', EUI Law Department Research paper 2014/01; W. Wils, *Efficiency and Justice in European Antitrust Enforcement* (Oxford: Hart Publishing, 2008).

[59] P. Van Cleynenbreugel, 'Institutional assimilation in the wake of EU competition law decentralisation', *Competition Law Review* 8 (2012) 285–312, at 312.

Legitimacy

It appears to me that legitimacy is not a legal principle in a strict sense although it can be linked to the rule of law and to legality. Instead it is a notion from the social sciences that revolves around the justification of and support for policies or particular policy measures. Fritz Scharpf has introduced a now widely shared distinction between procedure- (and participation-) based input legitimacy and substantive outcome legitimacy. In his view the EU is strong on the latter but not on the former.[60] This Scharpf ties in with his analysis that on the one hand the EU may be capable of promoting negative integration by shooting down protective State measures based on the strictures of EU law, but on the other hand it is unable to generate positive integration supporting public interests beyond market liberalization by adopting new measures at EU level.

Ingeborg Simonsson has carried out analysis of legitimacy with respect to EU cartel policy.[61] She refers to the general conceptual dichotomy pioneered by Scharpf but ultimately reaches a more specific conclusion: 'we have a paradoxical combination of high empirical legitimacy for uniform application of the law, but a shortage of normative rationality for uniformity'.[62] In terms of coherence this means that we cannot simply assume that maximum coherence matches maximum effectiveness and thereby maximizes legitimacy. Simonsson sees acceptance of local variation in combination with centralized prioritization as the solution—at least in the area of cartel control (to which I will return later).

Effectiveness

Ensuring the effective and uniform application of EU competition law—in order to protect competition in the internal market (which, as we will see, is the ultimate objective of EU competition law)—is the main intermediate objective of modernization as identified in Regulation 1/2003.[63] The question here is what effectiveness means. Following the standard account by Takis Tridimas, the effectiveness of EU law can be construed as a legal principle that is traditionally paired with equivalence to national law. This does not regard the colloquial notion linking effectiveness with achieving concrete results as much as the availability of a legal course of action to enforce any rights that are attributed by EU law.

Under the principle of effectiveness, the enforcement of EU law rights must not be made virtually impossible or excessively difficult by rules of national procedural law. This appears to be quite a weak standard. Under the principle of equivalence, EU law rights must be guaranteed to the same extent as the enforcement of comparable norms of national law. This standard appears to be stronger, except in those cases where the enforcement of national law falls short of a minimum

[60] Scharpf (n 20).
[61] Cf. eg I. Simonsson, *The Legitimacy of EU Cartel Control* (Oxford: Hart Publishing, 2010).
[62] Ibid at 350.
[63] Council Regulation 1/2003 (n 1), recital 1. Effectiveness reappears in recitals 5, 6, 8, 21, and 34.

standard of effectiveness. As a result, and as we will see in subsequent chapters, an EU minimum standard will sometimes be imposed.[64]

Effectiveness and equivalence are of special significance given the autonomy of national procedural law that must be reconciled with the primacy and direct effect of EU law from which they derive. This issue is of particular relevance because the dichotomy between EU substantive norms and national procedural rules is of central significance to the effective decentralization of antitrust. Tridimas places this kind of effectiveness in the context of the standard of judicial review, *locus standi*, the availability of interim measures, limitation periods, and compensation, in particular the right to claim damages for non-implementation.[65]

Taking a more contextual approach, in a seminal 1993 article Francis Snyder dealt with effectiveness in EU law in a broad sense, including legitimacy. While identifying seven distinct categories of effectiveness he discussed effectiveness primarily as including the dimensions of implementation, enforcement, and compliance.[66] Because it involves the actions of the subjects or targets of the rules concerned, compliance with competition law will be largely outside the scope of this book, apart from where it is relevant to the discussion on remedies such as fines (as well as other penalties such as incarceration), commitment decisions, and actions for damages. Implementation in terms of effective instruments, institutions, and procedures, as well as soft law guidance towards desired outcomes will all fall within the scope of my discussion. The same applies to enforcement by means of litigation and coordination (again in part by means of guidance), as well as the remedies just mentioned.

Effective enforcement is a central objective of the new system of antitrust modernization: its decentralization to the NCAs in Regulation 1/2003[67] and the cooperation between the NCAs and with the European Commission.[68] Although in Regulation 1/2003 it is mentioned alongside uniformity, effectiveness following modernization can be contrasted with the exclusive focus on uniformity of the prior authorization system. In the Regulation and, for instance, in the 2010 *VEBIC* Case[69] it appears that the notion of effectiveness concerns primarily (i) the availability of the necessary instruments, and (ii) their effective use in order to attain results. This is logical because effective enforcement requires adequate remedies with a substantial deterrent effect.

[64] See Case C-439/08 *VEBIC* (n 30); Case C-681/11 *Bundeswettbewerbsbehörde, Bundeskartellanwalt Schenker & Co et al.*, Judgment of 18 June 2013; and Directive 2014/104/EU (n 31).

[65] T. Tridimas, *The General Principles of EU Law*, 2nd edn. (Oxford: Oxford University Press, 2006). In the context of competition law see Case C-94/00 *Roquette Frères v Commission* [2002] ECR I-9011.

[66] Snyder (n 57) at 25. These are: (1) enactment of EU regulations into national law; (2) the application of EU regulations by the Member States; (3) the transposition of EU Directives; (4) implementation of EU law by the national civil service; (5) use of EU law by private actors; (6) recourse to litigation before national courts; and (7) enforcement of EU law by national courts.

[67] Council Regulation 1/2003 (n 1).

[68] Joint statement of the Council and the Commission on the functioning of the network of competition authorities, paras 2 and 5. Available at: <http://ec.europa.eu/competition/ecn/joint_statement_en.pdf>.

[69] Case C-439/08 *VEBIC* (n 30).

Table 1.3 Material standards of coherence

Standard	Effectiveness	Legitimacy
Procedure	Availability of legal recourse	Input legitimacy
Substance	Effective outcomes	Output legitimacy

In my view these two dimensions or readings of effectiveness are congruent with the two faces of legitimacy, as is summarized in Table 1.3. Arguably this is a simplification but in my view it is a justifiable one that will facilitate the application of these two concepts as the dual material standards of the degree of coherence achieved in EU competition law in what follows. Finally, at what could be considered as forming a meta-level analysis of effectiveness I will use the Commission's own assessments of the effectiveness of EU competition law and evaluate these in terms of how they score and how realistic they are.

6. Relationship to the Existing Literature

As far as I am aware, taking coherence as a starting point for a general account of competition law is new in itself. The intended innovation offered here is also provided by its scope: this is an attempt to understand competition law as a whole, as least from the prism of coherence. That is why it focuses not only on antitrust (the prohibitions on cartels and abuse of dominant position) but it also considers merger control and State aid as well as the sector-specific competition rules and their interrelationships.

In addition, the aim of this book is to gain a dynamic understanding of the development of the competition law system and therefore the direction in which it is moving, as well as its legitimacy, including with respect to the objectives of competition law such as the consumer interest. Given this, this book has a bearing on several bodies of literature that I will cover briefly: on coherence in EU law, general competition law, and sectoral competition law

Coherence studies in other areas of EU law

Some specialized literature with regard to coherence in EU law already exists, notably work edited by Sacha Prechal and Bert van Roermund on coherence in various areas of EU law, but not including EU competition law.[70] Their work was more interested in the convergence and divergence of legal concepts in national legal systems within the EU and EU law (and issues of legal terminology and translation) and more theoretical than what is presented here. The most pertinent

[70] S. Prechal and B. van Roermund, *The Coherence of EU Law: The Search for Unity in Divergent Concepts* (Oxford: Oxford University Press, 2008).

contribution to Prechal and van Roermund's volume is by Filomena Chirico and Pierre Larouche about law and economics.[71] They place coherence into context by debating whether regulatory competition is generally a problem and pointing out that the costs of uniformity may be high, even counterproductive. Removing the costs of divergence involves addressing externalities, eliminating transaction costs, and removing information imperfections. Rational decisions on doing so require a cost–benefit analysis that takes into account the benefits of the status quo and the costs of harmonization. The authors propose legal emulation—voluntary adoption of ideas or spontaneous harmonization—as preferable to a top-down harmonization model.

Second, there is a more recent (2013) monograph by Niamh Nic Shuibhne regarding coherence and free movement.[72] She links coherence with the values of fairness and integrity but defines it largely by means of its antithesis with fragmentation and the four drivers of the latter: (i) proliferation of principles; (ii) unsettled objectives of the market and free movement; (iii) protection of fundamental rights; and (iv) the structure of the Court. Also, Nic Shuibhne posits the existence of a legal continuum running from fragmentation, divergence, convergence, and coherence to legitimacy. The ranking of these values along this posited continuum is useful, although legitimacy appears to be a notion that is of a different nature than the other values.

Another area where coherence has been examined is with regard to foreign and security policy. Marise Cremona (2008) has proposed the existence of vertical (regarding the relationship between action by the EU or by the Member States) and horizontal (between the different EU policies and policy spheres) dimensions of coherence.[73] In addition, in Cremona's view a first level of coherence would be consistency, with an effective allocation of tasks as a second level and synergy between norms, actors, and instruments as a third. Although starting from the concept of coherence and applied to the common foreign and security policy, this approach comes close to that of studies regarding the coordination of regulatory policies (and competition).[74] As such, it fits with the analysis of the organizational side of EU competition law that I intend to undertake.

Finally, rounding the circle with the previous section on the argument concerning coherence, EU environmental law and legal theory are combined in an article by Leonor Moral Soriano.[75] He contrasts global (systemic) with local (branches of law such as EU environmental law) coherence, and theories dealing with coherence in the legal system with those dealing with coherence in the

[71] F. Chirico and P. Larouche, 'Divergence, functionalism and the economics of convergence' in Prechal and Van Roermund (n 70), at 463–94.

[72] Nic Shuibhne (n 38).

[73] M. Cremona, 'Coherence through law: what difference will the Treaty of Lisbon make?', *Hamburg Review of Social Sciences* 3 (2008) 11–36.

[74] See P. Larouche, 'Coordination of European and member state regulatory policy. Horizontal, vertical and transversal aspects', *Competition and Regulation in Network Industries* 5 (2004) 277–94.

[75] L. Moral Soriano, 'A modest notion of coherence in legal reasoning. A model for the European Court of Justice', *Ratio Juris* 16 (2003) 296–323.

legal reasoning of individual cases. He advocates the latter, local coherence, where he comes close to requiring balancing consistent with the approach to proportionality associated with the work of Robert Alexy.[76] This brings us back to the remarks on proportionality in the preceding section.

General competition law

A rich seam of legal literature on EU competition law and policy exists. Well-known examples informing competition policy and practice are Faull and Nikpay,[77] Bellamy and Child,[78] and Van Bael and Bellis.[79] Among textbook authors, Giorgio Monti adopts a conceptual approach.[80] Relevant examples of the purely scholarly literature on competition law are provided by Okeoghene Odudu,[81] Chris Townley,[82] and Tony Prosser.[83] This book will be more in line with the latter; that is, it will not offer a toolbox for legal practice nor a teaching text but instead elements of a conceptual framework intended to further academic analysis. It is in this direction that I intend to make my main contribution. While some of the findings in the following may also be relevant from a practical perspective, this is not their primary purpose.

Contextual material

There is increasing interest in work on the history of EU competition law, such as that of David Gerber,[84] Joanna Goyder, and Albertina Albors-Llorens,[85] and the recent volume edited by Kiran Patel and Heike Schweitzer.[86] This literature is characterized by a varying degree of grounding in the substance of competition policy and in theoretical sweep. Increasingly, non-lawyers are studying competition policy as well: the work by Michelle Cini and Lee McGowan is emblematic.[87] As in the historical accounts by competition lawyers, I will use

[76] R. Alexy, *A Theory of Constitutional Rights*, transl. J. Rivers (Oxford: Oxford University Press, 2002); R. Alexy and A. Peczenik, 'The concept of coherence and its significance for discursive rationality', *Ratio Juris* 3 (1990) 130–47.

[77] J. Faull and A. Nikpay (eds), *The EU Law of Competition*, 3rd edn. (Oxford: Oxford University Press, 2014).

[78] V. Rose and D. Bailey (eds), *Bellamy and Child: European Union Law of Competition*, 2013 edn. (Oxford: Oxford University Press, 2013).

[79] Van Bael and Bellis, *Competition Law of the European Community*, 5th edn. (Alphen aan de Rijn: Kluwer Law International, 2010).

[80] G. Monti, *EC Competition Law* (Cambridge: Cambridge University Press, 2007).

[81] O. Odudu, *The Boundaries of EC Competition Law: The Scope of Article 81* (Oxford: Oxford University Press, 2006).

[82] C. Townley, *Article 81 EC and Public Policy* (Oxford: Hart Publishers, 2009).

[83] T. Prosser, *The Limits of Competition Law: Markets and Public Services* (Oxford: Oxford University Press, 2005).

[84] Above n 6.

[85] J. Goyder and A. Albors-Llorens, *Goyder's EC Competition Law*, 5th edn. (Oxford: Oxford University Press, 2008).

[86] Above n 6.

[87] M. Cini and L. McGowan, *The Competition Policy in the European Union*, 2nd edn. (London: Palgrave MacMillan, 2008).

such material for contextual purposes. I do, however, want to avoid giving an exclusively or predominantly institutional account; instead I wish to come to grips with the substantive law as well, that is, the cases.

Competition law and economics

I will occasionally use the economic literature on competition law and policy but without any aim of making an original contribution.[88] The objective here is not presenting a legal and economics account of competition law but merely one which is informed by economic notions. In fact I will argue in part against an economics-based approach.

Sectoral competition law

Although I propose to carry out some sectoral work there will be limited overlap with specialized accounts of electronic communications such as that by Pierre Larouche,[89] Paul Nihoul, and Peter Rodford,[90] and with Maartje de Visser's study of antitrust and electronic communications networks and governance.[91] Nor will I emulate a more contextual account such as that on energy by Kim Talus,[92] or a more technical one on the same subject like that by Angus Johnston and Guy Block.[93] My objective here is neither to produce a reference work nor an encyclopaedic overview but instead to provide a comparative analysis of the various regimes on key points. Also, and as mentioned earlier, I will try to look beyond governance at the coherence of the substantive norms involved. For now I will first move from competition back to the concept of coherence.

7. Approach

In the main, my methodology will be based on a review of the literature and the case law, where relevant, including inputs from economics (efficiency, consumer welfare), philosophy of law (coherence as a legal concept) and political science (networks and hierarchies). The conceptual framework has already been set out in part with the help of the tables above: I want to study coherence at three levels,

[88] Eg M. Motta, *Competition Policy: Theory and Practice* (Cambridge: Cambridge University Press, 2004). D. Geradin, A. Layne-Farrar and N. Petit, *EU Competition Law and Economics* (Oxford: Oxford University Press, 2012).

[89] P. Larouche, *Competition Law and Regulation in European Telecommunications* (Oxford: Hart Publishing, 2000).

[90] P. Nihoul and P. Rodford, *EU Electronic Communications Law: Competition and Regulation in the European Telecommunications Market*, 2nd edn. (Oxford: Oxford University Press, 2011).

[91] Above n 22.

[92] K. Talus, *EU Energy Law and Policy: A Critical Account* (Oxford: Oxford University Press, 2013).

[93] A. Johnston and G. Block, *EU Energy Law* (Oxford: Oxford University Press, 2012).

external, and internally at systemic and component level while using two secondary criteria, effectiveness and legitimacy. Centralization (and the principle of unity of EU law) and decentralization (and subsidiarity) were identified as dimensions that are expected to be correlated with greater or lesser coherence, although the link with effectiveness and legitimacy is complex.

In addition I will work with two sectoral case studies in the two main sectors that are so far equipped with a specific competition regime: electronic communications and energy.

- Electronic communications has developed from a classical utilities model based on public monopolies to a vehicle for the information age. The interaction between EU liberalization and harmonization in this sector has already been studied extensively. My objective will be to look at the interaction between general and sector specific policy in their organizational and normative aspects.
- In the energy sector, there are similar concerns to those in electronic communications regarding third party access and market power, yet different concerns such as regarding security of supply (including in a geo-strategic sense), the environment, and even more persistent infrastructure bottlenecks also play a role here.

8. Chapter Outline

Following this introductory chapter there are nine further chapters in this book.

In Chapter II, starting from the European Coal and Steel Community (ECSC) Treaty I will chart how the (various elements of) the competition regimes of the EU were introduced in their historical context, under what conditions and constraints, and to what purpose. I sketch the structure, notably the instruments and institutions, of EU competition law. This involves identifying various phases of competition law and an interpretation of their general direction, including that of the current phase. In addition I want to identify the main drivers for change that were inherent in competition law and policy and those that were extraneous.

I argue that the middle ground between endogenous and exogenous factors will be formed by the development of EU law at large, of which EU competition policy is of course one manifestation (among an increasing number of such manifestations). Linked to this, I also look at the role of EU competition law in the context of European integration, that is to say I identify what it has contributed to this process and how. The resulting framework—the main legal instruments and their place within the treaties and secondary legislation—will also be outlined on order to provide a background to the following chapters. Therefore the questions examined here are: how can the development of the competition law regimes of the EU be characterized and explained; what variables are at play; and what does this predict about the future of these variables and regimes?

In Chapter III I define both the multiple objectives and the limits of the EU competition regimes both for each regime as such and in relation to other regimes. This involves the concepts of promoting integration and of consumer interest as well as possibly competing interests such as protection of the competitive process and/or economic freedom as objectives. The thesis that combating market power forms an intermediate objective in relation to all these goals will be examined.[94] The limits or boundaries of EU competition law are based on functional concepts such as undertaking and economic activity,[95] economic concepts like market power, as well as concepts that are judicially defined on a case-by-case basis such as effect on trade.

The main questions here are to what extent these multiple objectives and boundaries are settled and effective as centripetal mechanisms in shaping EU competition law. This is an issue because centrifugal forces as a result of decentralization and sectoral specificities (and more recently increasingly strong Euroscepticism) are also at play. The question how the internal market can function both as a meaningful objective and justification for EU competition policy will also be examined here.

Chapter IV charts the system of the main rules and exceptions of the EU competition regimes. This shows how EU antitrust relies to a large extent on primary law (the Treaty rules) supplemented by guidance, whereas merger control, State aid, and sectoral competition law rely more on secondary rules (regulations and directives), again supplemented by guidance. However, even in antitrust, secondary rules are emerging, such as the recent directive on damages for competition law infringements.[96] Hence, I will explore the question of whether this means procedural harmonization must follow from decentralized application of the EU competition rules.

As regards the working of rules and exceptions, the classical EU approach of combining broad prohibitions with a generous application of exceptions—and the legal exception regime that is key to EU antitrust—contrasts with the rule of reason approach (which can also be seen as a boundary issue). A clear parallel can be found in State aid with the *Altmark* criteria set out by the Court[97] versus the *Altmark* package of the European Commission.[98] I will examine the question whether the same trend applies sectorally, and the role of commitment decisions.

[94] L. Ortiz Blanco, *Market Power in EU Antitrust Law* (Oxford: Hart Publishing, 2011).

[95] O. Odudu, 'Economic activity as a limit to Community law', in C. Barnard and O. Odudu (eds), *The Outer Limits of European Union Law* (Oxford: Hart Publishing, 2009) 225.

[96] Proposal for a Directive of the European Parliament and of the Council on certain rules governing actions for damages under national law for infringements of the competition law provisions of the Member States and of the European Union, COM(2013) 404. Cf. eg Case C-360/09 *Pfleiderer AG v Bundeskartellamt* [2011] ECR I-5161.

[97] Case C-280/00 *Altmark Trans GmbH and Regierungspräsidium Magdeburg v Nahverkehrsgesellschaft Altmark GmbH* [2003] ECR I-7747.

[98] Most recently: Commission Decision of 20 December 2011 on the application of Article 106(2) of the Treaty on the Functioning of the European Union to State aid in the form of public service compensation granted to certain undertakings entrusted with the operation of services of general economic interest, OJ 2012, L7/3; Communication from the Commission—European Union framework for State aid in the form of public service compensation, OJ 2012, C 8/15.

In addition it appears that different types of interest can be used to claim exceptions under the different types of competition rules (such as the economic interest of the firm and the consumer under antitrust and the economic and equity interest of the EU under State aid, the both the economic and equity interests of the Member State under SGEIs). Finally, third party access will be studied as an example where different standards apply to the same type of competition issue, depending on the type of regime applied. I will also look at the question of whether this difference explains the emergence (and persistence) of sectoral regimes.

In Chapter V I deal with the different procedural regimes within EU competition law. The role of procedure in promoting material consistency will be examined. In addition I look at remedies. From a perspective of effectiveness, procedures and remedies can be construed as complements if procedures are seen as related to providing instruments and outcomes related to remedies. However, procedures also involve due process and protection of the rights of the defence, which play an important role with regard to legitimacy (input legitimacy) as well. In this context the Leniency Notice,[99] the Notice on Settlements,[100] the Guidelines on Fines,[101] and the new directive on the private enforcement of antitrust[102] will receive particular attention.

Chapter VI concerns the organizational side of EU competition law along with the rules governing this organization. I deal with issues such as formal coordination mechanisms (such as through the advisory committee) and regulatory competition,[103] although I intend to do so primarily in legal terms (such as powers of pre-emption and blocking powers). This also involves looking at the proportionality principle, which in EU law is generally applied in a different manner depending on its setting.

Antitrust is the primary focus, where the Commission, as guardian of the Treaties, with the ECN has the ultimate responsibility for developing policy, safeguarding efficiency and consistency.[104] This includes looking at the convergence rule of Article 3 of Regulation 1/2003 and the pre-emption power in the hands of the Commission in its Article 11(6) that serves to ensure coherent application,

[99] Commission Notice on Immunity from fines and reduction of fines in cartel cases, OJ 2006, C298/17.

[100] Commission Notice on the conduct of settlement procedures in view of the adoption of Decisions pursuant to Article 7 and Article 23 of Council Regulation (EC) No 1/2003 in cartel cases, OJ 2008, C167/1.

[101] Guidelines on the method of setting fines imposed pursuant to Article 23(2)(a) of Regulation No 1/2003, OJ 2006, C210/2.

[102] Proposal for a Directive of the European Parliament and of the Council on certain rules governing actions for damages under national law for infringements of the competition law provisions of the Member States and of the European Union, COM(2013) 404, 11 June 2013; Communication from the Commission on quantifying harm in actions for damages based on breaches of Article 101 or 102 of the Treaty on the Functioning of the European Union, COM(2013) 3440, 11 June 2013.

[103] P. Larouche, 'Coordination of European and Member State regulatory policy: horizontal, vertical and transversal aspects', in D. Geradin and N. Petit, *Which Regulatory Authorities in Europe?* (Cheltenham: Edward Elgar, 2005). B. Gabor, *Regulatory Competition in the Internal Market: Comparing Models for Corporate Law, Securities Law and Competition Law* (Cheltenham: Edward Elgar, 2013).

[104] Joint statement (n 68) para 9.

and Article 16 on uniform application respecting the primacy of the Commission by national courts and NCAs.

Chapter VII regards the role of the courts and their interaction with the European Commission. Here I primarily consider the coordination mechanism with regard to national courts that involve the European Commission's *amicus curiae* briefs and the power to pre-empt national judgments with its decisions, and the prejudicial procedures before the Court of Justice.

I deal first with a general feature of EU law—the pyramid of judicial review and judicial references with at its apex the General Court and the Court of Justice of the EU—in relation to a specific topic: the effect on the coherence of EU competition law. The questions I will ask are: (i) what are the main features of judicial review and prejudicial references regarding competition law, such as the standard of review applied; (ii) what are the consequences of this; and (iii) can we identify possible vectors for change? Second, I examine the role of national courts in their role as independent adjudicators of competition cases. The different perspectives of the CJEU, the General Court, and the Commission will be dealt with here as well.[105]

The two dimensions of EU competition law, mergers, and State aid, will be contrasted with antitrust in Chapter VIII. In particular their higher degree of centralization distinguishes them.

In Chapter IX I conduct comparative case studies on the sectoral regimes for electronic communications and for energy. This will focus on their organizational side and key cases, and will not comprise a full analysis of NRA, BEREC/ACER, and Commission decisions in these fields. Broadly, I will ask what are the key features of these regimes as regards their coherence, and how they compare and relate to general competition policy.

In the concluding chapter I draw together the answers to the research questions in the preceding chapters. I present my answer to the overarching question regarding what the centrifugal and centripetal tendencies are, which of these prevails on what occasion, and for what reason.

[105] See Joined cases C-501/06 P, C-513/06 P, C-515/06 P, and C-519/06 P *GlaxoSmithKline Services Unlimited v Commission of the European Communities (C-501/06 P)* and *Commission of the European Communities v GlaxoSmithKline Services Unlimited (C-513/06 P)* and *European Association of Euro Pharmaceutical Companies (EAEPC) v Commission of the European Communities (C-515/06 P)* and *Asociación de exportadores españoles de productos farmacéuticos (Aseprofar) v Commission (C-519/06 P)* [2009] ECR I-9291; Case C-67/13 P *Groupement des cartes bancaires (CB) v Commission*, Judgment of 11 September 2014.

II

History and Framework of EU Competition Law

1. Introduction

The introduction of competition rules into an international Treaty is rare, and until the adoption of the Treaty on the European Coal and Steel Community (ECSC) in 1951 it was unprecedented. The sectoral example set by the ECSC was followed by the 1957 Rome Treaty that established the European Economic Community (EEC). The EEC Treaty incorporated (i) antitrust rules, but unlike the competition regime in the ECSC added (ii) State aid provisions and lacked merger policy powers. By means of secondary law (Regulations and Directives), (iii) in 1989 merger powers were finally added and in the 1990s, (iv) sectoral competition rules for electronic communications and energy.

The emergence and application of these five sets of rules have evolved over time. In this chapter I will focus on antitrust. To set the stage, I will first give a short outline of the instruments that will be discussed. Next I provide an historical account of the development of these regimes. This involves setting out their purpose and the context in which they were introduced. At the same time I also provide the framework of the substantive rules including the instruments and institutions. Drawing on standard historical accounts I identify several phases of development of EU competition law and an interpretation of their general direction, including that of the current phase. This involves trying to identify the main drivers for change that were inherent in competition law and policy itself and those that were extraneous to it.

As part of this discussion, I also look at the role of EU competition law in the context of European integration, particularly integration through law.[1] This involves identifying what competition law has contributed to this process and in what manner this has occurred. Alongside coherence and effectiveness the main notion that is relevant in this regard is that of legitimacy. This includes not only output legitimacy in terms of results; that is, anticompetitive practices foiled. It

[1] Seminal: M. Cappelletti, M. Seccombe, and J.H.H. Weiler (eds), *Integration through Law: European and the American Federal Experience* (Berlin: De Gruyter, 1986); more recent is D. Augenstein (ed.), *Integration through Law Revisited: The Making of the European Polity* (Farnham: Ashgate, 2011).

also involves an increase in input legitimacy now that the EU antitrust rules have increasingly become 'the law of the land' throughout the EU and national competition authorities (NCAs) are involved in enforcing it.

As was set out in the general introduction to this book, the questions examined here are: how can the development of the competition law regimes of the EU be characterized and explained; what variables are at play; and what does this predict about the future of these variables and regimes with regard to the coherence of decisions and of the system as a whole?

2. The Framework: A Concise Overview of the Instruments

Antitrust: Anticompetitive agreements

Antitrust consists firstly of Article 101(1) of the Treaty on the Functioning of the European Union (TFEU) which prohibits anticompetitive agreements practices by undertakings, unless the limited conditions for an exception (and an exemption) set out in Article 101(3) TFEU are met.[2] The drafting of Article 101(3) TFEU (then Article 85(3) EEC) was a compromise that allowed for both a directly applicable exception system (favoured by France), and a prior authorization system (favoured by Germany). The open texture of the resulting text allowed a shift from the prior authorization to the legal exception system to occur in the context of the 2003 modernization of antitrust without requiring a Treaty amendment.

Under the original implementing legislation, Council Regulation 17 of 1962, the Article 101(3) TFEU exception was applied exclusively by the European Commission, based on a system of prior notification of the agreements concerned.[3] The key point of modernization under Council Regulation 1/2003 has been that the notification system and Commission exemption monopoly were replaced by a legal exception regime which is directly applicable, based on self-assessment by the undertakings concerned.[4] This has gone hand in hand with first, adopting an effects- (and more economics-) based approach, and second, a focus on hardcore cartels that is largely based on a successful system of leniency

[2] Article 85 EEC reads: (1) The following shall be prohibited as incompatible with the common market: all agreements between undertakings, decisions by associations of undertakings and concerted practices which may affect trade between Member States and which have as their object or effect the prevention, restriction or distortion of competition within the common market... (2) Any agreements or decisions prohibited pursuant to this Article shall be automatically void. (3) The provisions of paragraph 1 may, however, be declared inapplicable...which contributes to improving the production or distribution of goods or to promoting technical or economic progress, while allowing consumers a fair share of the resulting benefit, and which does not: (a) impose on the undertakings concerned restrictions which are not indispensable to the attainment of these objectives; (b) afford such undertakings the possibility of eliminating competition in respect of a substantial part of the products in question.

[3] Council Regulation No 17/62, First Regulation implementing Articles 85 and 86 of the Treaty, OJ 1962, 87 (Regulation 17).

[4] Council Regulation (EC) No 1/2003 of 16 December 2002 on the implementation of the rules on competition laid down in Articles 81 and 82 of the Treaty, OJ 2003, L1/1.

application by former cartel members.[5] However, there are various other escapes from the system of EU competition law system that start from the definition of undertaking[6] and include state instructions (the 'state action defence')[7] as well as inherent restrictions in the interest of a public interest objective.[8]

Apart from the implementation Regulation 1/2003, the Commission has adopted a panoply of secondary rules designed to deal with various infringements and exceptions to Article 101 TFEU. These will be discussed in the following.

Antitrust: Abuse of dominance

The second element of antitrust is the prohibition on the abuse of dominance in Article 102 TFEU. Here, market definition is key, as is establishing dominance and abuse. (The sector-specific rules for the network sectors are variations on this theme.) Dominance must always be assessed in relation to a specific product and geographic market. In addition, the Treaty does not include an exemption for dominance abuse, although based on the Commission's practice it is possible to invoke an efficiency-based objective justification as well as a meeting competition defence. In contrast to Article 101 TFEU there is no further secondary legislation on Article 102 TFEU (and the case law is comparatively scarce). More recently, the Commission's focus has been on exclusionary abuses, that is denying competitors access to the market (or foreclosure), more than on exploitative abuses, or squeezing out consumers.[9] Focusing on exclusion involves difficult assessments as there may be a fine line between vigorous competition on the merits, which is evidently thought desirable, and its equally vigorous anticompetitive variety. In addition, if consumer welfare is considered as a guiding objective (which it need not be, as we will see in subsequent chapters), it requires explanation why price gouging of consumers is not a priority but exclusion of competitors is. Presumably the reason is that it is more effective and less intrusive to solve retail problems by tackling competition issues at wholesale level and promoting competitive provision as the solution to issues of market power. This squares with the logic of promoting entry in the network sectors.

Antitrust: Application

For reasons that will be discussed at length later in this chapter, until May 2004 the application of EU antitrust law was largely concentrated in the hands of the

[5] The leniency programme is now based on Commission Notice on Immunity from fines and reduction of fines in cartel cases, OJ 2006, C298/17.

[6] Case C-205/03P *Federación Española de Empresas de Tecnología Sanitaria (FENIN) v Commission* [2006] ECR I-6295.

[7] Joined cases C-359/95P and C-379/95P *Commission and France v Ladbroke Racing Ltd* [1997] ECR I-6265.

[8] Case C-309 *J. C. J. Wouters, J. W. Savelbergh and Price Waterhouse Belastingadviseurs BV v Algemene Raad van de Nederlandse Orde van Advocaten* [2002] ECR I-1577.

[9] Communication from the Commission—Guidance on the Commission's enforcement priorities in applying Article 82 of the EC Treaty to abusive exclusionary conduct by dominant undertakings, OJ 2009, C45/7.

EU Commission. Today, the antitrust rules are applied by twenty-eight independent NCAs and by the European Commission, which also coordinates the NCAs, in part through the European Competition Network (ECN). In addition, the antitrust rules are also applied directly by national courts who may consul the Court of Justice on the correct interpretation of the EU law by means of prejudicial references. The EU's General Court hears appeals against Commission decisions, and its own rulings can be appealed on points of law by the Court of Justice. It is clear that this system of coordination and judicial review, which ultimately culminates at the Court of Justice, promotes coherence both internal (within EU competition law) and external (within EU law), of course only to the extent that the Court is consistent itself.

In particular, the Commission plays a pivotal role within this system. In the 2005 *Preinsulated Pipes* case the Court spelled out that in doing so the Commission is bound to pursue a competition policy, which would by definition have to be coherent.

> The supervisory task conferred on the Commission by Articles 85(1) and 86 of the EC Treaty (now Article 82 EC) [now Articles 101(1) and 102 TFEU] not only includes the duty to investigate and punish individual infringements but also encompasses the duty to pursue a general policy designed to apply, in competition matters, the principles laid down by the Treaty and to guide the conduct of undertakings in the light of those principles.[10]

It did so citing the 1983 *Musique Diffusion* case regarding the task of the Commission with regard to applying the EU antitrust provisions.

> That task certainly includes the duty to investigate and punish individual infringements, but it also encompasses the duty to pursue a general policy designed to apply, in competition matters, the principles laid down by the treaty and to guide the conduct of undertakings in the light of those principles.[11]

It remains to be examined whether the Commission has done so (at different times), and if so, how.

3. The Constitutional Status of Antitrust

Links with the internal market

There are at least three ways of looking at the constitutional dimension of the EU competition rules.

1. While this development may not be generally acknowledged, at least among EU lawyers the development of the system of the Treaties as interpreted by

[10] Joined cases C-189/02 P, C-202/02 P, C-205/02 P to C-208/02 P and C-213/02 P *Dansk Rørindustri A/S, Isoplus Fernwärmetechnik Vertriebsgesellschaft mbH and Others, KE KELIT Kunststoffwerk GmbH, LR af 1998 A/S, Brugg Rohrsysteme GmbH, LR af 1998 (Deutschland) GmbH, and ABB Asea Brown Boveri Ltd v Commission* [2005] ECR I-5425, para 170.

[11] Joined cases 100 to 103/80 *SA Musique Diffusion française et al. v Commission* [1983] ECR 1825, para 105.

the EU Courts is regarded as a process of constitutionalization.[12] As early as 1991 the Court itself identified the Treaties (then the EEC Treaty) as 'the constitutional charter of a Community based on the rule of law'.[13]

2. At an even more technical level, this can be squared with the notion of an economic constitution pioneered by the German school of Ordoliberalism where the idea is that the rule of law serves to contain interventions by the state in the market, but at the same time sets certain constraints on market forces in order to promote the functioning of the market.[14]
3. The ill-fated 2004 proposal for an explicit EU Constitution that was defeated in referenda in France and The Netherlands in 2005 (to be replaced by the 2007 Lisbon Treaty) included a provision explicitly stating that competition policy was one of the objectives of the EU. Instead the link between the legal basis for competition law and that of the internal market has become more important.

The primary legal basis for the competition rules is found in the Treaties which of course have developed over time with their successive renegotiations and amendments. It appears, however, that in spite of intense discussion not much has changed over time as far as the role of competition policy is concerned. In the EEC Treaty dating back to 1957, Article 3(g) listed among the activities of the Community 'a system ensuring that competition in the internal market is not distorted'. Article 1-III of the 2004 proposed Treaty establishing a Constitution for Europe stated among the Union's objectives that:

> The Union shall offer its citizens an area of freedom, security and justice without internal frontiers, and an internal market where competition is free and undistorted.

Presumably the purpose of this attempted elevation of competition law to a constitutional objective was to compensate for less competition-oriented developments in the Constitution such as the introduction in the next paragraph of the same article of the objective of a social market economy which, unlike the clause cited above, was incorporated in the Lisbon Treaty.

When, following the negative outcomes of the French and Dutch referenda, the Constitution was withdrawn and revamped to produce the 2007 Lisbon Treaty, the stature of the competition provision was allegedly one of the main casualties.[15]

[12] Cf. J.H.H. Weiler, *The Constitution of Europe: 'Do the New Clothes have an Emperor?' and other Essays on European Integration* (Cambridge: Cambridge University Press, 1999); M. Poiares Maduro, *We the Court: The European Court of Justice and the European Economic Constitution* (Oxford: Hart Publishing, 1998).

[13] Opinion 1/91 on the draft treaty establishing the European Economic Area [1991] ECR I-6079, para 21.

[14] W. Sauter, *EU Competition Law and Industrial Policy* (Oxford: Oxford University Press, 1997). D.J. Gerber, *Law and Competition in Twentieth Century Europe: Protecting Prometheus* (Oxford: Oxford University Press, 1998).

[15] A. Riley, 'The EU reform Treaty and the competition protocol: undermining EC competition law', *European Competition Law Review* 28 (2007) 703–7; F. Graupner, 'The battle over the role of European competition policy: now you see it, now you don't', *Competition Law Journal*

The outcome is that Article 3(1)b of the TFEU now states that the Union shall have exclusive competence in 'the establishing of the competition rules necessary for the functioning of the internal market'. Likewise Protocol 27 on the internal market and competition states 'that the internal market as set out in Article 3 of the Treaty on European Union includes a system ensuring that competition is not distorted'. This leads to the conclusion that the competition rules always were, and still are, primarily linked to the functioning of the internal market. To the extent that this link has been strengthened, this secures rather than weakens the position of competition policy because the internal market remains the defining project of European integration.

Unsurprisingly, therefore, the view from the EU institutions is that the Lisbon changes make little difference: competition policy was never an objective in its own right (although the draft constitution would have made it one) but an instrument to achieve the internal market. This it remains. Thus, in 2007 then Competition Commissioner Kroes reacted as follows:

> An Internal Market without competition rules would be an empty shell—nice words, but no concrete results. The Protocol on Internal Market and Competition agreed at the European Council clearly repeats that competition policy is fundamental to the Internal Market. It retains the existing competition rules which have served us so well for 50 years. It re-confirms the European Commission's duties as the independent competition enforcement authority for Europe. Now I would like to get back to the job.[16]

It is noteworthy here that the State aid rules are also covered. This view was essentially confirmed by the Court in *Commission v Italy* (2011):

> As to the seriousness of the infringement, the vital nature of the Treaty rules on competition must be recalled, in particular those on State aid, which are the expression of one of the essential tasks with which the European Union is entrusted. At the time of the Court's assessment of the appropriateness and the amount of the present penalty payment, that vital nature is apparent from Article 3(3) TEU, namely the establishment of an internal market, and from Protocol No 27 on the internal market and competition, which forms an integral part of the Treaties in accordance with Article 51 TEU, and states that the internal market includes a system ensuring that competition is not distorted.[17]

The symbolism contained in this is clear: there is to be no central role for competition in political terms. In practice, however, the impact of the antitrust decentralization process that is discussed below will be much more significant than such rearrangements.

6 (1997) 89–100; Cf. J. Goyder and A. Albors-Llorens, *Goyder's EC Competition Law*, 5th edn. (Oxford: Oxford University Press, 2008) 632–3.

[16] Statement by European Commissioner for Competition Neelie Kroes on results of June 21–22 European Council—Protocol on Internal Market and Competition, MEMO/07/250.

[17] Case C-496/09 *Commission v Italy* [2011] ECR I-11483. I am indebted to Ben van Rompuy's blog for these references. Available at: <http://kluwercompetitionlawblog.com/2011/11/25/>. Also cited in W. Sauter, 'Squaring EU competition law and industrial policy: the case of broadband', in J.M. Beneyto and J. Maíllo (eds), *Fostering Growth in Europe: Reinforcing the Internal Market* (Madrid: CEU ediciones, 2014).

The Lisbon Treaty and SGEI

As an aside, the Article 14 and Protocol 27 on services of general (economic) interest SGEI should be discussed here. The elaboration of SGEI in these two instruments provides the mirror image of what is sometimes (in my view wrongly, as we have just seen) considered the demotion of the competition rules in the 2007 Lisbon Treaty. Similarly, the elaboration of the provisions on SGEI has not had any noticeable repercussion. The two sets of changes are referred to jointly here because they were prepared in tandem in order to assuage the alleged doubts of the French and the Dutch following their negative votes on the draft Constitution. (Although in reality, few of the 'no' voters would probably have been aware that the EU even had policies on competition and SGEI.) However, partly as a result of these concessions, the Lisbon Treaty salvaged much of what had been set out in the doomed Constitution. Jointly they enabled the two governments concerned to save face vis-à-vis their electorates and to facilitate adoption of the Lisbon Treaty without further (potentially crippling) referenda.

It may also be that these changes reflect a growing general scepticism with regard to competition and a more positive view of SGEI. This would be paradoxical because SGEI act precisely as a means to reconcile public services with competition and promote their rationalization in accordance with market principles, not a free-for-all to justify public intervention. By adopting the SGEI model Member States are also accepting the primacy of competition law as the default rule for undertakings, and by using undertakings to provide public services they are showing that this is preferable to state ownership and public provision.

Conclusion on the role of competition law

Of the three constitutional dimensions cited above therefore only the first two are still relevant: that is, constitutionalization in the case law of the CJEU and the notion of the Treaties as providing an economic constitution. I will not be developing these as main themes in my analysis of the coherence of competition law in the EU. The direct effect and supremacy of EU law as legal principles, however, are self-evidently important to the effective functioning and legitimacy of EU competition policy, and they can be seen as expressing a constitutional force implied in EU law. I will return to this in Chapter III on the objectives of competition law. Meanwhile it will suffice for antitrust to be justified by its functional characteristics and practical objectives, and indeed by reference to the internal market, not by reference to aspirations of a higher order.

4. Competition Policy before 1957

I now turn to the historical development of EU competition law.

Sources of influence

It is possible to look for the origins or more properly at the inspiration of EU competition law in a range of sources and movements that pre-date the 1957 Rome Treaty.[18] In what I intend to be a loosely ranked ascending order of significance, these include the following five categories:

(i) Earlier national rules on competition and unfair trading practices (some dating back to the guild system of the *ancien régime*) throughout Europe which often pre-dated the Second World War and were frequently intended to promote orderly competition foremost, rather than free competition;

(ii) The German Ordoliberal school of law and economics which promoted the idea of free competition as a guiding principle of the economy and influenced the emergence of the post-war economic order of Germany as a social market economy;

(iii) Non-European sources, notably the antitrust laws of the United States (US) against cartels dating back to the 1890 Sherman Act;

(iv) Contemporary national sources that were themselves influenced by some of the former, such as 1957 German Act against restraints of competition (*Gesätz gegen Wettbewerbsbeschrankungen*), that followed upon cartel restraints imposed in Germany by the Allied occupation forces immediately after the Second World War. (Although given the timing involved, the influence here was on implementing Regulation 17/62 more than on the Treaty provisions concerning competition themselves.);

(v) Sources that formed part of the European integration effort themselves, notably the cartels prohibition and the rules on merger control in the ECSC Treaty in 1951.

I will not go into further detail regarding these various sources, however they do make clear that the EU competition rules were not created *ex nihilo* and can be traced back to distinct historical foundations. At national level, in parallel, the influence exercised varied from country to country, leading to a variety of national regimes that would become subject to spontaneous harmonization at a much later stage. Moreover, the vast majority of current Member States were not only not part of the original six States but were subjected to long decades of fascist dictatorship or communist misrule as intervening variables. Hence we should probably not attach too much importance to historic factors pre-dating the EU where, in successive enlargements, the desire to join the EU itself was the overwhelming motivation for accepting and adopting its rules, not least those on competition.

[18] See Goyder (n 15); K.K. Patel and H. Schweitzer (eds), *The Historical Foundations of EU Competition Law* (Oxford: Oxford University Press, 2013); L. Warlouzet, The rise of European competition policy, 1950–1991: A cross-disciplinary survey of a contested policy sphere, EUI Working papers RSCAS 2010/80.

In my view, it is the context of integration that is by far the most important historic influence that, moreover, continues to cast its unabated spell today. This also means that the ECSC rules are the most important precedent to integration. This is not to deny the influence of US antitrust laws in terms of the substantive norms that would eventually be applied, and the other factors listed above in preparing the ground for the principle of EU competition rules being accepted as legitimate forms of public policy. However, although in this sense these other factors may have influenced the direction and the shape of EU competition law, they could never have caused, justified, or explained its creation.

The ECSC example

As is well-known, the 1951 ECSC Treaty (which came into force in 1952 and expired fifty years later) was fundamentally an attempt to pool the dominant war industries of the time—coal and steel—between France and Germany. The purpose behind making this unprecedented move was practically to exclude any future belligerence between the two nations, not by crippling former foes but by each embracing the other via economic means.[19] In the words of the Schuman Declaration of 1950, uttered by the then French Minister of foreign affairs who announced the plan to create the ECSC, 'The solidarity in production thus established will make it plain that any war between France and Germany becomes not merely unthinkable, but materially impossible.'[20]

The Preamble of the ECSC Treaty itself makes this clear in more graphic detail by stating that the contracting parties were acting:

> to substitute for historic rivalries a fusion of their essential interests; to establish, by creating an economic community, the foundation of a broad and independent community among peoples long divided by bloody conflicts; and to lay the bases of institutions capable of giving direction to their future common destiny.

In this context, the wartime combinations of national industrial cartels would also have to be abolished or controlled. This gave rise to Articles 65 and 66 ECSC prohibiting cartels and introducing merger control as well as, in less explicit terms, prohibiting abuse of dominance in Article 66(7) ECSC. Antidumping measures were also provided. The explicit merger control powers for coal and steel are worth noting because they were withheld from the EEC for the economy at large until 1989.

The ECSC also set a number of related institutional precedents that were carried forward by the subsequent EEC and its successors, the European Community (EC) and European Union (EU). Not least among these were technocratic and sectoral government initiated by a supranational administrative body, the High

[19] A.S. Milward, *The Reconstruction of Western Europe 1945–1951* (London: Routledge, 1982); A.S. Milward, *The European Rescue of the Nation-State*, 2nd edn. (London: Routledge, 1999).

[20] Available at: <http://europa.eu/about-eu/basic-information/symbols/europe-day/schuman-declaration/index_en.htm>.

Authority, to be succeeded by the European Commission in the EEC and its successors, as well as government by the rule of law, administered in the final instance by a supranational Court of Justice. A Council of Ministers and an Assembly were precursors of the EU Council and European Parliament. A major difference is that in the EEC and its successors the administration of key industries (nor of minor industries for that matter) was not pooled in as coal and steel were under the ECSC. (For present purposes nuclear energy, governed by the 1957 Euratom Treaty, is not regarded as a key industry, in spite of earlier high expectations.) However, the EU has seen the emergence of harmonized competition-based regimes for key network based utilities, notably electronic communications and energy.

The emergence of EC competition law can be divided into three phases: the early years, the move toward a more economic approach, and modernization.

5. The Early Years

Why was an EU competition regime introduced?

The main reason why a competition regime was introduced in the 1957 EEC Treaty was directly derived from the internal market that was to be achieved not by pooling resources, as in the ECSC, but by removing state barriers to trade: quantitative restrictions and measures having equivalent effect. The instruments to promote this objective directly were the four freedoms: the free movement of goods, services, persons (including establishment), and capital.[21] An antitrust policy was introduced to avoid private undertakings (for instance, by means of cartels organized along national lines) reintroducing the restrictions that had been surrendered by public authorities. At the same time, State aid policy served to ensure that governments did not switch from throwing up tariff and non-tariff barriers to offering direct support of favoured undertakings financially.

This reasoning is set out in detail in the seminal 1956 Spaak Report drafted by an intergovernmental committee as an outline in preparation for the 1957 EEC Treaty.[22]

In the 1966 *Consten v Grundig* case, where it applied Article 85 EEC (now Article 101 TFEU) for the first time, the Court of Justice underscored this line of thought:

> an agreement between producer and distributor which might tend to restore the national divisions in trade between Member States might be such as to frustrate the most fundamental objections of the Community. The Treaty, whose preamble and content aim at abolishing the barriers between States, and which in several provisions gives evidence of a stern attitude with regard to their reappearance, could not allow undertakings to reconstruct such barriers. Article 85(1) [now Article 101(1) TFEU] is designed to pursue this

[21] C. Barnard, *The Substantive Law of the EU: The Four Freedoms*, 4th edn. (Oxford: Oxford University Press, 2013).

[22] '*Dans les conditions économiques du monde moderne, l'élargissement des marches et de la concurrence ne suffit pas à assurer la répartition la plus rationnelle des activités et le rythme le plus favorable d'expansion.*

aim, even in the case of agreements between undertakings placed at different levels in the economic process.[23]

In addition, the Court accepted the argument that where the purpose of an agreement was to partition markets, the effects need not be demonstrated: in the case at hand, German exports of consumer electronics to France had actually increased as a result of the contested agreement. This linked with the distinction between restrictions by object and by effect in the text of Article 85(1) EEC (now Article 101(1) TFEU) itself. (The contrast between restrictions between object and effect will be discussed in Chapter III.)[24]

The Court's ruling in *Consten v Grundig* therefore clearly shows that the Spaak Report's internal market-based rationale for competition policy in the EU context was alive and well and shared by the Court ten years later.[25] Similarly, in *Walt Wilhelm* in 1969, the Court emphasized that the primary aim of EU competition law, over and above promoting competition law itself, is the elimination of obstacles to the free movement of goods and safeguarding the unity of the internal market as the primary aim of EU competition law.[26] Note that the fact *Consten v Grundig* in 1966 was the first real test of the EU's competition policy showed that in practical terms not much had been achieved by that time, other than embarking upon an approach to vertical agreements which would determine the basic orientation of antitrust in the EU for the next forty years, only eventually to be regarded as fundamentally misconceived.

Market partitioning and vertical restraints

The integration-based perspective that saw antitrust foremost as an instrument to counteract market partitioning was to have far-reaching implications. The resultant emphasis on enabling parallel trade led to a fixation on fighting vertical

Le premier fait dont il convient de tenir compte, c'est la dimension atteinte par les entreprises, ou l'usage des ententes entre entreprises et, par suite, les pratiques de monopole, les facultés de discrimination, les possibilités de répartition du marché. Des règles de concurrence qui s'imposent aux entreprises sont donc necessaires pour éviter que des doubles prix aient le même effet que des droits de douane, qu'un dumping mette en danger des productions économiquement saines, que la répartition des marches se substitue a leur cloisonnement.

Le deuxième fait, c'est l'intervention étendue des Etats en vue de favoriser les entreprises de leur nationalité'. Il faut donc discerner les aides utiles à l' interêt general et à l' expansion de la production de celles qui ont pour objet et pour effet de fausser la concurrence.' Comité intergouvernemental créé par la Conférence de Messine, *Rapport des Chefs de délégation aux Minstres des Affaires étrangères* (Brussels: 1956), pp 16–17. The unofficial English summary and translation of this document leaves out these key passages.

[23] Joined cases 56 and 58/64 *Établissements Consten S.à.R.L. and Grundig Verkaufs-GmbH v Commission* [1966] ECR 429, at 340.

[24] See Case 226/11 *Expedia Inc. v Autorité de la concurrence et al.*, Judgment of 13 December 2012.

[25] Following modernization a similar statement can still be found in the Commission Notice: Guidelines on Vertical Restraints, OJ 2010, C 130/1, para 7: 'Market integration enhances competition in the European Union. Companies should not be allowed to re-establish private barriers between Member States where State barriers have been successfully abolished.'

[26] Case 14/68 *Walt Wilhelm et al. v Bundeskartellamt* [1969] ECR 1, para 9.

restraints that was not in line with their limited harmful nature in a more objective economic sense. It also claimed energy and resources from the Commission as the primary, almost sole enforcer of the competition rules that could have been spent more fruitfully elsewhere, notably fighting horizontal restraints, including cartels. Instead, the Commission gave priority to promoting intra-brand competition between different distributors of the same brand, above inter-brand competition between distributors of different brands.[27] This has sometimes been seen as the outcome of a struggle between Ordoliberals and Keynesians (a euphemism for social democrats) within the Directorate General of Competition (then DG IV) with the latter carrying the day then and subsequently, until relatively recently.[28]

The notification and authorization system

The development regarding parallel trade also fit with the system under the first enabling Regulation 17 adopted in 1962, tested before the Court for the first time in *Consten v Grundig*. The text of Articles 85 and 86 EEC (101 and 102 TFEU) did not state who would be in charge of applying them. Recent historical research holds that the text of Article 85 EEC (now Article 101 TFEU) reflected French thinking on decentralization and their views on legal exception, whereas Regulation 17, with its exemption system and centralization in the hands of the Commission, was more in line with the perspective taken by Germany.[29] Until Regulation 17 came into force in 1962, Article 88 EEC (now Article 104 TFEU) determined that it was the national authorities and not the Commission that decided on the application of the exemption provision in Article 81(3) EEC (now Article 101(3) TFEU).[30] This also enabled the national preferences for an exemption system in Germany and a legal exception system in France to persist up to the adoption of the Regulation. According to legal historians, this was the outcome of log-rolling to reach a French–German compromise that had linked the adoption of Regulation 17/62 (in a centralized form favoured by the German government) to proceeding with the development of the Common Agricultural Policy (strongly desired by the French).[31]

By force of Article 7(3) of Regulation 17, the Commission received exclusive competence to grant exemptions from the prohibition in Article 85(1) EEC (now Article 101 TFEU) under Article 85(3) EEC (now Article 101 TFEU).[32]

[27] This is now largely history, but not completely: parallel imports in the areas of pharmaceuticals and motor vehicle distribution remain live issues in EU competition policy today.

[28] S.M. Ramírez Pérez and S. van de Scheur, 'The evolution of the law on Article 85 and 86 EEC: Ordoliberalism and its Keynesian challenge', in Patel and Schweitzer (n 18), 19–53.

[29] Ibid, and L.F. Pace and K. Seidel, 'The drafting and the role of Regulation 17: a hard-fought compromise', in Patel and Schweitzer (n 18), 54–88. Cf. Goyder (n 15), 24–39.

[30] Article 88: Until the date of the entry into force of the provisions adopted in application of Article 87, the authorities of Member States shall, in accordance with their respective municipal law and with the provisions of Article 85, particularly paragraph 3, and of Article 86, rule upon the admissibility of any understanding and upon any improper advantage taken of a dominant position in the Common Market.

[31] Pace and Seidel (n 29).

[32] Council Regulation 17/62 (n 3).

Regulation 17 added a prior notification requirement (for new agreements, and a notification system allowing for a form of provisional validity for existing agreement)[33] and an authorization system for prior notification. The objectives of the new system as stated in the preamble of Regulation 17 were providing for a balanced system of competition law with effective supervision and a simple administration as well as uniform application.[34]

The Commission's monopoly on offering an exemption gave it a central and unique position of power within the competition law system while at the same time handicapping the other parties that played a role in its enforcement: NCAs and national courts. Incidentally, this high degree of centralization with a decision-making monopoly at the level of the European Commission was not unique for antitrust. In 1989 it was introduced for merger control for cases with an EU dimension, and it had always been the case for Article 107(3) TFEU clearance decisions under the State aid rules: in both cases (unlike for Article 101(3) TFEU), a centralized enforcement monopoly of the relevant EU rules remains in place today. In the shadow of the Commission's monopoly on finding aid compatible, the possibilities for complainants to obtain results in national courts are limited. This raises problems that are similar to those that were experienced in antitrust.

According to Article 4(1) of Regulation 17, exemptions could be retrospective or anticipatory but could only be granted following notification, however Article 4(2) provided an exception from the notification requirement for agreements (i) that were limited in scope to a single Member State, or (ii) where no more than two parties were involved and certain limited vertical restraints were involved, or (iii) that solely concerned standardization, joint research, and development or specialization, subject to certain market share and turnover thresholds. Although long neglected, this provision can be seen as the foundation for the economic approach that was to be adopted in the 1990s (and its scope was then extended to most vertical agreements).

De minimis, comfort letters, and block exemptions

In the 1969 *Völk v Vervaecke* case and the notice that was based on its reasoning, the Commission established the *de miminis* rule that an appreciable effect on competition was required for Article 85(1) EEC (now Article 101(1) TFEU) to apply.[35] In what was a very modern approach at the time, a 5 per cent market-share

[33] According to Article 7(1) of Regulation 17/62, above (n 3), the Commission was to fix the term for which invalidity of (clauses of) existing contract applied if the contracting parties had made amends.

[34] The Commission's White Paper on modernization of the rules implementing Articles 85 and 86 of the EC Treaty, COM(99) 101, OJ 1999, C132/1, para 14, cites an accompanying memorandum to Regulation 17 which listed (i) generating more information about the state of the markets, as well as (ii) ensuring a uniform regime, and (iii) an adequate measure of legal certainty.

[35] Case 5/69 *Franz Völk v SPRL Ets Vervaecke* [1969] ECR 295; Commission Notice of 27 May 1970 concerning agreements, decisions and concerted practices of minor importance which do not fall under Article 85(1) of the Treaty establishing the European Economic Community, OJ 1970,

threshold (and a turnover threshold of 20 million accounting units) was used to determine the scope for such agreements of minor importance.

However, as an unintended side-effect of the centralized authorization and notification system, the eventual result was nevertheless the submission of thousands of agreements for consideration by the Commission services (according to the 1999 White Paper by 1967 some 37,450 cases had accumulated),[36] creating a backlog that was not to be cleared over the forty years that this system lasted. Given the sheer volume involved, dealing with each of these cases by means of a formal individual decision was never a serious proposition.[37]

Instead, in the first place, the practice emerged of managing notifications by means of individual informal clearances, or comfort letters, which were not legally binding, and meant that *prima facie* the agreement concerned either did not restrict competition (leading to a negative clearance type exemption letter) or met the conditions of Article 81(3) EEC (now Article 101(3) TFEU, leading to an exemption-type comfort letter). Comfort letters did not have binding effect.[38] They speeded up the process but also eliminated the publication requirement (in all the official languages) as well as the formal consultation of the Advisory Committee of representatives of the Member States. This effectively meant signing away some of the procedural guarantees (and thereby input legitimacy) that the formal decision-making procedure had provided. The legality of the practice of issuing comfort letters was nevertheless confirmed by the Court in the 'perfume cases' (1980) although it also ruled that they merely constituted elements of fact for the national courts to take into account.[39]

In the second place, groups of agreements were cleared by means of block exemptions, which the Commission had been empowered to adopt by the Council Regulations 19/65, 2821/71, and 1534/91 based on Article 87 EEC (now Article 103 TFEU).[40] These block exemptions were issued for standard types of agreements, notably (i) vertical—exclusive distribution agreements or exclusive purchasing agreements,[41] respectively licensing and franchising;[42]

C64/1. Now: Notice on agreements of minor importance which do not appreciably restrict competition under Article 101(1) of the Treaty on the Functioning of the European Union, SWD(2014) 198 final.

[36] White Paper (n 34), para 24. [37] See Goyder (n 15).

[38] Case 99/79 SA *Lancôme and Cosparfrance Nederland BV v Etos BV and Albert Heyn Supermart BV* [1980] ECR 2511.

[39] Case 31/80 *NV L'Oréal and SA L'Oréal v PVBA 'De Nieuwe AMCK'* [1980] ECR 3775; Joined cases 253/78 and 1 to 3/79 *Procureur de la République et al. v Bruno Giry and Guerlain SA et al.* [1980] ECR 2327; Case 37/79 *Anne Marty SA v Estée Lauder SA* [1980] ECR 2481.

[40] Council Regulation 19/65/EEC of 2 March 1965 on application of Article 85 (3) of the Treaty to certain categories of agreements and concerted practices, OJ P 36; Council Regulation 2821/71/EEC of 20 December 1971 on application of Article 85 (3) of the Treaty to categories of agreements, decisions and concerted practices, OJ 1971, L285; Council Regulation 1534/91, below (n 44).

[41] Commission Regulation (EEC) No 1983/83 of 22 June 1983 concerning exclusive distribution agreements, OJ 1983, L173/1; Commission Regulation (EEC) No 1984/83 of 22 June 1983 concerning exclusive purchasing agreements, OJ 1983, L173/55.

[42] Commission Regulation (EEC) No 2349/84 of 23 July 1984 concerning patent licensing agreements, OJ 1984, L219/15; Commission Regulation (EEC) No 4087/88 of 30 November 1988

but also (ii) sectoral—motor vehicle distribution,[43] and insurance;[44] as well as (iii) horizontal—specialization agreements and research and development agreements.[45] If an agreement fulfilled all the conditions in a particular block exemption it was automatically cleared.

The various block exemptions, however, were originally highly specific and mutually exclusive, so undertakings were forced to choose a particular model and stick with that in order to obtain exemption under the competition rules, even if for commercial reasons a mixed form or even a wholly new format would have been preferred. At the time they were introduced, Valentine Korah, an early critic of this system, famously called this the 'straitjacket effect' of the block exemptions.[46] Even the Commission itself in the 1999 White Paper on modernization adopted this terminology to describe its own (former) practice.[47] Eventually, however, under the effects-based approach discussed later in this chapter, the block exemptions were bundled, notably in a single block exemption for vertical agreements.[48]

The results of the centralized system of antitrust

Institutionally a key merit of the notification and authorization system combined with an exemption monopoly was that it was highly coherent, at least in terms of the uniformity of EU law. Substantively, as we have seen, the system tended to be formalistic and somewhat inflexible, and from an economic point of view in parts self-contradictory and therefore not highly coherent at all. In terms of effective enforcement the results were in fact mixed. The Commission may have been effective in what it did (although this too may be debated) but as its actions were highly selective the overall effectiveness of EU competition law is debatable: hardcore cartels, the prohibition on dominance and abuse, as well as State aid enforcement were all areas that suffered from under-enforcement. The (input and output) legitimacy of this regime was also debatable, given its imperfect fit with economic reality.

concerning franchising agreements, OJ 1988, L359/46; Commission Regulation (EEC) No 556/89 of 30 November 1988 concerning know-how licensing agreements, OJ 1989, L61/1.

[43] Commission Regulation (EEC) No 123/85 of 12 December 1984 concerning motor vehicle distribution and servicing agreements, OJ 1985, L15/16.

[44] Council Regulation (EEC) No 1534/91 of 31 May 1991 on the application of Article 85(3) of the Treaty to certain categories of agreements, decisions and concerted practices in the insurance sector, OJ 1991, L143/1.

[45] Commission Regulation (EEC) No 417/85 concerning specialization agreements, OJ 1985, L53/1; Commission Regulation (EEC) No 418/85 of 19 December 1984 concerning research and development agreements, OJ 1985, L53/5.

[46] V. Korah, *An Introductory Guide to EEC Competition Law and Practice*, 4th edn. (London: Sweet and Maxwell, 1990).

[47] White Paper (n 34), para 78.

[48] Now Commission Regulation 330/2010/EU of 20 April 2010 on the application of Article 101(3) of the Treaty on the Functioning of the European Union to categories of vertical agreements and concerted practices, OJ 2010, L102/1; and Guidelines on Vertical Restraints, above (n 25).

To some extent (although this is sometimes exaggerated given the fixes based on comfort letters and block exemptions discussed above), the Commission was tied down by having to examine large numbers of relatively innocent agreements while lacking the resources to pursue hardcore cartels—cartels that were of course not notified but kept secret. According to the 1999 Modernisation White Paper, in thirty-five years and tens of thousands of notifications, only nine agreements were prohibited in the absence of a complaint,[49] although many more may have been modified and withdrawn, much as there have been few prohibitions in the context of merger review compared to notifications being withdrawn. In any event, as we shall see, in May 2004 the system of EU antitrust was modernized to address these flaws.

6. Towards an Effects-based Approach

A further dimension of modernization

Modernization had another dimension besides abolishing the exemption monopoly (and besides restocking the toolkit of the European Commission): regarding substance, it also included the introduction of a more effects-based approach in line with economic insights.[50] In adopting this more economic approach the Commission drew on the example of merger control which was characterized by a more streamlined form of administration and tight deadlines for decisions, prepared by teamwork integrating legal and economic analysis, and characterized by a relatively high degree of permeability to business views and economic argument. These developments were made possible by the introduction of a centralized (one-stop) system of *ex ante* merger control at EU level in 1989.[51] This will be discussed in Chapter VIII. Here the focus will remain on antitrust.

Introducing an effects-based approach to verticals

The different block exemptions regarding particular types of vertical agreement had been intended to enable particular types of agreement that were seen as efficient business practices and non-objectionable under Article 85(3) TFEU (now Article 101(3) TFEU). The resulting compartmentalized system of the EU approach to vertical agreements had been much criticized for its rigidity by practitioners and academic commentators alike, however.[52]

[49] White Paper (n 34), para 78.

[50] D.J. Gerber, 'Two forms of modernization in European competition law', *Fordham International Law Journal* 31 (2007) 1235–65.

[51] Council Regulation (EEC) No 4064/89 of 21 December 1989 on the control of concentrations between undertakings, OJ 1989, L395/1.

[52] See V. Korah, 'From legal form towards economic efficiency—Article 85(1) of the EEC Treaty in contrast to US Antitrust', *Antitrust Bulletin* 35 (1990) 1009; V. Korah, 'The future of vertical agreements under EC competition law', *European Competition Law Review* 19 (1998) 506–13; B. Hawk, 'System failure: vertical restraints and EC competition law', *Common Market Law Review* 32 (1995) 973–89.

The result was a comprehensive block exemption in the form of Regulation 2790/1999 for vertical agreements,[53] with the exception of motor vehicle distribution[54] which retained a separate regime. Regulation 2790/1999, which came into effect on 1 January 2000, clearly set out the new economic reasoning behind the approach to verticals:

> Vertical agreements of the category defined in this Regulation can improve economic efficiency within a chain of production or distribution by facilitating better coordination between the participating undertakings; in particular, they can lead to a reduction in the transaction and distribution costs of the parties and to an optimisation of their sales and investment levels...
>
> The likelihood that such efficiency-enhancing effects will outweigh any anti-competitive effects due to restrictions contained in vertical agreements depends on the degree of market power of the undertakings concerned and, therefore, on the extent to which those undertakings face competition.[55]

This approach, in other words, was based on the twin concepts of efficiency, as the goal to strive toward, and market power, as the risk to be controlled. The justification for taking this approach was based on the premise that sufficient experience had been gained with various forms of vertical restraints to allow for policy reform. The market power dimension was controlled by introducing a combination of a €100-million buyer turnover and 30 per cent supplier market-share thresholds (and a provision where parallel networks cover more than 50 per cent of a given market) that determined the applicability of the exemption. All agreements and clauses were, in principle, compatible except for a black list of prohibited clauses. In particular, retail price maintenance and various forms of territorial restrictions—which are sensitive in the EU integration context due to fears over market partitioning—remained off limits. Finally, Regulation 1216/1999 removed the prior notification requirement for vertical agreements by amending Regulation 17/62.[56]

The Verticals Guidelines (2000) that accompanied Regulation 2790/1999 showed the new orientation of EU antitrust law even more explicitly by referring

[53] Commission Regulation (EC) No 2790/1999 of 22 December 1999 on the application of Article 81(3) of the Treaty to categories of vertical agreements and concerted practices, OJ 1999, L336/21, and Commission Notice: Guidelines on Vertical Restraints, OJ 2000, C291/1. These have been succeeded by Commission Regulation (EU) No 330/2010 of 20 April 2010 on the application of Article 101(3) of the Treaty on the Functioning of the European Union to categories of vertical agreements and concerted practices, OJ 2010, L102/1, alongside Commission Notice, Guidelines on vertical restraints OJ 2010, C130/1.

[54] Commission Regulation (EEC) No 123/85, above (n 43); Commission Regulation (EC) No 1400/2002 of 31 July 2002 on the application of Article 81(3) of the Treaty to categories of vertical agreements and concerted practices in the motor vehicle sector, OJ L203/30; now Commission Regulation (EU) No 461/2010 of 27 May 2010 on the application of Article 101(3) of the Treaty on the Functioning of the European Union to categories of vertical agreements and concerted practices in the motor vehicle sector, OJ 2010, L 129/52.

[55] Regulation 2790/1999, above (n 53), paras 6 and 7.

[56] Council Regulation (EC) No 1216/1999 of 10 June 1999 amending Regulation No 17: first Regulation implementing Articles 81 and 82 of the Treaty, OJ 1999, L148/5.

directly to the consumer welfare standard. At the same time, this reasoning was combined with the more familiar standard of market integration:

> The protection of competition is the primary objective of EC competition policy, as this enhances consumer welfare and creates an efficient allocation of resources. In applying the EC competition rules, the Commission will adopt an economic approach which is based on the effects on the market; vertical agreements have to be analysed in their legal and economic context...
>
> Market integration is an additional goal of EC competition policy. Market integration enhances competition in the Community. Companies should not be allowed to recreate private barriers between Member States where State barriers have been successfully abolished.[57]

The balancing between consumer welfare and competing standards remains a live issue in EU antitrust: whereas the Commission (and the General Court) has tried to argue for consumer welfare as the dominant standard, the Court of Justice has insisted on parity with the protection of the competitive process and the position of competitors.[58] Chapter III returns to this issue.

Spreading the effects-based approach to horizontals and beyond

The new verticals Regulation can be seen as a turning point for the more economics-based substantive approach to antitrust. This approach has also been applied to horizontal restraints but, predictably, with less far-reaching results. There is now a single set of guidelines for horizontal restraints and market power plays a key role in the assessment of horizontal agreements.[59] This is the case except where hardcore cartels such as price fixing and market sharing are involved (which are normally caught even below the *de minimis* thresholds: 10 per cent market share for competitors and 15 per cent for non-competitors).[60] There are, however, still separate block exemptions in place for research and development and for specialization agreements.[61] Overall the impact of the new economic approach to

[57] Regulation 2790/1999, above (n 53), para 7.

[58] See Joined Cases C-501/06 P, C-513/06 P, C-515/06 P, and C-519/06 P *GlaxoSmithKline Services Unlimited, formerly Glaxo Wellcome plc v Commission* [2009] I-9291, para 63: 'Article 81 EC [now Article 101 TFEU] aims to protect not only the interests of competitors or of consumers, but also the structure of the market and, in so doing, competition as such.'

[59] Communication from the Commission: Guidelines on the applicability of Article 101 of the Treaty on the Functioning of the European Union to horizontal co-operation agreements OJ 2011, C11/1.

[60] Communication from the Commission: Notice on agreements of minor importance which do not appreciably restrict competition under Article 101(1) of the Treaty on the Functioning of the European Union, C(2014) 4136; Commission staff working document: Guidance on restrictions of competition 'by object' for the purpose of defining which agreements may benefit from the De Minimis Notice, SWD(2014)198. Another threshold is the effect on trade, generally set at 5 per cent market share and €40 million turnover. See Commission Notice: Guidelines on the effect on trade concept contained in Articles 81and 82 of the Treaty, OJ 2004, C101/81.

[61] Commission Regulation (EU) No 1217/2010 of 14 December 2010 on the application of Article 101(3) of the Treaty on the Functioning of the European Union to certain categories of research and development agreements Text with EEA relevance, OJ 2010, L335/36; Commission

horizontal agreements appears to have been limited, however in an unrelated development, cartel enforcement against anticompetitive horizontal practices has been very successful, largely dependent on leniency applications.[62]

In a Commission notice of 2009 the new economic approach has also been applied to exclusionary abuses under Article 102 TFEU, which may have been the high-water mark of its influence.[63] Since then, most recently in *Intel* (2014),[64] and several other cases on object versus effect such as *Allianz* (2012)[65] and *Expedia* (2013),[66] the European Courts seem to be giving more leeway for a form-based method.

7. Modernization

Three dimensions of modernization

The modernization of antitrust, strictly speaking, consisted of three elements: first, a more substantive economic approach, discussed in the previous section; second decentralization, revolving around procedural and jurisdictional changes, which I will discuss in the following. There is also a further third dimension which again forms a mixture of substance and procedure, such as a new focus on hardcore cartels based on leniency applications, as well as the reform of the instruments concerned, of which the introduction of enforceable commitment decisions is a good example.[67] This latter dimension can be labelled as the upgrading of the toolkit available to the European Commission.

Regulation (EU) No 1218/2010 of 14 December 2010 on the application of Article 101(3) of the Treaty on the Functioning of the European Union to certain categories of specialisation agreements Text with EEA relevance, OJ 2010, L335/43.

[62] Commission Notice on immunity, above (n 5).

[63] Communication from the Commission: Guidance on its enforcement priorities in applying Article 82 of the EC Treaty to abusive exclusionary conduct by dominant undertakings, OJ 2009, C45/7. N. Forwood, 'The Commission's "more economic approach"—implications for the role of the EU Courts, the treatment of economic evidence and the scope of judicial review', in C.-D. Ehlermann and M. Marquis (eds), *European Competition Law Annual 2009: Evaluation of Evidence and its Judicial Review in Competition Cases* (Oxford: Hart Publishing, 2011).

[64] Case T-286/09 *Intel Corp. v Commission*, Judgment of 12 June 2014. W.P.J. Wils, 'The Judgment of the EU General Court in Intel and the so-called more economic approach to Abuse of Dominance', *World Competition* 37 (2014) 405–34; P. Nihoul, 'The ruling of the General Court in Intel: towards the end of an effect-based approach in European competition law?', *Journal of European Competition Law & Practice* 5 (2014) 521–39; R. Subiotto, D.R. Little and R. Lepetska, 'The application of Article 102 TFEU by the European Commission and the European Courts', *Journal of European Competition Law & Practice* 6 (2015) 277–86.

[65] Case C-32/11 *Allianz Hungária Biztosító Zrt, Generali-Providencia Biztosító Zrt, Gépjármű Márkakereskedők Országos Szövetsége, Magyar Peugeot Márkakereskedők Biztosítási Alkusz Kft, Paragon-Alkusz Zrt., the legal successor of the Magyar Opelkereskedők Bróker Kft v Gazdasági Versenyhivatal*, Judgment of 23 March 2013.

[66] Case C-226/11 *Expedia Inc. v Autorité de la concurrence et al.*, Judgment of 13 December 2012.

[67] Some commentators regard the drive to promote private enforcement as the third branch. See J. Basedow, 'The modernization of European competition law: a story of unfinished concepts', *Texas International Law Journal* 42 (2007) 429–39.

Somewhat confusingly, in accounts about modernization the stress is often on the last two aspects because they are dealt with jointly in the Commission's 1999 White Paper,[68] and not on the former, that is to say the more economic approach, which the Commission dealt with separately. It is true, however, that although the economic approach and decentralization were introduced in parallel, they did not heavily depend on each other and they were each considered to be worthwhile pursuing in their own right. Finally, some accounts leave out the third or toolkit dimension as overly technical.

Because I have already touched upon the new economic approach, I will now follow the Commission's approach in its White Paper and focus on the decentralization of antitrust with some attention to the nuts and bolts of the upgraded toolkit, both under the heading of modernization. The parallel introduction of the new economic approach will return in the conclusion of this chapter.

Early attempts decentralization of antitrust

This topic is somewhat paradoxical since, from the adoption of Regulation 17/62 on, the early policy of the Commission was not to enhance the decentralization of antitrust. Quite the contrary, the policy was to centralize antitrust as much as possible in its own hands. This effort had been successful.

Nevertheless, although they were relatively restrained, prior to the introduction of the legal exception system in Regulation 1/2003 there had been some half-hearted earlier decentralization attempts: notably, the Commission issued separate notices on cooperation with national courts in 1993,[69] and with NCAs in 1997.[70] The reason why this was considered useful was because Article 85 and 86 EEC (now Articles 101 and 102 TFEU) were directly effective and could therefore be invoked between individuals.[71] The same held for the relatively rare exemptions that had been granted either in individual cases by the Commission or (more frequently) they were based on block exemptions.

Given the direct applicability of the prohibitions in Articles 85(1) and 86 EEC (now Articles 101(1) and 102 TFEU), in principle all national courts held concurrent powers to the Commission, as did at least those NCAs that had been authorized (at national level) to apply the EU competition rules. With the abovementioned notices, the Commission attempted to stimulate effectively coordinated application of Articles 85 and 86 EEC (now Articles 101 and 102 TFEU)

[68] White Paper (n 34).

[69] Notice on cooperation between national courts and the Commission in applying Articles 85 and 86 of the EEC Treaty, OJ 1993 C39/6; this was based on the case law in Case C-234/89 *Stergios Delimitis v Henninger Bräu AG* [1991] ECR I-935 confirming the supremacy of Commission Decisions with relation to national court proceedings and Case T-24/90 *Automec Srl v Commission* [1992] ECR II-2223 on the ability to prioritize (especially where a national court might resolve the substantive issue).

[70] Notice on cooperation between national competition authorities and the Commission in handling cases falling within the scope of Articles 85 and 86 of the EC Treaty, OJ 1997, C313/3.

[71] Case 127/73 *Belgische Radio en Televisie and société belge des auteurs, compositeurs et éditeurs v SV SABAM and NV Fonior* [1974] ECR 51, para 16.

by these national bodies. Bolstering the application of competition law, rather than expanding its reach is mentioned in the national authorities Notice, albeit without carrying much conviction.

This first attempt at decentralization was nevertheless doomed to fail because of the Commission's exemption monopoly under Article 85(3) EEC (now Article 101(3) TFEU), as imposed by Article 9(3) of Regulation 17/62.[72] National courts and competition authorities alike were required to suspend their proceedings once it became clear that the Commission might issue a ruling with regard to a particular agreement—a situation that could easily be triggered by a simple notification, and that could lead to an indefinite delay given the Commission's perennial backlog of such cases.[73]

Article 82 EEC (now Article 102 TFEU) cases were on the whole simply too complex for national authorities. This meant that there were few incentives for them to invest resources into enforcing EU competition law even if the national courts nominally enjoyed certain advantages such as the ability to award damages and to adopt interim measures. The unintended benefit of the failure of the earlier modest attempts at decentralization was that it demonstrated that a more radical approach would be required if effective decentralization was desired. This situation would only be remedied by the more recent modernization when Regulation 17/62 was replaced by Regulation 1/2003.

The Commission's 1999 White Paper: Alternatives

Proposals for radical reform had to wait until 1999 when the Commission adopted the White Paper that set out its policy proposals with regard to the reform of antitrust.[74] In this it explained the need for reform and sketched four alternative options for reform before selecting and elaborating just one: a legal exception system. It also went into detail on the need for consistent and uniform application of the competition rules and the need to intensify *ex post* control, in practice the toolkit for enforcement of the European Commission.

The objectives of reform were ensuring a better balance between the effectiveness of competition policy and the simplification of control, even although it is not self-evident that there should be a contrast between the two. The Commission spelled this out as follows:

> The Commission considers that, in seeking such a balance and in order to accomplish its institutional mission, it must have a procedural framework that enables it, in the first place, to refocus its activities on combating the most serious restrictions of competition and, secondly, to allow decentralised application of the Community competition rules while at the same time maintaining consistency in competition policy throughout the

[72] R. Wesseling, 'The Commission's Notices on decentralisation of EC antitrust law: in for a penny, not for a pound', *European Competition Law Review* 18 (1997) 94–7.

[73] Case 48/72 *SA Brasserie de Haecht v Wilkin-Janssen* [1973] ECR 77; Case C-234/89 *Delimitis*, above (n 69); Case C-344/98 *Masterfoods Ltd v HB Ice Cream Ltd* [2000] ECR I-11369.

[74] White Paper (n 34).

Community. Lastly, the Commission considers that the procedural framework should ease the administrative constraints on undertakings while at the same time providing them with sufficient legal certainty.[75]

The reasons for reform were set out as, first, the need to ensure effective supervision. This involved moving away from a reactive approach to notifications toward a proactive focus on the most serious cases, pursuing own-initiative procedures. Also decentralization was required given the impending enlargement of EU membership, which could lead to a doubling of the number of Member States (and languages used) and a further increase in socio-economic divergence. The second reason cited was the need to simplify administration: the existing system of block exemptions and comfort letters (although channelling the flood of notifications) did not provide adequate legal certainty to undertakings. At the same time, however, and somewhat in contradiction with the preceding claim, the Commission asserted that thirty-five years of centralized application of the competition rules had clarified the law for undertakings and national authorities alike. To a lesser extent, the Commission also identified the new economic approach and the need to focus on effects of market power as requiring change.

These arguments led to an analysis of four options for reform that relied on improving the authorization system, and one that replaced this system by the switch to a directly applicable legal exception system which was then advocated and elaborated in the remainder of the White Paper (alongside a number of significant procedural reforms). The options that were listed but were not selected for further elaboration were:

(i) interpreting Article 81(1) EEC (now Article 101(1) TFEU) as a rule of reason, regarding agreement with net benefits as not restrictive of competition and thereby obviating the need for an analysis under Article 81(3) EEC (now Article 101(3);[76]

(ii) decentralizing the exemption powers of Article 81(3) EEC (now Article 101(3) TFEU) to national authorities according to an allocation method based on the centre of gravity of the case involved (the favoured option of the German Cartel Office);

(iii) broadening the waiver of the notification requirement under Article 4(2) of Regulation 17 (as applied to verticals); and

[75] White Paper (n 34), para 42. Former Director General of DG Competition Claus Dieter Ehlermann criticized this point, stating that the sole objective should have been increasing the efficiency of EC antitrust policy. *The modernization of EC antitrust policy: a legal and cultural revolution*, EUI Working Paper RSC No 2000/17, para 67. Also published as C.D. Ehlermann, 'The modernization of EC antitrust policy: a legal and cultural revolution', *Common Market Law Review* 37 (2000) 537–90. Cf. J.S. Venit, 'Brave new world: the modernization and decentralization of enforcement under Articles 81 and 82 of the EC Treaty', *Common Market Law Review* 40 (2003) 545–80.

[76] See R. Wesseling, *The Modernisation of EC Antitrust Law* (Oxford: Hart Publishing, 2000). The cases cited in support of this approach are Case 258/78 *L.C. Nungesser KG and Kurt Eisele v Commission* [1982] ECR 2015, and Case 161/84 *Pronuptia de Paris GmbH v Pronuptia de Paris Irmgard Schillgalis* [1986] ECR 353.

(iv) procedural simplification such as abolishing the requirement for translation of certain documents and simplifying the Advisory Committee procedures.

These alternatives all have their advantages and disadvantages. Apart from practical objections such as the need to set up notification systems at national level where these did not yet exist, according to the White Paper the decentralized application of exemption decisions would in particular have posed 'a major risk to the uniform application of Community law'.[77] In his commentary on the White Paper former DG Competition director-general Claus Dieter Ehlermann has stated that the Commission considered this risk to be much greater than that resulting from an incoherent treatment of complaints.[78]

In a system governed by the rule of law with a presumption of innocence until proven guilty, it might be assumed that the Commission would in both settings be more worried about false positives than about false negatives, nor is it obvious why divergence would be worse for notifications than for complaints. It is true, however, that complaints were already decentralized without causing major worries, although this decentralization was in practice largely ineffective. This was so in large part because notifications to the Commission could block procedures and not all Member States had NCAs, and where NCAs existed, not all Member States had authorized them to apply Articles 85 and 86 EEC (now Articles 101 and 102 TFEU). Also, a divergence in terms of positive exemption decisions might result from national industrial policy goals and could in the implicit view of the Commission be more harmful.

I will not go into further detail on the merits of the four alternatives here because none of them was tabled for further debate or elaborated by the Commission. Instead I will now focus on the legal exception system that was eventually adopted.

A legal exception system

The White Paper proposed to ditch the exemption regime and to introduce a system of reading Article 85(3) EEC (now Article 101(3) TFEU) as a directly applicable legal exception, a change that did not require Treaty amendment but instead a modification of the enabling Regulation 17/62. Article 85 EEC (now Article 101 TFEU) as a whole would then become a directly applicable provision. According to the Commission this was now possible because since the 1960s the conditions for exemption have been clarified by the decision-making practice of the Commission and the EU courts.

At several points in its motivation for choosing a directly effective legal exception, the Commission referred to the parallel reform of the approach to vertical restraints and horizontal cooperation agreements, especially in the sense that this would further clarify the application of the EU competition rules. The

[77] White Paper (n 34), para 62, and Ehlermann (n 75), para 39.
[78] Ehlermann (n 75), para 97.

Commission also underlined that '[t]he approach taken to the application of Article 85 (now Article 101 TFEU) will continue to be rigorously economic'.[79] Freeing the Commission from its exemption monopoly would enable it to focus on the most serious infringements.

According to the White Paper, the directly applicable exception system approach that it proposed had three aspects: (i) ending the notification and authorization system, (ii) introducing decentralized application of the competition rules, and (iii) intensified *ex post* control. A guiding theme of the proposals was that decentralization must not lead to inconsistencies.

Coherence, consistency, and uniform application

The White Paper directly discussed three dimensions of coherence. First, this concerned the coherent nature of competition law prior to modernization in terms of its covering all economic sectors and (somewhat optimistically) in terms of the national policies set up in each Member State (as a result of spontaneous harmonization).[80] Second, it listed the role of centralized control in the hands of the Commission in ensuring this coherence, also by allowing a coherent body of case law on Article 85(3) EEC (now Article 101(3) TFEU) to emerge.[81] Third, looking forward, the White Paper referred to the need for coherence in the system of concurrent jurisdiction following modernization by (i) giving the Commission the power to remove cases from the NCAs, and by (ii) the requirement that national courts must avoid conflicts with Commission decisions.[82]

Throughout the proposals in the White Paper, consistency and uniform application, both elements of coherence, also received close attention. Regarding the relationship with national competition rules, consistency and uniform application were to be safeguarded by the general principle of primacy of EU law. Regarding EU competition policy, once the Commission has initiated procedures national authorities and courts would be bound (as before) to avoid conflicting decisions.[83] This means that the Commission could also claim cases and thereby assert its primacy with regard to new points of law or where there had been a risk of conflicting decisions at national level. Competition authorities would have to be authorized by their national governments to apply Article 85 and 86 EEC (now Articles 101 and 102 TFEU). *Amicus curiae* intervention by the Commission before national courts was to be enabled.

Coordination with a network of national authorities (somewhat unambitiously, with the benefit of hindsight) was envisaged by means of beefing up the Advisory Committee. Moreover, the White Paper pointed out that competition policy as a whole will continue to be developed and determined at EU level with a key role for the Commission. In its role of guardian of the Treaty, the Commission would

[79] White Paper (n 34), para 75. [80] Ibid, at para 4. [81] Ibid, paras 17 and 76.

[82] Ibid, executive summary, para 5.

[83] Case C-234/89 *Delimitis*, above (n 69); Case C-344/98 *Masterfoods*, above (n 73).

have special responsibility for ensuring consistent application of the competition rules and use its monopoly on proposing legislation to that effect. Regulations, notices, and guidelines would be its instruments to do this. In addition, specific procedural proposals such as the Commission's right to take a positive decision that no infringement exists and to conclude a case by taking commitment decisions were made.

An important reservation regarding consistency, however, is that procedural harmonization was not envisaged. This meant that, as before, the application of EU competition law in national proceedings would be governed by natural procedures including such issues as penalties and damages. This is less strange than it may seem at first sight because reliance on national procedural rules is a general feature of EU law that is not specific to competition law. An attempt at harmonization could have backfired against the modernization project as a whole (although limited attempts at agreeing a modicum of harmonization of procedures have been floated since then).[84]

Strengthening *ex post* enforcement

The Commission used the White Paper strategically to table not only a revised system for the application of Article 85(3) EEC (now Article 101(3) TFEU) but also to include a wish list of additional powers that it had long sought in order to strengthen its antitrust enforcement: the *ex post* cases, based on complaints and own-initiative cases, not on notifications. These included, for instance, the power to seal premises and to ask questions during onsite inspections. The level of fines for procedural violations was to be raised and it was proposed to have a separate category of fines for commitment decisions, along the lines of the system that existed with regard to obligations under the Merger Control Regulation. In addition a number of related smaller changes were advocated.

Reaction and evaluation

Unsurprisingly the commentary on the proposals, which were widely debated inter alia by the Member States, the European Parliament, industry, and antitrust lawyers, was varied.[85] On balance, however, it appears to have been generally positive, with the notable exception of the German *Monopolkommission*.[86] The latter argued essentially that (i) the proposed change went beyond the system established by the Treaty; (ii) that because Article 81(3) (now Article 101(3) TFEU)

[84] See L. Parret, *Side Effects of the Modernisation of EU Competition Law* (Nijmegen: Wolf Productions, 2011).

[85] See *White Paper on reform of regulation 17—Summary of the observations*. DG Competition document 20 September 2000. Available at: <http://ec.europa.eu/competition/antitrust/others/wp_on_modernisation/summary_observations.pdf>.

See also C.D. Ehlermann and I. Atanasiu (eds), *European Competition Law Annual 2000: The Modernisation of EC Antitrust Policy* (Oxford: Hart Publishing, 2001).

[86] Summary of observations, above (n 85), at 6.

required a declaration of inapplicability so a global exemption could not be issued; and (iii) that Article 81(3) did not fulfil the criteria for direct effect, of being sufficiently clear, precise, and unconditional.

A contrast was the supportive stance of the European Parliament, for instance, linking competition policy to the social market economy and the competitiveness of European industry as well as to the consumer interest, and emphasizing the need for guidance of national authorities.[87] It is difficult to imagine today such a broadly positive reaction taking place with regard to the increasing scope for antitrust even a few years later when as we have seen, curbing the position of competition within the framework of the Treaty—although effectively unsuccessful—became an objective of several Member States following the French and Dutch referenda that led to the demise of the Constitutional Treaty for the EU. Since then the general climate regarding support for the European project has not improved much. The timing of modernization can thus be regarded as having been fortuitous, to say the least.

In retrospect, and somewhat surprisingly, however, is that scaled down variations on notification and comfort letters were advocated even by seasoned observers as being desirable for reasons of legal certainty. [88] As we will see, this is one of the reasons why the Commission was eventually empowered to provide a formal finding of inapplicability in Article 10 as well as informal guidance more generally under Regulation 1/2003 (powers that have rarely been used).[89] Some critics found fault with the deterministic approach to reform taken by the Commission whereby just one of the possible options was preselected and developed for adoption, forestalling a more open debate on the four options sketched earlier.[90] Given that the Commission was arguing from a position of strength (full centralization) and was not under external pressure to reform other than possibly due to the impending enlargement (nor really under internal pressure because, in spite of what the Commission claimed, the notification system had become manageable), this critique seems optimistic.

A fundamental general point of criticism was that direct applicability of Article 81(3) EC (now Article 101(3) TFEU) imposed the duty to evaluate policy options on NCAs and above all on national courts (but what about the undertakings themselves in the course of self-assessment?) who would be ill-placed to do so.[91] I will return to the scope of the exception and the interests that must be balanced in that context in the following chapters.

[87] European Parliament Resolution on the Commission White Paper on modernization of the rules implementing Articles 85 and 86 of the EC Treaty (COM(1999) 101–C5-0105/1999–1999/2108(COS)), OJ 2000, C304/66.

[88] Ehlermann (n 75); M. Siragusa, 'A critical review of the White Paper on the reform of the EC competition law enforcement rules', *Fordham International Law Journal* 23 (1999) 1089–127.

[89] See recital 38 and Commission Notice on informal guidance relating to novel questions concerning Articles 81 and 82 of the EC Treaty that arise in individual cases (guidance letters), OJ 2004, C101/78.

[90] R. Wesseling, 'The draft regulation modernizing the competition rules: the Commission is married to one idea', *European Law Review* 26 (2001) 357–78.

[91] Ibid.

From my own point of view, the reasons given for reform were not fully convincing: not only was there no major pressure exerted by a backlog of notified cases any longer but also the law was not finally clear (all the less so given the new economic approach). Burdening the accession countries with their fledgling market economies and newly democratic governments by requiring them to enforce the competition rules themselves was not an obvious solution to problems flowing from enlargement. This suggests that the Commission was actually motivated mainly by the desire to enable more effective—including more widespread—enforcement. There was, however, tension between its objectives of effective and uniform application, simplifying administration, and decentralization. This tension would ultimately be largely addressed by means of the network of competition authorities, however that solution that was not yet clearly envisaged at the time when the modernization proposals appeared.

Regulation 1/2003: Three main points

After only two years of discussions and negotiations (compared to seventeen for the first Merger Control Regulation adopted in 1989) Regulation 1/2003 was adopted in December 2002 and came into force on 1 May 2004. This instrument as adopted largely reproduced what the Commission had proposed.[92] Because of its complexity I do not intend to provide a full discussion of the various aspects of Regulation 1/2003 here. Instead I will only cover three points: (i) the powers of the NCAs and national courts, (ii) those of the Commission, and (iii) how they are coordinated.

Empowering the national level

First, according to Articles 5 and 6 of Regulation 1/2003, the NCAs and national courts are empowered to apply Articles 81 and 82 EC (now Articles 101 and 102 TFEU). NCAs are to be empowered to require infringements to be ended, to order interim measures, to accept commitments, and to impose fines, as well as periodic penalty payments. In contrast, the provisions concerning national courts are limited to this empowerment clause, a role in procedural protection such as validating inspection decisions and the limitation clause in Article 16 of Regulation 1/2003.

According to Article 3 of Regulation 1/2003 where practices might affect trade between the Member State or abuses be prohibited by Article 82 EC (now Article 102 TFEU), the NCAs are required to apply Articles 81 and/or 82 alongside their national competition rules. As regards the relationship between national and EU competition law, Article 3(2) of Regulation 1/2003 prohibits the application of national competition law that forbids practices that may affect trade but are not

[92] The major exception being the power to issue new block exemptions under its own authority, which was not granted. Goyder (n 15), 624.

caught by Article 81(1) EC (now Article 101 TFEU) or fulfil the conditions of Article 81(3) EC (now Article 101(3) TFEU). The idea behind this rule is to promote convergence by creating a single standard of assessment, however stricter national rules regarding unilateral conduct are allowed. According to Article 3(3) of Regulation 1/2003 stricter national laws that pursue a different objective are also permitted.

The Commission's powers

Second, in the section on Commission decisions, in Article 7 the Commission received explicit powers to find and terminate infringements, including the potential to impose not only behavioural but also structural remedies: forcing undertakings to sell-off certain parts of their businesses (divestiture). In addition, the Commission was empowered by Regulation 1/2003 to impose interim measures in Article 8,[93] to adopt commitment decisions in Article 9 and a finding of inapplicability (a positive declaration of legality) in Article 10. In particular, the commitment decisions, adapted from the experience gained under the Merger Control Regulation,[94] amounted to a significant additions to its toolbox of instruments. It should be noted, however, that Commitment decisions adopted by the Commission do not affect the power of the NCAs and the national courts to apply Articles 81 and 82 EC (now Articles 101 and 102 TFEU).

The Commission's powers of investigation were also enhanced, as were its powers to impose fines. Notably this included new powers to question staff members and representatives of undertakings, to inspect the homes of such staff members and representatives, as well as to seal business premises. Fines for procedural infringements were increased substantially to 1 per cent of annual turnover, and for infringement of interim measures were set at 5 per cent of annual turnover.

Coordination between the EU and the national level

Third, having dealt with the national and the EU levels separately, Regulation 1/2003 covers the coordination between the two levels. In the first place there is a mutual duty to inform under Article 11. This requires the transmission of key documents by the Commission to the NCAs prior to taking its decisions and of the formal initiation of procedures by the NCAs to the Commission. In addition, NCAs are required to provide the Commission with the relevant information on a case at least thirty days before taking a formal decision. The Commission and the NCAs are authorized to exchange information to use in evidence.

[93] Interim measures under Regulation 17/62 had been based on Case 792/79 R *Camera Care Ltd v Commission* [1980] ECR 119.

[94] Albeit not based on legislation: see European Commission, Explanatory note, best practice guidelines: the Commission's model texts for divestiture Commitments and the trustee mandate under the EC Merger Regulation, 5 December 2013. Available at: <http://ec.europa.eu/competition/mergers/legislation/best_practice_commitments_trustee_en.pdf>.

The capping stone of the relationship between NCAs and the Commission is a priority right to the exercise of its powers that is assigned to the Commission in Article 11(6) of Regulation 1/2003. Mirroring the old Article 9(3) of Regulation 17/62, this means that if the Commission initiates proceedings for the adoption of a formal decision then the NCAs are relieved of their competence to act under Articles 81 and 81 EC (now Articles 101 and 102 TFEU). In addition, Article 10 decisions by which the Commission can make findings of inapplicability (which the NCAs cannot do)[95] likewise serves as an instrument promoting coherence because here too the Commission's action forecloses divergent decisions by national authorities.

Finally, Article 16 of Regulation 1/2003, under the heading of uniform application, provides that national authorities and courts cannot take decisions that run counter to a Commission decision, however this provision, which codifies the *Masterfoods* case,[96] does not mean they cannot take any decision at all. Unlike Article 11(6), this provision also applies to national courts, which is necessary to safeguard the primacy of Community law. This encroaches on the powers of national courts and requires strict scrutiny of the decisions involved by the EU courts. Jointly and paradoxically, the instruments provided in Articles 11(6) and 16 of Regulation 1/2003 give the Commission control over the decentralized system of EU competition law, by some measures (but in my view, not across the board) a stronger means of control than had existed under the prior centralized system.

Regulation 1/2003 and consistency

On the day that Regulation 1/2003 was adopted by the Council, the Commission and Council jointly adopted a statement on the functioning of the network of competition authorities.[97] Here they emphasized the role of the Commission as guardian of the Treaty bearing ultimate responsibility for developing policy and safeguarding efficiency and consistency. This explained why the Commission had been granted additional powers with respect to the NCAs, notably the power to claim cases at any stage and the blocking effect of its decisions, and the right to act as *amicus curiae* in order to safeguard coherence.

The statement also underlined the importance of effective and consistent application of the competition rules, and of effective enforcement. This shows how coherence of EU competition law was a concern and how it has been addressed. In Regulation 1/2003 the main mechanism was stated as follows:

> If the competition rules are to be applied consistently and, at the same time, the network is to be managed in the best possible way, it is essential to retain the rule that the

[95] Case C0375/09 *Prezes Urzędu Ochrony Konkurencji i Konsumentów v Tele2 Polska sp. z o.o., devenue Netia SA* [2011] ECR I-3055.

[96] Case C-344/98 *Masterfoods*, above (n 73).

[97] Available at: <http://ec.europa.eu/competition/ecn/joint_statement_en.pdf>.

competition authorities of the Member States are automatically relieved of their competence if the Commission initiates its own proceedings. Where a competition authority of a Member State is already acting on a case and the Commission intends to initiate proceedings, it should endeavour to do so as soon as possible. Before initiating proceedings, the Commission should consult the national authority concerned.[98]

Consistency is further promoted by notices that the Commission issued in 2004 on cooperation within the network of competition authorities and between the Commission and national courts.

Notices on cooperation with NCAs and national courts

In addition to the provisions contained in Regulation 1/2003 with regard to Commission primacy within the system, criteria for case allocation should ensure that in principle each case is dealt with by a single authority. Principles of case allocation are set out in the 2004 Commission Notice on cooperation within the network of competition authorities.[99] The general rule is that a single well-placed authority should deal with each case. In principle, the authority opening an *ex officio* case or receiving a complaint is thereby the relevant authority. Other criteria are likewise based on the existence of a material link between the infringement and the territory of a Member States:

(i) practices with substantial direct actual or foreseeable effects on competition with the territory, that are implemented or that originate within this territory;
(ii) the ability of the authority effectively to end the entire infringement;
(iii) and the ability of the authority to gather the necessary evidence.

In addition, there are criteria for cases suitable for parallel action, mainly where action by a single NCA would be insufficient effectively to end and sanction an infringement. The Commission is considered to be well-placed to act where there are multiple anticompetitive agreements and/or practices, including networks thereof, that have effects on competition in more than three Member States. The procedures for cooperation regarding case allocation and assistance are spelled out in this same notice.

The Notice on cooperation between the Commission and national courts focuses more on the relationship between national law and EU law.[100] In the first place, the Notice sets out the requirement that national courts must apply EU competition law alongside national law where there is an effect on trade between Member States. It recalls that within the bound of Article 3 of Regulation 1/2003, national courts cannot clear under national law agreements or practices that have

[98] Regulation 1/2003, above (n 4), preamble, para 17.
[99] Commission Notice on cooperation within the network of competition authorities, OJ 2004, C101/43.
[100] Commission Notice on the cooperation between the Commission and the courts of the EU Member States in the application of Articles 81 and 82 EC, OJ 2004, C101/54.

been found to infringe Article 81 EC (now Article 101 TFEU). With regard to abuse of dominance there is no similar convergence obligation. The Notice states that the absence of further harmonization procedures and sanctions, national procedural law remains applicable, although national law must provide for effective, proportionate, and dissuasive sanctions. Finally, the *amicus curiae* role of the Commission is spelled out: both that at the Commission's own initiative 'where the coherent application of Article 81 or 81 of the Treaty (now Articles 101 and 102 TFEU) so requires', based on Article 15(3) of Regulation 1/2003, and that at the request of national courts under Article 15(1).

Jointly with Regulation 1/2003, these documents on relations with the national authorities concerned provide the legal and institutional framework for modernization, in the sense of decentralization (and cooperation within the network) and the application of the new tools (leaving aside the new economic approach for now). I will now take a preliminary look at how antitrust modernization has turned out in practice by looking at the Commission's own evaluations.

Modernization: The results to date

The Commission itself has evaluated the functioning of regulation 1/2003 after five years in 2009[101] and after ten years in 2014.[102] In addition, a FIDE (*fédération internationale pour le droit européen*) report of 2008 has evaluated the results up until its publication.[103] Wearing his academic mantle, Wouter Wils, the Commission's Hearing Officer has declared modernization, or Regulation 1/ 2003, a success as NCAs are now deciding 90 per cent of EU competition cases and the ECN supports them well.[104] He sees more actions for damages before national courts. Finally, and somewhat surprisingly, the Commission has not handed down more decisions than it had done in the past in spite of being relieved from the notification burden, which may be explained by the burden having evaporated earlier or more difficult cases being handled more painstakingly.

In its 2009 Report the Commission noted that the competition rules had become the 'law of the land'. Whereas the instrument of commitments decisions under Article 9 of Regulation 1/2003 had been used widely, including structural commitments, the same did not apply to structural remedies under Article 7 procedures.

[101] Commission Communication, Report on the functioning of Regulation 1/2003, COM (2009) 206 and the accompanying Commission Staff Working Paper SEC(2009) 574.

[102] Commission Communication, Ten years of antitrust enforcement under regulation 1/ 2003: achievements and future perspectives, COM(2014) 453; and the accompanying Commission Staff Working Document, Ten years of antitrust enforcement under Regulation 1/2003, SWD(2014) 230; and the accompanying Commission Staff Working Document, Enhancing competition enforcement by the Member States' competition authorities: institutional and procedural issues, SWD(2014) 231.

[103] E. Gippini-Fournier, The modernisation of European competition law: first experiences with Regulation 1/2003. Community report to the FIDE Congress 2008, available at SSRN: <http:// ssrn.com/abstract=1139776>.

[104] W. Wils, 'Ten years of Regulation 1/2003 – a retrospective', *Journal of European Competition Law & Practice* 4 (2013) 293–301.

The Report noted that Article 10 findings of inapplicability and Article 11(6) claiming of cases by the Commission, intended as instruments for coherence had not been used. This was seen to reflect the smooth cooperation within the network of competition authorities (ECN) and according to the Network Notice.[105] It also reflected the fact that a model leniency programme would promote the application of the same substantive rules even if they were subject to divergent procedures and different sanctions.[106]

The ECN was seen by the Commission to have developed as a forum to ensure coherent application of EU competition law. Its dialogue at all levels of the organizations involved was seen to have contributed to a coherent approach to and application of the competition rules, fostering a common competition culture. It may be possible to conclude that the beginnings of input legitimacy would result. Among new issues discussed there that were not directly related to modernization was the 2003 *CIF* ruling where the Court of Justice held that NCAs were obliged to disapply national law that conflicted with competition law.[107] According to some commentators, the harmonious working relationships achieved within the ECN were sufficient to allow the Commission to take a more interventionist approach towards pursuing consistent application of the antitrust provisions.[108]

As discussed in Chapter I, the 2014 Report claims that the EU competition rules have now become the law of the land throughout the EU.[109] The Report uses figures to demonstrate a shift toward own initiative and complaint cases, commitment and prohibition decisions, and toward basic and manufacturing industries (traditionally the ones most troubled by hardcore cartels) as well as recently liberalized industries (notably energy, including excessive pricing by dominant energy producers). The 2014 Report also claims that enforcement by the NCAs, aided by policy development in the ECN, has developed in a broadly coherent manner.[110] The position of NCAs is thought to be developing toward more autonomy and effectiveness (suggesting respectively input and output legitimacy), backed up by safeguards to ensure independence and impartiality (suggesting input legitimacy). The 2014 Report also notes—after ten years of cooperation—spontaneous (voluntary) harmonization of the national procedural rules along the lines set out in Regulation 1/2003.

The area of fines is singled out as an example of divergence where effective deterrents are not always available at national level. This is indeed the case, although, as the 2014 Report cites, the Court of Justice had ruled in 2009 that the effectiveness of penalties is a precondition for the coherent application of EU competition law,[111] and in 2013 that decisions not to impose fines must be in line

[105] Above (n 99).

[106] Available at: <http://ec.europa.eu/competition/ecn/model_leniency_en.pdf> (2006). Now in a 2012 version, available at: <http://ec.europa.eu/competition/ecn/mlp_revised_2012_en.pdf>.

[107] Case C-198/01 *Consorzio Industrie Fiammiferi (CIF) v Autorità Garante della Concorrenza e del Mercato* [2003] I-8055.

[108] Goyder (n 15), 634.

[109] COM(2014) 453, above (n 102), paras 23.

[110] Ibid, paras 8, 23, and 43.

[111] Case C-429/07 *Inspecteur van de Belastingdisnet v X BV* [2009] ECR I-4833, para 37.

with the effective and uniform application of the EU's antitrust rules.[112] Other topics that are highlighted are leniency and (criminal) sanctions on individuals, the latter a topic where the Commission is lagging behind (some) Member States. There is a tension here between enforcement at the national and at the EU level.

Although providing the Commission with the authority to impose criminal sanctions is not discussed in the Report, it is in any event questionable whether the Commission could have the right to impose criminal sanctions until it takes on a prosecutorial role, separate from the administration of other policies. Damages are not highlighted in the Report but have been a key recent concern, also in relation to the inherent tension with leniency applications. Building on the case law of the Court of Justice (but in some respects at odds with it, as discussed in Chapter IV on procedures),[113] in April 2014 the European Parliament and Council have adopted a Directive on this topic.[114]

8. Conclusion

The general overview of the development of EU competition policy presented thus far shows an expansion of its scope to include new topics and sectors. At the same time there is a refocusing of method, like the more economic approach, and on themes like market power. The main development that combines several of these features is modernization.

Modernization

As we have seen, there are three main dimensions to modernization: (i) decentralization to national authorities and courts; (ii) a more economic approach based on the effects of the practices concerned; and (iii) the modernization of the instruments, or the toolkit, available to competition authorities. As far as coherence is concerned however these three variables are not all pulling in the same direction.

- *Decentralization* could be seen as posing a risk to coherence, that increases or decreases with the availability of effective overall coordination. At the same time it can also improve the effectiveness (scope) and legitimacy (both input and output) of EU competition law. The quality of the ECN, the Commission's success in picking the key cases to handle itself, and the

[112] Case C-681/11 *Bundeswettbewerbsbehörde, Bundeskartellanwalt v Schenker & Co et al.*, Judgment of 18 June 2013, para 36ff.

[113] Case C-453/99 *Courage Ltd v Bernard Crehan and Bernard Crehan v Courage Ltd et al.* [2001] ECR I-6297; Joined Cases C-295/04 to C-298/04 *Vincenzo Manfredi and Others v Lloyd Adriatico Assicurazioni SpA et al.* [2006] ECR I-6619.

[114] Directive 2014/104/EU of the European Parliament and of the Council of 26 November 2014 on certain rules governing actions for damages under national law for infringements of the competition law provisions of the Member States and of the European Union Text with EEA relevance, OJ 2014, L349/1.

success of *amicus curiae* efforts appear to be important compensating variables here, as is effective judicial review both at national and at EU level. As a preliminary assessment it certainly appears possible that due to the intensification of such controls that occurred in combination with decentralization, the degree of coherence has actually increased, although it might otherwise have decreased as a result of the risks of decentralization per se.

- The *more economic approach* on the one hand streamlines the enforcement efforts of the Commission and the NCAs, but on the other hand also makes their work more complex. It allows them to focus on hardcore cartels but because in an increasing number of cases complex economic evaluations are now involved it becomes more difficult for all parties involved (including undertakings) to know the law beforehand and to act accordingly. The work of national courts also becomes more complicated for the same reasons. Hence it is difficult to say what the net effect of the more economic approach on the coherence of EU competition law will be, although it may have elevated the quality of the application of EU competition law to a higher plane.
- *Modernization of the Commission's toolkit*, insofar as it strengthens the power of the Commission, and in particular to the extent that the latter forms the linch pin in ECN, tends to strengthen coherence in terms of effectiveness. It promotes the Commission as the central seat of control and its ability to decide difficult cases and thus set the general direction. However, the extent to which increased investigative powers raise issues of legal protection and therefore of input legitimacy remains to be examined.

Assessing the three dimensions of modernization jointly, we can say that the three dimensions of modernization achieved the modernization of EU competition law, thus raising it to the next level. A more exact analysis of the results will now be provided, starting with Chapter III on objectives and boundaries.

III

Objectives and Boundaries

1. Introduction

In this chapter my task is to identify the multiple goals and the various limits of the European Union (EU) competition regimes that define EU competition law, focusing on antitrust. Objectives and boundaries are to some extent opposites because the first define what competition law strives towards or seeks to achieve, whereas the second determine how far it may go in pursuing those goals. At the same time, an objective, if closely adhered to, also limits the scope of a policy. Both are to be distinguished from exceptions, where a rule clearly applies on its own terms but its application is suspended for a different reason. Beyond setting out the relevant parameters I intend to illustrate how objectives and boundaries interact.

Economic, non-economic, and EU-specific objectives

Following standard practice the organization of this chapter is by competition law objectives in general versus EU objectives, and economic objectives, notably the consumer welfare standard, versus non-economic objectives.[1] Under the heading of EU objectives, a category that combines economic and non-economic variables, I will address the important question of how the internal market can function as an objective and as a justification for EU competition policy.[2] Another significant question that arises here is whether the objectives of EU competition policy allow for or encourage the pursuit of non-economic public interest goals within the framework of competition law.[3] If they did, this would strain coherence,

[1] See I. Lianos, *Some reflections on the question of the goals of EU competition law*, CLES Working Paper Series 3/2013; D. Zimmer (ed.), *The goals of competition law*, papers of the 5th ASCOLA conference (Cheltenham: Edward Elgar, 2012); O. Odudu, *The Boundaries of EC Competition Law: The Scope of Article 81* (Oxford: Oxford University Press, 2006); R.B. Bouterse, *Competition and Integration: What Goals Count?: EEC Competition Law and Goals of Industrial, Monetary, and Cultural Policy* (Deventer: Kluwer, 1994)

[2] This chapter draws in part on my article 'The impact of EU competition law on national healthcare systems', *European Law Review* 38 (2013) 457–78 and on my (forthcoming) chapter in H. Hofmann and C. Micheau, *State Aid Law of the EU* (Oxford: Oxford University Press, 2016).

[3] S.A.C.M. Lavrijssen, 'The protection of non-competition interests; what role for competition authorities after Lisbon?', *European Law Review* 35 (2010) 634–59.

especially with regard to decentralized control. This question is distinct from that of whether non-economic goals can justify an exception; this will be dealt with in Chapter IV.

There are various ways of identifying the goals of EU competition law. These are: (i) starting by identifying the theoretical goals of competition policy at large ('why have competition law at all?'), which largely coincides with the economic objectives; (ii) looking at the specific context of the EU ('what do the Treaties and the policy statements say about its role?'); and (iii) looking at the case law ('what is the view of the Court?'). I will use all three methods, broadly in the order in which they have been presented here.

Legal boundaries

Objectives, if limited in number and in reach, can form a type of boundary in their own right. Legal boundaries, however, serve a different type of purpose: that of limiting the scope of the rules by defining what is categorically regarded as being inside and hence subject to the substantive rules, and what is beyond the reach of these rules and therefore inviolate. This is especially relevant with regard to the pursuit of public policies that cannot be accommodated within the competition rules.

There is a subtle difference between a finding that an event takes place outside a legal boundary and the finding that a rule has not been breached based on a substantive analysis within a legal boundary. In the former case the rule does not apply at all, so it could not have been breached, whereas in the latter the situation was covered by the rule, that is to say the general conditions for application of the rule were present but it was not breached because not all of the requirements for a breach were met. A third case is that of an exception: here a rule would be breached but this breach is excused because certain other compensating conditions are met, an example being the application of Article 101(3) Treaty on the Functioning of the European Union (TFEU). In a general sense, the constituent elements of the legal terms that form the competition rules, such as advantage, undertaking, agreements, decisions, or practices could each be seen as legal boundaries.

Economic boundaries

Finally, under the category of economic boundaries I will look primarily at appreciability and market power. Although they are formulated in legal terms as part of the competition law regime, these factors can legitimately be regarded as economic boundaries. This is because, unlike the legal boundaries discussed in the preceding section that are based on a binary kind of legal distinction (inside or outside a category), they depend on a stronger versus weaker quantifiable economic variable. This difference sets them apart. Under appreciability I will look more closely at the effect on trade and competition. There is also a range of criteria that can be based on quantitative thresholds, such as turnover or market share. Market power can be regarded as an economic boundary in its own right as well;

at the same time it is also related to the concept of appreciability which is why the two are grouped together here.

Coherence

As set out in the first chapter, the effectiveness and legitimacy of the various goals and boundaries of EU competition law and their pursuit will be used to address the qualitative achievement of the coherence standard. I intend to address three sets of questions regarding coherence as follows:

- The first questions aim to establish the facts: what are these multiple objectives and boundaries and to what extent they are settled law?
- A second question, geared toward coherence, is whether the objectives and boundaries are internally consistent and form part of an overarching whole in a logical sense?
- A further set of questions in this direction comprises: how are these objectives and boundaries to be seen from a perspective of the coherence of EU competition law; are there any which contribute or detract from this coherence, or are they neutral?

A set of objectives would appear to be more likely to be coherent if it is limited and closed, not extensive and open-ended, therefore I will seek to address the question of whether they are effective as centripetal mechanisms in focusing and determining the scope of EU competition law. This would promote the coherence and uniformity of EU competition law and this kind of coherence would appear to be served by having a single objective or a limited set of objectives.

In contrast, having multiple objectives in itself would appear to favour divergence, in particular if these objectives are not mutually consistent. Economists may claim that it is desirable that each individual policy objective is pursued by means of its own instrument. In EU competition law, that system can be argued to exist at the level of its components: for example, to control mergers we have a Merger Regulation, which was created *inter alia* to avoid having to use cartel policy or the control on abuse of dominance to police mergers. At the level of the overarching objectives, however, which hold for all types of competition law, this specificity would not be helpful. Also, if the intermediate objective pursued by merger control would then be to control mergers, this does not appear to tell us very much.

The risk of divergence is further increased by the existence of centrifugal forces that could lead to fragmentation. This is a result of decentralization, involving a multiplicity of actors at national level, of sectoral specificities as well as of a general background of rampant and often ill-founded Euroscepticism that threatens to undermine the drive for integration. Hence, I will examine that thesis that *ceteris paribus*, following modernization and following the introduction of sectoral regimes, there may be more reasons to limit the objectives and constrain the boundaries of EU competition law than had been the case while it remained a Commission monopoly. A further hypothesis is that the Commission itself in fact attempted to do so with the objective of consumer welfare, but failed because (i) the Court of Justice of the European Union (CJEU) from 2009 onward insisted on the existence of multiple objectives, and (ii) the high contracting parties to the 2007 Lisbon Treaty insisted on linking competition law first of all to the internal market.

To test for this we can check whether there has been a reduction in the number and scope of objectives following modernization, including the new economic approach. It seems, however, that whereas modernization succeeded in this respect the new economic approach has failed, at least with respect to the attempt to identify consumer welfare as the core value.

The question that is rather more difficult to answer is whether competition law is coherent in practice as the result of the application of objectives and boundaries. Having clear external boundaries would appear to promote coherence of competition policy by making competition law self-contained. Here I can only rely on selective illustrations from the case law. Hopefully the following chapters will provide a more satisfactory answer.

2. Economic Objectives

Efficiency and welfare

In this section I will discuss the following three economic objectives: (i) efficiency, (ii) consumer values, and (iii) combating market failures. As a caveat I should add that I am no economist and therefore my presentation of this side of the argument is strictly utilitarian. Although economics can accommodate equity concerns I will focus here on efficiency and welfare. These concepts have various meanings that I will briefly discuss.

In theoretical frameworks of competition law three types of efficiency generally play a role: (i) allocative efficiency, which ensures the maximum socially desirable output; (ii) productive efficiency, which ensures that resources accrue to the different production factors in such a way as to maximize output; and (iii) dynamic versus static efficiency, where the former takes the future into account whereas the latter concerns the status quo. Competition can be shown to benefit efficiency in all three dimensions.

There are two other types of efficiency that are frequently relevant to competition law. The first is Pareto efficiency, a state of allocation of resources in which it is impossible to make one person better off without making another individual worse off. The second is Kaldor–Hicks efficiency which relaxes this constraint insofar as there is a net positive result for some while others may as a consequence be left worse off. Neo-liberal views of efficiency tend to take the Kaldor–Hicks approach where parties that are better off could, in principle but need not in practice, compensate those that are worse off.

Market power can be shown to lead to increased monopoly profits along with a deadweight loss to total welfare involving both consumers and producers (so it is efficient neither in Pareto nor in Kaldor–Hicks terms) as well as to a loss in consumer welfare. It is therefore inefficient.

Debate among economists continues regarding the relevance of consumer versus total welfare as the appropriate objective for competition policy. In the United States, total welfare of the Kaldor–Hicks variety is frequently invoked as an antitrust objective covering benefits to producers as well as consumers.[4] Consumer welfare is generally associated with allocative efficiency. In the EU, consumer welfare has repeatedly been claimed as the overarching value of EU competition policy, albeit ultimately without success.[5]

Consumer values and efficiency in EU competition law

If consumer welfare is taken as the pre-eminent value of competition law then the effects of market behaviour on end-user prices are key to demonstrating infringements. This has the added benefit of clarifying both the test and the interest involved. Consumer welfare is mentioned explicitly in Article 101(3) TFEU (and Article 2(1)b of the Merger Regulation).[6] The Commission has repeatedly suggested that consumer welfare was a key objective of EU competition law, thus the 2000 Guidelines on vertical restraints stated that:

> The protection of competition is the primary objective of EC competition policy, as this enhances consumer welfare and creates an efficient allocation of resources.[7]

In its 2004 Guidelines on the application of Article 81(3) EC (now Article 101(3) TFEU) the Commission specified that:

> The objective of Article 81 [now Article 101 TFEU] is to protect competition on the market as a means of enhancing consumer welfare and of ensuring an efficient allocation of resources. Competition and market integration serve these ends since the creation and preservation of an open single market promotes an efficient allocation of resources throughout the Community for the benefit of consumers.[8]

Likewise, the 2009 Commission Guidance on the application of Article 102 TFEU to exclusionary abuses was replete with references to the consumer interest,[9] however the discussion as to whether the consumer interest is the ultimate objective of EU competition law was decided conclusively in the negative by the

[4] I. Lianos, Some reflections on the question of the goals of EU competition law, CLES Working Paper Series 3/2013, January 2013; J. Drexl, W. Kerber, and R. Podszun (eds), *Competition Policy and the Economic Approach: Foundations and Limitations* (Cheltenham: Edward Elgar, 2011).

[5] See K. Cseres, 'The controversies of the consumer welfare standard', *Competition Law Review* 3 (2007) 121–73.

[6] Council Regulation (EC) No 139/2004 of 20 January 2004 on the control of concentrations between undertakings, OJ 2004, L24/1.

[7] Commission Notice: Guidelines on Vertical Restraints, OJ 2000, C291/1 at para 7.

[8] Commission Notice: Guidelines on the application of Article 81(3) of the Treaty, OJ 2004, C101/97, para 13.

[9] Communication from the Commission: Guidance on the Commission's enforcement priorities in applying Article 82 of the EC Treaty to abusive exclusionary conduct by dominant undertakings, OJ 2009, C45/7.

finding of the CJEU in the pharmaceuticals case *GlaxoSmithKline* (2009).[10] Here it explicitly overruled the General Court (2006) which, following the view of the Commission, had claimed that the consumer interest was indeed the highest value of competition law. The General Court had held:

In effect, the objective assigned to Article 81(1) EC [now Article 101(1) TFEU], which constitutes a fundamental provision indispensable for the achievement of the missions entrusted to the Community, in particular for the functioning of the internal market... is to prevent undertakings, by restricting competition between themselves or with third parties, from reducing the welfare of the final consumer of the products in question.[11]

This also meant that showing the effects on final consumers was required to prove a restriction of competition. The CJEU, however, clarified its view that market structure and the position of competitors were objectives of equal rank:

like other competition rules laid down in the Treaty, Article 81 EC [now 101 TFEU] aims to protect not only the interests of competitors or consumers but also the structure of the market and, in so doing, competition as such. Consequently, for a finding that an agreement has an anti-competitive object, it is not necessary that final consumers be deprived of the advantages of effective competition in terms of supply or price.[12]

This case therefore also showed that competition law does not require direct effects on consumers, a perspective first clearly taken in *T-Mobile* that was decided in the same year.[13] Here the Court stated:

Article 81 EC [now Article 101 TFEU], like the other competition rules of the Treaty, is designed to protect not only the immediate interests of individual competitors or consumers but also to protect the structure of the market and thus competition as such.

Therefore... in order to find that a concerted practice has an anti-competitive object, there does not need to be a direct link between that practice and consumer prices.[14]

Regarding Article 102 TFEU, in *British Airways* the CJEU had ruled in 2007 that this provision 'is aimed not only at practices which may cause prejudice to consumers directly, but also at those which are detrimental to them through their impact on an effective competition structure'.[15] Likewise, in *Sot Lelos* (2008) the

[10] Joined Cases C-519/06 P, C-501/06 P, C-513/06 P, C-515/06 P and C-519/06 P *GlaxoSmithKline Services Unlimited v Commission (C-501/06 P)* and *Commission v GlaxoSmithKline Services Unlimited (C-513/06 P)* and *European Association of Euro Pharmaceutical Companies (EAEPC) v Commission (C-515/06 P)* and *Asociación de exportadores españoles de productos farmacéuticos (Aseprofar) v Commission* [2009] ECR I-9291; Case T-168/01 *GlaxoSmithKline Services Unlimited v Commission* [2006] ECR II-2969. Cf. Case T-213/01.

[11] Case T-168/01 *GlaxoSmithKline* (n 10), para 118. See Joined Cases T-213/01 and T-214/01 *Österreichische Postsparkasse AG, Bank für Arbeit und Wirtschaft AG v Commission* [2006] ECR II-1601, para 115: 'the ultimate purpose of the rules that seek to ensure that competition is not distorted in the internal market is to increase the well-being of consumers'.

[12] Joined Cases C-519/06 P, C-501/06 P, C-513/06 P, C-515/06 P, and C-519/06 P *GlaxoSmithKline* (n 10), para 63.

[13] Case C-8/08 *T-Mobile Netherlands BV, KPN Mobile NV, Orange Nederland NV and Vodafone Libertel NV v Raad van bestuur van de Nederlandse Mededingingsautoriteit* [2009] ECR I-4529.

[14] Ibid, paras 38–39.

[15] Case C-95/04 *British Airways Plc v Commission* [2007] ECR I-2331, para 106.

Court had held that the (limited) benefits to consumers of parallel trade could not be invoked as a justification of restraints imposed by a dominant undertaking.[16] Nevertheless, as the above quotation as well as other case law such as *Post Danmark* (2012) makes clear, the consumer interest is definitely one of the goals of EU competition law:

> Article 82 EC [now Article 102 TFEU] covers not only those practices that directly cause harm to consumers but also practices that cause consumers harm through their impact on competition.[17]

Also, it should be noted, in both *GlaxoSmithKline* and *T-Mobile* the Court explicitly extended the scope of its rulings to include 'the other competition rules of the Treaty', that is to say all of antitrust, as well as State aid (and arguably mergers, although these rules are not set out in the Treaty itself).

In addition it is worth emphasizing that the consumer in EU competition law is not the 'end-user' but can include all types of intermediate users and therefore undertakings operating downstream from the market where the infringement takes place as well. Finally, there is the issue of passing on harmful effects in the context of damages, which cannot be claimed at a particular level if passing on to a downstream (subordinate) level is possible. Kati Cseres (2007) claims that partly as a consequence of this broad definition of the standard of consumer harm, its application is so indeterminate that it is potentially detrimental.[18] Consumer interest then becomes primarily a rhetorical device to justify having competition policy.

Combating market failures

Following efficiency and consumer welfare, this final category of economic objectives concerns counteracting a suboptimal (inefficient) performance of markets that is due to failures such as information asymmetry, externalities, and non-competitive markets due to market power. It is evidently the last category, market power, which is of primary interest here. As we will see later, the requirement of existence of (a degree of) market power can also form a boundary that determines whether or not competition law is applicable. A clear example is significant market power (SMP), which in the context of electronic communications regulation is

[16] Joined Cases C-468/06 to C-478/06 *Sot. Lelos kai Sia EE et al. v GlaxoSmithKline AEVE Farmakeftikon Proionton, formerly Glaxowellcome AEVE* [2008] ECR I-7139, paras 52–57.

[17] See Case C-209/10 *Post Danmark A/S v Konkurrencerådet*, Judgment of 27 March 2012, para 20. Citing Case C-52/09 *Konkurrensverket v TeliaSonera Sverige AB* [2011] ECR I-527, para 24, which states that damage to consumers may not only be inflicted directly, but also via the detrimental effect on competition. See also Case C-202/07 P *France Télécom SA v Commission* [2009] ECR I-2369, para 105: 'since Article 82 EC [now Article 102 TFEU] refers not only to practices which may cause damage to consumers directly, but also to those which are detrimental to them through their impact on an effective competition structure... an undertaking which holds a dominant position has a special responsibility not to allow its behaviour to impair genuine undistorted competition on the common market'.

[18] Cseres (n 5).

taken as the basis for all competition-oriented intervention. The different types of economic objectives are linked. Therefore (a) protecting the structure of the market as well as the process of competition, which the CJEU has declared to be objectives of EU competition policy as we have just seen, are objectives that can serve the goal of (b) curbing market power as the primary instance of a market failure that harms competition, and thereby, ultimately (c) promote efficiency. As mentioned earlier, market power also forms a boundary for EU competition law and I will discuss it more at length in that context.

Less clearly a market failure in the strict economic sense, but sometimes seen as such, is under-provision of services that are deemed socially desirable. Effectively this opens the door to almost any kind of service provision under the heading of market failure. Fighting such market failure may for that reason not be accepted as an economic objective exception but as an exception on equity grounds. This category is nevertheless relevant to the exception for services of general economic interest (SGEIs) because only services which are already provided satisfactorily by the market cannot be the subject of an SGEI, and both economic and non-economic (or equity-based) exceptions are acceptable under the SGEI heading.[19]

3. Non-economic Objectives

Economic freedom

This is an objective that is often associated with the German Ordoliberal school of antitrust.[20] It is ranked as a non-economic objective because it is not efficiency-oriented. Here, freedom in the economic realm or freedom to compete is elevated to a value per se, which can be seen as a very strict assumption that market power is undesirable and potentially harmful. In the US setting this approach has been strongly criticized by the Chicago school.[21] It may yet be possible to link economic freedom to the objective of promoting competition as such, as we have seen above in the 2009 *GlaxoSmithKline* case,[22] however it is not clear that doing so would add to the idea of competition as such except by restricting it, arguably unnecessarily.

For instance, in the context of denying access, extending a right to compete to inefficient competitors is not obviously desirable—although the Commission will

[19] Communication from the Commission on the application of the European Union State aid rules to compensation granted for the provision of services of general economic interest, OJ 2012, C8/4, 48.

[20] See D.J. Gerber, *Law and Competition in Twentieth Century Europe: Protecting Prometheus* (Oxford: Oxford University Press, 1998). Some authors associate this freedom with neoliberalism as well, see F. Maier-Rigaud, 'Chapter 8. On the Normative Foundations of Competition Law—Efficiency, Political Freedom and the Freedom to Compete', in D. Zimmer (ed.), *The Goals of Competition Law* (Cheltenham: Edward Elgar, 2012). Cf. the comment by H. Schweitzer, ibid.

[21] R.H. Bork, *The Antitrust Paradox: A Policy at War with Itself* (New York, NY: Free Press, 1993); R. Posner, *Antitrust Law*, 2nd edn. (Chicago IL: Chicago University Press, 2001).

[22] Joined Cases C-519/06 P, C-501/06 P, C-513/06 P, C-515/06 P, and C-519/06 P *GlaxoSmithKline* (n 10).

also take into account network and learning effects that may enhance the efficiency of a competitor in the absence of anticompetitive constraints.[23] Meanwhile, throughout the substantive rules of competition law only efficient entry is generally protected, for instance as regards price squeezing (which protects those competitors who are only at least equally efficient as the dominant entity).[24] This is so under the 1998 *Bronner* test for market access to competitors' infrastructure in antitrust (also known as the essential facilities doctrine),[25] but also in the context of the access regime based on SMP in electronic communications regulation. In other words, there are limits to the special duty of care of dominant firms.[26] Promoting competition as such would therefore appear to signify 'competition on the merits', and at least implicitly between efficient competitors, not protecting the freedom of anyone who wants to enter the market. Protecting the freedom of all interested parties, for example in terms of imposing open access or network neutrality, is better done based on politically legitimized decision-making and public policy.[27]

Therefore economic freedom as an objective appears to be of limited practical significance, although invoking it publicly, like invoking the consumer interest, may well serve as a rhetorical tool for promoting the merits of competition law to a broader audience. At the level of the individual, economic freedom serves to promote choice[28] even though behavioural economics has cast considerable doubt on the rationality of the exercise of choice by consumers.[29]

Public policies and EU competition law

The next possible category of non-economic objectives of EU competition law (against which I will argue however) includes various types of public policies.

[23] Communication from the Commission: Guidance on its enforcement priorities in applying Article 82 of the EC Treaty to abusive exclusionary conduct by dominant undertakings, OJ 2009, C45/7, paras 23–24.

[24] Cf. C. Veljanovski, 'Margin squeeze: an overview of EU and national case law' (7 June 2012). *e-Competitions: Competition Laws Bulletin*, No. 46442. Available at SSRN: <http://ssrn.com/abstract=2079117>.

[25] Case C-7/97 *Oscar Bronner GmbH & Co. KG v Mediaprint Zeitungs- und Zeitschriftenverlag GmbH & Co. KG, Mediaprint Zeitungsvertriebsgesellschaft mbH & Co. KG and Mediaprint Anzeigengesellschaft mbH & Co. KG* [1998] ECR I-7791.

[26] Case 322/81 *NV Nederlandsche Banden Industrie Michelin v Commission* [1983] ECR 3461, para 10: 'A finding that an undertaking has a dominant position is not in itself a recrimination but simply means that, irrespective of the reasons for which it has such a position, the undertaking concerned has a special responsibility not to allow its conduct to impair genuine undistorted competition on the common market.'

[27] Available at: <https://ec.europa.eu/digital-agenda/en/net-neutrality-challenges>.

[28] See P. Nihoul, Freedom of choice: the emergence of a powerful concept in European competition law. Available at: <http://papers.ssrn.com/sol3/papers.cfm?abstract_id=2077694>. He refers especially to Case C-202/07 P *France Télécom SA v Commission* ECR 2009 ECR I-2369 and Case T-201/04 *Microsoft Corp. v Commission* [2007] ECR II-3601.

[29] See R.H. Thaler and C.R. Sunstein, *Nudge: Improving Decisions about Health Wealth and Happiness* (New Haven, CT: Yale University Press, 2008); D. Kahneman, 'Maps of bounded rationality: psychology for behavioral economics', *American Economic Review* 93 (2003) 1449–75.

Objectives, balancing, and exceptions

It is sometimes claimed that EU competition law has been used to pursue non-competition (or equity-based) public policy goals, however the (limited) case law that would support these claims seems to indicate that instead, such goals were thought to be valid concerns in the context of a balancing exercise between internal competition and external non-competition goals. In the 1977 *Metro* case, the Court held the following:

> The powers conferred upon the Commission under article 85(3) [now Article 101 TFEU] show that the requirements for the maintenance of workable competition may be reconciled with the safeguarding of objectives of a different nature and that to this end certain restrictions on competition are permissible, provided that they are essential to the attainment of those objectives and that they do not result in the elimination of competition for a substantial part of the common market.[30]

Subsequently in *Métropole* (1997), it stated:

> in the context of an overall assessment, the Commission is entitled to base itself on considerations connected with the pursuit of the public interest in order to grant exemption under Article 85(3) of the Treaty.[31]

Balancing typically takes place between competing policies and frequently between policies that are set at different levels, such as at EU and at national level. It does not presuppose a common or single set of objectives of these policies, hence, in my view, public policies that promote non-competition goals cannot be goals of competition law as such but can only serve to justify exceptions under Article 101(3) TFEU in antitrust, or under Article 107(3) TFEU in State aid, or in other contexts where a balancing exercise takes place.

Public policies at EU level

The following chapter will discuss the scope of grounds for exception in-depth.[32] For now, it appears obvious that EU competition law focuses on the economic justifications discussed above and the EU-specific objectives that are dealt with in the following discussion. Insofar as the activities concerned fall within the boundaries of EU competition law, non-economic public policies can play a role within EU competition law only in terms of warranting exceptions and only insofar as they reflect EU policies (such as environmental, cultural, and consumer

[30] Case C-26/76 *Metro v Commission* [1977] ECR 1875, para 21.

[31] Joined cases T-538/93, 542/93, 543/93 and 546/93 *Métropole Télévision v Commission* [1996] ECR II-649, para 118. Cf. Lianos (n 4), and G. Monti, 'Article 81 EC and public policy', *Common Market Law Review* 39 (2002) 1057–99.

[32] Cf. C. Townley, *Article 81 EC and Public Policy* (Oxford: Hart Publishers, 2009); O. Odudu, *The Boundaries of EC Competition Law: The Scope of Article 81* (Oxford: Oxford University Press, 2006); Monti (2002) (n 31); G. Monti, *EC Competition Law* (Cambridge: Cambridge University Press, 2007); H.H.B. Vedder, 'Of jurisdiction and justification: why competition is good for "non-economic" goals, but may need to be restricted', *The Competition Law Review* 6 (2009) 51–75.

policy). Whether this means that even then they have to conform to some goal of efficiency or whether they can, for instance, be covered by the internal market objective even where they fail the efficiency criterion remains to be seen. In any event, this is also the level at which the EU Commission could play a coordinating role between economic competition policy aims and horizontal EU objectives such as promoting the internal market and vertical (or sectoral) concerns.

What the effects would be on coherence is a complex issue: clearly limiting the scope of the objectives of and the exceptions to EU competition law would promote the unity and effectiveness of this body of law. In terms of the legitimacy of EU competition law, opinions would be likely to differ: from the perspective of competition law strictly speaking, clear choices enhance legitimacy and internal coherence, whereas from the wider perspective of EU integration and external coherence, more broadly accommodating political choices within competition law might in turn be considered to be more legitimate. The only point that I want to highlight at this stage is that public policies should be formulated as such by public authorities, not by private undertakings.[33]

Hence, such non-economic public policies at EU level cannot be qualified as objectives of EU competition law even though they may occasionally justify exceptions to it. That said, in my view, not even the latter is true for national public policies of any stripe.

Public policies at national level

It appears to me to be *a fortiori* obvious that the objectives of national public policy cannot form objectives of EU competition law. Allowing them to trump competition concerns would threaten the uniformity and coherence of EU competition law because different national policy concerns would be relevant in different Member States and to different degrees. This is not to deny that national competition authorities (NCAs) and national courts are capable of carrying out some form of balancing act with regard to broader policy concerns (as they may well be called upon to do) under their national competition law.

Chapter IV shows whether, for instance, in the Article 101(3) TFEU context national public policies trumps the objectives of EU law. It is already clear that this would lead to divergence and fragmentation. The main remedy would be frequent claims of cases by the Commission based on Article 11(6) of Regulation 1/2003, pre-empting NCAs.[34] Between twenty-eight Member States and myriad

[33] W. Sauter, 'Containing corporatism: EU competition law and private interest government', *European Competition Law Review* 36 (2015) 187–93.

[34] 'The initiation by the Commission of proceedings for the adoption of a decision under Chapter III shall relieve the competition authorities of the Member States of their competence to apply Articles 81 and 82 of the Treaty. If a competition authority of a Member State is already acting on a case, the Commission shall only initiate proceedings after consulting with that national competition authority.' Regulation 1/2003 Council Regulation (EC) No 1/2003 of 16 December 2002 on the implementation of the rules on competition laid down in Articles 81 and 82 of the Treaty, OJ 2003, L1/1.

possible policy concerns this might in any event not be effective and shooting down national policy concerns would most likely prove extremely costly for the Commission in terms of its broader legitimacy, as well as its political and regulatory capital. This would be the case even if it helped to safeguard the consistency or uniformity of EU competition law: hence the impact of an active exercise of the Commission's powers under Article 11(6) of Regulation 1/2003 on coherence would most likely be mixed. Other relevant dimensions are the boundaries of EU law that will be discussed below, and invoking SGEIs which is itself a powerful exception that will accommodate both efficiency and equity concerns formulated at national level.

4. EU-specific Objectives

As regards the objectives of EU competition policy, it is useful to distinguish between economic and non-economic goals as well as between the following three categories:

- the goals of competition law derived from general or abstract principles, as discussed earlier in this chapter: economic efficiency, consumer welfare, and economic freedom;
- from non-competition-oriented policies (although their validity is open to question); and
- the goals of EU competition law more specifically: policing the internal market, the process of competition, market structure.

Here I will discuss EU objectives. The antitrust and State aid provisions of EU law themselves do not set out explicit objectives, therefore they rely more heavily on the general objectives as set out in EU law, primarily the treaties as interpreted by the CJEU. The Merger Regulation is more explicit and mentions effective competition, market structure, and consumer welfare.[35] The aims of the rules on electronic communications[36] and energy[37] largely focus on setting out a harmonized framework; in the provisions on their scope they mention sustainable competition and the consumer interest, albeit not in a systematic way (for instance for electricity, but not for gas).

[35] Article 2(1) of Council Regulation (EC) No 139/2004 (n 6).

[36] Directive 2002/19/EC of the European Parliament and of the Council of 7 March 2002 on access to, and interconnection of, electronic communications networks and associated facilities, OJ 2002, L108/7: 'The aim is to establish a regulatory framework, in accordance with internal market principles, for the relationships between suppliers of networks and services that will result in sustainable competition, interoperability of electronic communications services and consumer benefits.'

[37] Directive 2009/72/EC of the European Parliament and the Council of 13 July 2009, concerning common rules for the internal market in electricity and repealing Directive 2003/54/EC, OJ 2009, L211/55, Article 1: 'This Directive establishes common rules...with a view to improving and integrating competitive electricity markets in the Community. It lays down the rules relating...open access to the market...It also lays down universal service obligations and the rights of electricity consumers and clarifies competition requirements.'

The internal market objective

As we have already seen in Chapter II, the EU's treaty framework has always linked competition policy to the internal market. Originally the stated aim was to see that the competition within the internal market (common market) was not distorted. Reversing the relationship, the CJEU has in the past on occasion not described the internal market as an objective of European competition law but has depicted competition law itself as a fundamental objective of the Community.[38] Post Lisbon, this view no longer corresponds to the treaties, where competition policy is now firmly linked to the internal market only, even if it ever did before.

The failed 2004 Constitution for Europe proposed an internal market where competition is free and undistorted as an objective of the EU itself. Following the 2007 Lisbon Treaty that came into force in 2009, the TFEU talks about an exclusive competence for the establishment of the competition rules necessary for the functioning of the internal market in Article 3(1)b TFEU and Protocol 27 ('the internal market as set out in Article 3 of the Treaty on European Union includes a system ensuring that competition is not distorted'). Consistent with this approach, the rules on antitrust, mergers, and State aid set out what practices are 'incompatible with the internal market', and the conditions under which they may be declared 'compatible with the internal market'. This confirms that whereas competition policy itself may not be an objective of the EU, safeguarding the internal market appears to be the overarching objective of EU competition law as set out constitutional level. This is clearly consistent with a view of the overall external coherence of EU competition law within the body of EU law as a whole. From the perspective of internal coherence of EU competition law, however, it is important to understand how the internal market objective functions in practice.

The structure of the market and the process of competition

In its case law the CJEU has defined the structure of the market and competition and the process of competition as objectives of EU competition law.[39] These goals appear to be closely linked to that of realizing the internal market, which makes them EU specific. A particular aspect which appears to be EU specific is the concern over market partitioning and enabling parallel trade, especially in the context of vertical (distribution) agreements. Systematically, market structure is a primary objective of merger control and of 'market making' policies in the electronic communications and energy sectors. It is associated with dominance and its sector-specific equivalent, significant market power (SMP). In this setting, the concept of workable competition as effective competition should also be mentioned, and this will be elaborated in Chapter IV.[40]

[38] Case C-289/04 P *Showa Denko KK v Commission* [2006] ECR I-5859, para 55; Joined cases T-259/02 to 264/02 and 271/02 *Raffeisen Zentralbank Österreich AG et al. v Commission* [2006] ECR II-5169, para 255. Cited in Lianos (n 4), 38.

[39] Joined Cases C-519/06 P, C-501/06 P, C-513/06 P, C-515/06 P, and C-519/06 P *GlaxoSmithKline Services*, above (n 10); Case C-8/08 *T-Mobile*, above (n 13).

[40] Case C-26/76 *Metro*, above (n 30).

Competitiveness

Finally, the concept of competition should be distinguished from the various references to competitiveness and competitive markets in the context of industrial policy and economic policy that were added by the 1993 Maastricht Treaty. Since Lisbon (2007), the notion of competitiveness has been joined with the social market economy to become a treaty objective.[41] If competition is seen as promoting competitiveness—for instance, by means of liberalization—the two notions are quite compatible. Frequently, however, there is a degree of tension because competitiveness taken as an industrial policy is associated with various forms of state intervention. I have dealt with this topic at length elsewhere, it is not necessary to do so here in the context of coherence.[42]

Which goals?

Summarizing briefly, there are three types of economic goals that characterize EU competition law: (i) market integration (including market structure and the process of competition), (ii) efficiency, and (iii) the consumer interest. Other views exist and are difficult to discount given the diversity of statements that can be found in the case law and the legislation, as well as in commentary on EU competition law. For example, Giorgio Monti lists economic freedom, market integration, and efficiency.[43] In the context of Article 101 TFEU, Okeoghene Odudu has advocated allocative efficiency and consumer welfare.[44]

To my mind, however, the combination of first, the linking of competition law to the internal market by the Lisbon Treaty (2007), and second, the 2009 Court judgments in *GlaxoSmithKline* and *T-Mobile* clinch the argument, at least regarding the pre-eminence of the internal market. In addition, Chapter II explained that the same reasoning would apply from a historical perspective, where from the outset, the competition rules intended to promote the internal market—a statement to which, for example, the Guidelines on vertical restraints (2010) still subscribe.[45] Finally, non-economic goals are in my view not included as objectives, but as we shall see in the next chapter, they may yet motivate exceptions.

[41] Article 3(3) TEU states: It shall work for the sustainable development of Europe based on balanced economic growth and price stability, a highly competitive social market economy, aiming at full employment and social progress, and a high level of protection and improvement of the quality of the environment.

[42] W. Sauter, *Competition Law and Industrial Policy in the EU* (Oxford: Oxford University Press, 1997); W. Sauter, 'Squaring EU competition law and industrial policy: the case of broadband', in J.M. Beneyto and J. Maíllo (eds), *Fostering Growth in Europe: Reinforcing the Internal Market* (Madrid: CEU ediciones, 2014).

[43] Monti (2002) (n 31).

[44] O. Odudu, *The Boundaries of EC Competition Law: The Scope of Article 81* (Oxford: Oxford University Press, 2006).

[45] 'Market integration enhances competition in the European Union. Companies should not be allowed to re-establish private barriers between Member States where State barriers have been successfully abolished.' Commission Notice, Guidelines on vertical restraints OJ 2010, C130/1, para 7. Version quoted in Monti (2002) (n 31).

What this appears to mean is that EU competition law has a number of goals that could strain its internal coherence, largely because there will be an objective to be found for most orientations of policy. Yet, the internal market objective is an excellent one as it grounds EU competition law in one of the core projects of the EU, external coherence, promoting consistency in that sense while inoculating it against further political intervention similar to that following the defeat of the draft Constitutional Treaty. In addition, given the diversity and range of the activities and interests of the EU, it was probably never a realistic prospect to have a single objective such as consumer welfare for its competition law regime. Finally however, not having politically defined non-economic goals (let alone open-ended ones) is a huge boon to coherence at all levels.

5. Legal Boundaries

Having looked at the objectives, we will now examine the boundaries of EU competition law. A more traditional expression for this is that these boundaries are jurisdictional criteria. In the case of boundaries, the parties and/or the practices involved are beyond the scope of competition law from the outset. Competition law is simply not applicable.[46] Where exceptions are involved parties are caught by the competition law rule, however they may be released based on special circumstances or following a balancing exercise, and this is considered in the next chapter.

The limits or legal boundaries of EU competition law are based on functional concepts and legal definitions such as the concepts of undertaking and of economic activity, economic concepts like market power as well as concepts that are judicially defined more on a case-by-case basis such as effect on trade.

The concept of undertaking

The notion of undertaking is of central importance in competition law because its rules only apply where undertakings are involved. This section focuses on the definition given to undertakings as it has been interpreted by the Court's case law and the Commission's practice. For this purpose, the following section will examine the notion of undertaking from a critical perspective, first in general terms and then in relation to two specific types of activity that are identified and discussed in recent European Commission guidance on this issue:[47] the exercise of public powers and social security.[48]

[46] On boundaries in competition law see Odudu (n 44); O. Odudu, 'Economic Activity as a limit to Community law', in C. Barnard and O. Odudu (eds), *The Outer Limits of EU Law* (Oxford: Hart Publishers, 2009) 225.

[47] Communication from the Commission on the application of the European Union State aid rules to compensation granted for the provision of services of general economic interest, OJ 2012, C8/4, and Communication from the Commission, draft Commission Notice on the notion of State aid pursuant to Article 107(1) TFEU.

[48] Cf. eg O. Odudu, 'The meaning of undertaking within 81 EC', *Cambridge Yearbook of European Legal Studies* (2005) 209–39; S. Stevens, 'Tax aid and non-profit organizations', *EC Tax Review* (2010) 156–69.

Notion of undertaking in competition law

The rules on antitrust and mergers apply directly and exclusively to undertakings. The State aid rules of the TFEU are targeted exclusively at the relationship between on the one hand, Member States (who are the addressees of the State aid rules), and on the other hand, undertakings (who must be the recipients for there to be an aid). Hence the definition of undertaking is key to determining the scope of the competition rules: in other words, to determine whether they apply to a particular entity (or rather, as we shall see, to a particular activity) at all.

The case law of the CJEU with respect to the notion of undertaking is functional in nature. In the first place, this means that definitions and classifications under national law are immaterial to the test that is applied by the Court.[49] This is necessary to avoid the same situation being treated differently under EU competition law in different Member States simply due to the fact that a certain activity is formally classified as public service in one Member State and as private enterprise in the other.

Second, this means that the Court does not look at the public or private status of the *entity* involved, which may take many different shapes, but instead it focuses on the type of activity that the entity carries out. Because undertakings carry out economic activities, the definition of undertaking rides on the definition of what constitutes an economic activity.

The concept of economic activity

The core of the definition of an undertaking within the meaning of State aid law is constituted by the concept of economic activity. The 1991 *Höfner* case is key here. In this case, dealing with job placement agencies, the Court stated that:

> in the context of competition law... the concept of an undertaking encompasses every entity engaged in an economic activity, regardless of the legal status of the entity and the way in which it is financed.[50]

In *Pavlov* (2000), a competition case regarding obligatory supplementary pension insurance for medical practitioners, the CJEU confirmed earlier case law to state that 'any activity consisting in offering goods and services on a given market is an economic activity'.[51] Therefore even individual doctors were regarded as constituting undertakings.

Moreover, to qualify as an economic activity it must be carried out at least potentially in competition. This potential is important: the Court in *Höfner* stated

[49] Cf. eg Case 118/85 *Commission v Italy* [1987] ECR 2599, paras 10–12.

[50] Case C-475/99 *Firma Ambulanz Glöckner v Landkreis Südwestpfalz* [2001] ECR I-8089, at 21.

[51] Joined cases C-180/98 to C-184/98 *Pavel Pavlov et al. v Stichting Pensioenfonds Medische Specialisten* [2000] ECR I-6451, para 75, citing Case 118/85 *Commission v Italy* [1987] ECR 2599, para 7, and Case C-35/96 *Commission v Italy* [1998] ECR I-3851, para 36; Cf. C-475/99 *Firma Ambulanz Glöckner v Landkreis Südwestpfalz* [2001] ECR I-8089, para 19.

The fact that employment procurement activities are normally entrusted to public agencies cannot affect the economic nature of such activities. Employment procurement has not always been, and is not necessarily, carried out by public entities.

It follows that an entity such as a public employment agency engaged in the business of employment procurement may be classified as an undertaking for the purpose of applying the Community competition rules.[52]

Thus, activities may be regarded as economic activities for the purposes of EU law in spite of the formal status quo in a given Member State.

In its guidance documents, however, the Commission takes a very different view: because similar activities may not always be carried out under the same conditions—that is to say, from time to time or in a different place—the issue as to whether a market and therefore an economic activity exists (and therefore an undertaking to which the State aid rules apply) has to be decided in the national context.[53] This conforms with what occurs in the context of free movement, and indeed in the context of SGEIs when applied to competition or State aid: reading across jurisdictions (applying EU rules on the basis that some Member States have less restrictive rules) is not allowed.

It is important that this interpretation, which is based more on national practice, distracts significantly from the impact of the functionalist approach. At the same time the guidance documents stress the relevance of potential competition, also in the case of in-house provision.[54] There thus appears to be a degree of friction between the various elements of the approach to the issue of economic activity on this count.

As regards the use of the concept of economic activity in the context of free movement, the general view also represented in the Commission's guidance is that this is different from that in the field of State aid,[55] and yet the case law (other than AG Opinions) to support this distinction is limited. The reason for this view is primarily that in the context of free movement economic activity is thought to be based on the concept of (potential) remuneration, whereas in the context of State aid law it requires (a potential for making) profit.[56] Based on the

[52] Case C-41/90 *Klaus Höfner and Fritz Elser v Macrotron GmbH* [1991] ECR I-1979, paras 22–23.

[53] Communication from the Commission on the application of the European Union State aid rules to compensation granted for the provision of services of general economic interest, OJ 2012, C8/4, para 12, and Communication from the Commission, draft Commission Notice on the notion of State aid pursuant to Article 107(1) TFEU, para 13.

[54] Communication from the Commission on the application of the European Union State aid rules to compensation granted for the provision of services of general economic interest, OJ 2012, C8/4, para 13, and Communication from the Commission, draft Commission Notice on the notion of State aid pursuant to Article 107(1) TFEU, para 14.

[55] Communication from the Commission on the application of the European Union State aid rules to compensation granted for the provision of services of general economic interest, OJ 2012, C8/4, para 15, and Communication from the Commission, draft Commission Notice on the notion of State aid pursuant to Article 107(1) TFEU, para 16, citing Case C-519/04 P *David Meca-Medina and Igor Majcen v Commission* [2006] ECR I-7006, paras 30–33; Case C-350/07 *Kattner Stahlbau GmbH v Maschinenbau- und Metall- Berufsgenossenschaft* [2009] ECR I-1513, paras 66, 72, 74, and 75.

[56] Cf. O. Odudu, "Economic activity as a limit to Community law", in C. Barnard and O. Odudu (eds), *The Outer Limits of European Union Law* (Oxford: Hart Publishing, 2010) 225–43, and the references cited there.

case law it is debatable whether making a profit is a strict requirement.[57] In any event, aside from the difference in the language used, profit and remuneration, or compensation—in the SGEI context with regard to State aid based on costs plus a reasonable rate of return, and therefore including a profit—are conceptually frequently barely distinguishable.

State action

The next boundary is imposed by the 'state action defence'. The rationale behind this boundary is that the EU Member States remain competent to pursue genuine public policies even at the expense of competition. However, I join Damien Gerard in pleading for the caveat that this is only so provided that any resulting restrictions on competition are, broadly speaking, necessary and proportional, much as ancillary restraints would be (or as Gerard claims, the internal market rules would require).[58] As a bottom line, it is generally accepted that in any event Member States are not allowed to rubber-stamp private restraints of competition and mask them as public policy in order to circumvent competition law. If they do so they infringe the useful effect (*effet utile*) of the competition rules, and thereby the Treaty.

At the same time private parties who are required to act in a manner that is predetermined by such public policies are not liable under the competition rules, but only insofar as their hands are actually tied. This corresponds to the question of whether or not there is sufficient scope left for competition to be distorted by the autonomous actions of private parties.[59] According to the Court in *Ladbroke* (1997):

> Articles 85 and 86 of the Treaty [now 101 and 102 TFEU] apply only to anti-competitive conduct engaged in by undertakings on their own initiative... If anti-competitive conduct is required of undertakings by national legislation or if the latter creates a legal framework which itself eliminates any possibility of competitive activity on their part, Articles 85 and 86 [now 101 and 102 TFEU] do not apply. In such a situation, the restriction of competition is not attributable, as those provisions implicitly require, to the autonomous conduct of the undertakings.[60]

This issue could arise, for instance, with regard to price regulation, however any remaining room for discounts or alternative sources of supply (parallel imports) could suffice here for a finding of competitive provision.

[57] Cf. eg Case C-49/07 *Motosykletistiki Omospondia Ellados NPID (MOTOE) v Elliniko Dimosio* [2008] ECR I-4863, para 27.

[58] D. Gerard, 'EU competition policy after Lisbon: time to review the "state action" doctrine?', *Journal of European Competition Law and Practice* 1 (2010) 202–10.

[59] Case 267/86 *Pascal Van Eycke v ASPA NV* [1988] ECR 4769; Joined cases C 359/95 P and C 379/95 P *Commission and France v Ladbroke Racing* [1997] ECR I-6265; Case C-198/01 *Consorzio Industrie Fiammiferi (CIF) v Autorità Garante della Concorrenza e del Mercato* [2003] ECR I-8055.

[60] Joined cases C-359/95 P and C-379/95 P *Ladbroke Racing* above (n 59), para 33. Cf. L. Hancher, 'Is private enforcement a viable means of tackling competition distortions caused by state action?', in E. Buttigieg (ed.), *Rights and Remedies in a Liberalised and Competitive Internal Market* (Malta: Gutemberg Press, 2012).

A significant case in this context was *GlaxoSmithKline* (2006, 2009),[61] already mentioned in the previous section in relation to the consumer interest. An important principle set out in the judgment of the General Court was that Article 101(1) TFEU (ex 81(1) EC) only applies to conduct engaged in by undertakings on their own accord. Thus, the investigation must start out by determining the impact of national regulations and whether those regulations leave any scope for competition that might be prevented, restricted, or distorted by autonomous conduct on the part of the undertakings.[62] At stake were agreements to limit parallel trade in pharmaceuticals. These were found to be anticompetitive because they eliminated one of the few remaining sources of competition in regulated markets.

At least in theory there is also a basis for EU intervention in national public policy that condones or imposes cartels.[63] This can constitute a breach of good faith by the Member State as a party to the TFEU. However, the so-called *effet utile* case law based on Article 4(3) TEU and Articles 101 and 102 TFEU has had limited practical effect. In *Belgian Dentists* (2008),[64] the Court found that a rule prohibiting advertising did not meet the standard for the infringement that it 'encourages, reinforces or codifies concerted practices or decisions by undertakings': it was seen as purely an act of public policy and therefore inviolate.

Inherent restrictions

Another contested category is that of inherent restrictions. In *Wouters* (2002),[65] the Court examined the role played by the Dutch bar association which was subject to a broadly stated public interest task and itself bound its members by (private) deontological rules that barred multidisciplinary partnerships between lawyers and accountants. The Court of Justice accepted that 'that regulation, despite the effects restrictive of competition that are inherent in it, is necessary for the proper practice of the legal profession' (notably its independence) and was not caught by competition law.[66] In *Meca-Medina* (2006), a similar approach was used with regard to anti-doping rules in sports, in part on health grounds.[67] Here the concept of (i) inherent restrictions was linked to (ii) the pursuit of a legitimate objective and (iii) a proportional application of the restrictions concerned: they had to be limited to what was necessary.[68]

[61] Joined cases C-519/06 P, C-501/06 P, C-513/06 P, C-515/06 P, and C-519/06 P *GlaxoSmithKline*, above (n 10).

[62] Case T-168/01 *GlaxoSmithKline*, above (n 10), paras 66–70.

[63] Case 267/86 *Van Eycke*, above (n 59).

[64] Case C-446/05 *Criminal proceedings against Doulamis* [2008] ECR I-1377, para 22.

[65] Case C-309/99 *J.C.J. Wouters, J.W. Savelbergh and Price Waterhouse Belastingadviseurs BV v Algemene Raad van de Nederlandse Orde van Advocaten* [2002] ECR I-1577.

[66] Ibid, para 110.

[67] Case C-519/04 P *David Meca-Medina and Igor Majcen v Commission* [2006] ECR I-6991. Cf. Case C-136/12 *Consiglio nazionale dei geologi v Autorità garante della concorrenza e del mercato and Autorità garante della concorrenza v Consiglio nazionale dei geologi*, Judgment of 18 July 2013; Case C1/12 *Ordem dos Técnicos Oficiais de Contas v Autoridade da Comcorrência*, Judgment of 28 February 2013.

[68] Ibid, paras 44–46.

These two cases suggest that the competition rules may occasionally be set aside on the basis of non-economic justifications. In my view this approach should not be regarded as a rule of reason because there is no balancing between pro- and anticompetitive effects of an agreement, but an agreement is judged to be out of bounds of the competition rules by definition based on the existence of a public interest in which certain restrictions are inherent. This could be a good way of dealing with bona fide non-economic (not efficiency-based) public interest objectives that can hardly be invoked under the Article 101(3) TFEU exception to the cartel prohibition. The bona fide nature of these objectives can then be tested based on the *effet utile* rule. So far, however, the inherent restrictions boundary rarely appears to come into play in EU competition law. At the same time it may be possible to distinguish between the public interest objective and disproportional private restraints of competition: an example is the (2012) *Compass* case.[69]

A recent example in this context is the General Court's 2014 ruling in *ONP*[70] where it confirmed the Commission's *ONP* (2011)[71] Decision concerning the branch organization of medical laboratories in France. ONP abused the regulatory powers that it enjoyed as part of the French market organization for the sector. In its Decision the Commission found that the inherent restrictions approach did not apply as the actions of the ONP were neither in the general interest nor necessary to guarantee the professional independence of its members. Moreover, it recalled that a distinction can be drawn between the competitive activities of an entity as an undertaking and those activities which it exercises as a public authority, and this is exactly what it did.[72] Accordingly, the General Court ruled that:

> The Commission had been correct in holding that it was not the task of a representative body of private persons to extend the scope of legal protection in order to protect the interest of a particular group when the legislature has set limits to the protection that is accorded and has left scope for a certain degree of competition.[73]

Thus the *Wouters* exemption did not apply. The Court, however, did not get around to ruling on the Commission's reasoning that the activities of an undertaking which are subject to competition should be examined separately from its exercise of public authority, and that these two cannot be assimilated in a manner that harms competition.[74] Finally it is worth mentioning the difference between ancillary restraints and inherent restrictions: the former serve to promote a private

[69] Case C-138/11 *Compass-Datenbank GmbH v Republik Österreich*, Judgment of 12 July 2012.

[70] Case T-90/11 *Ordre national des pharmaciens (ONP) et al. v Commission*, Judgment of 10 December 2014. See Sauter (2015) (n 33).

[71] *ONP* (Case 39510) [2010] C(2010) 8952 final, Commission Decision of 8 December 2010 based on Article 101 TFEU. Available at: <http://ec.europa.eu/competition/antitrust/cases/dec_docs/39510/39510_1203_3.pdf> accessed on 15 February 2013.

[72] With reference to case 107/84 *Commission v Germany* [1985] ECR 2655; Case T-128/98 *Aéroports de Paris v Commission of the European Communities* [2000] ECR II-3929; Case C-113/07 P *SELEX Sistemi Integrati SpA v Commission* [2009] ECR I-2207; and Case C-364/92 *SAT Fluggesellschaft mbH v Eurocontrol* [1994] ECR I-43.

[73] Case T-90/11 *ONP*, above (n 70), para 347.

[74] Sauter (2015) (n 33).

agreement and an efficient market outcome; the latter to promote a public interest pursued by a private agreement.

Collective agreements

In *Albany* (1999),[75]concerning compulsory affiliation to sectoral pension funds, the Court has determined that collective agreements between employers and workers that are intended to improve employment and working conditions by their nature and purpose do not fall within the scope of the competition rules. The reasoning was that collective bargaining was promoted by the Treaty (now Title IX, Articles 151–161 TFEU, ex 136–145 EC as amended) on social policy as well as at that time the 1991 Social policy agreement and social policy protocol (now transposed to Title IX). Thus, this boundary was derived from the general context of the treaties. This ruling has been applied to workers' sickness insurance schemes in *Van der Woude* (2000)[76] and more recently in *AG2R* (2011):

> a collective agreement concerning a healthcare insurance scheme which designates a single insurer in the event of subscription to that scheme, thereby excluding any possibility of affiliation to competing insurers, is excluded from the scope of Article 101(1) TFEU.[77]

This leaves Member States the opportunity to delegate decision-making in this field to the organized interests of employers and workers without falling foul of the *effet utile* rule based on Article 4(3) TEU (ex 10 EC, as amended) and Article 101 TFEU (ex 81 EC) that prohibits Member States' encouragement of antitrust infringements.[78] However, a collective agreement type of boundary rule does not exist for other kinds of organized interests that lack a similar basis in the Treaty.

In this context it is also worth noting that in *AG2R* (2011)[79] the fact that private parties effectively determined the scope of SGEIs for supplementary medical insurance in the French traditional bakery sector was also found to be compatible with EU law. The same had happened outside healthcare as regards supplementary pension insurance in *Albany* (1999).[80] SGEI thus appears to be a relatively flexible concept when it comes to accommodating national policies whereby private parties pursue public objectives.

[75] Case C-67/96 *Albany International BV v Stichting Bedrijfspensioenfonds Textielindustrie* [1999] ECR I-5751; Joined cases *C-115/97, C-116/97,* and *C-117/97 Brentjens' Handelsonderneming BV v Stichting Bedrijfspensioenfonds voor de Handel in Bouwmaterialen* [1999] ECR I-6025; and Case C-219/97 *Maatschappij Drijvende Bokken BV v Stichting Pensioenfonds voor de Vervoer- en Havenbedrijven* [1999] ECR I-6121.

[76] Case C-222/98 *Hendrik van der Woude v Stichting Beatrixoord* [2000] ECR I-7111.

[77] Case C-437/09 *AG2R Prévoyance v Beaudout Père et Fils SARL* [2011] ECR I-973, para 35.

[78] Case 267/86 *Van Eycke*, above (n 59).

[79] Case C-437/09 *AG2R*, above (n 77).

[80] Case C-67/96 *Albany*, above (n 75).

The compensation approach

The last legal boundary to be discussed concerns the compensation approach. In State aid a crucial role is played by the four so-called *Altmark* (2003)[81] criteria that are used to determine whether instead of an aid a form of compensation, such as a quid pro quo payment for a service, is concerned. These criteria are (i) that a public service obligation must in fact have been defined and legally assigned; (ii) that the parameters for compensation must be clear and set out in advance; (iii) compensation may not exceed costs and a reasonable rate of return; and (iv) the services must have been assigned either based on public procurement procedures or at the cost of a comparable efficient undertaking. This is a procedural test that does not go into effects.

A useful illustration is *BUPA* (2008),[82] which concerned the Irish risk equalization system for private medical insurance that was supplementary to the public insurance system. In what appears to have been a victory of theory over practice, the fact that a new entrant had to pay a multiple of its profits in subsidies to the incumbent under the scheme was held to be immaterial. The entrant accordingly withdrew from the market. *BUPA* was also noteworthy because the General Court relaxed the cost controls, stating that it was sufficient for costs to be verifiable and comparable after the fact. Moreover, services that did not cover the entire population but only a healthier and wealthier part of it and on a voluntary basis, were held to be acceptable as SGEIs. This was because the undertakings concerned in BUPA were under an obligation to accept all customers (open enrolment), at least those who could afford its fees.

In the more recent *CBI* case (2012),[83] the General Court used in effect the same standards as applied in *BUPA*: that there must be an act of entrustment of a universal service which is binding on the undertakings concerned and the parameters of compensation must be clear enough to prevent abuse, however it ruled that these had not been met by the Commission in its first stage State aid procedure and therefore it must conduct an in-depth investigation. This may lead to a renewed tightening of the *Altmark* standards by the General Court in relation to their earlier relaxation in *BUPA*.[84] The requirements of the compensation approach as applied here illustrate the interaction between the legal and economic boundaries of EU competition law.

6. Economic Boundaries

Market failure

The concept of a market failure can form a boundary to competition law. In its absence there would arguably be no economically sound reason to intervene

[81] Case C-280/00 *Altmark Trans GmbH and Regierungspräsidium Magdeburg v Nahverkehrsgesellschaft Altmark GmbH, and Oberbundesanwalt beim Bundesverwaltungsgericht* [2003] ECR I-7747.

[82] Case T-289/03 *British United Provident Association Ltd (BUPA) et al. v Commission* [2008] ECR II-81.

[83] Case T-137/10 *Coordination bruxelloise d'institutions sociales et de santé (CBI) v Commission (T-137/10)*, judgment of the General Court of 7 November 2012.

[84] Case C-280/00 *Altmark*, above (n 81).

in the market. Examples are externalities, information asymmetry, and network effects. More specifically to competition law, for instance, a failure of effective competition as a result of market power counts as a market failure. Increasingly the existence of a market failure is required for invoking exceptions as well, for instance in the State aid context.[85] As was mentioned earlier in the context of objectives, however, market failures cannot just be defined strictly as efficiency based. They can also be categorized more loosely to include equity concerns where the market underprovides certain socially desirable goods (such as education or environmental protection). If market failure is defined in the latter sense, that is if it covers non-economic (equity) reasons, this economic boundary is highly permeable. Finally, to be logically consistent, reliance on a market failure argument is only justified if it can be shown there is no government failure, whereby public intervention actually produces even worse results.

Appreciability

This second economic boundary is more quantitative in nature than qualitative. Once we are within the scope of the competition rules in a material sense the requirement of appreciability must still be met. The appreciability requirement can be understood as an economic boundary like market power, which is as a separate type of value or dimension with regard to the legal boundaries discussed earlier. Appreciability is relevant both to the effect on trade and to the restriction of competition that are required for the competition and State aid rules to apply. As we will see, these rules are not uniform across both areas of law.

Effect on trade

Unlike the two economic boundaries, the effect on trade and on competition appear in the text of Articles 101 and 102 TFEU itself, thus the effect on trade with regard to competition rules is a jurisdictional criterion. Although this criterion is to be applied on a case-by-case basis, its application is set out in Commission Guidelines (2004).[86] These Guidelines state that (i) a potential effect may suffice provided the undertakings involved have (ii) at least a 5 per cent market share and €40 million turnover. There is differentiation, however, between the scenarios involved where agreements covering several Member States or concerning imports and exports are usually by their very nature capable of effecting trade. It should be noted that agreements covering a single Member State or a significant part of it are capable of affecting trade if they raise significant barriers to entry—a foreclosure effect.[87] Agreements on purely local markets, even in border regions, do not appreciably affect trade.

[85] Case T-79/10 *Colt Télecommuncations France v Commission*, Judgment of 16 September 2013.

[86] Commission Notice, Guidelines on the effect on trade concept contained in Articles 81 and 82 of the Treaty [2004] OJ C101/81.

[87] Case C-234/89 *Stergios Delimitis v Henninger Bräu AG* [1991] ECR I-935.

According to the 2004 Guidelines, the notion that an agreement may affect trade

> implies that it must be possible to foresee with a sufficient degree of probability on the basis of a set of objective factors of law or fact that the agreement or practice may have an influence, direct or indirect, actual or potential, on the pattern of trade between Member States.[88]

Echoing the landmark 1974 internal market case, *Dassonville*, an effect on trade can be direct or indirect, actual or potential,[89] however the competition law concept of relevant market is not used in the Guidelines, not even with regard to dominant undertakings, where this would appear to be crucial; although leveraging market power from a dominated to a competitive market, for instance by bundling and tying, may also be an abuse it is not clear that this would equally be the case for, say, predation across relevant markets.[90] Hardcore cartels (price fixing and market sharing) that operate across borders will by definition affect trade. Finally, under Article 3(2) of Regulation 1/2003 where there is an effect on trade NCAs may not apply more strict national laws where there would not be a restriction of competition under EU competition law.[91]

Effect on competition

The appreciability of restrictions of competition is covered by the newly revised general *de minimis* Notice (2014),[92] based on turnover and market share, the turnover thresholds of the Merger Control Regulation, and the SGEI *de minimis* Regulation (2012),[93] and by the (2013) State aid *de minimis* Notice.[94] Like an effect on trade, an effect on competition is necessary for there to be a potential infringement of the antirust or State aid rules. However, the thresholds imposed by the State aid *de minimis* rules are based on aid levels instead of turnover and market definition and are relatively low—€200,000 over three years.

[88] Guidelines on the effect on trade, above (n 86), para 23.

[89] Case 8/74 *Procureur du Roi v Benoît and Gustave Dassonville* [1974] ECR 837, para 5.

[90] Case T-83/91 *Tetra Pak International SA v Commission* [1994] ECR II-755; T-201/04 *Microsoft*, above (n 28).

[91] Case C-226/11 *Expedia Inc. v Autorité de la concurrence et al.*, Judgment of 13 December 2012, paras 19–20.

[92] Communication from the Commission: Notice on agreements of minor importance which do not appreciably restrict competition under Article 101(1) of the Treaty on the Functioning of the European Union, OJ 2014, C291/1, replacing Commission Notice on agreements of minor importance which do not appreciably restrict competition under Article 81(1) of the Treaty establishing the European Community (de minimis) [2001] OJ C368/13.

[93] Commission Regulation (EU) No 360/2012 of 25 April 2012 on the application of Articles 107 and 108 of the Treaty on the Functioning of the European Union to de minimis aid granted to undertakings providing services of general economic interest [2012] OJ L114/8.

[94] Commission Regulation (EC) No 1407/2013 of 18 December 2013 on the application of Articles 107 and 108 of the Treaty on the Functioning of the European Union to *de minimis* aid, OJ 2013, L351/1.

In the 2012 *Expedia* case, the CJEU has clarified that Article 101(1) TFEU does not apply at all without an appreciable effect on trade and on competition.[95] Again, however, according to the Court in the 2012 *Expedia* case, this is so only provided they do not engage in hardcore restrictions (price fixing, output limitation, or market sharing). In such cases there is no need to demonstrate an effect on competition.[96] The *Expedia* case, where restrictions by object are per se violations and therefore by definition appreciable restrictions of competition, was followed by *Allianz* (2013),[97] where vertical restrains may be restrictions by object but must be examined in their economic and legal context:

> agreements...can be considered a restriction of competition 'by object' within the meaning of that provision, where, following a concrete and individual examination of the wording and aim of those agreements and of the economic and legal context of which they form a part, it is apparent that they are, by their very nature, injurious to the proper functioning of normal competition on one of the two markets concerned.[98]

The general *de minimis* Notice states that agreements between competitors with up to 10 per cent market share are not caught, nor are agreements between non-competitors with 15 per cent market share. This guidance, however, is binding only on the Commission, and not (at least not directly) on the NCAs.

The case law on which the criteria in the Notice are based is not always binding either. Thus, in *Bagnasco* (1999),[99] the CJEU held that coordination of current account interest rates by Italian banks did not have an appreciable effect in competition because changes in rates (at the discretion of the banks) were likely to be determined by objective factors such as developments in the money market. The banking services in question were found to have a limited effect on trade. An argument that restrictions by object were concerned would have been equally plausible.

In EU law there is, therefore, no absolute threshold for antitrust infringements (provided they affect trade). The merger control turnover thresholds which are too complex to discuss here in detail have two important exceptions: national mergers below the threshold can be dealt with at EU level and, vice versa, mergers with an EU dimension at national level, on request to the Commission. Finally, the SGEI *de minimis* Regulation provides a threshold for compensation of €500,000 over three fiscal years (and is therefore higher than that for State aid in general).

[95] Case C-226/11 *Expedia*, above (n 91), paras 16–17. [96] Ibid, paras 35–37.

[97] Case C-32/11 *Allianz Hungária Biztosító Zrt, Generali-Providencia Biztosító Zrt, Gépjármű Márkakereskedők Országos Szövetsége, Magyar Peugeot Márkakereskedők Biztosítási Alkusz Kft, Paragon-Alkusz Zrt., the legal successor of the Magyar Opelkereskedők Bróker Kft v Gazdasági Versenyhivatal*, Judgment of 23 March 2013, para 51.

[98] Case C-32/11 *Allianz Hungária Biztosító Zrt, Generali-Providencia Biztosító Zrt, Gépjármű Márkakereskedők Országos Szövetsége, Magyar Peugeot Márkakereskedők Biztosítási Alkusz Kft, Paragon-Alkusz Zrt., the legal successor of the Magyar Opelkereskedők Bróker Kft v Gazdasági Versenyhivatal*, Judgment of 23 March 2013.

[99] Joined cases C-215/96 and C-216/96 *Carlo Bagnasco et al. v Banca Popolare di Novara soc. coop. arl. (BNP) (C-215/96) and Cassa di Risparmio di Genova e Imperia SpA (Carige) (C-216/96)* [1999] ECR I-135.

Market power

Market power can be seen as a boundary issue of increasing importance: in its absence, restrictions are not relevant under the competition rules. The bottom line of market power is appreciability: the effect on competition and on trade has to be noticeable. At the other end of the spectrum of EU law relevance it is dominance, the ability to behave independently from competitors and trading counterparts. (The extremes are full competition and monopoly: what I want to discuss here is the categories that trigger applicability of the rules, not their opposites in economic terms.) Market definition and determining market share are the classical ways of determining market power. They also make the application of effects-oriented rules that rely on market share burdensome. Increasingly market power can also be derived directly from economic data—such as the ability to raise prices—using econometric methods. Examples of areas where the significance of market power has increased are the rules on vertical and horizontal restraints.[100]

A question that arises here is whether market power forms a boundary or whether combating market power forms an intermediate objective in relation to all the above-mentioned goals? This could certainly be argued, but not more forcibly than the fact that the enforcement of all rules of competition law forms similar intermediate objectives. To draw a distinction, the latter might be interpreted through the prism of market power, the existence of which would activate the relevant rules. This in turn gets back to the role of market power as a boundary, which I prefer.

The existence or otherwise of barriers to market entry serves to test arguments based on market power. An entry barrier is the opposite of a boundary. Where there are significant barriers to market entry, the existence of market power is more likely and its strength increased. In the absence of entry barriers the reverse holds: market power decreases.

Significant market power

As mentioned earlier in discussion on the rules on electronic communications, the main relevant concept in competition terms is that of SMP, which was based on that of dominance (but liberated from the requirement to prove abuse, and applied *ex ante* instead of *ex post*). In practice, proportionality requires that remedies address some identifiable risk of harm to competition and this also qualifies the *ex ante* character of the remedies to some extent.

Even before an SMP analysis is carried out, however, three criteria have to be met:

(a) the presence of high and non-transitory structural, legal or regulatory barriers to entry; (b) a market structure which does not tend towards effective competition within

[100] Guidelines on the application of Article 81(3), above (n 8); Commission Notice: Guidelines on Vertical Restraints, OJ 2010, C130/1; Commission Notice: Guidelines on the applicability of Article 101 of the Treaty on the Functioning of the European Union to horizontal co-operation agreements, OJ 2011, C11/1.

the relevant time horizon, having regard to the state of infrastructure-based and other competition behind the barriers to entry; and (c) competition law alone is insufficient to adequately address the identified market failure(s).[101]

These criteria have been applied by the Commission in its preselection of markets that have to be analysed, and have to be applied by the national regulatory authorities (NRAs) that wish to consider additional markets.

Countervailing market power

This is normally seen as countervailing market power on the other side of the market from an existing position of market power, that is to say the strong market position of a buyer could to a certain extent balance the market power of the seller, and vice versa. Whether countervailing market power is beneficial depends to a large extent on what the results are found in consumer markets (countervailing buying power in a consumer market itself is less likely): whether the benefits are passed on to end users.

7. Conclusion

This chapter raised the question of the role of the objectives of competition law in the context of the coherence of this body of law. A clear and limited number of objectives that are mutually consistent and can be organized in a hierarchical manner in order to resolve possible conflicts seems logically desirable because it increases the focus of the policy concerned. It is debatable whether EU competition law has such unity of purpose today, and whether it has ever had it in the past. The goals of EU competition law are numerous and although they are identifiable they are not clearly defined. In this sense at least the more economic approach has failed. The result is perhaps more favourable to flexibility than to coherence, albeit that in terms of legitimacy and effectiveness it has the saving grace of at least ensuring the survival of competition law. In Chapter II, I showed that at least since the Lisbon Treaty came into force in 2009, competition policy itself is not an objective of the Treaty. In my view it never was an objective, although an attempt to elevate it to this status was made in the context of the failed EU Constitution. This makes the internal market objective all the more important.

What seem to emerge are three sets of economic objectives: (i) those related to efficiency (ii) those related to consumers, and (iii) those related to the internal

[101] Commission Recommendation of 9 October 2014 on relevant product and service markets within the electronic communications sector susceptible to ex ante regulation in accordance with Directive 2002/21/EC of the European Parliament and of the Council on a common regulatory framework for electronic communications networks and services, OJ 2014, L295/79. Formerly Commission Recommendation of 17 December 2007 on relevant product and service markets within the electronic communications sector susceptible to ex ante regulation in accordance with Directive 2002/21/EC of the European Parliament and of the Council on a common regulatory framework for electronic communications networks and services, OJ 2007, L344/65.

market (including market structure and the competitive process). In particular, those in the latter category are specific to European integration and EU competition law and the CJEU has repeatedly declined the invitation to state whether the former two types of objectives are more important. Rather, since the defeat of the draft Constitution when the Lisbon Treaty came into force in 2009, the importance of the internal market has increased. The central nature of the internal market objective obviously helps to keep competition law grounded and connected with the broader integration project. With the benefit of hindsight, this return to first principles seems more convincing in its broader context rather than the narrow, perhaps blinkered focus on consumer welfare-based efficiency promoted by the Commission and the General Court, at precisely the time when Member States were bucking against the principle of having competition law at all.

At the same time, more integration does not equate to greater coherence of competition law even if greater coherence of competition law may mean more integration. Given the variance within the competition regime the next question becomes how much divergence the system can tolerate while still being considered coherent in terms of being effective and legitimate. In terms of coherence in a multilevel policy, the validity of multiple objectives increases the risks of divergence and fragmentation.[102] There is already such a risk at national level as a function of national competition law, which is addressed by Article 3 of Regulation 1/2003. Presumably, however, by definition there cannot be a requirement that national competition laws are not permitted to take broader objectives (and Article 3 gives more freedom where there are different objectives), such as equity related objectives into account, provided there is no effect on trade.

The risk of divergence arises even more seriously in the application of EU competition law if NCAs are required to balance multiple objectives (i) that are not *a priori* ranked in terms of precedence in the context of deciding on the applicability of exceptions, and (ii) where exceptions may be invoked based on national policy goals. It is self-evident that the problems are even worse where (iii) private equity goals are involved. I have already mentioned that I do not believe that such a requirement exists. We will examine this issue in detail in the next chapter on rules and exceptions in EU competition law.

As regards boundaries, the law here appears to be generally more transparent but not less complicated. We have seen that there are legal and economic boundaries in place. Among the former are the concepts of undertaking and economic activity, inherent restrictions, and the State action defence. These are not always consistent as, for example, the concept of undertaking as applied in different sectors shows. A comparable boundary in State aid is that of the concept of advantage, as spelled out by the CJEU in the 2003 *Altmark* Case, which has become the basis of the approach to compensation for public services under the State aid rules.[103]

[102] Lavrijssen (n 3).

[103] Case C-280/00 *Altmark Trans GmbH and Regierungspräsidium Magdeburg v Nahverkehrsgesellschaft Altmark GmbH, and Oberbundesanwalt beim Bundesverwaltungsgericht* [2003] ECR I-7747.

The economic boundaries mainly concern forms of market power, which conforms to the new economic approach (although the latter is contested by the recent emphasis on object-based infringements). Legal boundaries are an effective way of keeping public policies off limits provided, for instance, that the conditions of the state action doctrine are met. Here, equity goals can be defined and pursued by the Member States. At the same time the requirement of market power is playing an increasingly important role in ensuring that only economically significant behaviour comes within the scope of competition law.

IV

Rules, Exceptions, and Standards

1. Introduction

In the preceding chapters on the history and the objectives of EU competition law we have primarily encountered external coherence, that which connects EU competition law to EU law as a whole, largely through the internal market objective. The present chapter deals with internal coherence: at the level of EU competition law as a system and at the level of its individual components. I will discuss the essential framework of EU competition law in terms of its key rules and exceptions as well as, more selectively, a number of standards. This is not intended as a reference manual of EU competition policy but instead serves primarily to enable discussion regarding to what extent these rules and exceptions can be said to form a coherent whole, and what role they play individually.

Rules, rules of reason, and exceptions

First of all, the question is whether the conglomerate of competition rules—aside from its application in practice—forms a coherent (in other words functional) whole or a system at a general level. The relevant objectives and/or principles are assumed to promote the internal market by protecting a competitive market structure and the competitive process. I will assume that (i) multiple and divergent rules (exceptions and standards respectively), especially if applied at (ii) different levels of enforcement, will entail a risk of differentiation and fragmentation, whereas (iii) few and convergent rules under centralized control promote unity and coherence.

Second, however, in order for it to form a meaningful criterion, coherence is also understood as requiring effectiveness and legitimacy.[1] This means for instance that ostensibly simple rules that are in practice unenforceable or are so general as to be practically meaningless and require an ad hoc case-by-case analysis, do not meet these two additional qualitative conditions of coherence. Finally, legitimacy and effectiveness may entail a degree of flexibility. My second question is, therefore, whether and if so to what extent the conditions of legitimacy and effectiveness are met.

[1] M. Marquis, P. Lowe, and G. Monti (eds), *Effective and Legitimate Enforcement of Competition Law* (Oxford: Hart Publishing, forthcoming).

There appear to be two contrasting general approaches involved. EU competition law has a well-earned reputation of combining sweeping prohibitions with generous exceptions, first catching and then releasing its subjects with a warning, as does EU law at large. At the same time (as we have seen in the previous chapter's section on boundaries) the Court of Justice in particular has from time to time arguably used a 'rule of reason' type approach which involves a general test whether, on balance, the competition rules apply.

My intuition is that the latter is an example of a rule that is at face value attractive but in practice both too general to be effective, for example in terms of predictability and hence as a proportionate deterrence, and too deficient in terms of procedural and substantive due process to be legitimate. Nevertheless I will examine this alternative as well as the interaction between these two approaches. Secondary rules can either provide greater clarity and specificity or generate a mind-boggling proliferation of competition standards that is ultimately counterproductive. I will therefore examine the role of secondary legislation and of soft law guidance as a way of bridging open norms and decentralized practice, but not, in view of the available space and the overall purpose of this chapter, exhaustively.

Case studies of standards

As a type of example of standards I will review three issues in some more detail: effective or workable competition, market access, and proportionality. Workable competition is the intermediate goal of competition law. The issue of access is important under antitrust but even more so in the framework of the sector-specific rules on electronic communications and energy. Choosing this topic has the added advantage that market access is a key theme in settings of (exploitation) of market power and of market making. Proportionality is a recurrent theme throughout EU law (and for that matter national administrative and constitutional law) that has so far not been much discussed vis-à-vis competition law.[2] Thus, these three topics constitute respectively a normative standard (that is also an objective), a substantive standard, and a standard of review. The questions addressed will be whether the standards involved are coherent across settings and how this coherence is achieved.

2. Rules

Systemic (internal) coherence and EU competition law as a whole

As mentioned in Chapter II the rules on antitrust and state aid are set out in the Treaty on the Functioning of the European Union (TFEU) itself as primary rules of EU law, whereas those on mergers and the sector-specific frameworks were first

[2] However see J. Steenbergen, 'Proportionality in competition law and policy', *Legal Issues of Economic Integration* 35 (2008) 259–68; W. Sauter, 'Proportionality in EU competition law', *European Competition Law Review* 35 (2014) 327–32.

set out in secondary legislation. From the fact that secondary rules are based on primary law and because it takes time for the primary law to mature or its shortcomings to become obvious (as in the case of merger control that was originally based on applying the rules on antitrust), it follows logically that the secondary rules were not all adopted at the same time. In addition, within primary law antitrust matured before State aid did, in part due to a delay in adopting secondary legislation to complement and execute the treaty provisions involved. By now, however, at the most general level these primary and secondary rules can be considered to form a systematic (functional) whole at least to the extent that they jointly tackle the main categories of anticompetitive behaviour that are generally acknowledged: anticompetitive practices and dominance abuse by undertakings, the creation of positions of independent market power by mergers between undertakings, as well as anticompetitive advantages granted to undertakings by the Member States.

Unwritten EU law doctrines complement these provisions, such as that of *effet utile*, which prohibits Member States from infringing the competition rules, and that of (abuse of) collective dominance, which prohibits collusion by a close oligopoly. Such doctrines allow a degree of flexibility. Jointly these rules aim to police markets that are in principle competitive but where excesses have to be curbed. By contrast, for electronic communications and for energy there are supplementary rules which aim to create working markets where none existed before and where dominance is particularly entrenched based on previous statutory monopoly positions, vertical integration, and persistent network bottlenecks. These sectoral rules apply concurrently with the general competition rules. Taking EU competition law as whole, it would be difficult to identify a type of competition problem that could not be tackled by resorting to one of the types of rules available within it. (Although it is possible to have reservations regarding the merits of some of the competition problems identified, for example, as regards the proposed policy toward minority stakes and merger control. See Chapter VIII.) In other words there are at present no obvious gaps in terms of competition law instruments that are available in other developed markets' jurisdictions but not in the EU. Evidently this does not mean that the resulting powers are treated in a consistent manner, inter alia as there may be differences in view on how they should be applied.

With the exception of violations by object such as price fixing, output limitation, and market sharing with an effect on trade,[3] with regard to restrictions by effect for all instruments of EU competition law a degree of market power is necessary before the rules are triggered.[4] In all cases undertakings carrying out

[3] Communication from the Commission: Notice on agreements of minor importance which do not appreciably restrict competition under Article 101(1) of the Treaty on the Functioning of the European Union, OJ 2014, C291/1, paras 2 and 13, with reference to Case C-226/11 *Expedia Inc. v Autorité de la concurrence et al.*, Judgment of 13 December 2012. See also Commission Staff working document Guidance on restrictions of competition 'by object' for the purpose of defining which agreements may benefit from the De Minimis Notice, SWD(2014) 198.

[4] See L. Ortiz Blanco, *Market Power in EU Antitrust Law* (Oxford: Hart Publishing, 2013).

economic activities (that is to say active in markets, with regard to the provision of goods and services in exchange for consideration and at least potentially subject to competition), are involved. Leaving aside (for now) the difference between violations by object and by effect, these are common boundaries shared by the rules involved. There are no obvious inherent contradictions between the different instruments: some may be concerned more with market structure and others with anticompetitive practices but all are pulling in the same direction. They aim to achieve or protect effective competition, a standard we shall discuss more at length later in this chapter. Therefore, taken as a whole at face value and for our present preliminary purposes, at systemic level competition law can therefore be said to form a whole and an internally coherent one. This will be my basic hypothesis. We will see below whether there is convincing evidence that contradicts this position.

The antitrust rules

Antitrust covers two types of rules that are complementary: those concerning firms banding together to foreclose a market, and those concerning (in principle) single firms that dominate a market. The relevant rules are set out in Articles 101 and 102 of the TFEU. They have not changed in over five decades since the 1957 Rome Treaty and are relatively straightforward. Although a generous amount of guidance has nonetheless been published this mostly appears to concern the various exceptions to these rules and not their application in itself.[5] As we have seen in Chapter II, according to the case law of the Court of Justice, the set of objectives of the competition rules of the EU is the same.[6] This applies *a fortiori* to Articles 101 and 102 TFEU where the Court stated: 'Articles 85 and 86 [now Articles 101 and 102 TFEU] cannot be interpreted in such a way that they contradict each other, because they serve to achieve the same aim'.[7]

[5] Communication from the Commission Notice: Guidelines on the application of Article 81(3) of the Treaty, OJ 2004, C101/97; Council Regulation No 19/65/EEC of 2 March 1965 on application of Article 85 (3) of the Treaty to certain categories of agreements and concerted practices, OJ 1965, 36/533; Commission Regulation 330/2010 of 20 April 2010 on the application of Article 101(3) of the Treaty on the Functioning of the European Union to categories of vertical agreements and concerted practices, OJ 2010, L102/1; Council Regulation No 2821/71 on application of Article 85 (3) of the Treaty to categories of agreements, decisions and concerted practices, OJ 1971, L285/46; Commission Regulation No 1217/2010 of 14 December 2010 on the application of Article 101(3) of the Treaty on the functioning of the European Union to categories of research and development agreements OJ 2010, L335/36; Commission Regulation No 1218/2010 of 14 December 2010 on the application of Article 101(3) of the Treaty to categories of specialisation agreements OJ 2010, L335/43.

[6] See Joined Cases C-519/06 P, C-501/06 P, C-513/06 P, C-515/06 P, and C-519/06 P *GlaxoSmithKline Services Unlimited v Commission (C-501/06 P) and Commission v GlaxoSmithKline Services Unlimited (C-513/06 P) and European Association of Euro Pharmaceutical Companies (EAEPC) v Commission (C-515/06 P) and Asociación de exportadores españoles de productos farmacéuticos (Aseprofar) v Commission* [2009] ECR I-9291, para 63; and Case C-8/08 *T-Mobile Netherlands BV, KPN Mobile NV, Orange Nederland NV and Vodafone Libertel NV v Raad van bestuur van de Nederlandse Mededingingsautoriteit* [2009] ECR I-4529, paras 38–19.

[7] Case 6/72 *Europemballage Corporation and Continental Can Company Inc. v Commission* [1973] ECR 215, para 25.

Anticompetitive practices

Article 101(1) TFEU provides an anti-cartel rule prohibiting anticompetitive behaviour. This specifically (but not exclusively) regards price and quantity fixing, market sharing, and discrimination. The category of infringements is open-ended. They can be classified as either being prohibited by object, as the main purpose of the anticompetitive agreement, or by effect, as the anticompetitive result of an agreement. The burden of proof with regard to these two categories of classification of infringements is significantly different because demonstrating effects requires economic evidence.[8] Demonstrating intentions could in principle be accomplished based on (secret) agreements, such as the elusive 'smoking gun' that might be found in an on-site investigation, however the ability to derive the objective from the nature of the contested agreement or decision, such as fixing prices or sharing markets, is clearly a much lower threshold. An early statement to this effect is found in *Société Technique Minière* (1966):

> For the agreement at issue to be caught by the prohibition contained in article 85(1) [now Article 101(1) TFEU] it must have as its 'object or effect the prevention, restriction or distortion of competition within the common market'.
>
> The fact that these are not cumulative but alternative requirements, indicated by the conjunction 'or', leads first to the need to consider the precise purpose of the agreement, in the economic context in which it is to be applied. This interference with competition referred to in article 85(1) must result from all or some of the clauses of the agreement itself. Where, however, an analysis of the said clauses does not reveal the effect on competition to be sufficiently deleterious, the consequences of the agreement should then be considered and for it to be caught by the prohibition it is then necessary to find that those factors are present which show that competition has in fact been prevented or restricted or distorted to an appreciable extent.[9]

It sometimes appears as if restrictions by object are superseded by the need to demonstrate some form of effects in all instances. In *T-Mobile* (2009), however, the CJEU held that: 'there is no need to consider the effects of a concerted practice where its anti-competitive object is established'.[10] Appreciability has long appeared to be another potential escape. More recently in the 2012 *Expedia* case regarding online travel agency services, the CJEU has held

> the distinction between 'infringements by object' and 'infringements by effect' arises from the fact that certain forms of collusion between undertakings can be regarded, by their very nature, as being injurious to the proper functioning of normal competition...

[8] E. Loozen, 'The requisite legal standard for economic assessments in EU competition cases unraveled through the economic approach', *European Law Review* 39 (2014) 91–110; L. Parret, *Side Effects of the Modernization of EU Competition Law: Modernization as a Challenge to the Enforcement System of EU Competition Law and EU Law in General* (Nijmegen: Wolf Legal Publishers, 2010).

[9] Case 56/65 *Société Technique Minière (L.T.M.) v Maschinenbau Ulm GmbH (M.B.U.)* [1966] ECR 337, at 349.

[10] Case C-8/08 *T-Mobile*, above (n 6), para 30.

> It must therefore be held that an agreement that may affect trade between Member States and that has an anti-competitive object constitutes, by its nature and independently of any concrete effect that it may have, an appreciable restriction on competition.[11]

Thus it confirmed that the distinction between object and effect, and the relevant burden of proof (including with respect to appreciability) remained good law. Indeed according to the Court in this quotation from *Expedia*, in object cases the appreciability requirement is met by definition. This, as well as the relative clarity and efficiency of such cases, further adds to the attraction for the Commission and for national competition authorities (NCAs) in pursuing them.[12] Other recent case law (*Allianz*, 2013) supports the position in *Expedia* albeit that the existence of restrictions by object is to be determined based on a concrete and individual examination of the wording and the aim of the agreement concerned in its economic and legal context.[13]

Dominance abuse

Article 102 TFEU regards abuse of dominance, more specifically imposing unfair prices (such as excessive prices, predatory prices, or a price squeeze), limiting production, discrimination, and tying (or bundling). Again, the category of offences is open-ended. It is important to note that it is not illegal to possess a dominant position, nor is acquiring one—with the exception of doing so via a merger, which would then in principle be blocked. Thus an abuse is required to bring an undertaking within the scope of Article 102 TFEU. The other side of this argument is that the types of behaviour that may constitute abuses for a dominant undertaking (such as price discrimination or tying) are generally innocuous for undertakings that are not dominant.

It should be noted that this focus on abuse is at the core of the distinction with significant market power (SMP) in the sectoral regime for electronic communications which is applicable *ex ante* and does not require proof of an abuse. Evidently a proportionality requirement applies to the remedies imposed in this context, such as network access requirements. These remedies, however, are based on the need to promote the emergence of effective competition rather than aiming to remedy a threat to competition. This also means there does not have to be a direct link between particular remedies and 'abusive' behaviour.

Apart from the standard model of single firm dominance the concept of collective dominance (involving at least two different undertakings) has

[11] Case C-226/11 *Expedia Inc. v Autorité de la concurrence et al.*, Judgment of 13 December 2012, paras 36–37.

[12] See D. Bailey, 'Restrictions of competition by object under Article 101 TFEU', *Common Market Law Review* 49 (2012) 559–600.

[13] Case C-32/11 *Allianz Hungária Biztosító Zrt. et al. v Gazdasági Versenyhivatal*, Judgment of 14 March 2013, para 52 (dictum). See C.I. Nagy, 'The distinction between anti-competitive object and effect after Allianz: the end of coherence in competition analysis?', *World Competition* 36 (2013) 541–64.

gradually been developed in the case law.[14] Collective dominance can be distinguished with some difficulty from a concerted practice under the cartel prohibition, notably requiring a dominant position as opposed to merely an effect on trade and competition, in the case of a cartel. Apart from the requirement of jointly dominant market shares, since General Court's 2002 landmark *Airtours* case (concerning tour operators) proving collective dominance has involved meeting the following three cumulative conditions: (i) transparency; (ii) no threat of market entry; and (iii) the existence of an enforcement mechanism.[15]

The collective dominance doctrine can be seen as an attempt to bridge a perceived gap between the antitrust rules on anticompetitive practices (cartels) and those on dominance abuse. As such it is an illustration of a tendency of the system of EU competition law toward comprehensiveness as well as toward coherence—not allowing behaviour that is deemed anticompetitive to escape due to the inconvenient lack of a legal instrument but spawning new powers in response. At the same time this expansionist trend could also undermine coherence in the sense of consistency and legitimacy. Firms might justifiably ask, if we are not achieving single firm dominance by force of a merger or forming a cartel, why should we be persecuted under an ill-defined doctrine of collective dominance? Thus Commission merger decisions based on this approach were routinely challenged. Following *Airtours*, however, collective dominance has become an established dimension of EU competition law. This illustrates how the Court fulfils its role in the context of defining and expanding the doctrines of EU competition law.

The rule of reason

This is not an explicit written rule of antitrust, nor is it consistently applied in the case law or even generally accepted. Rules of reason can in fact be seen as alternatives to systems of written rules and exceptions. They are generally associated with enforcement in private suits before general (common law) courts, as in the United States, not as EU competition law still is, with enforcement largely carried out by specialized competition authorities. The rule of reason exception is nevertheless significant enough to warrant discussion in this section on rules of EU competition law.

[14] Joined cases T-68/89, T-77/89, and T-78/89 *Società Italiana Vetro SpA, Fabbrica Pisana SpA and PPG Vernante Pennitalia SpA v Commission* [1992] ECR II-1403; Joined cases C-68/94 and C-30/95 *France and Société commerciale des potasses et de l'azote (SCPA) and Entreprise minière et chimique (EMC) v Commission* [1998] ECR I-1375; Joined cases T-24/93, T-25/93, T-26/93, and T-28/93 *Compagnie maritime belge transports SA and Compagnie maritime belge SA, Dafra-Lines A/S, Deutsche Afrika-Linien GmbH & Co. and Nedlloyd Lijnen BV v Commission* [1996] II-1201.

[15] Case T-342/99 *Airtours plc v Commission* [2002] ECR II-2585. See G. Monti, 'The Scope of Collective Dominance under Articles 82 EC', *Common Market Law Review* 38 (2001) 131–57.

Does Article 101(1) TFEU contain a rule of reason?

Whether a rule of reason has ever been accepted in EU antitrust even implicitly is a matter of debate. The main historical instances of the application of the rule of reason in EU antitrust generally cited are *Nungessser* (1980)[16] and *Pronuptia* (1986),[17] where innovation in the areas of plant seeds and of store formats were involved. The restrictions concerned were found to be acceptable insofar as they were necessary with regard to a legitimate purpose, and therefore not regarded as restrictions of competition in the sense of Article 101(1) TFEU. Another instance is *Gøttrup-Klim* (1994),[18] where the necessity of the restrictive condition in relation to the legitimate purpose (a cooperative purchasing organization) is again stressed and not caught by Article 101(1) TFEU.

In the Commission's view, however, these instances do not illustrate the acceptance of a rule of reason but rather reflect the doctrine of ancillary restraints (see below). It took some time before the Court of Justice came out explicitly on the existence of a rule of reason and initially it did so in a circumspect manner. In *European Night Services* (1998) it added a layer of complexity by stating that the type of infringement is decisive. Restrictions can be dealt with under Article 101(1) TFEU only if they are restrictions by effect, but they must by their nature be considered under Article 101(3) TFEU if they are restrictions by object.[19] Thus in *Montecatini* (1999) the Court held:

> On this point, it need merely be stated that, even if the rule of reason did have a place in the context of Article 85(1) of the Treaty [now Article 101(1) TFEU], in no event may it exclude application of that provision in the case of a restrictive arrangement involving producers accounting for almost all the Community market and concerning price targets, production limits and sharing out of the market. The Court of First Instance did not therefore commit an error of law when it considered that the clear nature of the infringement in any event precluded the application of the rule of reason.[20]

Finally, in *Van den Bergh Foods* (2003), the General Court cut down the rule of reason theory explicitly.

> As regards HB's argument relating to application of the rule of reason in the present case, the Court would point out that the existence of such a rule in Community competition law is not accepted. An interpretation of Article 85(1) of the Treaty [now Article 101(1) TFEU], such as suggested by HB, is moreover difficult to reconcile with the structure of the rules prescribed by Article 85.

[16] Case 258/78 *L.C. Nungesser KG and Kurt Eisele v Commission* [1982] ECR 2015, para 58.

[17] Case 161/84 *Pronuptia de Paris GmbH v Pronuptia de Paris Irmgard Schillgallis* [1986] ECR 353, paras 16–17 and 27.

[18] Case C-250/92 *Gøttrup-Klim et al. Grovvareforeninger v Dansk Landbrugs Grovvareselskab AmbA* [1994] ECR I-4641, paras 34–35 and 45.

[19] Joined cases T-374/94, T-375/94, T-384/94, and T-388/94 *European Night Services Ltd (ENS), Eurostar (UK) Ltd, formerly European Passenger Services Ltd (EPS), Union internationale des chemins de fer (UIC), NV Nederlandse Spoorwegen (NS) and Société nationale des chemins de fer français (SNCF) v Commission* [1998] ECR II-3141, paras 136–137. See also case T-14/89 *Montedipe SpA v Commission* [1992] ECR II-1155, para 265.

[20] Case C-235/92 P *Montecatine SpA v Commission* [1999] ECR I-4539, para 133.

Article 85 of the Treaty expressly provides, in its third paragraph, for the exemption of agreements that restrict competition where they satisfy a number of conditions, in particular where they are indispensable to the attainment of certain objectives and do not afford undertakings the possibility of eliminating competition in respect of a substantial part of the products in question. It is only within the specific framework of that provision that the pro and anti-competitive aspects of a restriction may be weighed.[21]

This position seems clear: there is no rule of reason in EU competition law. In *O2 Germany* (2006), however, the General Court stated that the Commission was still required to carry out an analysis of the impact of a contested agreement on existing and potential competition under Article 101(1) TFEU. This was so, even if it was not required to carry out a full review of the positive and negative effects of the agreement on competition under Article 101(1) TFEU, and while the General Court repeated that a rule of reason had been deemed by the Community judicature not to have its place in Article 101(1) TFEU.[22] Again the distinction between restrictions by effect, where a full review of the state of competition is required under Article 101(1) TFEU, and by object, where it is not, appears key.

Ancillary restraints

A weaker version of the rule of reason is the doctrine on ancillary restraints. This covers certain types of restrictions that are directly related, necessary, and proportional to secure the benefits of an agreement that is pro-competitive in the overall market context. Such ancillary restraints are not caught by Article 101(1) TFEU. The main examples are non-compete clauses of limited duration and certain types of licensing and purchase and supply agreements. It is indicative of its reluctance to open this door too widely that the Commission has spelled out the relevant doctrine only with regard to concentrations,[23] although these principles also apply to Article 101(1) TFEU, thus this is a good example of a consistent approach between instruments.

Two main precedents of the modern approach to ancillary restraints under Article 101(1) TFEU are *Remia* (1985)[24] and *Métropole* (2001),[25] where the General Court stated 'the concept of an ancillary restriction covers any restriction which is directly related and necessary to the implementation of a main operation'.[26] In the

[21] Case T-65/98 *Van den Bergh Foods Ltd v Commission* [2003] ECR 2003 II-04653, para 106.

[22] Case T-328/03 *O2 (Germany) GmbH & Co. OHG v Commission* [2006] ECR 2006 II-1231, paras 68ff with reference to Case C-234/89 *Stergios Delimitis v Henninger Bräu AG* [1991] ECR I-935.

[23] Commission Notice on restrictions directly related and necessary to concentrations, OJ 2005, C56/23. Earlier: Commission Notice on restrictions directly related and necessary to concentrations, OJ 2001, C188/5; Commission Notice regarding restrictions ancillary to concentrations, OJ 1990, C203/5. See F.E. González Díaz, 'The notion of ancillary restraints under EC competition law', *Fordham International Law Journal* 19 (1995) 951–98.

[24] Case 42/84 *Remia BV et al. v Commission* [1985] ECR 2545, paras 18–20.

[25] Case T-112/99 *Métropole télévision (M6), Suez-Lyonnaise des eaux, France Télécom and Télévision française 1 SA (TF1) v Commission* [2001] ECR II-2459, paras 104–106. See also Case T-111/08 *MasterCard et al. v Commission*, Judgment of 24 May 2012.

[26] Case T-112/99 *M6*, above (n 25), para 104.

merger context there are many more instances. In *MasterCard* (2014) the Court of Justice elucidated the concept as follows:

> Where it is a matter of determining whether an anti-competitive restriction can escape the prohibition laid down in Article 81(1) EC [now Article 101(1) TFEU] because it is ancillary to a main operation that is not anti-competitive in nature, it is necessary to inquire whether that operation would be impossible to carry out in the absence of the restriction in question. Contrary to what the appellants claim, the fact that that operation is simply more difficult to implement or even less profitable without the restriction concerned cannot be deemed to give that restriction the 'objective necessity' required in order for it to be classified as ancillary,[27]

otherwise the prohibition of Article 101(1) TFEU would not be effective. It should be noted, however, that with necessity and proportionality the relevant criteria are very similar to those of the objective justification that can be applied even to hardcore restrictions in the context of Article 101(1) TFEU. (Evidently both types of restrictions, ancillary and hardcore, may exist within a single agreement.) In theory a clear distinction appears to exist between these two unwritten exceptions. Ancillary restraints normally relate to an agreement that is not itself and/or otherwise restrictive of competition. An objective justification on the other hand is required for an agreement that in itself is clearly restrictive of competition.[28] In practice there may be more similarities.

Inherent restrictions

More disruptive has been the 2002 *Wouters* case,[29] which was discussed in the previous chapter as a boundary issue.[30] Here essentially the existence of a bona fide public interest with regard to high-quality legal representation determined that the issue involved fell completely outside the scope of antitrust. The result is comparable to the way in which collective bargaining is excluded from antitrust based on an argument of the external coherence of competition law within the system of the Treaties (see the 1999 *Albany* case).[31] In my view this type of boundary case is clearly different from a balancing exercise between the pro- and

[27] Case C-382/12 P *MasterCard Inc. et al. v Commission*, Judgment of 11 September 2014, para 91.

[28] Other possible differences appear to be (i) the object or effect of the restrictions (with restrictions by object requiring an objective justification); (ii) in the nature of the restriction (mild restrictions, for instance because they are limited in time, may be ancillary restraints); and (iii) whether economic (ancillary restraint) on non-economic (objective justification) objectives are involved. However, so far none of these factors appears to have significant explanatory value. See also P. van Cleynenbreugel, 'Article 101 TFEU and the EU Courts: adapting legal form to the realities of modernization?', *Common Market Law Review* 51 (2014) 1381–436, at 1414.

[29] Case C-309/99 *J. C. J. Wouters, J. W. Savelbergh and Price Waterhouse Belastingadviseurs BV v Algemene Raad van de Nederlandse Orde van Advocaten* [2002] ECR I-1577.

[30] Cf. Case C-519/04 P *David Meca-Medina and Igor Majcen v Commission* [2006] ECR I-6991. Cf. Case C-136/12 *Consiglio nazionale dei geologi v Autorità garante della concorrenza e del mercato and Autorità garante della concorrenza v Consiglio nazionale dei geologi*, Judgment of 18 July 2013; Case C1/12 *Ordem dos Técnicos Oficiais de Contas v Autoridade da Concorrência*, Judgment of 28 February 2013.

[31] Case C-67/96 *Albany International BV v Stichting Bedrijfspensioenfonds Textielindustrie* [1999] ECR I-5751. See also Case C-219/97 *Maatschappij Drijvende Bokken BV v Stichting Pensioenfonds voor de Vervoer- en Havenbedrijven* [1999] ECR I-6121, and Joined cases C-115/97 to C-117/97

the anticompetitive aspects of an agreement such has been advocated as an alternative to the legal exception regime as the basis for the modernization of antitrust.[32]

The rule of reason and the legal exception regime

Arguably the rule of reason approach in EU antitrust law could have been buried definitively with the introduction of the legal exception system following modernization in 2004, which resolved the bottleneck issues inherent in the centralized notification and exemption regime that preceded it. However, in the Article 101 TFEU context it has persisted in the form of the notion of an objective justification that will be dealt with under exceptions below.

3. Exceptions

With regard to the various exceptions, three dimensions are involved: the nature of the interest, by whom it can be invoked, and who can decide.

Antitrust exceptions

Efficiency

In antitrust the main exceptions are economic in nature. These are efficiency under Article 101(3) TFEU and Article 102 TFEU. The Article 103(3) TFEU criteria are perhaps most widely known. The prohibition of Article 101(1) TFEU may be declared not applicable to an agreement and/or a practice:

> which contributes to improving the production or distribution of goods or to promoting technical or economic progress, while allowing consumers a fair share of the resulting benefit, and which does not:
> (a) impose on the undertakings concerned restrictions which are not indispensable to the attainment of these objectives;
> (b) afford such undertakings the possibility of eliminating competition in respect of a substantial part of the products in question.

In contrast, Article 102 TFEU on dominance abuse does not include a written exception, which appears to be logical given the need to demonstrate an abuse which might mean the behaviour was inexcusable. It turns out, however, that both an efficiency defence and the doctrine of objective justification provide for an exception here. These defences are found in soft law guidance and arguably in the Court's case law.[33]

Brentjens' Handelsonderneming BV v Stichting Bedrijfspensioenfonds voor de Handel in Bouwmaterialen [1999] ECR I-6025.

32 See R. Wesseling, *The Modernization of EC Competition Law* (Oxford: Hart Publishing, 2000).

33 Communication from the Commission: Guidance on its enforcement priorities in applying Article 82 of the EC Treaty to abusive exclusionary conduct by dominant undertakings, OJ 2009, C45/7, paras 28–31.

For Article 102 TFEU, the efficiency defence as set out in the 2009 Guidance on exclusionary conduct (foreclosure) must meet four cumulative conditions that are essentially identical to those spelled out in the Treaty itself under Article 101(3) TFEU that was quoted earlier:

- the efficiencies have been, or are likely to be, realized as a result of the conduct. They may, for example, include technical improvements in the quality of goods, or a reduction in the cost of production or distribution,
- the conduct is indispensable to the realization of those efficiencies: there must be no less anticompetitive alternatives to the conduct that are capable of producing the same efficiencies,
- the likely efficiencies brought about by the conduct outweigh any likely negative effects on competition and consumer welfare in the affected markets,[34]
- the conduct does not eliminate effective competition, by removing all or most existing sources of actual or potential competition.[35]

Remarkably, and in contrast to efficiencies in anticompetitive practices, for dominance abuse there is no explicit requirement that consumers share equitably in the resulting benefits. It is merely required that any losses incurred by such consumers are outweighed by the benefits to others, which is rather the reverse. (A Kaldor–Hicks-type efficiency test: see Chapter III.) There is no case law yet to show whether this is indeed how efficiencies should be interpreted here.

Policy objectives that can be defined in terms of efficiency improvements (such as can, for instance, often be claimed regarding environmental concerns) are not problematic under the exceptions to antitrust, given that the latter are economic in nature. It is still a matter for academic debate whether non-economic objectives can be accommodated under the antitrust exceptions. My personal view is that this is not the case (see further following).

Objective justification

The exception of objective justification is also addressed in the Commission's 2004 general guidance on the application of Article 101(3) TFEU,[36] as well as its 2010 guidelines on vertical restraints:

> Hardcore restrictions may be objectively necessary in exceptional cases for an agreement of a particular type or nature and therefore fall outside Article 101(1). For example, a hardcore restriction may be objectively necessary to ensure that a public ban on selling dangerous substances to certain customers for reasons of safety or health is respected.[37]

[34] Case C-23/14 *Post Danmark A/S v Konkurrencerådet*, Judgment of 6 October 2015, para 49.
[35] Guidance on exclusionary conduct, above (n 33), para 30.
[36] Guidelines on the application of Article 81(3), above (n 5), para 18.
[37] Commission Notice: Guidelines on vertical restraints, OJ 2010, C130/1, para 60.

The objective justification approach has surfaced in the 2011 *Pierre Fabre* case (although none was found there):

As regards agreements constituting a selective distribution system, the Court has already stated that such agreements necessarily affect competition in the common market... Such agreements are to be considered, in the absence of objective justification, as 'restrictions by object'.[38]

The notion of objective justification is also used in relation to the enforcement of Article 102 TFEU on dominance abuse as set out in the 2009 Guidance on exclusionary conduct.

In the enforcement of Article 82 [now Article 102 TFEU], the Commission will also examine claims put forward by a dominant undertaking that its conduct is justified. A dominant undertaking may do so *either* by demonstrating that its conduct is objectively necessary *or* by demonstrating that its conduct produces substantial efficiencies which outweigh any anti-competitive effects on consumers. In this context, the Commission will assess whether the conduct in question is indispensable and proportionate to the goal allegedly pursued by the dominant undertaking.[39]

The objective justification, for instance regarding a meeting competition defence, can be invoked as follows:

The question of whether conduct is objectively necessary and proportionate must be determined on the basis of factors external to the dominant undertaking.[40]

As is illustrated by this quotation, objective necessity should not be conflated with the notion of efficiencies that may be demonstrated both regarding Article 102 TFEU and in merger assessments using a four-part test that closely resembles that of Article 101(3) TFEU (see the next section).[41]

It may be questioned whether this way of addressing the objective justification involves (i) a rule of reason-type approach looking at the overall balance of an agreement as being pro- or anticompetitive, or (ii) it instead has more in common

[38] Case C-439/09 *Pierre Fabre Dermo-Cosmétique SAS v Président de l'Autorité de la concurrence and Ministre de l'Économie, de l'Industrie et de l'Emploi* [2011] ECR I-9419, para 39. See also para 60. Cf. Available at: <http://chillingcompetition.com/2011/10/18/case-c-43909-is-it-just-us-or-is-the-ecj-naming-the-eu-rule-of-reason/> and A. Svetlicinii, '"Objective justifications" of "restrictions by object" in Pierre Fabre: a more economic approach to Article 101(1) TFEU', *European Law Reporter* (2011) 348–53.

[39] Communication from the Commission: Guidance on its enforcement priorities in applying Article 82 of the EC Treaty to abusive exclusionary conduct by dominant undertakings, OJ 2009, C45/7, para 28, citing inter alia Case C-95/04 P *British Airways v Commission* [2007] ECR I-2331, paras 69 and 86. See also Case C-418/01 *IMS Health GmbH & Co. OHG v NDC Health GmbH & Co. KG* [2004] ECR I-05039.

[40] Guidance on exclusionary conduct, above (n 33), para 29. For a comprehensive view predating the guidance see E. Rousseva, 'The concept of "objective justification" of an abuse of a dominant position: can it help to modernise the analysis under Article 82 EC', *The Competition Law Review* 2 (2006) 27–72.

[41] Guidance on exclusionary conduct, above (n 33), paras 28–31; Guidelines on the assessment of horizontal mergers under the Council Regulation on the control of concentrations between undertakings, OJ 2004, C31/5, paras 76–88.

with an ancillary restraint that is necessary and proportionate to a legitimate objective, or (iii) whether there is no clear difference between the two. Ancillary restraints tend to be less restrictive (for instance in duration) whereas the objective justification relates to hardcore restraints, notably restrictions by object. An agreement that justifies ancillary restraints is typically not in itself restrictive and has positive economic objectives. In any event, as suggested by the references to public safety in the earlier quotation, where equity considerations are involved the objective justification may be used.

For public policy exceptions, however, the inherent restrictions approach (explicitly for Article 101 TFEU), the state action doctrine, and the exception for services of general economic interest (SGEIs) are also available. Finally, from the perspective of consistency the use of necessity and proportionality tests in each case is laudable but otherwise the proliferation of standards, boundaries, and exceptions seems confusing and risks being counterproductive.

National public policies

In my view, from a systemic perspective the difficulties of coordinating disparate national polies under the competition rules by NCAs mean that direct application of Article 101(3) TFEU requires that only competition values (economic or efficiency values) can be taken into account.[42] In addition, arguably the language of the provision concerned appears to be clear in this sense ('which contributes to improving the production or distribution of goods or to promoting technical or economic progress, while allowing consumers a fair share of the benefits'). Also in its guidance on the application of Article 101(3) TFEU and on vertical and on horizontal agreements, the Commission refers only to efficiency goals: hence equity concerns can only be taken into account insofar as they can be subsumed under efficiency goals.[43]

This means that under EU antitrust law NCAs are not to be saddled with balancing the economic interest in free competition with national equity-based industrial policy, energy policy, animal welfare, or environmental policies. Hence at national level, only economic arguments and specific EU objectives are to be taken into account, at least in the context of the application of EU competition law. This issue is linked with the debate about whether national polices other than competition policy are acceptable as a basis for exceptions to the competition rules.[44]

[42] U. Immenga, 'Coherence: a sacrifice of decentralisation', in C.-D. Ehlermann and I. Atanasiu, *European Competition Law Annual 2000: The Modernization of EC Antitrust Policy* (Oxford: Hart Publishing, 2001) 353–59.

[43] Guidelines on the application of Article 81(3), above (n 5); Commission Notice: Guidelines on Vertical Restraints, OJ 2010, C130/1; Commission Notice: Guidelines on the applicability of Article 101 of the Treaty on the Functioning of the European Union to horizontal co-operation agreements, OJ 2011, C11/1.

[44] S.A.C.M. Lavrijssen, 'The protection of non-competition interests; what role for competition authorities after Lisbon?', *European Law Review* 35 (2010) 634–59; H. Vedder, 'Of jurisdiction and justification. Why competition is good for "non-economic" goals, but may need to be restricted', *The Competition Law Review* 6 (2009) 51–75.

This does not preclude NCAs when applying national competition policies instead of Article 101 and 102 TFEU in the absence of an effect on trade from accommodating national public policy goals (just as the EU level of competition policy can accommodate EU level public policy objectives). The individual Member States are in principle free to add new concerns at the level of national competition policies. This also provides some flexibility as there are always likely to be significant constraints in terms of joint decision-making that impair adding new concerns as objectives or common policies at EU level.[45] This said, the measures concerned will have to respect the rules on State aid as well.

In this context, the merger rules form an exception with regard to national public policies. The legitimate interest taken into account as the baseline for EU merger control is that of safeguarding effective competition. However, Article 21(4) of the Merger Control Regulation explicitly allows Member States to take safeguard measures based on national public policies if the Commission finds them to be compatible with EU law.[46]

Finally, the SGEI concept allows both economic and non-economic (efficiency and equity) objectives to be taken into account, and it does this at the level of the interest of the Member State. (The term 'economic' in SGEI stands for the fact that it is provided by undertakings and does not pre-judge the nature or the objective of the service to be provided.)[47] Once again, this concerns an exception to competition law and not a source of alternative objectives for it.

EU level public policies

At EU level non-economic national objectives can be safeguarded if the manner in which they are pursued falls outside the scope, or boundaries, of EU competition law, as in the case of State action, inherent restrictions, and SGEI. We have seen that the exception of objective necessity, although it remains ill-defined, can also accommodate public policy concerns.

The State aid rules leave more room for non-economic policies, but this is so because in that field both the objectives of State aid and those of the policies that may be invoked to motivate an exception are at EU level. In addition, where State aid is concerned, the EU level has a monopoly on compatibility judgments, which makes it easier to control the application of such exceptions.

[45] F. Scharpf, 'The European social model: coping with the challenges of diversity', *Journal of Common Market Studies* 40 (2002) 645. C. Townley, 'Co-ordinated diversity: revolutionary suggestions for EU competition law (and for EU law too)', *Yearbook of European Law* 33 (2014) 1–51.

[46] Council Regulation (EC) No 139/2004 of 20 January 2004 on the control of concentrations between undertakings, OJ 2004, L24/1.

[47] U. Neergaard, 'Services of general economic interest: the nature of the beast', in M. Krajewski, U. Neergaard, and J. van de Gronden (eds), *The Changing Legal Framework for Services of General Interest in Europe: Between Competition and Solidarity* (The Hague: TMC Asser Press, 2009) 24; J.L. Buendia Sierra, 'Chapter 6: article 86', in J. Faull and A. Nikpay (eds), *The EU Law on Competition*, 2nd edn. (Oxford: Oxford University Press, 2007) 644.

The experience of State aid suggests that where EU equity-based policies are concerned it is up to the EU to do the balancing with the competition interest under the competition rules. So far there are no EU-defined SGEIs and Protocol 26 appears to imply that defining them is left to the Member States (although clearly there can be EU-defined universal service obligations). Or should we consider that giving EU policies other than competition priority (outside State aid) is anathema in EU law?

4. Secondary Law

This can be distinguished between hard law (regulations, directives, and decisions) and soft law (guidance notices and recommendations).[48] Without being exhaustive regarding their content I will now discuss their role within EU competition law.

Hard law

Arguably, secondary law is especially important outside antitrust: although Regulation 1/2003 plays a key role in setting out the procedural framework, the basic norms are found directly in the Treaty. That said, a series of Council regulations and Commission regulations sets out the conditions for block exemptions in antitrust, especially regarding the application of Article 101(3) TFEU to particular types of agreement.[49] In the age before modernization this also meant the notification requirement was lifted for agreements that fit within this framework and direct application of the exemption by national courts. Currently this is especially relevant with regard to vertical restraints (and motor vehicle distribution in particular). A similar system is in place for State aid, with a general block exemption and series of sector-specific exemptions, as well as a specific regime for public service compensation.[50]

[48] L. Senden, *Soft Law in European Community Law* (Oxford: Hart Publishing, 2004).

[49] See Council Regulation 2821/71/EEC of 20 December 1971 on application of Article 85(3) of the Treaty to categories of agreements, decisions and concerted practices, OJ 1971, L285/6; Commission Regulation 1217/2010/EU of 14 December 2010 on the application of Article 101(3) of the Treaty on the Functioning of the European Union to certain categories of research and development agreements, OJ 2010, L335/36; Commission Regulation 1218/2010/EU of 14 December 2010 on the application of Article 101(3) of the Treaty on the Functioning of the European Union to certain categories of specialisation agreements, OJ 2010, L335/43; Council Regulation 19/65/EEC of 2 March 1965 on application of Article 85 (3) of the Treaty to certain categories of agreements and concerted practices, OJ 6/3/1965, p 36; Commission Regulation 330/2010/EU of 20 April 2010 on the application of Article 101(3) of the Treaty on the Functioning of the European Union to categories of vertical agreements and concerted practices, OJ 2010, L102/1.

[50] Commission Regulation (EU) No 651/2014 of 17 June 2014 declaring certain categories of aid compatible with the internal market in application of Articles 107 and 108 of the Treaty, OJ 2014, L187/1.

Soft law

Guidance, or soft law, is non-binding but indicative of what a binding ruling might (or might not) entail. It can be seen as essential in helping NCAs and national courts apply EU competition law in a decentralized manner. Against this background the 2004 modernization package that accompanied Regulation 1/2003 included a range of soft law measures to cushion its impact.[51] As is spelled out in *Expedia* (2012), such guidance is binding only on the Commission itself insofar as it limits the exercise of its discretion, but it is not binding on NCAs: 'a Commission notice, such as the *de minimis* notice, is not binding in relation to the Member States'.[52] That is so unless they have independently bound themselves to applying the Commission's guidance or have duplicated it for domestic purposes, in which case the binding effect is still not that of the Commission's Notice itself.

Of course, guidance is also crucial to undertakings, in particular following decentralization based on Regulation 1/2003 whereby they became responsible for self-assessment under the directly effective legal exception of Article 101(3) TFEU, as well as in the context of Article 102 TFEU. Within the framework of decentralization a further level of soft law in the form of Commission guidance to undertakings regarding novel applications of Articles 101 and 102 TFEU by way of informal guidance letters was foreseen; however, at the time of writing (that is to say over a ten-year time period) not a single instance of such guidance has occurred.

By contrast, an example of soft law guidance that has been widely used since its introduction in 1996 (updated and renewed in 2006) is the Leniency Notice. This sets out the terms under which undertakings that provide information on cartels (to which they have generally been a party themselves) are rewarded with immunity and/or reduced fines.[53]

The implications for coherence

We have found what appears to be a scattershot range of exceptions to the competition rules which do not provide a clear norm or systematic set of norms. Unlike what could be said with respect to the rules themselves—that they at least covered the likely scenarios of restrictions of competition in a comprehensive manner—the exceptions do not appear to complement each other very well at all. The single exception could be the blanket function of SGEIs which can be invoked to cover

[51] Guidelines on the application of Article 81(3), above (n 5); Commission Notice: Guidelines on the effect on trade concept contained in Articles 81 and 82 of the Treaty, OJ 2014, C101/81; Commission Notice on cooperation within the Network of Competition Authorities, OJ 2004, C101/43. Commission Notice on the cooperation between the Commission and the courts of the EU Member States in the application of Articles 81 and 82 EC, OJ 2004, C101/54; Commission Notice on informal guidance relating to novel questions concerning Articles 81 and 82 of the EC Treaty that arise in individual cases, OJ 2004, C101/78.

[52] Case C-226/11 *Expedia*, above (n 11), paras 27–29.

[53] Commission Notice on immunity from fines and reduction of fines in cartel cases, OJ 2006, C298/17.

most instances where a plausible public interest is involved. Yet even that does not cover all instances where an exception may be warranted. At the same time at national level there may be real temptations to accommodate national policies on equitable or efficiency grounds. Also, having a relatively tidy set of rules matters less if the exceptions are slipshod. In sum: the risk of counterproductive divergence, or fragmentation, is real here.

5. Standards

Having discussed rules and exceptions, distinguishing standards from norms or rules is not a clear cut task; moreover it would seem to be foolhardy to attempt a general overview of all applicable standards in competition law or even just those in antitrust. Hence I will attempt to cover only a few that would enable a discussion of the role of standards without setting off on a wild goose chase. The three standards that I propose to examine in some more degree of detail are the standard of proof with regard to (i) effective or workable competition, (ii) market access, and (iii) proportionality. I have already discussed the standard for restrictions by object or effect in previous sections. Other examples of standards that will not be pursued here are dominance (that was discussed in part under boundaries), abuse, transparency, non-discrimination, and bundling.

Various types of competition

Workable or effective competition is one of the types of standards with regard to competition that are employed in EU competition law. So are competition on the merits and effects on competition—the latter will not be covered here as I have already discussed it as a boundary in Chapter III. These standards are not necessarily found in the economic literature on industrial organization but they play a role in the secondary competition law legislation as well as the case law of the Court.

Effective competition

Perfect competition and monopoly are the ideal types familiar in textbook justifications of antitrust rules. Whereas monopoly appears in competition practice (although perhaps not always equally persistent, aside from publicly awarded legal monopolies), perfect competition seems to be only a theoretical construct, not much use as a practical standard for competition law. In the 1977 *Metro I* case, the concept of workable competition instead was defined as follows:

> The requirement contained in Articles 3 and 85 of the EEC Treaty [now articles 3(1)b and 101 TFEU] that competition shall not be distorted implies the existence on the market of workable competition, that is to say the degree of competition necessary to ensure the observance of the basic requirements and the attainment of the objectives of the Treaty,

in particular the creation of a single market achieving conditions similar to those of a domestic market.

In accordance with this requirement the nature and intensiveness of competition may vary to an extent dictated by the products or services in question and the economic structure of the relevant market sectors...

The powers conferred upon the commission under Article 85 (3) [now Article 101(3) TFEU] show that the requirements for the maintenance of workable competition may be reconciled with the safeguarding of objectives of a different nature and that to this end certain restrictions on competition are permissible, provided that they are essential to the attainment of those objectives and that they do not result in the elimination of competition for a substantial part of the common market.[54]

The result is therefore a more realistic and practical standard.[55] Today we would associate the attainment of the objectives of the Treaty mentioned by the CJEU in this quotation with safeguarding the internal market in line with Article 3(1)b TFEU ('the establishing of the competition rules necessary for the functioning of the internal market'). However, in the case law the concept of workable competition is found far less often than that of effective competition, which is similar, but which is included in the wording of the Merger Control Regulation in its Article 2 where the test to be met is set out.[56]

In State aid the relevant standard is not workable or effective competition but whether there is an effect on competition in a market where there is trade between Member States,[57] as one of the four criteria that must be met before there can be an aid. This is much closer to the appreciability criterion in antitrust than it is to workable competition and also serves a different function: it is a jurisdictional criterion and can as such be regarded as a boundary issue.[58] For State aid, however, this threshold is even lower than *de minimis* in antitrust: in principle it is sufficient that there is a market in which undertakings are engaged in economic activity, and the general *de minimis* rules for State aid have a cut-off at €200,000 over three years.[59] This is in contrast with a 5 per cent market share and €40 million

[54] Case 26/76 *Metro SB-Großmärkte GmbH & Co. KG v Commission* [1977] ECR 1875, paras 20–21. See also case T-88/92 *Groupement d'achat Édouard Leclerc v Commission* [1996] ECR II-1961 Joined cases 209 to 215 and 218/78 *Heintz van Landewyck SARL et al. v Commission* [1980] ECR 3125; Case 75/84 *Metro SB-Großmärkte GmbH & Co. KG v Commission* [1986] ECR 3021.

[55] C.M. Bender, G. Götz, and B. Pakula, 'Effective competition: its importance and relevance for network industries', *Intereconomics* 46:1 (2011) 4–10.

[56] Council Regulation on the control of concentrations between undertakings, above (n 46), recital 6: 'Community law must...include provisions governing those concentrations which may significantly impede effective competition in the common market or in a substantial part of it'. See also Article 2(1)(a) and 2(2) regarding effective competition.

[57] Communication from the Commission (2014), Draft Commission Notice on the notion of State aid pursuant to Article 107(1) TFEU, para 6.3. Citing Case T-288/97 *Regione Friulia Venezia Giulia v Commission* [2001] ECR II-1619, para 41.

[58] Communication from the Commission: Notice on agreements of minor importance which do not appreciably restrict competition under Article 101(1) of the Treaty on the Functioning of the European Union, OJ 2014, C291/1. A more generous regimes exists for public service compensation. See above (n 50).

[59] Commission Regulation (EU) No 1407/2013 of 18 December 2013 on the application of Articles 107 and 108 of the Treaty on the Functioning of the European Union to de minimis aid, OJ 2013, L351/1. For public services compensation a more generous regime applies.

turnover for an appreciable effect on competition in antitrust (because such agreements have no effect on trade).[60]

Competition on the merits

This somewhat obscure notion is closely linked to the application of the prohibition on the abuse of dominance. The peculiarity of dominance abuse is precisely that it prohibits types of behaviour that are acceptable business practice for non-dominant undertakings. The ambiguity of this position is notable in the case law on competition on the merits. Competition on the merits is linked to the notion of the special responsibility of dominant undertakings.[61] It is also linked to the even more fundamental notion that an abuse is an objective concept that can be distinguished from 'normal' forms of competition which may include 'meeting competition'.[62] However, even the Guidelines on exploitative abuses do not contain more information about the substance of competition on the merits.

The case law is inconclusive. In *Intel* (2014), the General Court stated that:

> an undertaking in a dominant position has a special responsibility not to impair, by conduct falling outside the scope of competition on the merits, genuine undistorted competition in the common market[63]

This also means that not all competition based on price is warranted.[64] For a dominant undertaking, eliminating a competitor may be an infringement.[65] It does not mean, however, that the requirement of competition on the merits involves protecting (all) competitors. In *Post Danmark* (2012) the Court held that:

> Competition on the merits may, by definition, lead to the departure from the market or the marginalisation of competitors that are less efficient and so less attractive to consumers from the point of view of, among other things, price, choice, quality or innovation.[66]

In the context of the Organisation for Economic Co-operation and Development (OECD), proposals have been tabled on giving competition on the merits substantive meaning by connecting it with actual tests such as the profit sacrifice test, the no economic sense test, the equally efficient firm test, and various consumer

[60] Commission Notice on agreements of minor importance which do not appreciably restrict competition under Article 101(1) of the Treaty on the Functioning of the European Union, OJ 2014, C291/1.

[61] Case 322/81 *NV Nederlandsche Banden Industrie Michelin v Commission* [1983] ECR 3461, para 57.

[62] Case T-203/01 *Manufacture française des pneumatiques Michelin v Commission* [2003] ECR II-4071, para 54.

[63] Case T-286/09 *Intel Corp. v Commission*, Judgment of 12 June 2014, para 205. See Case T-321/05 *AstraZeneca AB and AstraZeneca plc v Commission*, Judgment of 1 July 2010, para 355.

[64] See for instance Case T-336/07 *Telefónica, SA and Telefónica de España, SA v Commission*, Judgment of 29 March 2012, para 172; Case C-280/08 P *Deutsche Telekom AG v Commission* [2010] ECR I-9555, para 177.

[65] Case T-228/97 *Irish Sugar plc v Commission* [1999] ECR II-2969, para 111.

[66] Case C-209/10 *Post Danmark A/S v Konkurrencerådet*, Judgment of 27 March 2012, para 22.

welfare balancing tests.[67] These have not been adopted in the EU Guidelines. For now the general suggestion is one of having cake (a criterion) and eating it too (not specifying how and when it applies in a consistent manner).

Market access and refusal to supply

The second category of standards examined relates to access. This is one of the key problems in competition law which we see reflected in antitrust (refusal to supply as an abuse of dominance), to a lesser extent in merger control and in State aid, and to a greater extent in the sector-specific regimes for electronic communications and for energy. For these sectoral regimes, mandated access is actually the basic tool for market making, promoting competition, and curbing market power. In antitrust, on the other hand, there is more scepticism regarding access requirements. The main issue is how to avoid discouraging investment in innovation and efficient delivery by undertakings with market power while ensuring that they do not dampen competition to such an extent that efficient market entry is harmed by monopoly power.

Refusal to supply

In both cases an important role is played by the notion of essential facilities, meaning the existence of dominance astride a bespoke infrastructure cannot be replicated even by an efficient competitor. Key precedents in this respect based on antitrust (dominance abuse) are the 1995 *Magill TV Guide* case[68] and especially the 1998 *Bronner* case.[69] In *Magill* the role of innovation and the consumer interest were stressed to plead in favour of granting access, however in *Bronner*, the bar for mandatory access was raised to a very high level: it would only be granted where replication based on the same volume of production as that of the incumbent was not feasible. Constraints on the total volume of demand meant that reaching the same production level would often be excluded in any event, hence smaller but efficient producers would not obtain access (and hypothetical ones that were equally large as the incumbent might not need it).

IMS Health (2004), following the *Magill* line, is the case that set the current standard on access as: (i) indispensability to innovation, (ii) elimination of competition, and (iii) the absence of an objective justification.[70] A final notable judgment on refusal to supply primarily because it confirmed the existing approach in a case

[67] 'What is competition on the merits?', *OECD Policy Brief*, June 2006, with a description of the tests mentioned above.

[68] Joined cases C-241/91 P and C-242/91 P *Radio Telefis Eireann (RTE) and Independent Television Publications Ltd (ITP) v Commission* [1995] I-743.

[69] Case C-7/97 *Oscar Bronner GmbH & Co. KG v Mediaprint Zeitungs- und Zeitschriftenverlag GmbH & Co. KG, Mediaprint Zeitungsvertriebsgesellschaft mbH & Co. KG and Mediaprint Anzeigengesellschaft mbH & Co. KG* [1998] ECR I-7791.

[70] Case C-418/01 *IMS Health*, above (n 39).

with high institutional stakes for the EU institutions (both the Commission and the General Court) is *Microsoft* (2007). This case concerned, inter alia, the refusal of Microsoft to supply and authorize the use of interoperability information.[71] The standard applied (and met) here was that of *IMS*.[72]

Meanwhile, the Commission sketched its general approach to access in its 2009 Communication on exclusionary conduct.[73] Before a refusal to supply can be regarded as an abuse under Article 102 TFEU, essentially three conditions have to be met: (i) the product or service must be necessary (indispensable) to compete effectively on a downstream market, meaning that effective replication is not feasible; (ii) the refusal would (immediately or eventually) eliminate effective competition on the downstream market; and (iii) it would lead to consumer harm, a condition which is often construed in terms of the dampening of innovation. As regards the third condition the Commission asserts that it will conduct a balancing exercise to determine whether for consumers imposing the obligation to supply would be more or less harmful than not doing so.

Margin squeeze

Margin squeeze is mentioned alongside refusal to supply in the Communication on exclusionary conduct, but the applicable conditions are not spelled out there. Presumably, margin squeeze is a related abuse or a more specific form of refusal to supply. It is caused by the fact that there is not enough room between wholesale purchasing prices and retail selling prices to allow even an efficient competitor to survive in the market. In the first place, the three abovementioned conditions have to be met. Second, the wholesale price that is offered by the dominant (vertically integrated) firm to the (input-dependent) downstream competitor must be excessive in the sense just mentioned, resulting in a negative or in any event economically unsustainable margin between the two.[74]

Under the heading market access and refusal to supply, we therefore see a range of standards in antitrust to which we should add the sectoral standards for third party access. At the same time it is clear that efficient entry, innovation, and the effect on consumers are common threads. In addition, the antitrust access standards provide a backstop for regulatory intervention. General competition law thus functions as a safety net for sector specific intervention—used by the Commission to correct wayward NRAs even although it has no competence to act directly under the sectoral rules itself.

[71] Case T-201/04 *Microsoft Corp. v Commission* [2007] ECR II-3601.

[72] See C. Ahlborn and D.S. Evans, 'The Microsoft judgment and its implications for competition policy towards dominant firms in Europe', *Antitrust Law Journal*, 75 (2009) 887–932.

[73] Guidance on exclusionary conduct, above (n 33), paras 75–90.

[74] Case C-295/12 P *Telefónica SA and Telefónica de España SAU v Commission*, Judgment of 10 July 2014; Case C-280/08 P *Deutsche Telekom AG v Commission* [2010] ECR I-9555.

The proportionality standard

Within the realm of legal standards, proportionality also clearly deserves attention. This includes not only an attempt to identify the standard used in different settings (such as a state aid clearance by the Commission, or the national application of an efficiency defence in an abuse of dominance setting), but also how it relates to coherence if we assume that like teleology it is beneficial to distinguish this category from coherence rather than to conflate the two terms. Moreover, proportionality is linked both to legitimacy as it concerns the standard for the realization of a legitimate objective, and to effectiveness. The least restrictive means that is still effective is typically the most stringent norm to be applied under this test. Proportionality of EU law enforcement on the one hand and of the use of exceptions on the other might form necessary constraints that promote coherence.

Coherence also forms the mildest form of a proportionality test under the internal market: whether goals are pursued in an internally consistent and systematic manner.[75] This can be considered to be the bottom line of what may be expected of a policy in terms of good governance.[76] Proportionality is required both of the Commission in its enforcement actions and of Member States and undertakings in particular in the framework of exceptions.

The general proportionality standard

The standard version of the test is set out in the free movement case, *Fedesa* (1990). This consists of four elements that can be grouped under the categories of necessity and balancing. The latter is also seen as proportionality in the strict sense. It is not encountered much in free movement but, as we will see below, it is relevant in EU competition law.

Under *necessity* comes:

1. an appropriate (or suitable) measure
2. in pursuit of a legitimate objective (legality—this is sometimes not counted as a separate step in the test), and
3. among the appropriate measures, that which constitutes the least restrictive effective means.

Finally, under the *balancing* test we encounter proportionality in the strict sense:

4. not manifestly disproportionate in terms of a costs versus benefits balance.

These steps are not always applied in a cumulative manner. In particular, under step 3 concerning the choice of means, the least restrictive means standard is often

[75] Case C-169/07 *Hartlauer Handelsgesellschaft mbH v Wiener Landesregierung and Oberösterreichische Landesregierung* [2009] ECR I-1721, para 63.

[76] Sauter (n 2); and W. Sauter 'Proportionality in EU law: a balancing act?', *Cambridge Yearbook of European Legal Studies* (2012–13) 439.

replaced by a not manifestly disproportionate test, and in most instances step 4, balancing or proportionality per se, is often left out completely.

In EU law, Member States are as a rule subject to the relatively mild manifest disproportionality test, although in harmonized areas a least restrictive means test may be applied. Member States are generally only directly involved in EU competition law concerning State aid and SGEIs (*effet utile* cases are so far rare and likely to remain so). With regard to SGEIs, a manifest disproportionality standard is the rule. In State aid control however, as we have seen above, there is full balancing test.

The proportionality standard in antitrust

What we see here is that in cases like *Alrosa* (2010)[77] and *Mastercard* (2012),[78] concerning the Commission's powers with regard to remedies, after a formal finding of infringement under Article 7 of Regulation 1/2003 a least restrictive means (strict) test is applied, whereas its decisions on pursuing commitments under Article 9 of that Regulation are only reviewed against the milder standard of manifest disproportionality.

As regards the use of site inspections in order to investigate antitrust infringements, the Commission enjoys a broad margin of discretion,[79] however it must ensure that they do not constitute a 'disproportionate and intolerable interference' in relation to the aims that they pursue. Thus the power to initiate an inspection has to be justified as being proportionate to the need for the information sought, and not in terms of the severity of infringement suspected.[80] This appears to be a necessity test based on suitability and least restrictive means.

Perhaps surprisingly, the test for undertakings is (even) stricter. As is well known, Article 101(3) TFEU sets four cumulative conditions for the directly effective legal exception from the cartel prohibition in Article 101(1) TFEU. These are (i) the creation of efficiencies, (ii) which are passed on to consumers, (iii) with only indispensable restrictions, and (iv) no elimination of all competition in the market. The test for indispensability checks whether the least restrictive standard is met, but the test of the negative and positive effects of an agreement on consumers can be seen as a classic balancing requirement; that is, the application of proportionality in the strict sense. This balancing is therefore the relevant difference with the test under Article 101(1) TFEU, as the necessity requirement is found in relation to both provisions.

Taken together, this suggests the application of a proportionality test under Article 101(3) TFEU which is as detailed as that found in *Fedesa*,[81] and more

[77] Case C-441/07 P *Commission v Alrosa Company Ltd* [2010] ECR I-5949, paras 36–42.

[78] Case T-111/08 *MasterCard*, above (n 25), paras 323–324.

[79] Cf. Joined Cases T-289/11, T-290/11, and T-521/11 *Deutsche Bahn et al. v Commission*, Judgment of 6 September 2013; Case T-135/09 *Nexans France SAS and Nexans SA v Commission*, Judgment of 14 November 2012.

[80] Cf. Case T-339/04 *France Télécom SA v Commission* [2007] ECR II-526.

[81] Case C-331/48 *The Queen v Minister of Agriculture, Fisheries and Food and Secretary of State for Health, ex parte: Fedesa et al.* [1990] ECR I-4023, para 13.

demanding than that in *Gebhard* (1995) in the free movement context.[82] Unlike either of these free movement-based tests, balancing actually appears to apply in the context of Article 101(3) TFEU and Article 107(3) TFEU. Moreover it requires a detailed or in any event substantiated economic assessment.

Thus we see that the proportionality test in EU competition law consists of a series of partly overlapping tests that are applied as alternatives instead of cumulatively. The Member States are generally subject to manifest disproportionality testing in the case of SGEIs and to strict balancing under the State aid rules. The standard(s) to which the Commission is held in the context of competition law differs with the degree of intrusiveness of the measure involved but still stops short of balancing. In contrast, private parties (undertakings) in the framework of competition law are subjected to the strictest proportionality requirements: both LRM and balancing of costs and benefits.

6. Conclusion

In this chapter I have loosely examined the main rules and exceptions as well as a number of standards of EU competition law. Against this background I have also looked at public interest exceptions. As a general observation, the EU system of competition law appears to be comprehensive in terms of providing a rule to tackle each type of competition problem and a range of exceptions to these rules. This raises two questions: (i) why the electronic communications and energy sectors have been subjected to specific regimes whereas other sectors have not and while the competition rules continue to apply in parallel (this issue will be tackled in Chapter IX), and (ii) whether divergence between different instruments of competition law is more or less serious than within one instrument between different levels of its application.

It is my view that a rule of reason, which would provide a systematic alternative to the legal exception system, does not exist in EU competition law. The Court of Justice has been quite clear on this and on closer inspection the exceptions involved are different ones. This is to be welcomed because the rule of reason appears to be too open-textured to allow for a consistent application across different levels of enforcement and judicial control. The same is true for allowing public interest justifications within the legal exception regime. Where national equity-based policies are nonetheless genuinely desirable and require proportional exceptions to the competition rules, Member States can revert to the State action

[82] Case C-55/94 *Reinhard Gebhard v Consiglio dell'Ordine degli Avvocati e Procuratori di Milano* [1995] ECR I-4165, para 37. There, the Court stated there are four requirements that must be fulfilled by restrictions when a Member State hinders or makes less attractive the exercise of the Treaty freedoms: (i) they must be applied in an non-discriminatory manner; (ii) they must be justified by imperative requirements in the general interest; (iii) they must be suitable for securing the attainment of the objective which they pursue; and (iv) they must not go beyond what is necessary in order to attain it.

doctrine, removing the practices concerned from the scope of the competition rules, or to SGEIs.

EU competition law is equipped with a range of standards reaching from the vague (effective competition and competition on the merits) to the varied (refusal to supply and the conditions for mandatory third party access). The latter is arguably the most important element of the abovementioned sectoral regimes, where I will try to make more sense of these parallel standards. Finally, with proportionality we see a standard that derives from a general principle of EU law that is applied in a differentiated manner (differently to different parties) in EU antitrust. This reinforces both external and internal coherence.

V

Procedures and Remedies

1. Introduction

There are two sides to the twin topics of this chapter. On the one hand, procedures and remedies can jointly be seen as the tools that are used to shape and implement effective enforcement of competition law and thereby give it practical meaning. They impose structure on the parties involved and can be abstracted to a certain extent from the substantive or material norms that I have discussed in the preceding chapters. On the other hand, procedures and remedies are concerned with autonomous legal values such as due process and the rights of the defence, as well as the legality and proportionality of enforcement action, which serve to protect the defendant as well as the overall legitimacy of the process of competition law enforcement.

Therefore, procedures and remedies can be linked to effectiveness and legitimacy, both regarding inputs (process) and outputs (deterrence), but they are also subject to (and themselves express) the restraints imposed by the rule of law. They can be described as checks and balances. These restraints act within the framework of legitimacy as well as within that of effectiveness, although arguably they pull in different directions: for instance more guarantees of due process may enhance (input) legitimacy while hampering effective enforcement (and thereby output legitimacy). A related dimension is formed by the requirement that competition law must remain within its boundaries not just in relation to undertakings but also with regard to the sovereign powers of the Member States, the most important crucible in this respect being the policy on State aid. This refers to the balance of power between the different levels of governance in the EU.

In this chapter I will not only look at the effectiveness and legitimacy of EU competition law as discussed earlier but also at the balance between the rights of the undertakings involved in competition proceedings on the one hand and those of the investigating authorities at national and at EU level on the other. First I will discuss procedures with regard to antitrust. Here I will use the example of leniency applied by the European Commission at EU level versus damages actions by private parties before national courts. Next I will look at the various types of remedies using the example of infringements versus commitments.

The larger questions that I will address are as follows. The first is how the balance is struck between uniformity and effectiveness on the one hand, and due process, the rights of the defence and legitimacy on the other. Effectiveness and legitimacy are therefore contrasted. The second question is whether the result is a coherent system, and in what direction this system is developing.

2. Procedures

What role for procedures in EU competition law?

Procedural law formally determines the manner in which a procedure must be pursued. The role of the rules on procedure in EU competition law can be described as prescribing the steps that must be taken in the appropriate legal form in order to ensure that the process involved may have legally valid results within the overall framework of applicable norms, including in terms of the respective rights and duties of the parties involved in the procedure.

Procedural law has long been a specialized field of study in competition law in its own right.[1] Like the standards discussed in earlier chapters, the procedures of EU competition law are manifold. Some are not set out in primary law but are defined in practice and/or soft law (instruments like Commission notices)—market definition is one of them.[2] Another is the system of checks and balances that is applied to the pursuit of competition cases within the Commission, which combines prosecutorial and administrative adjudicative functions.[3] The main check and balance is evidently that provided though judicial review by the General Court and the Court of Justice, however the appeals process (and the system of preliminary rulings) is the same as for other cases in EU law.

EU procedure and national law

An important point of departure for EU competition law is that as far as procedural law is concerned, its application at national level is largely if not almost exclusively a matter for the Member States, at least provided that the result is equally effective as is the application of national law. Of course, this stricture still constitutes cold

[1] See, for instance: N. Khan, *EU Antitrust Procedure*, 6th edn. (London: Sweet & Maxwell, 2012); L. Ortiz Blanco (ed.), *EU Competition Procedure*, 3rd edn. (Oxford: Oxford University Press, 2013); G.L. Tosato and L. Bellodi (eds), *EU Competition Law: Volume I, Procedure: Antitrust—Merger—State Aid*, 2nd edn. (Deventer: Claeys and Casteels, 2014); L. Parret, *Side effects of the modernisation of EU competition law. Modernisation as a Challenge to the Enforcement System of EU Competition Law and EU Law in General* (Nijmegen: Wolf Legal Publishers, 2011). More generally: K. Lenaerts, I. Maselis, and K. Gutman, J.T. Nowak (ed.), *EU Procedural Law* (Oxford: Oxford University Press, 2014). More specific: C. Harlow and R. Rawlings, 'Modernisation, cooperation, enforcement: competition', in C. Harlow and R. Rawlings, *Process and Procedure in EU Administration* (Oxford: Hart Publishing, 2014) 196–219.

[2] Commission Notice on the definition of the relevant market for the purposes of Community competition law, OJ 1997, C372/5.

[3] A type of system that was ruled to be compatible with the fair trial requirement of Article 6 of the European Convention on Human Rights in ECtHR, Appl No 43509/08, *Menarini Diagnostics S.R.L. v Italy*, Judgment of 27 September 2011.

comfort if national laws were not effectively applied either. With regard to the distinction between substance (EU law) and procedure (determined by national law) as applied in national courts, Imelda Maher raises the question even more pointedly: 'the issue remains whether the hybridity of common and divergent rules is sufficient not just for the coherence of the law but also for its standing as "good" law'.[4]

In an earlier paper, however, Maher had noted that procedural autonomy 'allows national authorities to be consistent within their own jurisdictions whether they are applying the EC [now EU] rules or their own domestic competition laws'.[5] This shows that we have two legal systems that are to some extent competing, including on the dimension of internal consistency, while at the same time there is overlap between them. In any event, in spite of the principle of national procedural autonomy, the EU courts are not promoting a passive role for EU competition law in this respect. In its 2010 *VEBIC* decision, the Court of Justice intervened where national procedural rules fell below the standard that was required for an effective application of Articles 101 and 102 TFEU regarding legal recourse for the national competition authority (NCA) involved (an entity which in Belgium, where this case originated, was itself a court).[6]

In addition, there is a degree of harmonization taking place: most recently (2014) the Directive on (private actions regarding) Damages, an example that will be discussed in more detail below.[7] For the NCAs there are checks and balances in place not only at national level but also at EU level in particular, given the Commission's ability to claim a case at any stage of the proceedings in Article 11(6) and even for national courts given the binding nature of the Commission's decisions in Article 16 of Regulation 1/2003.

Finally, the influence of the European Competition Network (ECN) plays a role regarding de facto procedural harmonization. How coordination of this system, that combines features of a network with features of a hierarchy, works will be the subject of the next chapter, as is the role of the advisory committee of representatives of the Member States (that also fit under the examination of coordination), which for the decision of individual antitrust cases is composed of representatives of the NCAs.

Elements of procedure

The procedures of EU competition law can be grouped sequentially from the complaint or *ex officio* action leading to the opening of a case, from the statement of

[4] I. Maher, 'Competition law modernization: an evolutionary tale', in P. Craig and G. de Búrca (eds), *The Evolution of EU Law*, 2nd edn. (Oxford: Oxford University Press, 2011) 717–42, at 733.

[5] I. Maher, 'Functional and normative delegation to non-majoritarian institutions: the case of the European Competition Network', *Comparative European Politics* 7 (2009) 414–34, at 428.

[6] Case C-439/08 *Vlaamse federatie van verenigingen van Brood- en Banketbakkers, Ijsbereiders en Chocoladebewerkers (VEBIC) VZW* [2010] ECR I-12471. N. Petit, 'The judgment of the European Court of Justice in *VEBIC*: filling a gap in Regulation 1/2003', *Journal of European Competition Law & Practice* 2 (2011) 340–4.

[7] Directive 2014/104/EU of the European Parliament and of the Council of 26 November 2014 on certain rules governing actions for damages under national law for infringements of the competition law provisions of the Member States and of the European Union, OJ 2014, L349/1.

objections to the hearing and the eventual finding of infringement and through to the procedural aspects of remedies from fines to actions for damages.[8] This assumes all steps are completed, although some cases may be closed at an earlier stage, for instance following a rejection of a complaint, or are concluded based upon a commitment decision. Cartel infringement decisions may have been settled by the parties, facilitating proof of an infringement that in this context is essentially obtained by means of an admission.

The relevant procedures could also be grouped as dealing with the requirements for undertakings, steps in the process, dealing with legal protection for undertakings (such as the right to be heard and access to the file), and the exercise of the powers of the authorities involved—the Commission, NCAs, national and EU courts—as well as with the coordination between them. In addition, they can of course be grouped according to the type of procedure, based on the nature of the competition policy instrument involved, antitrust (public enforcement and private action), mergers and State aid.

The objective here is to provide a short description of the main elements of antitrust procedure and to chart the relevant features of centralization and decentralization. The procedures and the remedies of mergers and State aid and of the sectoral regimes will be discussed for comparative purposes in Chapters VIII and IX.

Some general principles

The allocation of cases

Regulation 1/2003 itself does not provide rules for case allocation,[9] although its Article 13 provides for the suspension or termination of proceedings once another NCA has already taken up the case or has dealt with an agreement.[10]

Instead, case allocation is left to the ECN, guided by the Joint statement of the Council and the Commission on the functioning of the network of competition authorities,[11] and the Commission Notice on cooperation with the network of competition authorities of 2004.[12] Apparently the former served to assuage the

[8] Ortiz Blanco (n 1). The main procedural documents are Council Regulation (EC) No 1/2003 of 16 December 2002 on the implementation of the rules on competition laid down in Articles 81 and 82 of the Treaty, OJ 2003 L1/1; Commission Regulation 773/2004 of 7 April 2004 relating to the conduct of proceedings by the Commission pursuant to Articles 81 and 82 of the EC Treaty, OJ 2004, L123/18; and Commission Notice on best practices for the conduct of proceedings concerning Articles 101 and 102 TFEU, OJ 2011, C308/6.

[9] See S. Brammer, 'Concurrent jurisdiction under Regulation 1/2003 and the issue of case allocation', *Common Market Law Review* 42 (2005) 1383–424.

[10] This rule even applies where an NCA has rejected a complaint based on its priority policy (so has not dealt with the substance). Case T-355/13 *easyJet Airline Co. Ltd v Commission*, Judgment of 21 January 2015. See also Case T-201/11 *Si.mobil telekomunikacijske storitve d.d. v Commission*, Judgment of 17 December 2014, D. Viros, '*Si.mobil Telekomunikacijske*: the rejection of complaints as tool to manage decentralized enforcement within the ECN', *Journal of European Competition Law & Practice* 6 (2015) 415–17.

[11] Available at: <http://ec.europa.eu/competition/ecn/joint_statement_en.pdf>.

[12] Commission Notice on cooperation within the Network of Competition Authorities OJ 2004, C101/03.

fears of the NCAs—especially the *Bundeskartellamt*—that had been afraid of a prepotent role of the Commission within the ECN.[13] This guidance determines that the centre of gravity principle is applied to case allocation, which means that in principle a single (that is to say the best placed) NCA deals with each case, where coordinated efforts between several NCAs remain an exception, and that where three or more NCAs are involved the Commission will in principle take the case itself.

All case allocation takes place in the shadow of the crucial caveat that, based on Article 11(6) of the Regulation, the Commission can in any event claim any case at any point of the procedure at Member State level. By initiating its own case it 'shall relieve the competition authorities of the Member States of their competence to apply Articles 81 and 82 [now Articles 101 and 102 TFEU] of the Treaty'. According to the Joint Statement such claims by the Commission serve primarily to enforce a consistent application of the EU competition rules on points of law, and to prevent conflicting decisions from being taken, thus this manner of pre-emption can be seen as being intended to promote coherence.

The burden of proof

Article 2 of Regulation 1/2003 determines explicitly that the party alleging the infringement of the rules has to prove its existence, as do the parties invoking an exception (such as that of Article 101(3) TFEU) its applicability.[14] The distinction between restrictions by object and by effect that was discussed in Chapter III is salient here. For both object- and effects-based cases there is the requirement of an appreciable effect on trade, in essence to demonstrate that an EU dimension is involved.[15] Essentially, the difference between object and effect infringements means that to prove object restrictions neither appreciability nor, for that matter, any effects have to be shown (provided there is an effect on trade).

In contrast, for restrictions by effects, appreciable negative effects on competition have to be shown. Appreciability involves both qualitative (for instance market share based) and qualitative (are the measures suitable to restrict competition?) dimensions. The bottom line is that imposed by the *de minimis* Notice.[16] On top of this hurdle of appreciable effect on competition, demonstrating restrictions by effect in most cases requires providing economic proof of negative effects which can be supported and contested using economic arguments. The reliance on economic evidence is in line with what has been called the new economic approach.[17]

[13] W. Wils, 'Ten years of Regulation 1/2003—a retrospective', *Journal of European Competition Law & Practice* 4 (2013) 293–301, at 295.

[14] More subtle: C. Volpin, 'The ball is in your court: Evidential burden of proof and the proof-proximity principle in EU competition law', *Common Market Law Review* 51 (2014) 1159–85.

[15] This is based on a 5 per cent market share and €40 million threshold. Commission Notice: Guidelines on the effect on trade concept contained in Articles 81 and 82 of the Treaty, OJ 2004, C101/81.

[16] Notice on agreements of minor importance which do not appreciably restrict competition under Article 101(1) of the Treaty on the Functioning of the European Union, OJ 2014, C 291/01.

[17] See J. Basedow and W. Wurmnest (eds), *Structure and Effects in EU Competition Law* (Deventer: Kluwer, 2011). N. Forwood, 'The Commission's "more economic approach"—implications

Economic evidence

The use of economic evidence is a topic that sits halfway between the content and the process of EU competition law proceedings. The Commission services have drafted informal best practice guidelines on dealing with economic evidence in the context of antitrust cases.[18] Such evidence is essential especially in cases where infringements by effect rather than restrictions by object must be demonstrated. This also means that there is less legal certainty, in advance, on what behaviour is allowed and what prohibited by EU competition law. At the same time it means that where there was less *ex ante* certainty or none, the burden of proof to demonstrate the existence of an infringement is commensurately higher.

This said, both the General Court in the recent Article 102 TFEU case, *Intel* (2014),[19] and the Court of Justice in Article 101 TFEU cases such as *Cartes Bancaires* (2014),[20] suggest that economic evidence is not always preponderant in deciding competition cases. They may instead turn on legal arguments. It suggests that the debate between the proponents of the new economic approach and those advocating legal certainty has not been resolved, in any event not in favour of the former. However, if it is true that legal standards are easier to generalize and to apply, in particular in national judicial proceedings where dealing with comprehensive and contradictory economic evidence (the so-called battle of the reports) is more problematic than it may be at EU level, then from a systemic point of view the more recent trend can be seen as a positive one.

Rights of the defence

Human rights context

The rights of the defence are protected by the European Convention on Human Rights (ECHR), notably its Article 6 on the right to a fair trial.[21] These rights are then fleshed out in EU law, the provisions of which are interpreted by the Court

for the role of the EU Courts, the treatment of economic evidence and the scope of judicial review', in C.-D. Ehlermann and M. Marquis (eds), *European Competition Law Annual 2009: Evaluation of Evidence and its Judicial Review in Competition Cases* (Oxford: Hart Publishing, 2011) 255–70.

[18] DG Competition, Best practices for the submission of economic evidence and data collection in cases concerning the application of Articles 101 and 102 TFEU and in merger cases. Staff working paper (see <http://ec.europa.eu/competition/consultations/2010_best_practices/best_practice_submissions.pdf>). See also: Communication from the Commission on quantifying harm in actions for damages based on breaches of Article 101 or 102 of the Treaty on the Functioning of the European Union, OJ 2013, C167/19.

[19] Case T-286/09 *Intel Corp. v Commission*, Judgment of 12 June 2014. See W.P.J. Wils, 'The judgment of the EU General Court in Intel and the so-called more economic approach to abuse of dominance', *World Competition* 37 (2014) 405–34; and P. Nihoul, 'The ruling of the General Court in Intel: towards the end of an effects-based approach in European competition law', *Journal of European Competition Law & Practice* 5 (2014) 521–30.

[20] Case C-67/13 P *Groupement des cartes bancaires (CB) v Commission*, Judgment of 11 September 2014.

[21] Convention for the Protection of Human Rights and Fundamental Freedoms as amended by Protocols No 11 and No 14, Rome, 4 November 1950.

of Justice in the light of the ECHR. In EU competition law this notably includes inter alia (i) access to the file,[22] (ii) legal privilege,[23] and (iii) the oral hearing by the hearing officer.[24] The ECHR principle of equality of arms is often cited in this context.[25] This principle of balance also reflects the equilibrium between effective enforcement (and output legitimacy) and the rights of the defence and input (or process) legitimacy.

The EU system is supported by the ruling of the European Court of Human Rights in *Menarini* (2011).[26] Looking at the comparable Italian system of competition law enforcement, this court ruled that this was subject to the abovementioned Article 6 because it involved criminal sanctions. At the same time, insofar as the decision involved was subject to full judicial review, the administrative law nature of enforcement (instead of say a prosecutorial model before a judge) was acceptable. As we shall see in Chapter VII, in the EU context judicial review is in fact applied to different standards in the same case, ranging from full review of the facts and their qualification to marginal review of complex economic assessments. Nevertheless it is generally assumed that the *Menarini* standard is met.

Initiation of proceedings

Following an initial assessment (which may include requests for information addressed to the parties or even on-site inspections) concluding that a case merits further investigation, the European Commission can decide to initiate proceedings in a competition case either on its own initiative (*ex officio*) or in reaction to a complaint. A decision to initiate proceedings notifies and identifies the parties (the latter, if it is made public, often in a press release) and defines the scope of the case.[27]

Regulation 1/2003 covers the initiation of proceedings by the Commission in its Article 11(6), where the main consequence is spelled out: if the Commission initiates proceedings it thereby relieves the NCAs of the competence to apply Articles 101 and 102 TFEU to the case at hand. If, however, pursuant to Article 11(3) of Regulation 1/2003 an NCA had already informed the Commission that it had opened formal investigations in a particular case, then the Commission would have to consult them before initiating proceedings in that case itself (see also section above on allocation of cases).

[22] Commission Notice on the rules for access to the Commission file in cases pursuant to Articles 81 and 82 of the EC Treaty, Articles 53, 54, and 57 of the EEA Agreement and Council Regulation (EC) No 139/2004, OJ 2005, C325/7.

[23] Commission Notice on best practices, above (n 8), at 15. Case 155/79 *AM & S Europe Limited v Commission* [1982] ECR 1575; Case C-550/07 P *Akzo Nobel Chemicals Ltd and Akcros Chemicals Ltd v Commission* [2010] ECR I-8301.

[24] Decision 2011/695/EU of the President of the European Commission of 13 October 2011 on the function and terms of reference of the hearing officer in certain competition proceedings, OJ 2011, L275/29.

[25] M. Botta, 'Commission acting as plaintiff in cases of private enforcement of EU competition law: *Otis*', *Common Market Law Review* 50 (2013) 1105–18.

[26] *Menarini* case (n 3).

[27] Ortiz Blanco (n 1), paras 5.33–5.50.

The initiation of proceedings as such is dealt with in greater detail in the Commission's implementing Regulation 773/2004. As far as the parties that are suspected of an infringement are concerned, this is the moment when they are formally notified that there are such suspicions in their regard and that the Commission is carrying out investigations with a view to adopting a decision under Chapter III of Regulation 1/2003. Such decisions can involve a finding of infringement, imposing interim measures, accepting commitments, or, more rarely, a finding of inapplicability (of which there are no examples so far). The initiation of proceedings itself, like issuing a statement of objection, is merely a step in preparation of a decision and is not itself a challengeable act.[28]

Proceedings are initiated no later than once the Commission issues a statement of objections or requests the parties to express in writing their interest in engaging in settlement discussions (see following).

Damages versus leniency

The 2014 Directive on Damages is a (thus far) unique measure of procedural harmonization in a realm that is traditionally left to the judicial systems of the Member States. The Directive explicitly serves to ensure coherence and predictability, indicating a need for legal certainty.[29] As it also concerns remedies it is dealt with in more detail in the remedies section. Here I will limit myself to some remarks on leniency. Leniency is relevant because the Damages Directive establishes absolute protection for submissions made in the context of leniency or settlement applications: access to such information cannot be claimed by parties who wish to pursue follow-up actions.[30]

This also forms an important step in the harmonization of the rules of evidence in the application of EU competition law,[31] however it is evidently inspired less by a desire for harmonization in general or to promote the rights of the defence in particular than by the effectiveness of the Commission's leniency programme. The latter would suffer if the information submitted there would eventually put leniency applicants at risk of claims for damages not just in the EU (which is the main thrust of the Damages Directive) but possibly also in the United States. Exposure to competition law enforcement in the US would be even more dangerous given the existence of (not just criminal sanctions including incarceration but also of) triple damages there.

Thus three dimensions of balance all play a role with respect to this issue: the balance between (i) the Commission and the defendants, (ii) the rights of the defendants and those of claimants in damages actions, and (iii) the effectiveness of central and public antitrust enforcement and decentralized private enforcement. The results suggest that the balance has come down in favour of the Commission, the leniency applicants, and centralization.

[28] Ortiz Blanco (n 1), at 240.

[29] Directive 2014/104/EU, above (n 7). Recital 46.

[30] Ibid.

[31] I. Vandenborre and T. Goetz, 'EU competition law procedural issues', *Journal of European Competition Law and Practice* 5 (2014) 648–55.

Powers of investigation

If in a coherence context the rights of the defence can be justified by procedural legitimacy, the powers of investigation of the Commission come under the heading effectiveness. In what is to some extent a zero-sum game, it is clear that these two must coexist in an uneasy balance.

Sector inquiries and requests for information

Apart from carrying out horizontal sector inquiries into sectors of the economy or types of agreements, the Commission can makes requests for information from undertakings for the purposes of carrying out its antitrust duties (Articles 17 and 18 of Regulation 1/2003). In material terms, sector inquiries in recent years have become an important tool to launch in-depth investigations into the workings of a sector which is then generally followed up (or accompanied by) inspections and further proceedings to establish individual infringements of Articles 101 and 102 TFEU. Accompanied by press releases and statements, they place a particular sector in the antitrust spotlight for an extended length of time. Requests for information are a way of obtaining the necessary material for establishing an antitrust infringement by means of formal correspondence.

Inspections

Where a suspicion of a competition infringement exists, based on a Commission decision (delegated to the Commissioner responsible for competition), the officials authorized by the Commission may perform inspections of undertakings in order to collect evidence.[32] This covers the right to enter and search business premises and any other premises where a reasonable suspicion exists that records relevant to the inspection may be kept. This right to carry out inspections includes the homes of officers of the undertakings that are under investigation. A prior judicial authorization at national level may be required as a matter of national law for all inspections, and in the case of other than business premises, the subjects of the investigation have the right to have the Commission decision reviewed by the Court of Justice.[33]

Although 'fishing expeditions' are not allowed, the demands on the enabling decision for an inspection to be authorized are not very stringent. In the 2014 *Nexans* case the Court of Justice held that for a Commission decision ordering an inspection to be valid it was not necessary to define the relevant market precisely in order to qualify legally the suspected infringements or to indicate the exact time period involved.[34]

[32] Permission from a national court is required for inspections at national level in most Member States. See ECN working group on cooperation issues and due process, investigative powers report, 31 October 2012.

[33] Regulation 1/2003, above (n 8), Article 21(2).

[34] Case C-37/13 P *Nexans and Nexans France SAS v Commission*, Judgment of 25 June 2014. See Vandenborre and Goetz (n 31).

Internal checks and balances

In addition to the formal procedural requirements discussed earlier, the Competition Directorate-General of the Commission (DG COMP) has introduced a number of informal internal checks and balances. These serve for the Commission to remain critical of its own methods not only more generally but also to avoid tunnel vision in individual cases. This development is often associated with three merger cases that the Commission lost before the General Court in 2002 (rulings which were essentially confirmed insofar as pursued before the Court of Justice).[35]

Today the internal checks and balances involve peer review (also called 'the fresh pair of eyes') of the efforts of the case team and the economic guidance provided by the Chief Economist's office,[36] as well as the independent role of the Hearing Officer (all within DG COMP),[37] the role of the legal service and associated services (outside DG COMP, but within the Commission),[38] as well as final decision-making by the plenary College of Commissioners (rather than by delegation to the Commissioner for Competition). Internal quality control here coincides with the interest of defendants to be confronted only with well-founded and considered procedures.

Regarding the Hearing Officer, the right to be heard is linked to Article 41 of the EU Charter of Fundamental Rights (as is access to the file).[39] Since the entry into force of the Lisbon Treaty on 1 December 2009, this provision is justiciable. By being attached directly to the member of the Commission responsible for competition, the Hearing Officer has a degree of independence within DG COMP. However, he is still an official of the European Commission and not an independent outsider in the sense of a court or a tribunal. The hearing is therefore a purely administrative procedure.

[35] This involves the following three sets of cases: (i) Case T-342/99 *Airtours v Commission* [2002] ECR II-02585; (ii) Case T-5/02 *Tetra Laval BV v Commission* [2002] ECR II-4381, Case C-12/03 P *Commission v Tetra Laval BV* [2005] ECR I-987; and (iii) Case T-310/01 *Schneider Electric v Commission* [2002] ECR II-4071, Case T-77/02 *Schneider Electric v Commission* [2002] ECR II-4201 Case T-351/03 *Schneider Electric v Commission* [2007] ECR II-2237, Case C-440/07 P *Commission v Schneider Electric SA* [2009] ECR I-6413.

[36] P. Marsden, 'Checks and balances: EU competition law and the rule of law', *Competition Law International* 5 (2009) 24–8. DG COMP: Proceedings for the application of Articles 101 and 102 TFEU: Key actors and checks and balances. Available at: <http://ec.europa.eu/competition/antitrust/key_actors_en.pdf>.

[37] Decision of the President of the European Commission of 13 October 2011 on the function and terms of reference of the hearing officer in certain competition proceedings, OJ 2011, L275/29.

[38] Article 23(3) of the Rules of Procedure of the Commission, OJ 2000, L308/26, as amended by Commission Decision 2010/138/EC, OJ 2010, L55/60.

[39] Charter of Fundamental Rights of the European Union, OJ 2000, C364/01. Article 41(2) on the rights to good administration includes: 'the right of every person to be heard, before any individual measure which would affect him or her adversely is taken; the right of every person to have access to his or her file, while respecting the legitimate interests of confidentiality and of professional and business secrecy'.

3. Remedies

General context

The remedies that are discussed here apply to the European Commission because national remedies are predominantly determined by national law. Remedies in competition law can be said to constitute the legal rules that provide for and impose the consequences of findings of infringement (or agreements by parties to enter into commitments that render such findings superfluous) that are either punitive, restorative, or designed to prevent future recurrence of past suspected or definitively established infringements (or a combination of such measures).

As is suggested by this working definition, in principle competition law remedies are related to a finding of infringement, with fines as the classic example. In some cases remedies automatically ensue from the infringements with which they are connected. The main example is Article 101(2) TFEU that makes (those parts of) agreements that violate the anti-cartel rule in Article 101(1) TFEU automatically void. Similarly, under the State aid rules, an aid that is not notified is by definition illegal and must be repaid just like if an aid is (found to exist and) not compatible with the internal market.

In recent years, however, the range of remedies in EU competition law, more specifically antitrust, has become more varied. Following the example of merger control, under Article 7 of Regulation 1/2003 structural remedies (the requirement or agreement to sell off parts or branches of an undertaking that is subject to competition law scrutiny) and behavioural remedies have become antitrust remedies as well. Similarly, in line with the example from mergers, commitment decisions (which may include the offer of structural remedies) are now explicitly covered in Article 9 of Regulation 1/2003.

Based on an inversion of the adage *ubi jus ibi remedium*, it has been debated whether the existence of an appropriate remedy determines if an infringement can be found (in particular in the context of Article 102 TFEU), however such a theory would be at odds with the discretionary powers that the Commission and NCAs enjoy as well as with the existence of substitutionary remedies, notably fines. As is claimed by Ioannis Lianos, what is needed is logical coherence between the wrong found and its remedy, which can be established by means of the proportionality test.[40] I will go into this test in more detail later in this chapter.

[40] I. Lianos, 'Is the availability of "appropriate" remedies a limit to competition law liability under Article 102 TFEU? The mischiefs of "discretionary remedialism" in competition law', in F. Etro and I. Kokkoris (eds), *Competition Law and the Enforcement of Article 102* (Oxford: Oxford University Press, 2010) 165–85. I. Lianos, Competition law remedies in Europe: which limits for remedial discretion? CLES Research Paper Series, 2/2013 January 2013; I. Lianos, 'Competition law remedies in Europe', in I. Lianos and D. Geradin (eds), *Handbook on European Competition Law: Enforcement and Procedure* (Cheltenham: Edward Elgar, 2013) 362–455.

Categories of remedies in the various areas of EU competition law

To some extent the different categories of remedies are complementary in nature, and in some respects they are alternatives. The choice of particular types of remedy may also have implications for judicial review. As discussed later, the CJEU has full jurisdiction concerning the imposition of fines and periodic penalty payments, however this level of scrutiny does not apply to other types of remedies. This is logical because, for instance, a commitment decision does not include a finding of an infringement but concludes that there are no longer grounds for Commission action, and it is at least conceptually a voluntary undertaking by the undertaking or undertakings concerned.

In antitrust cases under Article 7 TFEU, if infringements are found they are in principle fined and subject to an order to cease and desist under an injunction (a requirement to terminate the infringement). Such a finding may also lead to the imposition of structural remedies or divestiture (forced sales of parts of an undertaking), to behavioural remedies such as an access requirement, as well as to private suits for damages.

In State aid the main remedy is repayment of the aid, although private remedies for damages are also possible here. Under the merger rules there are no direct infringements of the original rules but only procedural violations (such as of the standstill requirement or of the obligation to notify) and violations of terms and conditions imposed and or undertaken in the context of a merger clearance (for instance a divestiture commitment). Nevertheless merger remedies play an important role in cases where they may resolve the competition concerns raised by a particular transaction.[41] In this sense they correspond with commitment decisions in antitrust, which they pre-date and have inspired.[42]

I will now look at the various types of remedies in turn. Leniency is not a remedy in any strict sense, but because it is closely related to the practice of applying remedies (essentially it functions as a modifier of remedies, as do settlements) I will deal with it against this background. Mixing the chronological sequence with the legal status and degree of severity involved I will present this material in the following order. The logical starting point for any discussion of remedies is the difference between findings of infringements versus commitments, which play an increasing role. Next I chart automatic annulment, which has treaty status, fines, and periodic penalty payments, which are subject to the fullest review by the European courts, leniency and settlement procedures, structural and behavioural remedies. Finally I will discuss damages as the most recent addition to the competition law toolbox, which is in many ways the most

[41] Commission Notice on remedies acceptable under Council Regulation (EC) No 139/2004 and under Commission Regulation (EC) No 802/2004, OJ 2008, C 267/1.

[42] Commission Notice on the conduct of settlement procedures in view of the adoption of Decisions pursuant to Article 7 and Article 23 of Council Regulation (EC) No 1/2003 in cartel cases, OJ 2008, C167/1; Commission Regulation (EC) No 622/2008 of 30 June 2008 amending Regulation (EC) No 773/2004, above (n 8), as regards the conduct of settlement procedures in cartel cases, OJ 2008, L171/3.

decentralized, that is to say to the level of individual claimants under civil law proceedings in national courts.

Commitments versus findings of infringements

Commitments offered by undertakings and secured by way of a Commission decision under Article 9 of Regulation 1/2003 are not remedies in the classical sense. They can be seen as an extension of the Commission's right to prioritize its cases.[43] Although they are intended to assuage competition concerns, they do not form a sanction imposed after an infringement has been comprehensively proven in a manner designed to be judicially unassailable in an adversarial process. Quite the contrary: commitments aim to forestall the need for such proof and any finding that an infringement took place while simultaneously establishing more competitive market practices.

Here especially the contrast between findings of infringement under Article 7 of Regulation 1/2003 and commitment decisions under Article 9 of that regulation plays a role.[44] In *Alrosa* (2010), the CJEU has set out the essential distinction between the two:

> Those two provisions of Regulation No 1/2003 . . . pursue different objectives, one of them aiming to put an end to the infringement that has been found to exist and the other aiming to address the Commission's concerns following its preliminary assessment.[45]

In addition, the Commission does not hold commitments to be appropriate in cases where it believes imposing a fine is required, whereas settlement procedures are perfectly suited to cartel cases, meaning that substantively the two categories do not show much overlap.[46]

It should be noted, however, that given the possibility of accepting a settlement under Article 7 in cartel cases,[47] and of mitigating the fines for reasons of leniency imposed following the finding of an infringement under the same provision,[48] Articles 7 and 9 of Regulation 1/2003 are in reality not so far apart as they might initially seem. It has been suggested that the proportionality principles

[43] M. Wathelet, 'Commitment decisions and the paucity of precedent', *Journal of European Competition Law & Practice* 6 (2015) 553–5, at 553.

[44] See E. Hjelmeng, 'Competition law remedies: striving for coherence or finding new ways', *Common Market Law Review* 50 (2013) 1107–38. See also the Commission's Competition policy brief, 'To commit or not to commit: deciding between prohibition and commitments', Issue 3, March 2014.

[45] As cited in Hjelmeng, above (n 44), Case C-441/07 P *Commission v Alrosa Company Ltd* [2010] ECR I-5949, para 46.

[46] Commission Notice on best practices, above (n 8), para 116.

[47] Commission Regulation (EC) No 622/2008 of 30 June 2008 amending Regulation (EC) No 773/2004, above (n 8), as regards the conduct of settlement procedures in cartel cases, OJ 2008, L171/3. Commission Notice on the conduct of settlement procedures in view of the adoption of Decisions pursuant to Article 7 and Article 23 of Council Regulation (EC) No 1/2003 in cartel cases, OJ 2008, C167/1.

[48] Commission Notice on Immunity from fines and reduction of fines in cartel cases, OJ 2006, C298/17.

may impose stricter limits on the Commission in the context of Article 7 than of Article 9 of Regulation 1/2003.[49] Article 7 directly implies least restrictive means testing, which is the most demanding proportionality standard applied today in judicial review under EU competition law. In the case of Article 9, under the general principle of proportionality the Court only reviews whether the Commission's assessment is manifestly incorrect.[50]

Although commitment decisions may involve a greater degree of discretion for the Commission, from a broader or systemic perspective they have the drawback that they fail to clarify the law.[51] From the point of view of the undertaking involved, following a commitment decision it is in a stronger position vis-à-vis third parties because there is no finding of an infringement for them to bring follow-on actions.[52] From the opposite perspective, one advantage of a Commission infringement decision is that it opens the door to private enforcement at national level.

Another final aspect of commitment decisions is their use to achieve divestment by undertakings in cases where the internal market legislation has failed to do so—so far notably in the energy sector.[53] This is comparable to the use of commitments (and of pressure on the home Member States of the undertakings involved to liberalize their domestic legislation and by implication support EU level liberalization) in merger proceedings in the electronic communications sector that took place in the 1990s.[54] In both energy and electronic communication services, promoting market access is the overriding concern. This seems to be in line with the predominant foreclosure (exclusion) concern of the approach to dominance in the Commission's 2009 Article 102 Guidance paper,[55] which may have been the high water mark of the new economic approach that has more recently been called into question by the 2014 *Intel* judgment of the General Court.[56]

Annulment

As automatic annulment of cartel agreements is provided for in Article 101(2) TFEU itself ('Any agreements or decisions prohibited pursuant to this Article

[49] Hjelmeng (n 44), at 1008–9.

[50] W. Sauter, 'Proportionality in EU competition law', *European Competition Law Review* 35 (2014) 327–32, at 330–1.

[51] Wathelet, above (n 43) however cites Case C-202/06 P *Cementbouw Handel & Industrie BV v Commission* [2007] ECR I-12129.

[52] R. Whish, 'Editorial. Motorola and Samsung: an effective use of Article 7 and Article 9 of regulation 1/2003', *Journal of European Competition Law and Practice* 8 (2014) 603–4.

[53] Hjelmeng (n 44), at 1020–21. COMP/39402, *RWE*, Decision of 19 March 2009; Case COMP/39315, *ENI*, Decision of 29 September 2010.

[54] *Atlas* and *GlobalOne* decisions of 17 July 1996, OJ L 239 of 19 September 1996, pp. 23 and 57. See P. Larouche, *Competition Law and Regulation in European Telecommunications* (Oxford: Hart Publishing, 2002).

[55] Communication from the Commission: Guidance on its enforcement priorities in applying Article 82 of the EC Treaty to abusive exclusionary conduct by dominant undertakings, OJ 2009, C45/7.

[56] Case T-286/09 *Intel*, above (n 19).

shall be automatically void'), it takes pride of place among the remedies available in EU competition law, however its direct effect is difficult to square with the procedural autonomy of the Member States. The latter expect to retain responsibility for determining the civil law consequences of competition law infringements, thus this provision shows that the tension between the EU and national levels as regards effective remedies can not only be found in the text of the TFEU itself but dates back to the original Rome Treaty. Nevertheless the case law on this provision is scarce. It appears to suggest that the main issue is severability: whether it will suffice that the key infringing clauses of the agreement concerned are void, or that instead the agreement as a whole is declared void because in the absence of the infringing clauses it can no longer be said to constitute a valid agreement representing the will of both contracting parties. In practice, private parties trying to escape from contractual commitments that could conceivably infringe the competition rules, but primarily because their business case soured, frequently attempt to rely on Article 101(2) TFEU (the 'Euro-defence').

Fines

Fines are the primary and traditional sanction (and remedy) available for the enforcement of the competition rules at EU level. They are not, however, the most draconian: several Member States allow for criminal sanctions against officials of undertakings that are found guilty of competition law infringements (including incarceration, in the case of Austria, Ireland, Germany, and the United Kingdom), and as we have already seen Article 7 of Regulation 1/2003 itself allows for structural remedies. The fines imposed by the Commission are subject to soft law guidance.[57] Article 261 TFEU[58] and Article 31 of Regulation 1/2003[59] provide that the CJEU has unlimited jurisdiction to review decisions on fines that the Commission has adopted pursuant to Article 23 of that Regulation.

Fines are intended to combine a specific and a general deterrent effect in order not only to sanction the undertaking that is fined but also to discourage other undertakings from engaging in similar illegal behaviour. Fines are based on the value of the sales to which the infringement relates and the duration of the infringement. The resulting amounts are adjusted according to the presence of any aggravating circumstances (such as recidivism, refusal to cooperate or the

[57] Guidelines on the method of setting fines imposed pursuant to Article 23(2)(a) of Regulation No 1/2003, OJ 2006, C210/2.

[58] Article 261 TFEU (formerly Article 229 EC) reads: 'Regulations adopted jointly by the European Parliament and the Council, and by the Council, pursuant to the provisions of the Treaties, may give the Court of Justice of the European Union unlimited jurisdiction with regard to the penalties provided for in such regulations.'

[59] Council Regulation (EC) No 1/2003 of 16 December 2002 on the implementation of the rules on competition laid down in Articles 81 and 82 of the Treaty, OJ 2003 L1/1. Article 23 states: 'The Court of Justice shall have unlimited jurisdiction to review decisions whereby the Commission has fixed a fine of periodic penalty payment. It may cancel, reduce or increase the fine or periodic penalty payment imposed.'

instigation of infringements) and/or of mitigating circumstances such as cases where infringements have been cause by negligence, or were encouraged by public authorities.

Under EU competition law the leniency rules, which evidently have an impact on the level of the fines imposed, are dealt with separately (see further following).

Periodic penalty payments

This is a type of fine that is linked to the failure to provide specific performance on the part of the undertaking(s) involved of duties specified by the Commission. The objective is of course not to collect fines but to apply financial pressure in order to change the behaviour of the undertakings. Periodic penalty payments are subject to the same level of scrutiny (full judicial review) by the European courts as are regular fines.

Leniency and settlement

The instrument of leniency (or immunity from, and reduction of, fines) has been employed by the Commission since 1996[60] in order to trade lower sanctions for individual undertakings against inside information on anticompetitive agreements enabling it to enhance (greatly) the effectiveness of its anti-cartel enforcement. Today, the majority of cartel cases at EU level are pursued on this basis.[61] Its application is based on a soft law instrument that guides the parties to leniency applications in their submissions and the Commission in its resulting actions.[62]

Settlement procedures have likewise been introduced to allow more efficient pursuit of cartel cases and are also based on the reward of undertakings for admitting and terminating infringements as well as pursuing compliance.[63] The opportunity to establish an (uncontested) precedent may likewise apply, although surely the strongest precedents are the ones confirmed upon appeal to the EU Courts and not those plea-bargained by undertakings with the European Commission (including, no doubt, a commitment not to appeal the resulting decision).

[60] Commission Notice on the non-imposition or reduction of fines in cartel cases, OJ 1996, C207/4.

[61] From 1 May 2004 to 31 December 2013 there were fifteen *ex officio* EU cartel cases compared to forty-four leniency EU cartel cases. See Commission Staff Working Document Ten Years of Antitrust Enforcement under Regulation 1/2003, SWD (2014) 230/2, Accompanying the document: Communication from the Commission to the European Parliament and the Council, Ten Years of Antitrust Enforcement under Regulation 1/2003, Achievements and Future Perspectives, para 16, figure 3.

[62] Commission Notice on immunity, above (n 48).

[63] Commission Notice on the conduct of settlement procedures in view of the adoption of Decisions pursuant to Article 7 and Article 23 of Council Regulation (EC) No 1/2003 in cartel cases, OJ 2008, C167/1 and Council regulation (EC) No 622/2008 of 30 June 2008 amending regulation (EC) Bo 773/2004, as regards the conduct of settlement procedures in cartel cases, OJ 2008, L171/3.

The application of leniency can be distinguished from settlement procedures because the former applies to informing on others and the latter to self-incrimination. Nevertheless, where this is not logically excluded in principle it is possible for an undertaking to qualify for both regimes, which may then be applied cumulatively and can accordingly lead to allowing a more significant reduction of fines of 10 per cent in the case of settlement alone but of up to full immunity under leniency.

Structural remedies versus behavioural remedies

These two types of remedies have been imported into EU antitrust from the context of merger control although the logic there is different: in merger settling, structural remedies (divestment) are the preferred solution that make a clean break and do not require burdensome and often ineffectual monitoring and enforcement action as behavioural remedies would. In antitrust, divestiture is considered an ultimate remedy (that has so far rarely been applied) and a behavioural remedy much more in line with traditional practices such as a requirement to cease and desist anticompetitive behaviour, like a refusal to deal.

In antitrust both types of remedy are specifically named in Article 7 of Regulation 1/2003, as if to underline their availability following modernization. Here it is stated that such remedies must be proportional to the infringement and necessary to bring it effectively to a halt.

Damages: Case law versus legislation

One of the main recent innovations of EU competition law, in particular in terms of procedural harmonization is the 2014 Damages Directive (mentioned earlier).[64] This followed on the *Courage and Crehan* case (2001)[65] and *Manfredi* (2006)[66] where the Court established that the possibility of private damages suits was required to ensure the effectiveness of EU competition law:

> the full effectiveness of Article 81 EC [now Article 101 TFEU] and, in particular, the practical effect of the prohibition laid down in Article 81(1) EC [now Article 101(1) TFEU] would be put at risk if it were not open to any individual to claim damages for loss caused to him by a contract or by conduct liable to restrict or distort competition.[67]

More recently, in *Otis* (2012), the CJEU has accepted that even the European Commission itself could act as a private plaintiff in damages suits.[68] The Damages Directive as adopted did not extend the *Masterfoods* rule[69] with regard to primacy

[64] Directive 2014/104/EU above (n 7).

[65] Case C-453/99 *Courage Ltd v Bernhard Crehan and Bernard Crehan v Courage Ltd et al.* [2001] ECR I-6297, para 26.

[66] Case C-295/04 *Vincenzo Manfredi v Lloyd Adriatico Assicurazioni SpA* [2006] ECR I-6619.

[67] Ibid, para 60.

[68] Case C-199/11 *Commission v Otis NV et al.*, Judgment of 6 November 2012. See Botta (n 25).

[69] Case C-344/98 *Masterfoods Ltd v HB Ice Cream Ltd* [2000] ECR I-11369, para 57.

of Commission decisions in antitrust matters over national courts (set out in Article 16 of Regulation 1/2003 on uniform application) to include decisions by NCAs having binding effect on national courts, as had originally been proposed. In any event, it is difficult to see how this solution could have been justified as legitimate or even considered to be workable in a system where judicial review of NCA decisions would have to be carried out by those same national courts.

There is inherently a degree of tension between effective private enforcement and the effectiveness of a leniency-based public enforcement policy. This is, for instance, because access to the file for private litigants may discourage leniency applications but also because leniency applicants are by definition self-identified as having infringed the competition rules, which will handicap them in court in the context of private actions for damages against them. This uneasy balance is found in the Commission's leniency Notice:

> The fact that immunity or reduction in respect of fines is granted cannot protect an undertaking from the civil law consequences of its participation in an infringement.[70]

However, it also notes that public disclosure of documents or statements received in the context of leniency applications would harm the protection of inspections and investigations. Indeed Article 6(6) of the 2014 Damages Directive provides that:

> Member States shall ensure that, for the purpose of actions for damages, national courts cannot at any time order a party or a third party to disclose any of the following categories of evidence: (a) leniency statements; and (b) settlement submissions.[71]

This legislative limitation stands in stark contrast to the judicial broadening of the scope for third party disclosure claims following the 2014 *Kone* judgment where the Court held that customers of non-cartel members may claim damages in cases of so-called umbrella pricing (where price followers shelter under the cartel umbrella).[72] The Damages Directive also eliminates the scope for the balancing of the interests concerned on this issue that had earlier been suggested in *Pfleiderer* (2011)[73] and *Donau Chemie* (2013),[74] albeit explicitly due to the absence of regulation at the time.

Thus in *Pfleiderer* the Court held that:

> it is, in the absence of binding regulation under European Union law on the subject, for Member States to establish and apply national rules on the right of access, by persons adversely affected by a cartel, to documents relating to leniency procedures.[75]

[70] Commission Notice on immunity, above (n 48), para 39.

[71] Directive 2014/104/EU, above (n 7).

[72] Case C-557/12 *Kone AG et al. v ÖBB-Infrastruktur AG*, Judgment of 5 June 2014. See Vandenborre and Goetz (n 31), at 649–50

[73] Case C-360/09 *Pfleiderer AG v Bundeskartellamt* [2011] ECR I-5161, para 23.

[74] Case C-536/11 *Bundeswettbewerbsbehörde v Donau Chemie AG et al.*, Judgment of 6 June 2013.

[75] Case C-360/09 *Pfleiderer*, above (n 73), para 23. See Vandenborre and Goetz (n 31).

Likewise in the same case the Court held that:

> the provisions of European Union law on cartels, and in particular Regulation No 1/2003, must be interpreted as not precluding a person who has been adversely affected by an infringement of European Union competition law and is seeking to obtain damages from being granted access to documents relating to a leniency procedure involving the perpetrator of that infringement. It is, however, for the courts and tribunals of the Member States, on the basis of their national law, to determine the conditions under which such access must be permitted or refused by weighing the interests protected by European Union law.[76]

We therefore see a significant degree of procedural harmonization by means of legislation on this point precisely where the Court of Justice by means of introducing a balancing test has sought to respect national procedural autonomy.

The Damages Directive

In November 2014, the European Parliament and Council adopted the Damages Directive, elements of which have already been discussed.[77] The Damages Directive is to be implemented by December 2016. Paraphrasing its Article 1, it sets out rules designed to foster undistorted competition in the internal market by ensuring equivalent protection throughout the Union for anyone who has suffered competitive harm. It is the most important example of harmonization on remedies in EU antitrust law to date and does not just seek to promote private enforcement but equally to balance public and private enforcement, as we have seen in the case of denying access to information obtained from leniency and settlement applicants.

In striking this balance, the Directive aims at regulating 'the coordination of those two forms of enforcement in a coherent manner', notably to avoid divergence that could jeopardize the internal market.[78] This connection is necessary because as harmonization legislation there must be a link with achieving the internal market. The latter is presented somewhat implausibly as the possible result of undertakings preferring to establish themselves and to trade outside Member States which effectively enforce the right to compensation.[79] It might equally have been thought that undertakings less bent on breaking the law would wish to avoid Member States where the antitrust rules are not enforced effectively. In reality, however, neither the relative strength nor weakness of antitrust enforcement is likely to be a decisive factor in commercial decisions regarding where to trade or produce within the EU. Arguably therefore, the argument of why the internal market requires a damages directive is weak.

The Directive applies to infringements of EU competition law and national competition law in parallel where there is an effect on trade. National rules

[76] Case C-360/09 *Pfleiderer*, above (n 73), para 32.
[77] Directive 2014/104/EU above (n 7).
[78] Ibid, recital 6. [79] Ibid, recital 8.

regarding compensation with regard to an infringement of Articles 101 and 102 TFEU must respect the familiar principles of effectiveness (not making it excessively difficult or practically impossible to exercise the relevant right) and equivalence (not less favourable than according to comparable national actions). Taking its distance from the system exercised in the United States, the Directive is not to lead to overcompensation due to punitive or multiple damages. Instead, damages are limited to (i) actual loss (*damnum emergens*), (ii) loss of profit (*lucrum cessans*), and (iii) interest. This approach is in line with EU practice, which is predominantly based on public enforcement, but blocks a truly deterrent damages system.

Regarding the disclosure of evidence, we have already seen that Article 6(6) of the Damages Directive excludes leniency statements and leniency submissions from the categories of evidence which national courts can order a party or third party to disclose. A similar but milder exception applies with regard to joint and several liability, which is the general rule for undertakings that have infringed EU competition law. Leniency applicants are likely to be the preferential target of litigation under such a rule because they are generally the first party for which the decision of the competition authority finding an infringement becomes final (as it will be difficult if not impossible for them to appeal). Therefore, under the Damages Directive a leniency applicant is jointly and severably liable only in relation to its own purchasers or providers, and to other injured parties only where full compensation cannot be obtained from the other undertakings that were involved in the same breach. Similarly, in order to promote out-of-court settlements, co-infringers who have not settled cannot recover a contribution from infringers who have settled consensually out of court.

In addition, the Damages Directive provides minimum standards for limitation periods, not to begin before the infringement has ended and not shorter than five years. A passing-on defence is allowed in order to avoid overcompensation in those cases where undertakings wishing to claim damages were able to shoulder their own customers with overcharges originally imposed on themselves by the undertakings that infringed EU competition law. Finally, the Directive states that it shall be presumed that cartel infringements cause harm, albeit a rebuttable presumption.

A *Masterfoods*-type rule requiring national courts to respect NCA decisions in the same way they must do under Article 16(1) of Regulation 1/2003 and which would have added a whole new dimension to the allocation of power in antitrust at national level did not survive the drafting process.[80] Instead, the Damages Directive thus provides a complete catalogue of compensation issues and a showcase of the balancing act between the EU and national levels on procedural and remedies issues that remains to be tested in practice. At the same time the Damages Directive already calls for supplementary guidelines by the Commission on quantifying damages, in order to guarantee coherence and predictability.[81]

[80] Case C-344/98 *Masterfoods*, above (n 69).

[81] Communication from the Commission on quantifying harm in actions for damages based on breaches of Article 101 or 102 of the Treaty on the Functioning of the European Union, OJ

4. Proportionality and Remedies

In EU law as elsewhere the legal principle of proportionality requires an appropriate balance between the means and ends of public policies. The test applied ranges from a mild manifest disproportionality test to a stricter least restrictive means test and even a full cost–benefit analysis.

As is the case for any EU policy, the acts of the Commission in the context of competition law are subject to scrutiny based on proportionality.[82] At the same time the degree of harmonization here is very high as competition policy can be seen as a de facto common policy of the EU with an uncommon degree of control in the hands of the Commission, which not only formulates but executes this policy directly and coordinates the NCAs in their decentralized application of the rules. The main instances of proportionality testing that are relevant in competition cases concern the Commission's powers of on-site investigation and its power to impose fines as well as its powers with regards to remedies.

Another category of the application of proportionality in the framework of competition law remedies is that of Commission enforcement decisions. Here again the powers of the Commission are under review, not the behaviour of undertakings. Article 7 of the Regulation 1/2003 includes an explicit proportionality test, stating that the Commission may impose on undertakings

> any behavioural or structural remedies which are proportionate to the infringement committed and necessary to bring the infringement effectively to an end.[83]

Article 9 of the same Regulation provides that the Commission may make commitments by undertakings that are intended to remedy competition problems binding on them, and does not include an explicit reference to proportionality. In *Alrosa* (2010), the Court has specified that therefore the applicable proportionality tests differ: whereas Article 7 directly implies least restrictive means testing, in the case of Article 9 under the general principle of proportionality the Court only reviews whether the Commission's assessment is manifestly incorrect.[84]

> The specific characteristics of the mechanisms provided for in Articles 7 and 9 of Regulation No 1/2003 and the means of action available under each of those provisions are different, which means that the obligation on the Commission to ensure that the principle of proportionality is observed has a different extent and content...
>
> Article 7... expressly indicates the extent to which the principle of proportionality applies in situations covered by that article... the Commission may impose on the undertakings

2013, C167/19 and Commission Staff Working Document of 11 June 2013—Practical Guide on Quantifying Harm in Actions for damages based on breaches of Article 101 or 102 of the Treaty on the Functioning of the European Union, SWD (2013) 205.

[82] This section is based on my paper 'Proportionality in EU competition law', *European Competition Law Review* 36 (2014) 327–32.

[83] Council Regulation (EC) No 1/2003 of 16 December 2002 on the implementation of the rules on competition laid down in Articles 81 and 82 of the Treaty, OJ 2003, L1/1.

[84] Case C-441/07 P *Commission v Alrosa Company Ltd* [2010] ECR I-5949, paras 36–42.

> concerned any behavioural or structural remedies which are proportionate to the infringement committed and necessary to bring the infringement effectively to an end.
>
> Application of the principle of proportionality by the Commission in the context of Article 9…is confined to verifying that the commitments in question address the concerns it expressed to the undertakings concerned and that they have not offered less onerous commitments that also address those concerns adequately.[85]

This approach would also be in line with the fact that competition policy is a Community policy with a significant degree of harmonization. In *Mastercard* (2012), the Court again identifies least restrictive means testing of Article 7 decisions.[86] We thus see a strict review of remedies and a more limited review of Commission discretion with regard to policy decisions to resolve cases by other means, and with the consent of the parties.

The Commission likewise has a wide margin of discretion in setting fines in competition cases. At the same time the EU courts have full jurisdiction with regard to fines but without so far exercising this competence to its limits.[87] In the Commission's 2006 Guidelines on the setting of fines, reference is made to a proportion of the value of sales of the infringing undertaking(s).[88] However, this is not the limit of the relevance of proportionality because in its own words the General Court 'is under a duty to verify whether the amount of the fine imposed is proportionate in relation to the gravity and duration of the infringement…and to weigh the gravity of the infringement and the circumstances invoked by the applicant'.[89] Here, although the 10 per cent worldwide turnover threshold as a maximum amount for antitrust fines is by definition somewhat arbitrary, it can also be seen as a hardwired proportionality requirement.

We thus see a range of tests being applied to Commission legal acts that range from necessity to manifest disproportionality but, unlike those that apply to private parties, involve neither balancing nor economic justification. This means that a significant degree of discretion is retained within a norm embedded in general EU law, ensuring external coherence as well as a degree of input legitimacy.

5. Convergence

It is a general tenet of EU law that unless they are explicitly harmonized, procedures remain national so long as they enable effective enforcement of EU law. At the same time we observe both spontaneous harmonization and Court-inspired convergence.

[85] Ibid, paras 38, 39, 41.

[86] Case T-111/08 *Mastercard and Others v Commission*, Judgment of 24 May 2012, paras 323–324.

[87] Cf. Case C-386/10 P *Chalkor AE Epexergasias Metallon v Commission* [2011] ECR I-13090. Case C-272/09 P *KME Germany AG et al. v Commission* [2011] ECR I-12860.

[88] Guidelines on the method of setting fines imposed pursuant to Article 23(2)(a) of Regulation No 1/2003, OJ 2006, C210/2.

[89] Cf. eg Case T-368/00 *General Motors Nederland BV and Opel Nederland BV v Commission* [2003] ECR II-4495, para 189; citing Case T-229/94 *Deutsche Bahn v Commission* [1997] ECR II-1689, para 127 and Case C-333/94 P *Tetra Pak v Commission* [1996] ECR I-5951, para 48.

Effective and uniform application

Recital 1 of Regulation 1/2003[90] cites the uniform and effective application of EU competition law as necessary to ensure that competition in the internal market is not distorted. In *Tele2 Polska* (2011), the Court referred to this recital to support the argument that, unlike the Commission (which may make a finding of applicability under Article 10 of Regulation 1/2003), the NCAs cannot take negative declaratory decisions to state that no infringement of EU competition law has occurred:

> Such a 'negative' decision on the merits would risk undermining the uniform application of Articles 101 TFEU and 102 TFEU, which is one of the objectives of the Regulation highlighted by recital 1 in its preamble, since such a decision might prevent the Commission from finding subsequently that the practice in question amounts to a breach of those provisions of European Union law.[91]

In what has been called 'institutional assimilation' in *VEBIC* (2010), the Court held that national procedural autonomy was subject to the demands of effectiveness of EU law, requiring reforms to the Belgian system of competition law enforcement which did not allow the Belgian competition authority (itself an adjudicative body) to defend its appeals in court.[92]

Uniformity is also the object of Article 16 of Regulation 1/2003, which determines that national courts ruling on antitrust matters cannot take decisions running counter to a decision adopted by the Commission. This is a codification of the 2000 *Masterfoods* ruling of the CJEU.[93]

Uniformity is far from complete, however. For instance, national Courts are not always bound by decisions of the NCAs, unlike the case vis-à-vis the Commission under Article 16 of Regulation 1/2003 on the uniform application of EU competition law. As mentioned earlier, the Commission proposed to include a harmonization of this issue in the Damages Directive[94] but failed.[95]

Soft law coordination

There are various instruments of soft law guidance that were adopted by the Commission to accompany Regulation 1/2003 in the context of self-assessment in accordance with the direct effect of Article 101(3) TFEU by undertakings. These instruments are only binding upon the Commission itself (as a result of legitimate expectations). The NCAs may draw inspiration from such documents or they may

[90] Regulation 1/2003, above (n 8).

[91] Case C-375/09 *Prezes Urzędu Ochrony Konkurencji i Konsumentów v Tele2 Polska sp. z o.o., devenue Netia SA* [2011] I-3055, para 28.

[92] Case C-439/08 *VEBIC*, above (n 6). See P. Van Cleynenbreugel, 'Institutional assimilation in the wake of EU competition law decentralisation', *Competition Law Review* 8 (2012) 285–312.

[93] Case C-344/98 *Masterfoods*, above (n 69), para 57.

[94] Directive 2014/104/EU, above (n 7).

[95] M. Botta, 'Commission acting as plaintiff in cases of private enforcement of EU competition law: Otis', *Common Market Law Review* 50 (2013) 1105–18, at 1116.

be obliged to follow them as a matter of national law or spontaneous harmonization. NCAs are not, however, as a matter of EU law bound by such documents.[96] Vice versa in *Schenker* (2013): the CJEU held that not even an earlier interpretation of EU law adopted by an NCA could protect the undertaking concerned from a subsequent finding of anticompetitive conduct by another NCA (or by extension by the Commission).[97] According to Sven Völcker this means that

> The Court appears to be far more interested in establishing the supremacy of the principle of 'uniform and effective application of EU competition law' than acknowledging a fundamental legal principle such as *nulla poena sine culpa*.[98]

In my view, however, seen in combination with the Damages Directive as dropping the requirement that national courts could be pre-empted by decisions of NCA, the ruling in *Schenker* (2013) that NCA views are not binding on other NCAs means that in sum there now is less, not more, scope for coordination (or at least for imposing conformity). Instead there is more freedom that may be effective in the enforcement of the individual case but is unlikely to guarantee more uniformity within the system as a whole or greater coherence. At the same time this degree of slack may make the system more workable. Arguably, however, that comes at the expense of predictability and legal certainty for private parties.

6. Conclusion

Procedures and remedies under EU competition law largely concern the EU Commission in its role as competition authority on the one hand, and private parties either as suspected of infringements or as plaintiffs, including in damages cases at national level, on the other. The national courts and NCAs do not play a significant role here with regard to EU procedural law and remedies because the latter have not been harmonized. At national level they remain within the realm of the twenty-eight national jurisdictions within the EU, insofar as they effectively guarantee the enforcement of EU competition law under norms no less stringent than for comparable applicable law. In exceptional cases, however, effective enforcement of EU law norms nevertheless requires amendment of national procedures. This was shown in *VEBIC*,[99] where the applicable national norms did not discriminate but fell instead below the minimum that was acceptable for the defective enforcement of EU competition law.

[96] Case C-360/09 *Pfleiderer* above (n 73), (procedure); Case C-226/11 *Expedia Inc. v Autorité de la concurrence et al.*, Judgment of 13 December 2012 (substance). S.B. Völcker, '*Ignorantia lex non excusat* and the demise of national procedural autonomy in the application of EU competition rules: *Schenker*', *Common Market Law Review* 51 (2014) 1497–520.

[97] Case C-681/11 *Bundeswettbewerbsbehörde, Bundeskartellanwalt v Schenker et al.*, Judgment of 18 June 2013. See Völcker (n 96).

[98] Ibid, at 1510.

[99] Case C-439/08 *VEBIC*, above (n 6).

Unsurprisingly therefore, so far there has been a limited degree of harmonization, notably the 2014 Damages Directive.[100] This is noteworthy inter alia because it prefers to protect the Commission's leniency policy over the rights of access to the file for purposes of informing individual damages claims at national level. That is remarkable because both leniency and individual damages claims are purportedly in the interest of promoting the effectiveness of EU competition law. Even more remarkable is that the Directive in effect corrects the direction of the case law of the European courts on this issue (such as *Pfleiderer*),[101] which had consistently promoted the interest of individuals claiming damages. In the Directive this is replaced in favour of centralized control by the Commission, and protecting its leniency and settlement tools.

At the same time, in the same Damages Directive the effort to bind national courts not to contradict NCA decisions that had been mooted in drafts, has been extirpated from the final version that was adopted. Materially this seems to be the right outcome as the result would have been a muddle with regard to judicial review and the separation between the executive and judicial branches. The *Masterfoods*[102] rule codified in Article 16 of Regulation 1/2003, as well as the Commission's authority to claim any case based on Article 11(6) of that same Regulation, both secure the pre-eminence of the Commission that is necessary to speak of an EU-wide system. This does not mean that *Masterfoods*-type rules need apply at every level: we may see a network with a hierarchical level elevating only the centre, not necessarily a pyramid where NCAs block each other, or trump national courts, as a matter of course.

Tackling the questions set out in the introduction to this chapter, it is clear that indeed with regard to procedures and remedies a balance is struck between uniformity and effectiveness, and due process, the rights of the defence, and (input) legitimacy. Over time, and following painful defeats before the General Court (albeit in merger control), the Commission has paid more respect to due process as well as internal procedures that benefit quality control. At the same time it appears to have emphasized its own control over that of the NCAs, an issue that I will examine more in depth in the next chapter. Contrasting effectiveness and legitimacy as the two competing values of the resulting system seems justified.

The second question I asked was if the result is a coherent system, and in what direction it is developing. This too will be picked up again in the next chapter. For now I will only observe that it appears to be a system with a light touch, where at least procedure and remedies are not much used for coordination purposes, as conceivably they might have been if more harmonization had been pursued. Instead, the Commission tries to keep its hands free, which suggests it is less interested in steering the NCAs in a particular direction by means of command and control than in effectively remaining the pre-eminent independent competition authority in the EU.

[100] Directive 2014/104/EU, above (n 7).

[101] Case C-360/09 *Pfleiderer* above (n 73).

[102] Case C-344/98 *Masterfoods*, above (n 69).

VI

Networks, Hierarchy, and Coordination in Antitrust

1. Introduction

Unlike the topics of the preceding chapters, that of the present one is not primarily based on legal categories. Its concern is the governance structure of EU competition law and its functioning, however the legal instruments involved in structuring the enforcement of EU competition law by the national competition authorities (NCAs) and the EU Commission and the interaction between these bodies within the European Competition Network (ECN) will be discussed. I also intend to look at the national courts and their interaction with the EU Commission. The role of the EU courts as the ultimate arbiters of EU competition law will be examined separately in the next chapter.

According to the 2002 joint statement of the Council and the Commission on the functioning of the network of competition authorities, within the ECN the co-operation between the NCAs and the Commission is based on principles of equality, respect, and solidarity. The independence of the participants is stressed. However, within the ECN, the Commission, as guardian of the Treaties,[1] has the ultimate responsibility for developing policy, safeguarding efficiency and consistency.[2] There is an inherent tension here between on the one hand the idea of a network, characterized by softer forms of coordination such as mutual information and discussion of issues, and on the other hand the application of principles of hierarchy, associated with more formal kinds of coordination such as pre-emption.

Examining the functioning of network-based governance in EU competition law requires looking at the convergence rule regarding national competition law of Article 3 of Regulation 1/2003[3] and the pre-emption power in the hands of the

[1] More prosaically: 'The Commission shall promote the general interest of the Union and take appropriate initiatives to that end. It shall ensure the application of the Treaties, and of measures adopted by the institutions pursuant to them. It shall oversee the application of Union law under the control of the Court of Justice of the European Union.' Article 17(1) Treaty on European Union.

[2] Joint Statement of the Council and the Commission on the functioning of the network of Competition Authorities, 16 December 2002, paras 7 and 9. Available at: <http://ec.europa.eu/competition/ecn/joint_statement_en.pdf>.

[3] Council Regulation (EC) No 1/2003 of 16 December 2002 on the implementation of the rules on competition laid down in Articles 81 and 82 of the Treaty, OJ 2003 L1/1.

Commission in its Article 11(6) that serves to ensure coherent application, as well as Article 16 on uniform application respecting the primacy of the Commission by national courts and NCAs.

In a sense this chapter will involve an assessment of how Regulation 1/2003 has worked and whether it has worked well. The challenge is which benchmarks to use in order to justify making this judgement. I will start by examining the benchmarks suggested by the Commission itself in the context of its own five- and ten-year evaluations, conducted in 2009 and 2014 respectively, and to evaluate these critically.[4] Then I will try to put them in context.

The main questions asked are the following:

What constitutes the EU competition law network for antitrust (ECN), why was it created, and what are the main rules by which it operates? This involves looking in particular at the role of hierarchy, and how this squares with the concept and practice of a policy network, and examining what, by contrast, is the role of coordination.

How does the network perform in terms of outcomes? In terms of coherence, what are the effects on the effectiveness and consistency of EU competition law, and on its legitimacy? Another question will be whether there any measurable outputs that can be compared before and after modernization.

Finally, regarding the ECN, I will examine what are the effects of cooperation within the network on the different actors involved: DG Competition (DG COMP) and its role, as well as the NCAs in their national context. For instance, do we observe greater independence from the national governments versus more interdependence with other ECN members and the EU Commission?

The structure of the chapter is as follows:

- First, I will look at the organizational dimension of the enforcement of EU competition law in the ECN along with the rules that determine this organization. This involves dealing with formal and informal coordination mechanisms such as those regarding case allocation. I will also examine regulatory competition, although I intend to do so primarily in legal terms and not as an exercise in political economy, for instance by focusing on powers of preemption and veto or blocking powers. In particular, the different levels of competition law enforcement play a role here.[5]
- Second, I will look at outcomes as reported by the members of the network itself, and at the effect of the network on its members.

[4] G. Monti, 'A plea for "extraterritorial" antitrust enforcement by national competition authorities', paper presented at the Fourth ACELG Annual Conference (14 November 2014).

[5] G. Monti, 'Independence, interdependence and legitimacy: the EU Commission, national competition authorities and the European Competition Network', EUI Law Department Research paper 2014/01; C. Harlow and R. Rawlings, 'Modernisation, cooperation, enforcement: competition', in C. Harlow and R. Rawlings, *Process and Procedure in EU administration* (Oxford: Hart Publishing, 2014) 196–219; Y. Svetiev, 'Networked Competition Governance in the EU: Centralization, Decentralization, or Experimentalist Architecture?', in C. Sabel and J. Zeitlin (eds), *Experimentalist Governance in the European Union: Towards a New Architecture* (Oxford: Oxford University Press, 2010) 79–120.

Throughout this chapter, I again focus on antitrust. Mergers and state aid—which are not formally decentralized to national bodies—are covered separately in Chapter VIII, and networks in energy and electronic communications in Chapter IX.

2. The European Competition Network: Forum for Coherent Application of EU Law

Pre-existing cooperation

Prior to the creation of the ECN in 2002 the Commission already engaged in cooperation with national competition authorities and had published a notice on this topic in 1997.[6] This was based on the application of different systems of competition law (EU versus national law) at the two levels but nevertheless included principles of case allocation. At this time NCAs were encouraged to focus on cases with mainly national effects and that could not be exempted so the Commission's exemption monopoly did not play a blocking role (notably regarding Article 102 TFEU). As discussed in Chapter II regarding matters with an EU dimension, cooperation was nevertheless hamstrung by the exemption monopoly of the Commission, and on other matters there was little to gain for NCAs except intellectual guidance and moral support.

There was no question of the possibility of networks of NCAs at this stage. Under Regulation 17/62 even the Advisory Committee that looked at the Commission's draft antitrust Decisions was predominantly staffed by representatives of the relevant national ministries, although some brought along their NCAs (where they already existed) and exceptionally an NCA might turn up unaccompanied.[7] By contrast, Article 14(2) of Regulation 1/2003 specifies that for the discussion of individual cases, representatives of the NCAs must be present on the Advisory Committee. For general policy matters they may be accompanied by other (non-NCA) representatives.

Outside practical matters such as assistance with on-site investigations by the Commission, there are no indications that under the exemption system of Regulation 17/62 cooperation between the authorities at national level and the Commission ever really took off. (One instance to the contrary may be the Commission's cooperation with the Italian NCA to split up the prosecution of a cement cartel case.)[8] Nevertheless, the example provided by the Commission

[6] Commission Notice on cooperation between national competition authorities and the Commission in handling cases falling within the scope of Articles 85 or 86 of the EC Treaty, OJ 1997, C313/3. D.M.B. Gerard, 'Public enforcement: the ECN—network antitrust enforcement in the European Union', in I. Lianos and D. Geradin (eds), *Handbook on European Competition Law: Enforcement and Procedure* (Cheltenham: Edward Elgar, 2013) 181–227.

[7] EEC Council Regulation No 17: First Regulation implementing Articles 85 and 86 of the Treaty OJ 1962, 13/204, Article 10.

[8] G. Monti, 'Managing decentralized antitrust enforcement: Toshiba', *Common Market Law Review* 51 (2014) 261–79. Cf. Case C-219/00 P *Cementir—Cementerie del Tirreno v Commission*

may have promoted spontaneous harmonization of national competition law or the European model as well as creating a breeding ground for the ideas behind Regulation 1/2003. At least the preamble of the Regulation speaks of the development of a Community competition policy that 'helped to disseminate a common competition culture' within the EU.

Creation of the ECN

Regulation 1/2003 is based on a system of parallel competences regarding the application of Articles 101 and 102 TFEU for the European Commission, at EU level, and the NCAs, each within the confines of their own Member State. Although an effect on interstate trade is a requirement for Articles 101 and 102 TFEU to apply,[9] it is a point of discussion as to what extent the NCAs can enforce EU antitrust law against infringements outside their national territory, for instance by taking extraterritorial turnover into account when imposing fines.

From the outset of modernization it was clear that some form of cooperation would be required.[10] That is because lifting the Commission's monopoly on Article 101(3) TFEU exemptions (by replacing this with a directly effective legal exception) opened the way to full enforcement at national level. This option was then made mandatory when Article 5 of Regulation 1/2003 charged the NCAs of the Member States with carrying out this task.[11] (Meanwhile its Article 6 likewise empowered national courts to apply Articles 101 and 102 TFEU.) However, while Regulation 1/2003 does provide for information exchange and primacy rules (or powers of pre-emption) in the relationship between the Commission and the NCAs, it does not provide much detail on topics such as case allocation and more general coordination.

To address such practical issues, the European Competition Network was formed on 16 December 2002 when Regulation 1/2003 was adopted.[12] On that same day, the existence of the ECN was confirmed by the abovementioned joint statement by the Council and Commission on the functioning of the network of competition authorities. This document was supplemented by a 2004 Cooperation Notice,[13] which codifies and extends the 2002 joint statement by the Council and the Commission on the functioning of the ECN. The idea behind this approach

(Joined Cases C-204/00 P, C-205/00 P, C-211/00 P, C-213/00 P, C-217/00 P, C-219/00 P) [2004] ECR I-123.

[9] Commission Notice: Guidelines on the effect on trade concept contained in Articles 81 and 82 of the Treaty, OJ 2004, C101/81.

[10] C.-D. Ehlermann and I. Atanasiu (eds), *European Competition Law Annual 2002 Constructing the EU Network of Competition Authorities* (Oxford: Hart Publishing, 2005).

[11] Although Article 35 of Regulation 1/2003 also determined that the Member States should designate the relevant authorities and empower them to apply Articles 101 and 102 TFEU under national law.

[12] Joint Statement (n 2).

[13] Commission Notice on cooperation within the network of Competition Authorities, OJ 2004, C101/3.

was that the joint statement would set out the principles and the Cooperation Notice the operational aspects.

The NCAs

A discussion of the ECN requires paying some prior attention to the organization of the NCAs. The ECN is constituted by the NCAs of the twenty-eight Member States of the EU and the European Commission (or in practice its DG COMP). The NCAs in turn are designated by the Member States under Article 35 of Regulation 1/2003, subject to the general EU law principle of effectiveness and equivalence that requires they must be equipped to carry out their EU law tasks of enforcing Articles 101 and 102 TFEU at least as effectively as the enforcement of the relevant national law. The same applies to the obligation, for that purpose, for the Member States to provide for effective, proportionate, and dissuasive sanctions.

EU law, however, does not explicitly require minimum guarantees of independence for the NCAs nor of the effectiveness of their operations by providing adequate staffing and financing,[14] although the *VEBIC* case (2010) could arguably be used as a basis for challenging manifest inadequacies.[15] This is unlike some sectoral regulators such as in the energy, electronic communications, and transport fields where EU law does demand such guarantees, which is partially explained by the need to stay at arm's length from incumbents.[16] It should be added that in any event in at least some cases NCAs are also the responsible sectoral authorities, or deal with consumer protection and/or public procurement. Only a minority of NCAs deal strictly with antitrust and merger control.[17] Nevertheless in 2010 the heads of the NCAs have issued a joint call for effective funding.[18]

The minimum set of powers of the NCAs (as well as the maximum, as is suggested by the 2011 *Tele2 Polska* case)[19] is established in Article 5 of Regulation 1/2003 and comprises the ability to adopt decisions requiring that an infringement be brought to an end, ordering interim measures, accepting commitments, and imposing fines and periodic penalty payments as well as any other sanctions that are provided for in their national law. In addition, under Article 5, an NCA

[14] Commission staff working document, Enhancing competition enforcement by the Member States' competition authorities: institutional and procedural issues, accompanying the Commission Communication, Ten years of antitrust enforcement under Regulation 1/2003: achievements and future perspectives, SWD(2014) 231, at 13.

[15] Case C-439/08 *Vlaamse federatie van verenigingen van Brood- en Banketbakkers, Ijsbereiders en Chocoladebewerkers (VEBIC) VZW* [2010] ECR I-12471.

[16] See also case C-614/10 *Commission v Austria*, Judgment of 16 October 2012; Case C-288/12 *Commission v Hungary*, Judgment of 8 April 2014.

[17] Ten years of antitrust enforcement (n 14), at 9.

[18] Resolution of the Meeting of Heads of the European competition authorities of 16 November 2010, Competition authorities in the European Union—the continued need for effective institutions. Available at: <http://ec.europa.eu/competition/ecn/ncas.pdf>.

[19] Case C-375/09 *Prezes Urzędu Ochrony Konkurencji i Konsumentów v Tele2 Polska sp. z o.o., devenue Netia SA* [2011] I-3055.

may decide that there is no ground for it to act, a type of decision that (unlike a Commission finding under Article 10 of Regulation 1/2003) neither binds other NCAs nor national courts, nor the Commission. This has been described as being a very rudimentary rule which seeks to combine substantive coherence with national procedural autonomy.[20]

There are now two basic organizational types of NCAs: the majority are those which are based on the model of a single administrative authority (which may or may not have a functional separation between investigative and decision-making activities); and a minority (in Austria, Estonia, Ireland, Sweden, Denmark, and Finland) that operates based upon a judicial model. In the latter case, an administrative authority is responsible for investigations and a court is responsible for deciding on the evidence presented by that authority. An earlier type of arrangement with separate administrative authorities responsible for investigations and for decisions has in all cases (in Estonia, France, Spain, Belgium, Luxemburg, and Malta) been replaced by one of these two models.[21] It is up to the Member States to designate their NCAs provided they can act effectively to carry out their duties.[22]

Objectives

The objective of the ECN, as set out in the 2002 joint statement, is to ensure that the EU competition rules are applied 'effectively and consistently'. Achieving such effectiveness and consistency can be seen as the greatest challenge to the new system.[23] As we have seen in Chapter III, Regulation 1/2003 sets the same goal but says 'effectively and uniformly': hence this uniformity is now toned down with a functional equivalent that may be more appropriate in a multifocal perspective. These are therefore the standards we should hold this system to from a coherence perspective. In the 2004 Cooperation Notice the objectives set out are considerably more general and framed in more operational terms: (i) to form a forum for discussion and debate, (ii) to provide a framework for cooperation, and (iii) to create and maintain a common competition culture in Europe.

Arguably the ECN started as a mere information network that has graduated to become a policy network. The Commission's five- and ten-year evaluations suggest that the ECN has in fact become central to the implementation of the modernization effort. The role of the ECN is also noteworthy because, even as a policy network, it does not have automatic legal status and the power to adopt binding rules in EU law. At the same time its activities effectively reach beyond coordination.

[20] Commission staff working paper accompanying the Communication from the Commission, Report on the functioning of Regulation 1/2003, SEC(2009) 574, at 61.

[21] Staff working document, SWD(2014) 231, (n 14), at 5–6.

[22] Case C-53/03 *Synetairismos Farmakopoion Aitolias & Akarnanias (Syfait) and Others v GlaxoSmithKline plc and GlaxoSmithKline AEVE* [2005] ECR I-4609; Case C-439/08 *VEBIC*, above (n 15).

[23] I. Maher, 'Functional and normative delegation to non-majoritarian institutions: the case of the European Competition Network', *Comparative European Politics* 7 (2009) 414–34, at 428.

The Commission services document underpinning the Commission's five-year report on the experience with Regulation 1/2003 has described the ECN as a forum to promote the coherent application of EU competition law.[24] The latter implies both consistency and systemic cohesion with relation to common goals, and presumably these goals are those set out in Chapter III.

In order to examine these claims, I will now look at some examples of formal rules governing the ECN along with some examples of the substance of such rules. I will then consider informal rules, hierarchy, and consistency.

Formal coordination

Examples of formal rules

Aside from its powers of pre-emption under Regulation 1/2003 itself, the Commission is the only member of the ECN who can propose new competition legislation at EU level. In practice it is also the only member which adopts notices on the interpretation of EU competition law (although arguably individual NCAs could do so). This gives it a privileged position within the network. By virtue of Regulation 1/2003 the NCAs are bound mainly to apply Articles 101 and 102 TFEU. They are not necessarily legally required to apply by analogy all secondary legislation or guidance documents such as Commission notices on issues of EU competition law. In some jurisdictions, such as The Netherlands, they may be required to follow the EU approach even as a matter of national competition law. Moreover, in national proceedings all NCAs are likely to be required to provide an explicit justification for departing from the approach set out in Commission notices.[25] However, procedural rules and sanctions remain predominantly the realm of national law. Also, EU law may be applied in parallel with divergent (although subject to the strictures of Article 3 of Regulation 1/2003) national law. Thus, EU competition law will not always have a uniform impact at national level.

One method for solving this problem is providing joint statements promising conformity with a policy which is then explicitly signed up to by the individual NCAs. This somewhat improvised approach has been resorted to in the 2004 Cooperation Notice. The NCAs need not have signed, especially to the extent that they are meant to be independent from national politics, but they did. However, it is not clear what sanctions would follow if an ECN member decided to retract its support or to flout the agreement that it had signed up to. This method clearly illustrates that there is still a grey area between the obligation to apply Articles 101 and 102 TFEU, the desirability of a uniform approach to doing so in practice, and the need to coordinate practical aspects of cooperation.

A further example of coordination in the form of common rules is the ECN Model Leniency Programme of 2006 as revised in November 2012.[26] Leniency is

[24] Commission staff working paper SEC(2009) 57, (n 20), paras 264–268. See Ten Years of antitrust enforcement under regulation 1/2003, COM(2014) 453, paras 8 and 23.

[25] Monti (2014) (n 5), at 16.

[26] Available at: <http://ec.europa.eu/competition/ecn/mlp_revised_2012_en.pdf>.

in essence a policy to exchange with an informant leading to the elimination of a cartel for full or partial immunity from fines for the infringement concerned. The model leniency programme is intended both to promote the adoption of leniency programmes at national level and to facilitate the coordination between them. It provides for soft harmonization of the existing programmes and alleviates the burdens on undertakings associated with multiple leniency filings in cross-border cartel cases. This shows that while Regulation 1/2003 harmonizes substance and not procedure, in practice the ECN also works to harmonize procedure.

Finally, a relatively rare example of formal coordination in the shape of secondary legislation that is precisely intended to take effect at national level—but in the national courts—is the 2014 Damages Directive, dealing with issues such as the availability of information in damages cases derived from a leniency application or a settlement as well as limitation periods and joint and several liability.[27] Under the terms of the Directive such information will not be made available. There is tension here in particular between centralized cartel policy of the EU Commission and the policy of some of the NCAs which relies heavily on leniency and the stated desire to promote private damages actions at national level as a means of effective enforcement.

This is a good example of how different interests may exist at different levels of enforcement and between different methods of enforcement. It also shows that in the end the interest of centralized enforcement—by the Commission and the NCAs—is favoured even if it required further secondary legislation to do so and to limit the effect of the case law of the Court of Justice (see above Chapter V on the balance between lenience and private damages actions).

In practice we therefore see a range of instruments being applied but with a focus on coordination and communication.

Principles of case allocation

An important aspect of the Cooperation Notice are the principles on case allocation, which decide when NCAs will act alone or in parallel, and when the Commission will take on a case. From the perspective of the undertakings involved, case allocation is of great significance in terms of the applicable procedures and sanctions, which differ between Member States,[28] yet it cannot serve as a basis for private parties to claim a right to be prosecuted in one jurisdiction rather than another.[29] For the ECN members it determines their case load and who has priority. In fact, Firat Cengiz states that 'the ECN could best be described as an informal jurisdiction allocation regime surrounded with information exchange

[27] Directive 2014/104/EU of the European Parliament and of the Council of 26 November 2014 on certain rules governing actions for damages under national law for infringements of the competition law provisions of the Member States and of the European Union, OJ 2014, L349/1.

[28] See S. Brammer, 'Concurrent jurisdiction under Regulation 1/2003 and the issue of case allocation', *Common Market Law Review* 42 (2005) 1383–424.

[29] Case T-339/04 *France Télécom SA v Commission* [2007] ECR II-521, para 80.

mechanisms, rather than a multi-level policy network'.[30] This perception is predicated on a view of networks as largely non-hierarchical and more spontaneous in nature than is the ECN which is characterized by the same author as highly structured and juridified (and, I would add, potentially subject to close control by the European Commission). That may not be the final word on this matter, however the point regarding the centrality of case allocation is clear.

The idea developed in the Cooperation Notice is that cases are handled by the most 'well-placed' authority. An NCA is regarded as well placed to take a case if (i) the agreement concerned has a substantive effect on its territory or originates there, (ii) the NCA can effectively terminate the entire infringement, and (iii) it has access to the necessary evidence. Up to three NCAs may decide to coordinate their action in cases where these conditions do not hold. The Commission is considered to be well placed in cases with effects on competition in more than three Member States. The difference with the 1997 system mentioned earlier is thus considerable, given the fully concurrent powers of the NCAs and the Commission. It is, however, important to stress that the Notice also deals with the instances where the Commission may unilaterally claim cases outside the context of (consensual) case allocation (see further below).

Informal coordination and information exchange

Informal coordination is by its very nature difficult to observe outside the closed circle of the ECN. This obviously makes the scope and impact of coordination difficult to chart. It may reasonably be assumed, however, to be based on information exchange between the network members and a monitoring mechanism on the side of the Commission.

The framework for information exchange

Information exchange at the beginning of the procedure is based on Article 11(2) of Regulation 1/2003 regarding the transmission of the most important documents pertaining to its procedures for the Commission, and Article 11(3) whereby the NCAs inform the Commission 'without delay' about the first formal investigative measure in their own procedures. This also serves to detect parallel procedures in the interest of case allocation. Under Article 12 of Regulation 1/2003 information, including confidential information can be exchanged, but may only be used to apply Articles 101 and 102 TFEU (and therefore not national competition laws) with respect to the subject matter for which it was collected: thus, in the same case.[31]

[30] F. Cengiz, 'Multi-level governance in competition policy: the European Competition Network', *European Law Review* 35 (2010) 660–77, at 666.

[31] Contrasting views are found in D. Reichelt, 'To what extent does the co-operation within the European competition network protect the rights of undertakings?', *Common Market Law Review* 42 (2005) 745–82; and K. Dekeyser and E. De Smijter, 'The exchange of evidence within the ECN

Policy discussions within the ECN

The ECN provides a forum to discuss both horizontal and sectoral competition policy issues, albeit at different levels: (i) the Director General's meeting discusses major policy issues (such as the policy on exclusionary abuses); (ii) the ECN Plenary serves for the discussion of horizontal antitrust issues and the ability of NCAs to implement them at the level of officials (such as horizontal and vertical restraints); (iii) working groups deal with horizontal issues such as leniency and sanctions; and finally (iv) there are subgroups that do not deal with horizontal issues but instead work on particular sectors such as banking, healthcare, or media, and discuss for instance sector inquiries in these sectors.

In the Commission services working paper underpinning the 2009 five-year review of Regulation 1/2003 by the European Commission, this four-tier structure and constant dialogue are credited with having 'promoted a coherent approach and the coherent application of the EC [now EU] antitrust rules'.[32] This paper also credits the discussions with realizing 'the final objective of promoting a common competition culture in Europe'.[33] The Commission services working paper does concede that this internal coherence is not combined with a significant degree of external transparency, an issue that it says has been raised by commentators from the legal and business community.

This raises the question of whether the observed limited transparency is necessary for or even beneficial to the degree of coherence that has been attained. Presumably the argument would be that policy discussions within this body of antitrust enforcers must be shielded from full public scrutiny in order to allow a frank exchange and avoid lobbying pressures. Arguably, if the information necessary to mount an effective legal defence in individual cases is available then other classes of information may not need to be shared beyond the ranks of antitrust enforcers.

Hierarchy

A characteristic feature of the system of parallel powers that are exercised by the EU and national levels, organized by means of the ECN, is that it interacts with several elements of hierarchy. These cement the EU Commission's status as rather more than a *primus inter pares*, which could mean agenda-setting powers, chairing sessions, and casting a deciding vote. The principle of hierarchy between national and EU law, and of the European Commission over the NCAs and even over national courts, is expressed clearly at several points in Regulation 1/2003:[34]

and how it contributes to the European co-operation and co-ordination in cartel cases', *Legal Issues of Economic Integration* 32 (2005) 161–74.

[32] Commission staff working paper SEC(2009) 574, above (n 20), paras 248–268: 'The ECN as a forum to promote coherent application' at 72 and 74.

[33] Ibid, at 74.

[34] The Commission only listed three main mechanisms: (i) Article 3(1) regarding the requirement for NCAs to apply Articles 101 and 102 TFEY where there is an effect on trade; (ii) Article 11(4) on the obligation to notify draft NCA decisions to the Commission; and (iii) the Commission's

- Article 3(1) which requires NCAs and national courts to apply Articles 101 and 102 TFEU in each case where they apply national competition law and where there may be an effect on trade.
- Articles 3(2) and 3(3) on the relationship with national competition law that determines stricter rules of national law are only allowed for unilateral behaviour, provided there is an effect on trade and unless the rules in point serve a different purpose. The Commission has identified this as an instrument promoting convergence.[35] At the same time, and to the contrary, these rules suggest that the Member States have won some leeway here.
- Article 10, whereby only the Commission is authorized to make a finding of inapplicability of Articles 101 and 102 TFEU.[36] The Commission has associated this power with coherence (adding that the extensive efforts of the ECN had made its application unnecessary so far).[37]
- Article 11(4), which requires NCAs to notify their draft decisions based on Articles 101 and 102 TFEU to the Commission at least thirty days before they are adopted. This promotes consistency and gives the Commission the opportunity to apply Article 11(6) before the NCA concerned adopts a formal decision.
- Article 11(6) on the initiation of proceedings by the Commission unilaterally relieving NCAs of their competence to apply Articles 101 and 102 TFEU in the same case. Here too the Commission explicitly sees this as an instrument aiming at coherence.[38] It is also an ultimate remedy.
- Article 16, which codifies the *Masterfoods*[39] rule that not only NCAs (Article 16(2)) but also national courts (Article 16(1)) must respect prior Commission decisions when interpreting EU competition law. Courts must even respect prospective Commission decisions, for instance by staying proceedings. An example appears to be the United Kingdom litigation by search engine Foundem against Google, in the light of the Commission's ongoing investigations into the practices of the latter undertaking.

Article 11(4) of Regulation 1/2003 requires NCAs to inform the Commission by submitting their draft decisions under Articles 101 and 102 TFEU (to bring an infringement to an end, to accept commitments or withdraw the benefit of a block exemption) to the Commission. The Commission itself states that it has developed a practice of submitting observations to NCAs which may be oral or in

authority to relieve an NCA of its duties under Article 11(6). Commission staff working paper SEC(2009) 574, above (n 20), at 74.

35 Report on the functioning of Regulation 1/2003, COM(2009) 206, above (n 20), at 6.

36 Case C-375/09 *Tele2 Polska*, above (n 19), para 28, with regard to Article 102 TFEU; Case C-681/11 *Bundeswettbewerbsbehörde, Bundeskartellanwalt Schenker & Co et al.*, Judgment of 18 June 2013, para 42 with regard to Article 101 TFEU.

37 Report on the functioning of Regulation 1/2003, COM(2009) 206, above (n 20), at 20.

38 Ibid, at 7.

39 Case C-344/98 *Masterfoods Ltd v HB Ice Cream Ltd* [2000] ECR I-11369.

writing, not containing new information or evidence that would affect the position of the parties, but—therefore at least implicitly—on points of policy and law. The NCAs take such points into account as they consider appropriate.[40]

The Commission likewise provides the Member States with information about its own investigations, but the relationship is unequal. This information procedure effectively allows the Commission the possibility of intervening by initiating proceedings of its own, thereby relieving the NCA concerned of its competence to apply Articles 101 and 102 TFEU as was mentioned earlier. Needless to say, this nuclear option is unlikely to be used often, and in fact it does not appear to have been used so far (that is to say in over ten years), however there are possible undeclared exceptions such as the e-Book investigation that was moved from the Office of Fair Trading to the Commission.

However, presumably the capability of doing so provides the Commission with leverage that it can use to persuade NCAs and thereby to ensure their decisions are generally consistent with the Commission's interpretation of EU competition law. (There is an analogy here with the Article 7 procedure in electronic communications—see Chapter IX.) This means that the NCAs' decisions are taken in the shadow of a Commission claim under Article 11(6) of Regulation 1/2003. The fact that such Commission decisions must be submitted for discussion to the Advisory Committee, which is composed of NCA representatives, does not fundamentally change the equation, as theirs is by definition only an advisory function and they lack the power to alter the Commission's decisions. Similarly, under Article 16 of Regulation 1/2003 the decisions of national courts are taken under the shadow of Commission decisions, including forthcoming ones. Unlike the NCAs, however, they can still address preliminary questions to the CJEU to get a conclusive view on the Commission's approach.

Consistency

The 2004 Cooperation Notice sets out an efficient division of work and an effective and consistent application of the EU competition rules as its objectives.

At the same time the 2004 Cooperation Notice has provided more clarity on when the Commission may invoke Article 11(6) of Regulation 1/2003. There is a distinction between non-contentious events, where the Commission claims a case at the allocation stage as I have discussed above, and cases claimed at a subsequent stage, which are limited to cases where (i) there is a risk of conflicting decision being taken by network members, (ii) there is a risk of conflict with settled case law (but only in rare cases will this regard the qualification of facts such as market definition), (iii) there are undue delays, (iv) the Commission must develop EU competition policy to promote effective enforcement, and (v) other cases, where the NCAs concerned do not object.

[40] Commission staff working paper SEC(2009) 574, above (n 20), at 75.

Here too there is a suggestion of symmetry (or at least restraint) because the Cooperation Notice also states that the Commission will 'normally' not adopt a decision which conflicts with that of an NCA, provided that it has been properly informed in line with Article 11 of Regulation 1/2003 and that it has not exercised its right to pre-empt under Article 11(6).[41] However, the Commission will override this rule if an EU interest is at stake. Moreover, in the *France Télécom* case (2007) the General Court (citing the Cooperation Notice) recalled that the allocation of cases does not create individual rights for the undertaking involved in an infringement to have its case dealt with by a particular authority.[42]

Output

Aside from the function of informal coordination and of case allocation, the ECN collaborates in order to formulate and adopt recommendations which are based on best practices and desiderata in the antitrust enforcement field.[43] Two examples are the (2006 and 2012) Leniency Notice,[44] and the 2013 ECN Recommendations on investigative and decision-making powers.[45] In addition, the NCAs have started cooperation outside the ECN context, but in parallel, with regard to mergers (Merger Notice[46]). According to the Commission:

> These Recommendations are intended to serve as advocacy tool which NCAs can use vis-à-vis policymakers to help ensure that they are equipped with an effective competition toolkit.[47]

Thus, part of the output of the ECN is a type of advocacy intended to establish effective competition tools in a very practical sense.

The ECN as a network

More generally, in its five-year evaluation the Commission has claimed that '[t]he network is an innovative model of governance for the implementation of Community law by the Commission and Member State authorities'.[48] In its

[41] 2004 Cooperation Notice, above (n 13), para 57.

[42] Case T-339/04 *France Télécom*, above (n 29), para 80.

[43] ECN Recommendation on Investigative Powers, Enforcement Measures and Sanctions in the context of Inspections and Requests for Information; ECN Recommendation on the Power to Collect Digital Evidence, including by Forensic Means; ECN Recommendation on Assistance in Inspections conducted under Articles 22(1) of Regulation(EC) No 1/2003; ECN Recommendation on the Power to set Priorities; ECN Recommendation on Interim Measures; ECN Recommendation on Commitment Procedures; ECN Recommendation on the Power to Impose Structural Remedies.

[44] ECN Model leniency programme, (2006) as revised in November 2012. Available at: <http://ec.europa.eu/competition/ecn/mlp_revised_2012_en.pdf>.

[45] ECN recommendation on investigative powers, enforcement measures and sanctions in the context of inspections and requests for information, December 2013.

[46] EU Merger Working Group, Best practices on cooperation between EU National Competition Authorities in merger review, 8 November 2011 Available at: <http://ec.europa.eu/competition/ecn/nca_best_practices_merger_review_en.pdf>.

[47] Commission Communication, Ten years of antitrust enforcement under Regulation 1/2003: achievements and future perspectives, COM(2014) 453, at 9.

[48] Report on the functioning of Regulation 1/2003, COM(2009) 206, above (n 20), at 10.

ten-year report the Commission emphasizes the key role played by the NCAs but highlights the need for effective independence, adequate financing and staffing levels, and appropriate sanctions. The ECN appears to differ from comparable networks in energy and electronic communications where the Commission is not a member as such and where central agencies such as the Agency for the Cooperation of Energy Regulators (ACER) and the Body of European Regulators of Electronic Communications (BEREC), albeit in embryonic form, have been created. (The comparison between these networks will be elaborated in Chapter IX.)[49]

Both commentators from political science, such as Stephen Wilks,[50] and lawyers, like Alan Riley,[51] suggest that paradoxically, the decentralization to NCAs that formed one of the main changes introduced by the modernization of antitrust has led to an increase in the powers of the Commission. With regard to the ECN, Wilks argues that 'it offers an exceptionally powerful model of policy enforcement which reflects the politics of competition policy and the normative coherence of the policy community'.[52] Also, he states regarding the Commission that '[r]ather than "centralizing" European competition policy it has "Europeanized" the national competition regimes' with powers that are the equivalent of a transnational agency.[53] As far as the powers are concerned this appears to be an understatement: I cannot think of a similarly equipped transnational agency in the EU or elsewhere.

Effectiveness and equivalence versus regulatory competition?

So far therefore the suggestion is that the policy network has enhanced the effectiveness and consistency and thereby indirectly the impact of EU antitrust law and even the role of the Commission. An important question that I have not addressed so far is to what extent coherence can be squared with regulatory competition and the degree of freedom that may be desirable to allow for local particularities and/or experimentation? Logically, at some point the energy afforded to striving towards uniformity may be expected to become counterproductive—perhaps one reason why in the ECN context the objective of consistency is used instead of uniformity.[54]

49 More broadly see D. Coen and M. Thatcher, 'Network governance and multi-level delegation: European networks of regulatory agencies', *Journal of Public Policy* 28 (2008) 49–71; S. Lavrijssen and L. Hancher, 'Networks on track: from European regulatory networks to European regulatory "network agencies" ', *Legal Issues of European Integration* 34 (2008) 23–55.

50 S. Wilks, 'Agency escape: decentralization or dominance of the European Commission in the modernization of competition policy?', *Governance* 18 (2005) 431–52; S. Wilks, 'Agencies, networks, discourses and the trajectory of European competition enforcement', *European Competition Journal* 3 (2007) 437–64.

51 A. Riley, 'EC antitrust modernization: the Commission does very nicely—thank you! Part 1: Regulation 1 and the notification burden', *European Competition Law Review* 24 (2003) 604–15; A. Riley, 'EC antitrust modernization: the Commission does very nicely—thank you! Part 2: Between the idea and the reality: Decentralisation under Regulation 1', *European Competition Law Review* 24 (2003) 657–72.

52 Wilks (2007) (n 50), at 463.

53 Wilks (2005) (n 50), at 437.

54 F. Chirico and P. Larouche, 'Divergence, functionalism and the economics of convergence' in S. Prechal and B. van Roermund, *The Coherence of EU Law: The Search for Unity in Divergent Concepts* (Oxford: Oxford University Press, 2008) 463–94.

In part this issue depends largely on the definition of effectiveness that is used. The mildest minimum standard expressed, for instance, in the free movement context in the *Metallgesellschaft* case in 2001 is just that national law 'must not render practically impossible or excessively difficult the exercise of the rights conferred by Community [now EU] law'.[55] In my view, this demonstrates how well the effective judicial protection demanded by Article 19(1) TEU works.[56] In the competition context it is also found in the follow-on private actions for damages case law of the CJEU.

By contrast, in *Schenker* (2013) with regard to the powers of NCAs to impose fines on firms that had negligently or intentionally breached EU competition law, the CJEU ruled that in the context of application of Article 5 of Regulation No 1/2003, national conditions 'should be at least as stringent as the condition laid down in Article 23 of Regulation No 1/2003 so as not to jeopardise the effectiveness of European Union law'.[57] Similarly in *VEBIC* (2010) an EU standard was set.[58]

Here it is the EU measure itself that literally sets the effectiveness standard. The distinction between these two examples might be explained by the public enforcement context in the (strong) latter case versus that of the rights of private parties in the (weak) former. Whether such a distinction is justifiable is another matter. Another distinction is that between a national norm (and equivalence) and an EU norm imposed directly.

At the same time, regulatory competition is to do with not pursuing consistency for its own sake but instead in pursuit of defined goals that may on occasion be reached using alternative but equivalent (equally effective) means. Together with effectiveness, equivalence (no less effective treatment than comparable cases under national law) is a boundary principle of EU competition law. We have already seen that equivalence is the rule with regard to procedural law as well as with national competition law regarding practices that do not affect interstate trade.

Here, the *Toshiba* case (2012) on the applicability of the framework of Regulation 1/2003 to situations pre-dating accession of a Member States is relevant.[59] The judgment has been criticized by Giorgio Monti as supporting an overly inclusive *ne bis in idem* rule where Article 16 of Regulation 1/2003 (on uniformity) is interpreted in such a manner as to pre-empt national law, whereas Article 3(2) of Regulation

[55] Joined Cases C-297/98 and C-410/98 *Metallgesellschaft Ltd and Others (C-397/98), Hoechst AG, Hoechst UK Ltd (C-410/98) v Commissioners of Inland Revenue, H.M. Attorney General [2001]* ECR I-1727, para 85.

[56] See K. Lenaerts, 'Effective judicial protection in the EU'. Available at: <http://ec.europa.eu/justice/events/assises-justice-2013/files/interventions/koenlenarts.pdf>.

[57] Case C-681/11 *Schenker*, above (n 36), para 36. Also: 'As regards immunity from or not imposing a fine, in order for such treatment—which is moreover at issue in the main proceedings—not to undermine the effective and uniform application of Article 101 TFEU, it can be accorded in strictly exceptional situations only, such as where an undertaking's cooperation has been decisive in detecting and actually suppressing the cartel.' Ibid, para 49.

[58] Case C-439/08 *VEBIC*, above (n 15).

[59] C-17/10 *Toshiba Corporation et al. v Úřad pro ochranu hospodářské soutěže*, Judgment of 14 February 2012. Monti (2014), above (n 5).

1/2003 makes clear that the national rules on unilateral conduct are not even required to conform in terms of the norm applied itself. Monti also claims that for 'controlled decentralization' to succeed further, legislation is needed, whereas the more radical alternative of 'uncontrolled decentralization' could be attempted instead.

Relevant here too are *Schenker* (2013)[60] as well as *Orange* (2014)[61] and *easyJet* (2015).[62] In *Schenker*, the CJEU ruled that because national competition authorities lack the power to adopt a negative decision (unlike the Commission under Article 10 of Regulation 1/2003), there is no infringement of (in this case) Article 101: 'they cannot cause undertakings to entertain a legitimate expectation that the conduct does not infringe that provision'.[63] Likewise in *Orange* the General Court held that a commitment decision or a decision to close an investigation by an NCA does not bar the Commission from opening proceedings against the undertaking involved even on the same facts.

By contrast, in *easyJet*, the Dutch NCA had rejected purely on priority grounds a complaint based on Article 102 TFEU and the equivalent domestic competition law provision. Subsequently the Commission likewise rejected the same complaint with regard to Article 102 TFEU based on Article 13(2) of Regulation 1/2003 merely on the ground that an NCA had already dealt with the case. The CJEU confirmed that to do so was within the Commission's powers. The result looks a lot as if the Commission is having its cake and eating it too: there is no pre-emptive effect of NCA decisions, but even their prioritization decisions will provide full cover to the Commission for not taking up a complaint, while not blocking the Commission from taking it up anyway if it adopts a different view.

Finally, as far as I am aware there is no widespread notion that regulatory competition and intellectual leadership outside DG COMP is regularly displayed within the ECN. This does not exclude the fact that it may sometimes occur (such as by the French NCA regarding online sales or the Dutch NCA on sustainability issues), but it does suggest that it is not a dominant feature within the system and it certainly is not clearly observable. I will return to this issue in Chapter IX when examining the sectoral networks.

3. The Outcomes of Modernization

There are various possible ways of charting the outcomes of modernization. One is to look at the outputs in terms of actual competition cases including their content. In the next chapter I will look at the *amicus curiae* briefs and opinions of the

[60] Case C-681/11 *Schenker*, above (n 36).

[61] Case T-402/13 *Orange v Commission*, Judgment of 25 November 2014.

[62] Case T-355/13 *easyJet Airline Co. Ltd v Commission*, Judgment of 21 January 2015. See also the ECN Recommendation on the power to set priorities Available at: <http://ec.europa.eu/competition/ecn/recommendation_priority_09122013_en.pdf>.

[63] Case C-681/11 *Schenker*, above (n 36), at 42. For Article 102, the leading case is Case C-375/09 *Tele2 Polska*, above (n 19).

Commission based on Article 15(3) of Regulation 1/2003 and the related national court cases. These fall firmly within the scope of the functioning of Regulation 1/2003 and I would expect them to raise the most important questions from the perspective of coherence. A much more indirect way is to look briefly at some of the leading cases of the General Court and the Court of Justice providing guidance to NCAs and to the Commission that is relevant to the functioning of the ECN. This I will do below.

At a more abstract level, the outcomes of competition procedures have been charted by the European Commission and the NCAs themselves where they have used considerable quantitative data. I will start with a short discussion of the latter.

Reports from the network participants

The European Commission its services (DG COMP) have reported on the five-year (2009, a report that was required by Article 44 of Regulation 1/2003) and ten-year (2014, on its own initiative) anniversaries of the entry into effect of Regulation 1/2003. The tone of these reports is uniformly upbeat. The five-year report (2009) states three important related claims in this respect.

> The EC competition rules have to a large extent become the '*law of the land*' for the whole of the EU. Cooperation in the ECN has contributed towards ensuring their coherent application. The network is an innovative model of governance for the implementation of Community law by the Commission and Member State authorities.[64]

The assertion that EU competition law has become the (i) law of the land is therefore combined with (ii) its coherent application and (iii) a new mode of governance. In the ten-year report (2014), the Commission repeats the 'law of the land' claim and advances it further by stating that:

> the work carried out by the ECN has become increasingly important to ensure coherent enforcement and to allow stakeholders to benefit from a more level playing field.[65]

A level playing field is clearly one of the dimensions of coherence that is of interest to the parties that are subject to the relevant rules. The Commission underscores that a dynamic development of close cooperation within the ECN underpins the coherent application of EU competition law throughout the EU.[66] Such claims, if accurate, would be good news for legal certainty (and hence legitimacy) as well as effectiveness.

However, evaluating these claims is relatively complicated. One element of evidence is that the formal hierarchical instruments discussed earlier have not been used yet, which could indicate a high degree of agreement on the interpretation of the applicable norms. We do not know to what extent, however, their use has

[64] Ibid, at 9–10.

[65] Ten years of antitrust enforcement (n 14), at 9.

[66] Ibid, at 11.

been contemplated or threatened bilaterally or even within the ECN context: we are not privy to the discussions within the ECN. This means that to a large extent I will have to rely on public documents such as the two reports just quoted and on the case law.

As I have already mentioned, the Commission staff working paper that accompanies the 2009 five-year report explicitly details 'the ECN as a forum to promote coherent application',[67] and discusses work on horizontal issues as well as coordination on individual cases and decisions.

> Overall, it clearly results from the feedback received by the Commission... that the mechanisms provided by Article 11 of Regulation 1/2003 function very well and have led to the largely coherent and consistent application of the EC [now EU] competition rules in the ECN over the last five years. The concerns related to a major risk of incoherent and inconsistent application of EC competition law in a decentralized system that have been raised at the time of the adoption of the modernization package have certainly not been realized.[68]

Although the Commission also acknowledges that a few cases showed inconsistencies, it does not identify them or the issues concerned. The *amicus curiae* cases may be instructive in this regard. I will first look at the general data provided by the Commission

Types of Commission and NCA competition decisions

For the ten-year period 2003–2014 the Commission reports having taken 122 decisions where it applied Articles 101 and/or 102 TFEU, the latter sometimes in conjunction with Article 106 TFEU on legal monopolies and services of general economic interest. (This means rejections of complaints were not counted.) Of these decisions, 73 per cent involved Article 101 TFEU and 48 per cent, almost half of all Commission decisions, involved cartels. (Only 9 per cent of decisions involved vertical restraints.) Three-quarters of cartel decisions were based upon leniency applications, the remainder being accounted for by *ex officio* investigations. This is consistent with claims that the Commission has been able to focus more on its priorities, namely the most serious antitrust infringements of which cartels are the most egregious example.[69] That in turn means that one of the main objectives of EU antitrust modernization appears to have been realized.

During the same time period, the NCAs notified 665 envisaged enforcement decisions to the Commission (see Figure 6.1). The joint pattern for the NCAs (which may well obscure significant differences between individual NCAs) is that Article 102 TFEU cases, on dominance, are most numerous at 36 per cent; cartels at 27 per cent measure only half the comparative share reached by the Commission. This is with only 34 per cent of cartels coming in under a leniency programme, again

[67] Commission staff working paper SEC(2009) 574, above (n 20), paras 244–268.

[68] Ibid, para 260.

[69] Ten years of antitrust enforcement, (n 14), at 4: 'The Commission and the NCAs have prioritised the most serious and harmful anticompetitive practices, in particular, cartels'.

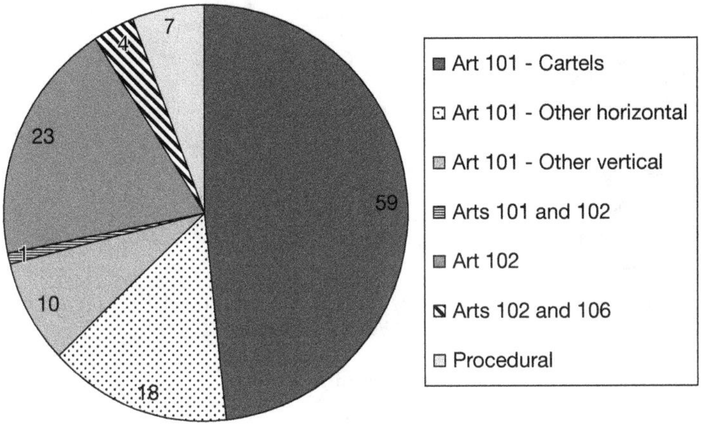

Figure 6.1 Commission decisions following modernization.
Commission staff working document SWD(2014)230, at 6.

about half of that reported by the Commission itself. A relatively large share of 18 per cent of the total number of NCA cases (double that of the Commission) is accounted for by vertical agreements. The dominance cases brought by the NCAs in large part involved the utilities sectors: energy, telecommunications, and transport, with, for example, refusals to deal by vertically integrated monopolists.

To some extent these figures suggest that the decision-making mix of the NCAs (analysed jointly) is somewhat more traditional, and (possibly wholly appropriately) biased toward the utilities and to some extent verticals, whereas the Commission is ahead of the curve, or at least headed in the direction it had set out as its objective for modernization (see Figure 6.2). This could also be interpreted as representing a division of labour.

Regarding Article 102 TFEU, the Commission has acted against exclusionary abuses (foreclosure) in 84 per cent of its decisions, and only in 16 per cent (or 5 actual cases over 10 years) against exploitation.[70] This is in line with its general approach to Article 102 TFEU in recent years and the focus on exclusion expressed most explicitly in its 2009 paper on that topic.[71] However, this economics-centred approach has more recently been called into question by the General Court in *Intel* (2014).[72] The NCAs appear to have been more even-handed with regard

[70] An example is Case T-301/04 *Clearstream Banking AG, Clearstream International SA v Commission* [2009] ECR II-3155.

[71] Communication from the Commission: Guidance on its enforcement priorities in applying Article 82 of the EC Treaty to abusive exclusionary conduct by dominant undertakings, OJ 2009, C45/7.

[72] Case T-286/09 *Intel Corp v Commission*, Judgment of 12 June 2014. See P. Nihoul, 'The ruling of the General Court in Intel: towards the end of an effects-based approach in European competition law', *Journal of European Competition Law & Practice* 5 (2014) 521–30; W.P.J. Wils, 'The judgment of the EU General Court in Intel and the so-called more economic approach to abuse of dominance', *World Competition* 37 (2014) 405–34.

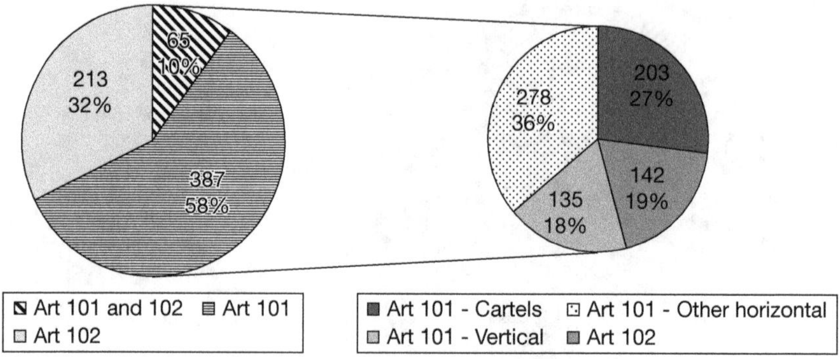

Figure 6.2 NCA decisions following decentralization.
Commission staff working document SWD(2014)230, at 7.

to exploitation, in part because taken together with cases in which both types of abuses were found these account for 27 per cent of their Article 102 TFEU decisions. Such cases were found particularly in the energy, media, and transport (airport services) sectors.

The Commission also reports that industrial products (especially chemicals) no longer form the lion's share of cartel activity, that cartels are more diverse, more sophisticated, and more likely to operate globally. In this context there is increasing cooperation between the European Commission and the International Competition Network (ICN). In addition, the data collected are increasingly voluminous, reflecting the more general societal trend of having to deal with 'big data' in order to produce workable conclusions instead of relying on a convenient 'smoking gun' (which now cartel participants are usually more circumspect is generally unavailable). In the lore of antitrust enforcement, the smoking-gun expression refers to a preferably handwritten note detailing the most incriminating aspects of an illegal cartel arrangement by one of its participants, providing conclusive evidence.

The net gains for modernization

When compared with pre-modernization data, the above figures show a considerable net gain for antitrust enforcement as a result of modernization. In a 2013 paper, Wouter Wils found an eightfold increase in the number of substantive decisions based on Articles 101 and 102 TFEU. In terms of numbers, however, nearly all the gains are realized by the new cases brought by the NCAs that were not there prior to modernization (so every NCA decision counts as a gain), and not by additional cases brought by the Commission. Wils has shown that the number of Article 101 and 102 TFEU decisions taken by the Commission has barely increased since modernization: under Regulation 17/62 the Commission on average adopted 7.5 prohibition decisions and 2 exemptions per year, and under Regulation 1/2003 on average it adopted 7 prohibition decisions and 3 commitment decisions per year.[73]

An increase would have been expected, at least based on the Commission's own argument that modernization was necessary to liberate the Commission services from dealing with dreary and frequently pointless notifications that kept them away from more productive work on the key antitrust infringements. There are numerous possible explanations for this phenomenon and Wils presents several of them, for instance that the Commission services now have to focus more on state aid and merger cases, where they retain an exemption monopoly, with its incumbent curse of having to deal in some form with all the notified cases (which might be called the water-bed theory of administrative priority setting). Also, the increased stress on economic analysis in competition cases might make case handling more time consuming, and some of this time may be taken up by the management of the competition policy network.

Alan Riley has described abolition of the notification procedure as not the radical step that it was presented to be but 'merely the abolition of an already irrelevant procedure with marginal impact on the operation of EC [now EU] competition rules'.[74] From personal experience as a case handler in the final years of Regulation 17/62 (which may not be representative for its entire duration) but well before modernization was a *fait accompli*, I can confirm that the notification burden was then deliberately greatly overstated for rhetorical purposes whereas in practice it did not keep DG COMP from setting different priorities and acting on them. I therefore believe that the absence of a gap resulting from the disappearance of the notification work is largely explicable by the fact that there was little significant notification work being done anymore.

That does not mean there has been no change. The types of cases DG COMP is now handling are more complex and time consuming, its internal quality checks are more rigorous (factors that Wils mentions as well), as are the standards required by the General Court and the CJEU. Difficult infringement cases are no longer typically pursued by an overworked and lonely case handler on the basis of formal correspondence with the undertaking concerned but in a more hands-on manner by entire teams with economic expertise on board. As the total number of staff has remained largely constant, this more intense effort is consistent with the number of decisions remaining broadly constant as well. It is also easily compatible with a picture of an unchanged quantity but possibly higher quality of decisions, as well as with the modernization narrative of the Commission taking its responsibility as *primus inter pares*. More is not always better here.

Finally, it is not clear what the gains from modernization have been in real terms such as annual consumer savings as a percentage of gross domestic product

[73] W. Wils, 'Ten years of Regulation 1/2003—a retrospective', *Journal of European Competition Law & Practice* 4 (2013) 293–301.

[74] A. Riley, 'EC antitrust modernization: the Commission does very nicely—thank you! Part one: Regulation 1 and the notification burden', *European Competition Law Review* 24 (2003) 604–15, at 604.

(GDP). In recent years such data are being collected in several jurisdictions (EU, some NCAs, and the United States) for competition policy at large. The available figures for the period 2008–2013 suggest modest percentages ranging between 0.087 and 0.37 of GDP for the European Commission, which appears to be broadly in line with the findings for the other competition authorities surveyed. However, there are likely to be more significant indirect effects including those based on deterrence, improved quality, and choice.[75]

Types of procedure and/or instrument

Among the procedural innovations of Regulation 1/2003, the most significant is that enabling the Commission to adopt commitment decisions under its Article 9. These are particularly effective because the breach of a commitment may be penalized directly without a requirement of establishing a further substantive infringement of the competition rules. A stark example is the €561 million fine that the Commission imposed on Microsoft in 2013 for violating the terms of its 2009 commitments with regard to third party browser access, with which the abuse of dominance case regarding tying of Internet Explorer had been concluded.[76] Over the ten-year period under discussion, the Commission took thirty-three Article 9 commitment decisions compared to seventy-seven Article 7 prohibition decisions, the latter especially in cartel cases when commitments would be inappropriate (unlike settlements, about which see further following).

Commitment decisions may be behavioural (such as an access obligation) or structural (such as divestment of certain activities) and have so far been mainly behavioural in nature. Nevertheless, the Commission reports that the increasing use of structural commitments represents convergence with its practice in merger cases (where structural commitments are the norm and behavioural commitments seen as second-best).[77] Under Article 7 of Regulation 1/2003 the Commission has been explicitly empowered to impose (rather than accept an offer by the undertaking concerned as under Article 9) behavioural as well as structural remedies. In *Alrosa* (2007), on restrictive practices and dominance abuse in the diamond sector, the General Court ruled that due to the principle of proportionality, the commitments that Commission achieves under Article 9 of Regulation 1/2003 may not go beyond the remedies that it could have imposed under its Article 7.[78]

[75] F. Ilkovitz and Adriaan Dierx, 'Ex post evaluation of competition policy enforcement: what can we learn from the literature and from the experience of competition authorities? *Competition Policy Brief*, June 2015; and European Commission, Ex-post economic evaluation of competition policy enforcement: a review of the literature. Available at: <http://ec.europa.eu/competition/publications/reports/expost_evaluation_competition_policy_en.pdf>.

[76] COMP/39.530—Microsoft (tying), Commission Decision of 6 March 2013.

[77] Commission staff working document, Ten years of antitrust enforcement under regulation 1/2003, accompanying the document Commission Communication, Ten years of antitrust enforcement under Regulation 1/2003: achievements and future perspectives, SWD(2014) 230, at 56–57. Further statistics are available at <http://ec.europa.eu/competition/ecn/statistics.html>.

[78] Case T-170/06 *Alrosa v Commission* [2007] ECR II-2601; Commission staff working paper SEC(2009) 574, above (n 20), at 33–4.

However, on appeal in 2010, the Grand Chamber of the Court of Justice ruled that the purpose and the scope of Articles 7 and 9 of Regulation 1/2003 were different. Moreover:

> Undertakings which offer commitments on the basis of Article 9 of Regulation No 1/2003 consciously accept that the concessions they make may go beyond what the Commission could itself impose on them in a decision adopted under Article 7 of the Regulation after a thorough examination.[79]

This would appear to make the use of commitments more attractive to the Commission, however, so far structural remedies have been rare, although some were imposed in the energy sector as commitment decisions.[80]

Similarly, Article 10 of Regulation 1/2003 which enables the Commission to adopt a finding of inapplicability in exceptional cases (that is to say without re-introducing the Commission's exemption power under Article 101(3) TFEU that was abolished by modernization), has so far not been applied yet. Article 10 explicitly states that such a decision must be required by the public interest. An Article 10 decision is binding on national courts and NCAs and has become the only way for the Commission to activate Article 101(3) TFEU.

However, the NCAs have no Article 10 powers themselves. Instead they are empowered more narrowly by Article 5 of Regulation 1/2003 to decide that there are no grounds for action in cases where the conditions for the application of Article 101 and/or 102 TFEU are not met. Unlike the Commission's Article 10 Decision, such NCA decisions are not binding on other NCAs, nor on national courts, and not on the Commission either, yet they may fall under the *ne bis in idem* rule (see further following). Unlike NCAs, national courts are able to apply Article 101 TEFU fully, including Article 101(3) TFEU.

The fact that with regard to NCAs the Commission has a monopoly over findings of inapplicability of EU law under Article 10 (even if national competition law provides otherwise) was settled in the *Tele2 Polska* case (2011) as far as Article 102 TFEU is concerned.[81] With regard to Article 101 TFEU, the same outcome was reached concerning Article 101(3) TFEU in *Schenker* (2013).[82]

Finally, it is worth highlighting that in the 2009 Commission services report that forms the basis for its five-year evaluation, the point is made that as an *ex ante* measure ensuring consistency Article 10 has been overtaken by events. This is because the ECN has proven to be such an unexpectedly successful forum for discussing issues of competition policy.[83] Soft forms of coordination (albeit in the shadow of binding rules) therefore appear to have obviated the need for the

[79] Case C-441/07 P *Commission v Alrosa Company Ltd.* [2010] ECR I-5949, para 48.

[80] Case COMP/39.402—RWE Gas Foreclosure, Commission Decision of 18 March 2009; Case COMP/39.388—German Electricity Wholesale market and COMP/39.389—German Electricity Balancing Market, Commission Decision of 26 November 2008.

[81] Case C-375/09 *Tele2 Polska*, above (n 19), para 28.

[82] Case C-681/11 *Schenker & Co*, Judgment of 18 June 2013.

[83] Commission staff working paper SEC(2009) 574 (n 20), at 36.

Commission's use of its primacy and pre-emption tools. The counterfactual is difficult to construe with confidence: hence whether soft coordination would have worked in the absence of the possibility of hard intervention remains an open question.

Effects of the ECN on the position of its network members

Effects on the NCAs

As discussed in Chapter II, prior to modernization there had been widespread spontaneous harmonization of national competition rules to the EU standard, however it is clear that the stature of the NCAs—some of which were expressly created for this purpose—has increased with (i) their ability (and duty) to apply Articles 101 and 102 TFEU, (ii) with their membership of the ECN, and (iii) through their direct relationship with the European Commission, as opposed to contacts through the intermediacy of national governments and their respective ministries. The latter is illustrated by the fact that by force of Article 14 of Regulation 1/2003, NCAs now sit on the Advisory Committee, instead of Ministry representatives, although the latter may join in for the discussion of general matters (as opposed to the discussion of individual cases).

This growth in stature both in the domestic and in the EU setting is to do with the application of norms that are developed at EU level and in the context of the network of peers that is the ECN. This means it takes the NCAs to some extent outside the national context and insulates them to a certain measure from the pressure and influences (political or otherwise) to which they are subject within that context. In addition, Article 5 of Regulation 1/2003 provides a minimum set of powers (including that to accept commitments) that helps the effectiveness of NCAs.

The ECN provides a forum for debate and consensus building where members obtain valuable input, often based on practical experience, that they could not easily obtain within their national legal frameworks (least of all where an international dimension is involved). Best practices are developed and shared in this manner. This in turn helps NCAs to build up a position of enhanced independence vis-à-vis their national governments not only with respect to the application of EU law but also with regard to the application of national competition law in cases that lack an EU dimension.

From a political science perspective, Wilks sees a risk of incoherence and leadership challenges within the ECN, the absence of which is 'explained by the value that the NCAs place upon their domestic independence which is enhanced by the ECN' as well as by the creation of a persuasive common competition discourse.[84] In the ECN, the discussion on the enforcement methods applied is connected with effective powers needed, leading to a lobby for a standardized minimum set

[84] Wilks (2007) (n 50), at 455.

of instruments as well as for the allocation of adequate resources.[85] In sum: the NCAs can use their participation in ECN to bolster their position in the national context. In more abstract terms, it enhances both their legitimacy and effectiveness.

Effects on the European Commission

The Commission too is an ECN member, albeit to say the least as a *primus inter pares*. As we have seen, it even disposes of the legal tools to override the other members in the pursuit of actual cases: it can enforce its primacy by pre-empting conflicting decisions. In addition, its decisions are binding on the other members (NCAs), whereas the decisions of the NCAs are valid only within their own Member States and do not have such binding force on the Commission or on each other.[86]

For the Commission the ECN is not merely a network a network of peers but also a constituency on which it can draw for a measure of support in formulating and executing its policies. The NCAs form the hands and feet of the Commission in the twenty-eight Member States: it can therefore have a broader effect than if it would have to act as the sole enforcer of EU competition policy. This is illustrated by the figures on the numbers of decisions cited earlier: for every Commission decision there are between five and six such decisions taken by NCAs. The Commission's policy notices are amplified by NCAs following suit and its decisions can trump national courts. Unlike some may have feared at the outset of modernization, the power of the Commission appears to have increased rather than decreased.[87]

This new context raises questions regarding the role and position of DG COMP. Other DGs within the Commission lack a similar body of specialized law, a similarly independent role in executing it, and a network of satellites at national level applying these rules as well. (Although DG Connect and DG Energy may come close with the electronic communications and energy regulation networks.) The increasingly specialized activities that DG COMP carries out and its increasing clout create some friction with the activities of the college of Commissioners as a whole—for instance, when large multinational corporations are involved with the EU across multiple policy dimensions. Nevertheless there is a risk that in the College of Commissioners the increased competition policy powers enjoyed by the Commission may be influenced by political considerations. If this risk actually does increase over time this is likely to lead to renewed pleas for DG

[85] Such as Resolution of the Meeting of Heads of the European competition authorities of 16 November 2010, Competition authorities in the European Union—the continued need for effective institutions, available at: <http://ec.europa.eu/competition/ecn/ncas.pdf>.

[86] Maher (n 23), at 428.

[87] See for instance C.-D. Ehlermann and I. Atanasiu (eds), *European Competition Law Annual 2002: Constructing the EU Network of Competition Authorities* (Oxford: Hart Publishing, 2005).

Competition to become an independent authority itself, perhaps structured as part of a European public prosecutor's office.[88]

However, while this arrangement might work for antitrust and State aid (although in the latter case, the subjects of enforcement would be the Member States) it would not work for mergers where there are in principle no infringements to prosecute and consequently the process involved is less adversarial at least in principle (although, for instance, a decision to block a merger might be challenged in an adversarial process). If the coherence between these three branches of competition policy is to be taken seriously the transformation of DG COMP into a public prosecutor would therefore be problematic on this count.

What effects on coherence?

The Commission has claimed that modernization has led to the growth of a culture of competition, and that competition law is now 'the law of the land' throughout the EU.[89]

Jointly, the abovementioned effects lead to the construction of an EU policy sphere on competition. As we have seen, in the modernization framework as specified in the 2002 joint statement by the Council and the Commission, effectiveness and consistency are the leading objectives of the ECN structure.[90] This is pursued by a mixture of hard (Commission primacy, or pre-emption) and soft (exchange of information and best practices) instruments. The effects of these instruments on coherence are intended to be positive, and as we have seen earlier, the Commission services have claimed that they clearly are.

Nevertheless it is difficult to estimate to what extent this effort has been successful, both because we lack a methodology to establish a baseline and because we do not have a reliable counterfactual to construe what would have happened in the absence of modernization. Just as increasingly effective competition law enforcement is spreading globally outside the context of the EU, so it might have spread and intensified at national level within the EU, even in the absence of modernization. As mentioned, widespread spontaneous harmonization of national competition law already occurred prior to modernization. In addition, some form of coordination might have been construed even in the absence of common enforcement of EU competition rules at national level.

Be this as it may, it must be assumed that (i) applying the same rules and (ii) striving toward doing so consistently and (iii) having instruments to enforce that

[88] There is, in fact, a 2013 proposal to create such an office, albeit so far only with relation to prosecuting fraud against the EU budget. Commission Communication, Proposal for a Council Regulation on the establishment of the European Public Prosecutor's Office, COM(2013) 534. Earlier, C.-D. Ehlermann, 'Reflections on a European cartel office', *Common Market Law Review* 32 (1995) 471–86; S. Wilks and L. McGowan, 'Disarming the Commission: the debate over a European cartel office', *Journal of Common Market Studies* 33 (1995) 259–73.

[89] Commission Communication, Ten years of antitrust enforcement under Regulation 1/2003: achievements and future perspectives, para 23.

[90] Joint Statement, above (n 2), para 2.

consistency can only have enhanced coherence. In addition, the common goal has been safeguarding the internal market. Steering such a coherent system by intellectual leadership and coordination combined with primacy and pre-emption tools enhances the effectiveness of the Commission. The fact that for NCAs procedures and remedies remain governed by national law is a possible source of divergence, although on leniency an effort at voluntary harmonization has been made, and formal harmonization has been achieved regarding damages. Most likely, however, this type of effort will be limited to problems requiring coordinated action by the NCAs. There does not appear to be any sign of harmonization for its own sake, even if regulatory competition on either form or substance likewise appears to be absent.

4. Conclusion

We have seen the workings of the Commission, the NCAs, and the network which they constitute in common, the ECN. As background, it is useful to recall the way Alan Riley summed up modernization in 2003:

> In essence the Commission pulled off a political masterstroke, it has used the abolition of a procedure it has known for years was a dead letter, to give the appearance of a radical commitment and willingness to change to impress the Member States. Simultaneously it has given the impression of wanting to undertake significant decentralization, while in fact giving very little away and achieving a significant degree of centralized control and supervision over the NCAs. And in return it has sought and obtained a major refurbishment and increase in its own direct powers.[91]

This is to some extent a caricature and, given the time of its writing, it was not informed by the actual working of the ECN or for that matter of modernization at large, yet I largely concur with this view as an assessment of the outset of modernization. Since then, however, events have moved on and, as I have set out in this chapter, it is clear that not just the Commission is profiting from the new system but also that the NCAs are empowered both by modernization and by collaborating in the ECN. Moreover, the objectives of modernization appear to have been reached, at least in large part: a uniform (or consistent, depending on the source) and effective application of EU law to priority cases, meaning the most serious infringements.

So far at least the picture that emerges from the Commission's reporting on the functioning of the ECN is overwhelmingly positive. In their 2009 report, underpinning its five-year evaluation, the Commission Services also stated that 'the Regulation reconciled the requirements of substantive coherence with the existing procedural diversity amongst European Competition Authorities'.[92] Another

[91] A. Riley, 'EC antitrust modernization: the Commission does very nicely—thank you! Part two: between the idea and the reality: decentralization under Regulation 1', *European Competition Law Review* 24 (2003) 657–72, at 672.

[92] Commission staff working paper SEC(2009) 574, above (n 20), at 61.

claim is that a 'common competition culture' has now been founded in Europe.[93] More prosaically but not less importantly, the overall productivity regarding the application of Articles 101 and 102 TFEU has increased significantly, primarily due to the new cases brought by the NCAs (albeit that this may in part be cases that would otherwise have been dealt with under national law). The Commission's output in quantity has not increased, but the quality of its output arguably has. This too can count as output legitimacy.

The ECN is clearly a policy network with elements of cooperation and hierarchy in place. The latter, the Commission's pre-emption powers, have so far not been used, at least not explicitly. So far, coordination (perhaps in the shadow of pre-emption) has sufficed to keep the system going in the direction that is consistent with the Commission's views. This means that the network has been a force favouring convergence and coherence, and notably its goals of effectiveness and consistency. It may give these goals priority over promoting policy experiments at national level in a pattern of decentralization, as Giorgio Monti has observed,[94] but at least this is consistent with EU competition law's dominant objective of protecting the internal market.

[93] Ibid, at 74.

[94] Monti (2014) (n 5), at 19. Y. Svetiev, 'Scaling experimentalism: from convergence to informed divergence in transnational competition policy', in J. Zeitlin (ed.), *Extending Experimentalist Governance?: The European Union and Transnational Regulation* (Oxford: Oxford University Press, 2015) 169–95.

VII

National Courts, the Commission, and the CJEU

1. Introduction

As we have seen in previous chapters, modernization aims to promote the effectiveness and the uniformity of EU antitrust law. Effectiveness and uniformity can be seen as aspects of coherence. In the literature it has been observed that four significant safeguards of uniformity play a role in this respect: the preliminary ruling procedure before the Court of Justice, the principle of sincere cooperation found in Article 4(3) Treaty of the European Union (TEU), the cooperation mechanisms in Article 15 of Regulation 1/2003,[1] and the duty to avoid conflicting decisions in its Article 16.[2] In this chapter we will look at those aspects that concern national courts and the Court of Justice of the European Union (CJEU) as well as the relationship between the Commission and national courts under Regulation 1/2003.

I will deal, first, with a general feature of EU law: the pyramid of judicial review and judicial references with the CJEU at its apex, more specifically with regard to EU antitrust law, the General Court and the CJEU.[3] The questions here are: (i) what are the main features of judicial review and prejudicial references regarding EU competition law; (ii) what is the standard that is applied; (iii) what are the consequences of this in relation to the coherence of EU competition law; and (iv) can we identify vectors for change?

Second, I will examine the role of national courts in their role as independent adjudicators of competition cases. How does the interaction between the Commission and the national courts on Articles 101 and 102 Treaty on the Functioning of the European Union (TFEU) work and how does this differ from

[1] Council Regulation (EC) No 1/2003 of 16 December 2002 on the implementation of the rules on competition laid down in Articles 81 and 82 of the Treaty, OJ 2003, L1/1.

[2] M. Jaeger, 'Standard of review in competition cases: can the General Court increase coherence in the European Union judicial system', in T. Baumé *et al.* (eds), *Today's Multilayered Legal Order: Current Issues and Perspectives. Liber Amicorum in Honour Of Arjen W.H. Meij* (Zutphen: Paris Publishers, 2011), 115–40, at 115.

[3] With the Civil Service Tribunal these two bodies form the Court of Justice of the European Union. See Article 19(1) TEU: 'the Court of Justice of the European Union shall include the Court of Justice, the General Court and specialised courts'.

the relationship the Commission has with the NCAs? How can these modes of interaction be explained? Here I will examine the formal relationships as well as the Commission's intervention in actual national cases by means of *amicus curiae* briefs (*ex officio*) and opinions (on demand by the national courts) mentioned in Article 15 of Regulation 1/2003.

Finally, I will look at the role of the EU courts in EU competition law. This means looking at the objectives and standards of EU competition law through the prism of its final arbitrator, the Court of Justice. The different perspectives of the General Court and the Commission will be dealt with here as well.[4] The discussion will focus on the effect of the judicial dimension on the coherence of EU competition law. The latter in turn will be attuned to the objectives of effectiveness and legitimacy—the rule of law.[5]

2. The Judicial Architecture of the EU

This is not the place for a general discussion of the EU's judicial architecture, nor do I claim to be well-equipped to provide it.[6] Instead I will set out briefly some general characteristics of the interaction between the EU courts and national courts, as well as between EU courts and the European Commission. This is intended to facilitate the discussion that follows on the role of both the national and the EU courts with respect to EU competition law.

National courts are themselves integrated within the system of EU courts insofar as they directly apply effective provisions of EU law, such as Articles 101 (following modernization) and 102 TFEU. They are in this sense EU courts themselves and in that capacity they are bound to follow the interpretation of EU law provided by the highest EU court, the Court of Justice, as well as that of the General Court insofar as this has not been overruled by the former. Thus, a hierarchical principle applies to the judicial architecture of the EU that takes the form of a pyramid, although it is less stringent than the comparable edifices of national law.

The decisions of even the highest national courts cannot be appealed before the Court of Justice or the General Court so the measure of control exercised is indirect. Comparative research has shown that even leading cases like

4 See Joined cases C-501/06 P, C-513/06 P, C-515/06 P and C-519/06 P *GlaxoSmithKline Services Unlimited v Commission of the European Communities (C-501/06 P) and Commission of the European Communities v GlaxoSmithKline Services Unlimited (C-513/06 P) and European Association of Euro Pharmaceutical Companies (EAEPC) v Commission of the European Communities (C-515/06 P) and Asociación de exportadores españoles de productos farmacéuticos (Aseprofar) v Commission (C-519/06 P)* [2009] ECR I-9291; Case C-67/13 P *Groupement des cartes bancaires (CB) v Commission*, Judgment of 11 September 2014.

5 N. MacCormick, *Rhetoric and the Rule of Law: A Theory of Legal Reasoning* (Oxford: Oxford University Press, 2009); T. Bingham, *The Rule of Law* (London: Penguin Books, 2011). See also Chapter I, this book.

6 P. Craig, *EU Administrative Law*, 2nd edn. (Oxford: Oxford University Press, 2012) 261–88.

Tetra Laval[7] are often not cited by national courts, although on substance the national case law on Articles 101 and 102 TFEU tends to be consistent with that of the CJEU.[8] One explanation that is sometimes suggested is the influence of the NCAs in national proceedings who adhere to the line set out by the Commission and the CJEU.

Be it direct or indirectly effective, this hierarchy is in the interest of promoting the effectiveness and the unity of EU law. To facilitate this process, the possibility for national courts to ask the Court of Justice for a preliminary reference on points of EU law based on Article 267 TFEU establishes a direct channel of communication between the EU and the national level.[9] In particular, national courts whose judgments are (in the procedure at hand) not subject to further appeal are required to use such references, unless the issue of EU law involved is clear or has previously been clarified.[10]

The control of the CJEU is much more direct for Commission decisions enforcing Articles 101 and 102 TFEU, which may be appealed first before the General Court and subsequently, on points of law only, before the Court of Justice. Combined with the system of preliminary references to the Court of Justice by national courts who similarly hear appeals regarding NCA decisions, this two-stage system of judicial review ensures that the ultimate authoritative interpretation of EU competition law rests in the hands of the CJEU.

It trickles down to the national level via the (highest) national courts, and is imposed on competition authorities at all levels across the EU including (by appeals against its decisions before the General Court and the Court of Justice) on the Commission at its centre. At the same time there is a parallel channel of control that runs via the Commission.

The Commission plays an important role not only because it initiates much innovation in EU competition law and exercises the role of *primus inter pares* within the European Competition Network (ECN), as we have seen in the previous chapter. Both under the *Masterfoods* ruling (2000)[11] and its codification in Article 16 of Regulation 1/2003, it can also trump, or more accurately pre-empt, the judgments of national courts in competition matters. Because the Commission is not a court but instead an administrative body, this is a remarkable limitation of judicial autonomy, albeit one deemed necessary to ensure the unity of the system

[7] Case T-5/02 *Tetra Laval BV v Commission* [2002] ECR II-4381; Case C-12/03 P *Commission v Tetra Laval BV* [2005] ECR I-987.

[8] S. Lavrijssen, A. Gerbrandy, and O. Essens, 'European and national standards of review: differentiation or convergence', in O. Essens, A. Gerbrandy, and Saskia Lavrijssen (eds), *National Courts and the Standard of Review in Competition Law and Economic Regulation* (Groningen: Europa publishing, 2009) 265–92.

[9] Recommendations to national courts and tribunals in relation to the initiation of preliminary ruling proceedings, OJ 2012, C338/1. K. Lenaerts, 'The unity of European law and the overload of the ECJ—the system of preliminary rulings revisited', in I. Pernice, J. Kokott, and C. Saunders (eds), *The Future of the European Judicial System in a Comparative Perspective: 6th International ECLN–Colloquium/IACL Round Table Berlin, 2–4 November 2005* (Baden-Baden: Nomos, 2006) 211–39.

[10] Case 283/81 *Srl CILFIT and Lanificio di Gavardo SpA v Ministry of Health* [1982] ECR 3415.

[11] Case C-344/98 *Masterfoods Ltd v HB Ice Cream Ltd.* [2000] ECR I-11369.

of EU competition law (to avoid conflicting decisions) and linked to the EU law duty of sincere cooperation.

Finally, as we will see in detail later, the Commission plays an advisory role with respect to the national courts. Thus, both the Commission and the CJEU have direct links with the national courts and in fact only the General Court is not similarly connected in an institutional manner—although of course through its rulings it plays an important substantive role in regards to content of EU competition law.[12]

Below I will first look at the role of national courts in EU competition law and at their interaction with the European Commission. Next we will examine the advisory function.

3. The Role of the National Courts in EU Competition Law

There is an important distinction to be made here between, on the one hand, the period prior to modernization, and on the other hand, the period after that, which is the focus of my discussion.

National courts prior to Regulation 1/2003

Unlike the Commission (empowered in Article 105 TFEU) national courts have traditionally derived their power to apply Articles 101 and 102 TFEU immediately from the direct effect of these Treaty rules.[13] It is therefore not surprising that interaction between the EU Commission and national courts on the application of European competition law pre-dates modernization by some margin, with a first Commission notice on this subject published in 1993 (pre-dating even the 1997 Notice on cooperation with NCAs mentioned in the previous chapter).[14] This dealt with the implications of leading cases at the time, mainly *Delimitis* (1991), regarding the ability of a national court to apply what is now Article 101(1) TFEU, and *Automec II* (1992), on the ability of the Commission to prioritize its antitrust enforcement.[15] The Notice sets out the basic distinction that whereas the Commission is bound to act in the public interest, national courts must safeguard the subjective rights of private individuals.

Clearly, in its 1993 Notice the Commission had civil law courts acting in contractual disputes in mind and not administrative law courts dealing with appeals

[12] Jaeger (2011) (n 2), at 116.

[13] Joined cases 56 and 58/64 *Établissements Consten S.à.R.L. and Grundig-Verkaufs-GmbH v Commission* [1966] ECR 299; Case 127/73 *Belgische Radio en Televisie and société belge des auteurs, compositeurs et éditeurs v SV SABAM and NV Fonior* [1974] ECR 313.

[14] Notice on cooperation between national courts and the Commission in applying Articles 85 and 86 of the EEC Treaty, OJ 1993, C39/6.

[15] Case C-234/89 *Stergios Delimitis v Henninger Bräu AG* [1991] ECR I-935 and Case T-24/90 *Automec Srl v Commission* [1992] ECR II-2223.

against NCAs' decisions (such as on fines or rejections of complaints), let alone national courts acting as NCAs themselves. Because Articles 101(1) and 101(2) as well as Article 102 TFEU were directly effective, there was in fact a clear role for national courts in contractual disputes based on arguments of competition law, albeit frequently regarding contracts that one of the parties wished to have struck down for commercial reasons. As the Notice pointed out, national courts enjoyed the power to determine the civil law effects of Article 101(2) TFEU, that is to say which parts of an infringing agreement were to be considered void. Generally, national courts could apply EU and domestic law in combination and could also adopt interim measures and award damages as well as costs, which the Commission could not do (or at least not easily, in the case of interim measures[16]).

Nevertheless, because the application of Article 101(3) TFEU remained a Commission monopoly, the national courts were frequently hamstrung by the possibility that the Commission might grant an exemption. This problem was only partially resolved by means of block exemptions, which were directly applicable by the national courts as well although they were criticized on other grounds, such as their having a straitjacket effect.[17] Directly effective or not, Article 102 TFEU is a separate issue because the evidentiary burden involved was practically insurmountable by private parties before national courts. Therefore again, in practice only, proceedings initiated by the Commission were likely to have a chance of success.

National courts since Regulation 1/2003

There are at least four reasons why national courts are of increasing relevance for EU competition law since Regulation 1/2003 came into force:

- First, because European competition law is increasingly enforced by NCAs, whose decisions are subject to appeal before national courts (normally administrative in nature), the latter have naturally become more involved in EU competition law since modernization. Some NCAs are themselves national courts, and in some cases decisions on matters such as fines are reserved for national courts, with the NCA taking on a prosecutorial role.
- Second, the direct effect of Articles 101 and 102 TFEU has not changed, but it may nevertheless be expected that recourse to these provisions by private parties, before national courts, has become more frequent since modernization. This too will add to the case load of the national courts, generally under civil law.
- Third, whenever they have recourse to national competition law national courts will now also have to apply EU competition law, unless they can argue that interstate trade is not affected.

[16] Case 792/79 *Camera Care Ltd v Commission* [1980] ECR 119.

[17] See for instance V. Korah and D. O'Sullivan, *Distribution Agreements under the EC Competition Rules* (Oxford: Hart Publishing, 2002).

- Last but not least, individual actions for damages in national courts, again under civil law, can be based on findings of infringement at EU level. Such actions are promoted by the 2014 Damages Directive.[18]

These dimensions will be covered below as part of the discussion of the formal legal framework, which is followed by that on the soft law that governs the relationship between the European Commission and national courts within the framework of EU competition law.

Based on Regulation 1/2003 and the case law of the CJEU, the national courts of the Member States at present have the following powers:[19]

- Regarding Article 101 TFEU, the power
  - to apply Article 101(1) TFEU and to declare whether agreements fall within its scope or outside it.[20]
  - to apply Article 101(2) TFEU and to declare what parts of an agreement that is at odds with Article 81(1) TFEU are void.
  - to apply Article 101(3) TFEU and to declare whether the four conditions for application of the legal exception have been met.
- Regarding Article 102 TFEU, the power
  - to find an abuse of dominance (including finding whether an objective justification applies).
  - to award damages to claimants with regard to a breach of EU competition law.[21]

In addition, a national court normally has the power to award (interim and normal) injunctive relief in competition cases.

Legal framework for interaction between the Commission and national courts

National courts have been explicitly empowered to apply Articles 101 and 102 TFEU by Article 6 of Regulation 1/2003. This provision seems at least to some extent spurious given the direct effect of Articles 101 and 102 TFEU, and falsely suggests that they are on similar footing as the NCAs (empowered by Article 5 of Regulation 1/2003) when clearly they are not, except those courts which are NCAs themselves.

[18] Directive 2014/104/EU of the European Parliament and of the Council of 26 November 2014 on certain rules governing actions for damages under national law for infringements of the competition law provisions of the Member States and of the European Union OJ 2014, L349/1.

[19] J. Goyder and A. Albors-Llorens, *Goyder's EC Competition Law*, 5th edn. (Oxford: Oxford University Press, 2009), at 544–5.

[20] Case 127/73 *BRT v SABAM*, above (n 13); Case C-234/89 *Delimitis*, above (n 15).

[21] Case C-453/99 *Courage Ltd v Bernard Crehan and Bernard Crehan v Courage Ltd et al.* [2001] ECR I-6297, para 36.

As we will see later in this chapter, the legal framework in place for the relationship between national courts and the Commission is not very extensive. A more informal network comparable to that of the ECN does not exist for national courts either. This is logical because for national courts it is their independence which is crucial, not hanging together to avoid hanging separately for reasons of consistency, as is the case for the NCAs. Moreover, especially since the foundational EU case law establishing the doctrines of supremacy and direct effect,[22] national courts have already enjoyed a special relationship with the EU level: that with the CJEU by means of preliminary references for authoritative guidance on points of EU law.

Primacy under Regulation 1/2003

There are a number of provisions in Regulation 1/2003 which govern the relationship between national courts and the EU Commission. The most important of these is the extended *Masterfoods* (2000) rule embodied in its Article 16, mentioned earlier.[23] This is a conflicts rule that gives primacy (or a right of pre-emption) to the European Commission. It does so because it requires that national courts refrain from ruling in conflict with Commission decisions, to the point of staying their proceedings where the Commission has initiated proceedings and is contemplating a decision but has not yet formally decided. Article 16(1) of Regulation 1/2003 reads:

> When national courts rule on agreements, decisions or practices under Article 81 or Article 82 of the Treaty [now Articles 101 and 102 TFEU] which are already the subject of a Commission decision, they cannot take decisions running counter to the decision adopted by the Commission. They must also avoid giving decisions which would conflict with a decision contemplated by the Commission in proceedings it has initiated. To that effect, the national court may assess whether it is necessary to stay its proceedings. This obligation is without prejudice to the rights and obligations under Article 234 of the Treaty [now Article 267 TFEU].

The reference to Article 267 TFEU means that if, for instance, an action for annulment has been brought regarding the Commission decision at hand, then the national court may address a request for a preliminary ruling to the CJEU on the point of EU law involved.

The primacy rule contained in Article 16 of Regulation 1/2003 imposes a strict curb on the independence of national courts in competition matters. In principle the Commission could even block national courts from taking a decision by

[22] Case 26/62 *NV Algemene Transport- en Expeditie Onderneming van Gend & Loos v Netherlands Inland Revenue Administration* [1962] ECR 3; Case 6/64 *Flaminio Costa v E.N.E.L.* [1964] ECR 114.

[23] Case C-344/98 *Masterfoods*, above (n 11), para 60: 'where a national court is ruling on an agreement or practice the compatibility of which with Articles 85(1) and 86 of the Treaty [now Articles 101 and 102 TFEU] is already the subject of a Commission decision, it cannot take a decision running counter to that of the Commission, even if the latter's decision conflicts with a decision given by a national court of first instance'.

initiating proceedings in a case where it has become aware that an outcome which the Commission would consider to be deleterious to EU competition law might otherwise emerge in a national judicial procedure under Articles 101 and 102 TFEU. Effectively Article 16 confers on the Commission the same power of pre-emption regarding the national courts as it enjoys vis-à-vis the NCAs in Article 11(6) of Regulation 1/2003.

At the same time it is also clear that this draconian rule ought to be highly effective in guaranteeing the unity and effectiveness of EU competition law. The escape routes are not obvious. At most, national courts can try to influence the outcome of an undecided case by submitting a preliminary reference to the CJEU, which evidently trumps the Commission's interpretation of EU law. However, given the delay involved in engaging in a preliminary procedure it is doubtful whether doing so would actually be practical in a significant number of cases.[24]

Cooperation under Regulation 1/2003

Article 15 of Regulation 1/2003 is entitled 'cooperation with national courts'. In the first place, under Article 15(1) national courts may request the Commission for information or for an opinion on questions of EU competition law. Under Article 15(2) national courts are to send the Commission copies of their written judgments where they have decided on the application of Articles 101 and 102 TFEU (a practice more honoured in the breach than in the observance: see later in this chapter). Based on Article 15(3) of Regulation 1/2003, the NCAs may submit observations regarding the application of Articles 101 and 102 TFEU before the national courts in their own Member State. Likewise, based on Article 15(3) and in the interest of *coherence* in the application of Articles 101 and 102, the European Commission may act as *amicus curiae*. This is the single example of explicit use of the concept of coherence in Regulation 1/2003 and a significant one as all *amicus curiae* briefs must meet this standard: whether they are necessary as required by the interest of coherence.

Finally, the Commission makes oral observations with the permission of the court concerned. It appears plausible that there can be interaction between this soft power of persuasive (or even just informative) intervention in national proceedings in Article 15 and the hard backstop of Article 16 of Regulation 1/2003 already discusssed.

[24] Between 2010 and 2014 the average duration for a preliminary ruling to be handed down by the Court of Justice from the moment it is requested ranged from 16.1 to 15 months. In the General Court, competition cases took 45.7 months to complete in 2010 and 45.8 months in 2014. For State aid cases, the figures were 32.4 months in 2010 and 32.5 months in 2014. See Court of Justice of the European Union, *Annual Report 2014: Synopsis of the Work of the Court of Justice, the General Court and the Civil Service Tribunal* (Luxembourg: Publications Office of the EU, 2015). Critical: T. Jenkins and G. Bushell, 'Justice denied or simply delayed? Consequences of excessive delay at the EU's General Court', *Journal of European Competition Law & Practice* 6 (2015) 3–14.

Article 15(3) paragraph 2 of Regulation 1/2003 provides for the provision to the Commission (as well as NCAs) by the national courts of documents necessary to assess cases in the interest of making an *amicus curiae* intervention. These provisions do not prejudice broader powers to act as *amicus curiae* that the NCAs may individually enjoy within their domestic jurisdiction.

In its five-year report on the application of Regulation 1/2003, the Commission identifies the abovementioned instruments as devices that are intended to promote the coherent application of the competition rules by the national courts.[25] In addition, there is soft law governing the relationship between the Commission and the national court, as there has been since the 1993 Notice on cooperation between national courts and the Commission. I deal with this shortly before moving on to examining the Commission's *amicus curiae* briefs in detail.

Soft law and the national courts

As part of the modernization package, the Commission in 2004 adopted a Notice on cooperation with national courts regarding Articles 101 and 102 TFEU,[26] which replaced the 1993 Notice. The 2004 Notice is broader: where in 1993 courts were more or less limited to competition arguments raised in contractual disputes between private parties, in 2004 courts were also acting as review courts for NCA decisions, and in some Member States they were acting as NCAs themselves. At the same time, the game had changed due to the 2000 *Masterfoods* ruling of the CJEU[27] and its codification in Article 16 of Regulation 1/2003.

This clearly required more intense coordination between national courts and the Commission, and the 2004 Notice sets out a framework for the Commission to act as *amicus curiae*, providing opinions on request or at its own initiative (although only the latter is considered an *amicus curiae* brief in Article 15(3) of Regulation 1/2003 itself). Also, it reminds national courts of their duty under Article 15(2) of the regulation to submit copies of their judgments where they have applied Articles 101 and 102 TFEU. This is an obligation that is not seriously observed in practice because at the time of writing, ten years later, the courts of the majority of Member States had not submitted copies of any decisions to the Commission at all whereas other sources clearly show that such cases do exist.[28]

Since Regulation 1/2003 came into force on 1 May 2004 the Commission has intervened as *amicus curiae* before national courts at its own initiative thirteen times based on Article 15(3) and has provided opinions on request from national

[25] Communication from the Commission of 29 April 2009, Report on the functioning of Regulation 1/2003, COM(2009) 206, at 8.

[26] Commission Notice on the co-operation between the Commission and the courts of the EU Member States in the application of Articles 81 and 82 EC, OJ 2004, C101/54.

[27] Case C-344/98 *Masterfoods*, above (n 11).

[28] See <http://ec.europa.eu/competition/elojade/antitrust/nationalcourts/>. For at least ten of the non-reporting Member States the OCL database nevertheless contained court cases based on Articles 101 and 102 TFEU, which strongly suggests there is significant underreporting.

courts in twenty-six proceedings (so twice as frequently) based on Article 15(1).[29] The Commission services document that accompanies the ten-year report of 2014 mentions that a number of *amicus curiae* briefs has led national courts to submit preliminary references to the CJEU.[30] To give an indication of the range of issues that are invoked in the context of the coherent application of EU competition law, I will now take a more detailed look at the Commission's *amicus curiae* briefs and opinions.

4. The Commission's *Amicus Curiae* Briefs

These *amicus curiae* briefs are short commentaries on issues of EU competition law arising before national courts that are generally drafted, and signed, by individual members of the Commission's legal service. In at least one set of proceedings (at different levels of jurisdiction) the Commission has even retained local counsel to draft and submit its advice, a novelty presumably explained by the technical nature (national tax law) of the matter at hand: this occurred in the Dutch case on the tax deductability of cartel fines discussed later in this chapter. If the Commission were to do so more frequently it would greatly increase the number of cases in which it could intervene (given the time constraints of the legal service), but might detract from the authority assigned to such briefs.

Tax deductability of cartel fines

At a meta-level, the question is when the Commission is allowed to submit an *amicus curiae* brief based on Article 15(3) of Regulation 1/2003 on coherence grounds. This issue was raised in proceedings in The Netherlands and became the subject of a preliminary reference by a Dutch appeals court to the CJEU in 2007.[31] The underlying substantive issue was whether the fines that the Commission had imposed on a member of a plasterboard cartel could be considered to be tax deductible as a matter of national law, an outcome which (if answered in the affirmative) would obviously weaken the impact and the deterrent nature of such fines.[32] In The Netherlands at the time, whether deductability was possible remained an

[29] Data from Commission Staff Working Document, Ten years of antitrust enforcement under Regulation 1/2003 SWD(2014) 230, para 22. Available at: <http://ec.europa.eu/competition/court/overview_en.html>.

[30] Commission Staff working paper, SWD(2014) 230, at 73. This refers to Case C-681/11 *Bundeswettbewerbsbehörde, Bundeskartellanwalt v Schenker & Co. et al.*, Judgment of 18 June 2013; Case C-427/07 *Inspecteur van de Belastingdienst v X BV* [2009] ECR I-4833; and Case C-439/09 *Pierre Fabre Dermo-Cosmétique SAS v Président de l'Autorité de la concurrence and Ministre de l'Économie, de l'Industrie et de l'Emploi* [2011] ECR I-9419.

[31] Commission *amicus curiae* briefs of 24 September 2009, with the Gerechtshof Amsterdam, and of 16 December 2010, with the Hoge Raad der Nederlanden.

[32] The substantive case was decided at the highest level in Case C-407/08 P *Knauf Gips KG v Commission* [2010] ECR I-6375 and Case C-413/08 P *Lafarge SA v Commission* [2010] ECR I-5361. Here the Commission decision was largely upheld.

open question regarding both cartel fines under national competition law and EU fines.

In the preliminary reference, however, the question was whether an *amicus curiae* brief could be submitted that did not regard the application of Articles 101 and 102 TFEU themselves, but rather the procedural phases following this application. Hence we are at the threshold here between (EU-based) substance and (national-law based) procedural law. In its ruling in *Belastingdienst v X* (2009),[33] the CJEU found that an amicus curiae brief was acceptable here, based on the following reasoning:

> there is an intrinsic link between the fines and the application of Articles 81 and 82 EC [now Articles 101 and 102 TFEU]
>
> The effectiveness of the penalties imposed by the national or Community competition authorities on the basis of Article 83(2)(a) EC [now Article 103(3)(a) TFEU] is therefore a condition for the coherent application of Articles 81 EC and 82 EC.
>
> In proceedings relating to the penalties in respect of anti-competitive practices provided for in Article 83(2)(a) EC, the decision that the court seised must give is capable of impairing the effectiveness of those penalties and therefore might compromise the coherent application of Articles 81 EC or 82 EC.[34]

Thus, the effectiveness of Articles 101 and 102 TFEU required the Commission's intervention on coherence grounds, even although the actual application of Articles 101 and 102 TFEU (which had already been applied when the fines were imposed) was not at issue. Eventually in 2011, the Dutch *Hoge Raad* duly confirmed an appeals court decision that EU cartel fines were not tax deductible under Dutch law, just as six months earlier it had ruled for the first time that cartel fines imposed national under national law were not deductible.[35] Although this cannot be deduced from the text of the decision regarding the deductibility issue under national competition law, it appears reasonable to assume that the interpretation of the national tax law provisions in the light of EU law has also coloured the interpretation of the implications for national competition law that were not formally touched by the *amicus curiae* brief. In any event a consistent—and coherent—result was arrived at concerning the treatment of cartel sanctions that comprised not only the interpretation of EU law but also that of national competition law.

Nevertheless, the issue on the substance of deductability is not yet settled EU law because it has not been confirmed by the CJEU which, in *Belastingdienst v X*, had only ruled on the narrow issue whether the *amicus curiae* brief was admissible. In a similar case where an *amicus curiae* brief was filed by the Commission in 2012, however, the Belgian constitutional court (when likewise confronted with the issue of potential tax deductability of EU cartel fines) turned down a suggestion by the Commission in its brief to file a preliminary reference. Instead,

[33] Case 427/07 *Belastingdienst*, above (n 30). [34] Ibid, paras 36–38.

[35] Hoge Raad, 12 August 2011, LJN: BO6770 (EU fines) and Hoge Raad 7 January 2011, LJN: BL0214 (Dutch fines).

it ruled itself that such deductability was excluded,[36] on the ground that allowing tax deductability of EU cartel fines under Belgian law would be a breach of EU law because it would handicap the effectiveness and coherence of Articles 101 and 102 TFEU.[37] According to the Belgian constitutional court, it would also offend the requirement of loyal cooperation under Article 4(3) TFEU that requires national law to be interpreted in a manner that is as far as possible in conformity with EU law.[38]

In both these Dutch and the Belgian cases, the outcomes arrived at by the national courts in question are in line with the Commission's *amicus curiae* brief. The links between coherence and effectiveness, and between coherence and loyal cooperation in the interest of consistency, illustrate how a power to persuade that at first sight appears to be a light touch can have significant consequences even in an area—procedural law and sanctions—that nominally remains reserved to the national level. This particular discussion also shows that a preliminary reference was needed to establish the principle that the Commission's intervention was legitimate.

Severability of cartel decisions

A similar example of an *amicus curiae* brief leading to national law conforming with the EU precedent—admittedly in a case where (as before on tax deductability of fines) no strong national precedents appear to exist—regards the limitation periods for damages claims of private parties following on public findings of cartel infringements. At least in theory, the EU favours such private enforcement, however just as happened in the case of the Damages Directive in relation to disclosure of information that was derived from leniency applications and settlements,[39] in practice, public enforcement tends to take priority.

Thus in the 2014 *Deutsche Bahn v Morgan* case the Supreme Court of the United Kingdom was called upon to decide whether, for purposes of calculating the start of a two-year limitation period for damages claims under UK law, a Commission decision in which a cartel was fined should be regarded as a bundle or a series of individual decisions vis-à-vis the targeted parties. Under the latter interpretation, these individual decisions could either be appealed or not, and if they were not the limitation period would begin to run straightaway. Under an alternative interpretation, the Commission decision would be regarded as a unified whole and the limitation period would only start after all appeals against the decision had been exhausted.

[36] Grondwettelijk Hof, 20 December 2012, nr. 5285, Case 161/2012; Citing Case T-10/89 *Hoechst AG v Commission* [1992] ECR II-629.

[37] Commission *amicus curiae* brief of 8 March 2012, in No 5285 *Tessenderlo Chemie NV v Belgian State*.

[38] Citing Case C-115/08 *Land Oberösterreich v ČEZ as* [2010] ECR I-10265.

[39] Directive 2014/104/EU, above (n 18).

In the case at hand the undertaking that was the subject of a damages claim was the leniency applicant in the competition case. It was therefore not in a position to appeal the Commission decision—and if Commission decisions were to be regarded as a bundle of individual decisions then the limitation period with regard to its part of the decision would already have expired, making a damages claim impossible.

Citing EU case law from *Wood Pulp* (1993) onward to the effect that the bundle theory had already been accepted as a matter of EU law,[40] the UK Supreme Court held that to rule there could be different results as a matter of national law would be at odds with the general requirement of consistency between EU and national law. A divergent outcome would also fall foul of the requirement that there should be an effective domestic remedy for breaches of EU law because unless a decision was overturned as a whole, variation would be introduced in this respect at national level. The UK Supreme Court accepted the Commission's view that the consistent interpretation meant that a Commission cartel decision could be partially overturned by the courts at EU level[41] and therefore not with regard to parties who had not appealed the decision. It would then remain valid with regard to those parties. This meant that the latter could nevertheless (at least within the period of limitation) be sued for damages based on a cartel infringement although 'it might be difficult for a claimant to provide that it had suffered any loss caused thereby'.[42] The net effect for the damages claimant in the case at hand was that the limitation period had expired and his claim was blocked.

Again, the national court was therefore careful to take a coherent approach, albeit based on general EU law principles of consistent interpretation and effectiveness.[43]

Damages claims versus leniency

As seen in Chapter V, significant tension exists between the need to collect evidence for private damages suits in follow-on actions on the one hand, and protecting the confidentiality of leniency applications on the other. Claimants of damages must try to remedy a situation of asymmetric information (notably to prove the counterfactual of what prices would have been in the absence of a cartel agreement), whereas leniency applicants may be the subject of retribution and,

[40] Joined cases C-89/85, C-104/85, C-114/85, C-116/85, C-117/85, and C-125/85 to C-129/85 *A. Ahlström Osakeyhtiö et al v Commission* [1993] I-1307; Case C-310/97 P *AssiDomän Kraft Products AB v Commission* [1999] ECR I-5363 and Case T-462/07 *Galp Energía España SA v Commission*, Judgment of 16 September 2013.

[41] Commission *amicus curiae* brief of 18 February 2014, in Case UKSC 2012/0209 *Morgan advanced materials PLC and Deutsche Bahn et al.*

[42] UK Supreme Court, *Judgment Deutsche Bahn AG and others (repondents) v Morgan advanced materials Plc (formerly Morgan Crucible Co Plc) Appellant*, 9 April 2014 [2014] UKSC 24, para 27.

[43] 'The refusal under that domestic scheme of civil relief against the addressees who had not appealed would on its face infringe the European principles that domestic law should reach results consistent with legal rulings binding at the European level and that there should be an effective domestic remedy for breaches of European law established at the European level.' Ibid, para 22.

more importantly, increased vulnerability to damages claims. To start with, as seen in *Deutsche Bahn v Morgan*, leniency applicants will normally not appeal the Commission's infringement decision, so they are the first cartel participant that can effectively be sued.

With regard to encouraging damages claims as well as leniency applications, the ultimate objective is that of promoting the effective enforcement of the EU competition rules. As we now know, the legislative balance has swung in favour of leniency applications in the 2014 Damages Directive.[44] In 2012, the UK High Court of Justice, Chancery Division, was advised by an *amicus curiae* brief that access to leniency information was to proceed under the balancing test set out in the 2011 *Pfleiderer* case of the CJEU.[45] The UK regarded the suggestion that *Pfleiderer* applied and that EU law did not preclude English courts from ordering disclosure as *actes clairs*, and hence not requiring a preliminary reference.[46]

Other *amicus curiae* briefs

Although they have not been numerous, *amicus curiae* briefs have dealt with a relatively wide variety of other topics. By way of illustration and insofar as linguistically accessible to me (the language used is always that of the procedure and translations are generally not provided), these are briefly covered here in reverse chronological order.

Effect on trade

The most recent example was the Commission's intervention in 2012 on the interpretation of the Guidelines on the effect on trade between Member States of competitive restraints on telecommunications in the French overseas provinces and territories as not capable of being based on a single criterion, such as in this case the geographic coverage of the network concerned.[47]

[44] Directive 2014/104/EU, above (n 18).

[45] Commission *amicus curiae* brief of November 2011 (no exact date), with reference to Case C-360/09 *Pfleiderer AG v Bundeskartellamt*, Judgment of 14 June 2011. In *Pfleiderer*, the CJEU states that: 'in the consideration of an application for access to documents relating to a leniency programme submitted by a person who is seeking to obtain damages from another person who has taken advantage of such a leniency programme, it is necessary to ensure that the applicable national rules are not less favourable than those governing similar domestic claims and that they do not operate in such a way as to make it practically impossible or excessively difficult to obtain such compensation... and to weigh the respective interests in favour of disclosure of the information and in favour of the protection of that information provided voluntarily by the applicant for leniency. That weighing exercise can be conducted by the national courts and tribunals only on a case-by-case basis, according to national law, and taking into account all the relevant factors in the case.' Ibid, paras 30–31.

[46] High Court of Justice Chancery Division, *National Grid Electricity Transmission Plc v ABB Ltd et al.*, Judgment of 4 April 2012.

[47] Commission Notice—Guidelines on the effect on trade concept contained in Articles 81 and 82 of the Treaty OJ 2004, C101/81, para 90: 'Where an agreement forecloses access to a regional market, then for trade to be appreciably affected, the volume of sales affected must be significant

Legitimate expectations

In a 2011 *amicus curiae* brief, the Commission advised the Austrian *Oberste Gerichtshof* that legitimate expectations of a cartel participant with regard to not having infringed Article 101 TFEU could not be based on a prior legal assessment which made no reference to this provision (and in fact pre-dated its applicability in the Austrian context).[48] In addition, the Commission held that an NCA empowered by Article 5 of Regulation 1/2003 to find and fine cartel agreements was entitled, in exceptional circumstances such as when dealing with a leniency application, to refrain from imposing a fine on the undertaking concerned. This view was also taken by the CJEU on a preliminary reference in this matter which gave rise to *Schenker* (2013). There, the CJEU ruled that because NCAs cannot adopt a negative decision, their views cannot give rise to legitimate expectations justifying the non-imposition of a fine for a cartel infringement.

Legal exception

Another example was the nature of the test applied under Article 101(3) TFEU to negotiated capacity reductions of Irish slaughterhouses in 2010,[49] which had also led to a preliminary reference to the CJEU decided in the 2008 *Irish Beef* Case.[50] The latter had clarified that such reductions negotiated among competitors constituted restrictions by object. In its *amicus curiae* brief, the Commission quoted the General Court in *SPO* (1995) to the effect that 'it is impossible to distinguish between normal competition and ruinous competition. Potentially any competition is ruinous for the least efficient undertaking.'[51]

Exclusion of Internet sales

In 2009 the Commission advised the French *Cour d'appel de Paris* on the interdiction of Internet sales within a selective distribution network of cosmetics by Pierre Fabre as being a restriction by object and on the strict limitation of the application of the notion of objective justification under Article 101(1) TFEU.[52] This case gave

in proportion to the overall volume of sales of the products concerned inside the Member State in question. This assessment cannot be based merely on geographic coverage. (etc).' Advising the French Cour de Cassation, 31 January 2012, in Case Nr 140 FS-P+B.

[48] Commission *amicus curiae brief* before the Austrian Oberste Gerichtshof, 11 September 2011. No related national decision is available on the Commission's site. However see Case C-681/11 *Schenker*, above (n 30) and the Austrian decision 16OK 4/13 of 2 December 2013.

[49] Commission *amicus curiae* brief before the Irish High Court of 30 March 2010, in *Competition Authority v The beef industry development society limited and Barry Brothers (Carrigmore) Meats limited*. Case subsequently withdrawn.

[50] Case C-209/07 *Competition Authority v Beef Industry Development Society Ltd and Barry Brothers (Carrigmore) Meats Ltd* [2008] ECR I-8637.

[51] Commission *amicus curiae* brief before the Irish High Court of 30 March 2010, para 34, quoting Case T-29/92 *Vereniging van Samenwerkende Prijsregelende Organisaties in de Bouwnijverheid* (SPO) [1995] ECR II-289, para 294.

[52] Commission *amicus curiae* brief of 11 June 2009, in Case RG 2008/23812 before the Cour d'appel de Paris. Judgment of the Cour d'appel de Paris of 29 October 2009, in case 2008/23812.

rise to a preliminary reference in 2011 in the celebrated *Pierre Fabre* case,[53] where the CJEU likewise found that:

> Article 101(1) TFEU must be interpreted as meaning that, in the context of a selective distribution system, a contractual clause requiring sales of cosmetics and personal care products to be made in a physical space where a qualified pharmacist must be present, resulting in a ban on the use of the internet for those sales, amounts to a restriction by object within the meaning of that provision where, following an individual and specific examination of the content and objective of that contractual clause and the legal and economic context of which it forms a part, it is apparent that, having regard to the properties of the products at issue, that clause is not objectively justified.[54]

The *Cour d'appel* in its 2013 judgment followed the Commission's approach, finding an infringement and no objective justification.[55]

Motor vehicle distribution

In the first Commission *amicus curiae* brief on record, of 2006, it also intervened before the *Cour d'appel de Paris* in a procedure regarding a qualitative selective dealer network.[56] The subtlety of the Commission's arguments was superfluous as the subsequent ruling turned on bookkeeping fraud concerning illegal sales committed by the complaining dealer who had been excluded from the preferred network, so in this case at least the competition arguments were immaterial.[57]

The Commission's opinions

Upon request from the national courts concerned the Commission provides opinions on matters of law concerning the application of Articles 101 and 102 TFEU. The number of opinions requested and provided, reaching thirty over the entire period since modernization in early 2015, is roughly double that of the *amicus curiae* briefs discussed here, however they are more concentrated among a few Member States with twelve opinions being requested in Spanish courts and ten by Belgian courts.

As in the *amicus curiae* briefs, in its opinions the Commission stresses that only the CJEU can provide a binding interpretation by way of a preliminary ruling. It also states that the national court is obliged to request such a preliminary ruling if there is no appeal against its decisions unless the law is clear because the Court has already ruled upon the point concerned or the interpretation is obvious. Also, the Commission does not come down in favour of one of the parties to a dispute

[53] Case C-439/09 *Pierre Fabre*, above (n 30). [54] Ibid, para 47.

[55] Cour d'appel de Paris, Judgment of 31 January 2013, in case 2008/23812.

[56] Commission amicus curiae brief of 2 November 2006, before Cour d'appel de Paris, Affaire garage Gremeau/Daimler Chrysler France.

[57] Cour d'appel de Paris, Judgment of 7 June 2007, Case 05/17909.

although in practice its reasoned opinion may favour the position of one party more than that of another.

It is beyond the scope of this chapter to detail the Commission's opinions and the impact on national judgments. Anecdotal evidence from the Belgian cases examined shows that the national court in one case took a more strict interpretation on vertical distribution and applied a lower threshold for dominance abuse than might have been expected of EU Courts, and in another the court complained of not having received from the Commission the advice on the legality of dominance being extended to ancillary activities that it had requested.[58] Therefore, thus far the impact of Commission opinions in terms of numbers and geographical distribution, as well as possibly content, appears to be limited.

5. The Role of the EU Courts

The role of the General Court and CJEU with regard to EU competition law has been much debated in the recent literature.[59] This is largely because the complexity of the economic issues involved is increasing and the norms imposed by human rights law are becoming more pertinent and stringent. The important issues here are the standard of review, notably in relation to the so-called new economic approach, and the shift from controlling administrative discretion to protecting individual rights.

Institutional set-up and legal basis

Since the onset of European competition law, the single most important change with regard to the role of the EU Courts has been the creation of the Court of First Instance (following the entry into force of the Lisbon Treaty in 2009, called the General Court) in 1988. Its competence has been expanded by successive Treaty amendments; notably, this has included from the outset appeals against Commission decisions in competition cases. The Court of Justice functions as a supreme appellate court with regard to the rulings in competition cases by the General Court, albeit restricted only to points of EU law and not dealing with assessment of fact. In addition, just as it does in relation to non-competition

[58] Rechtbank van Koophandel, Dendermonde, Case 2856/2008 of 3 November 2010; and Cour d'appel de Bruxelles Case 2009/6075 of 3 September 2009.

[59] See for instance: D. Bailey, 'Scope of judicial review under Article 81 EC', *Common Market Law Review* 41 (2004) 1333–60; D. Geradin and N. Petit, Judicial Review in European Union Competition Law: A Quantitative and Qualitative Assessment, TILEC Discussion Paper Series 2011/8; A. Meij, 'Judicial Review in the EC Courts: Tetra Laval and Beyond', in Essens *et al.* (2009), at 7–22; H. Schweitzer, 'Judicial review in EU competition law', in D. Geradin and I. Lianos (eds), *Handbook on EU Antitrust Law: Enforcement and Procedure* (Cheltenham: Edward Elgar, 2013) 491–539; H. Schweitzer, 'The European competition law enforcement system and the evolution of judicial review', in C.-D. Ehlermann and M. Marquis (eds), *EUI Competition Law Annual 2009, Evaluation of Evidence and its Judicial Review in Competition Cases* (Oxford: Hart Publishing, 2011) 79–146.

matters, the Court of Justice deals with competition matters that arise in requests for a preliminary ruling at national level, allowing it to ensure consistency in the approach taken by national courts, again on points of EU law.

The CJEU may quash decisions of the General Court in whole or in part, and the General Court may likewise strike down Commission decisions. However, neither court may decide instead of the Commission after setting aside the latter's decision—something that high administrative courts are generally entitled to do under national jurisdictions in the Member States. Instead, the case is referred back to the Commission to correct the decision if it is deemed salvageable, or to take a new decision. This system can be seen as a reflection of the institutional balance within the EU. This is characterized by functionally separate roles for the Commission, which must apply the competition rules and develop competition policy, and the CJEU, which controls the legality of the Commission's actions but does not engage in competition policy itself.[60] An exception to this rule is formed by the fines that the Commission imposes in competition cases, where the CJEU has unlimited jurisdiction (see below) and may therefore replace the Commission's assessment with its own.

The relevant legal basis for the review of Commission decisions is found in Article 263 TFEU where it is stated that the CJEU shall review the legality of acts of the European Commission

> on grounds of lack of competence, infringement of an essential procedural requirement, infringement of the Treaties or of any rule of law relating to their application, or misuse of powers.

As has been widely observed, these are standards of judicial review that are familiar from French administrative law (and that were modelled after the *recours pour excès de pouvoir* before the French *Conseil d'État*[61]). At the same time, Article 261 TFEU determines that the CJEU may be given unlimited jurisdiction with regard to penalties by means of a Regulation of the European Parliament and Council, which has in fact been done in Article 31 of Regulation 1/2003 where it is stated that it may cancel, reduce, or increase the fine or periodic penalty payment imposed.

Marginal versus comprehensive review on substance

In broad strokes it is possible to characterize two standards of judicial review as being applied by both the General Court and the Court of Justice.[62] The first is full, comprehensive review. In line with EU human rights law as well as with Article 261 TFEU in combination with Article 31 of Regulation 1/2003 this applies with regards to fines in antitrust cases under EU law. The second is marginal review, which is applied to cases where the Commission is required to make a

[60] Geradin and Petit (n 59), at 19.
[61] Meij (n 59), at 7.
[62] Cf. Craig (n 6), 400–45.

complex economic assessment—or broadly, where it exercises policy making powers. Marginal review dates back to the earliest competition case law of the Court where it held in *Consten and Grundig* (1966):

the exercise of the commission's powers necessarily implies complex evaluations on economic matters. A judicial review of these evaluations must take account of their nature by confining itself to an examination of the relevance of the facts and of the legal consequences which the commission deduces therefrom. This review must in the first place be carried out in respect of the reasons given for the decisions which must set out the facts and considerations on which the said evaluations are based.[63]

Thus, the powers of review of the CJEU are at least to some extent limited by the enforcement powers exercised by the Commission.[64] The General Court does not, therefore, examine whether the Commission reached the correct conclusion. Instead it checks whether or not the Commission reached its conclusion in a legally correct manner.[65] This latter approach of marginal review does not mean writing a blank cheque to the Commission: its discretion is not boundless. Marginal review has become an increasingly rigorous test in EU law, and not just in the area of competition.[66]

Marc Jaeger, President of the General Court but writing in a private capacity on the standards of legal review in EU competition law,[67] called attention to the following 2005 ruling of the Court of Justice in the *Tetra Laval* case,[68] triggered by a merger review procedure:

Whilst the Court recognises that the Commission has a margin of discretion with regard to economic matters, that does not mean that the Community Courts must refrain from reviewing the Commission's interpretation of information of an economic nature. Not only must the Community Courts, inter alia, establish whether the evidence relied on is factually accurate, reliable and consistent but also whether that evidence contains all the information which must be taken into account in order to assess a complex situation and whether it is capable of substantiating the conclusions drawn from it. Such a review is all the more necessary in the case of a prospective analysis required when examining a planned merger with conglomerate effect.[69]

[63] Joined cases 56 and 58/64 *Consten and Grundig*, p. 347.

[64] Bailey (2004) (n 59), at 1327.

[65] Ibid, at 1328.

[66] Craig (n 6) lists the following examples: (i) risk regulation, based on Case T-13/99 *Pfizer Animal Health SA v Council* [2002] ECR II-3305; (ii) competition, based on C-12/03 P *Commission v Tetra Laval* [2005] ECR I-987; and (iii) fundamental rights, based on Joined cases C-402/05 P and C-415/05 P *Yassin Abdullah Kadi and Al Barakaat International Foundation v Council and Commission* [2008] ECR I-6351.

[67] M. Jaeger, 'The standard of review in competition cases involving complex economic assessments: towards the marginalisation of the marginal review?', *Journal of European Competition Law & Practice* 2 (2011) 295–314; Meij (n 59). See also B. Vesterdorf, 'Judicial review in EC competition law: reflections on the role of the Community Courts in the EC system of competition law enforcement', *Global Competition Policy* 1 (2005) 3–27. On the general impact of the *Tetra Laval* standard on the application of competition law in national courts, see Essens *et al.* (n 8).

[68] Case C-12/03P *Tetra Laval*, above (n 7).

[69] Ibid, para 39.

Tetra Laval has led to abundant commentary. However, in Jaeger's view, as in that of former Judge Arjen Meij, instead of being an intensification of the judicial review of economic assessments, the objective of the General Court in this case was to specify the standards of proof, although these may well be said to form two sides of the same coin.[70]

The ruling in *Tetra Laval* shows that different standards of review apply at different stages of the case: there is one standard for the finding of the facts, and another for their appraisal. Meij has stated clearly that comprehensive review applies to the interpretation of the conditions for applying the relevant provisions—Articles 101 and 102 TFEU—as well as the accuracy and reliability of the facts, their consistency and completeness as well as whether they are able to substantiate the conclusions drawn from them are subject to comprehensive review. This effectively means that only the appraisal of complex issues requiring economic (or other scientific) analysis is subject to marginal review. Successively this means (i) a comprehensive review of the facts, (ii) a marginal review of their economic assessment (such as in the case of Article 102 TFEU regarding market definition, which review may nevertheless be detailed, as in the 2007 *Microsoft* case)[71], and (iii) a comprehensive review again of their qualification in terms of Articles 101 and 102 TFEU.[72]

Unlimited jurisdiction: The standard of judicial review on fines

As we have seen, Article 261 of the Treaty in conjunction with Article 31 of Regulation 1/2003 itself provides that the CJEU shall have unlimited jurisdiction with regard to fines. This is reflected by the fact that (only as regards to this element of Commission antitrust decisions) the CJEU may replace the Commission's decision with its own judgment.

At the same time, the Court of Justice has held that the Commission itself has a wide discretion as regards the choice of factors that it takes into account in order to determine the amount of fines. This may also reflect the need for the Commission to have a fining policy, inter alia in view of ensuring a deterrent effect. To this end the Commission has adopted guidelines.[73] In doing so, however, it has also limited its own discretion because when diverging from its own guidelines it must justify such a departure in such a manner as meets the requirements of the principle of equal treatment.[74] The CJEU may judge the Commission's fines at least in part by their conformity with the fining guidelines but is not itself

[70] Jaeger (n 67), at 299; citing Meij (n 59), at 19.

[71] Case T-201/04 *Microsoft Corp. v Commission* [2007] ECR II-3601, paras 479ff, citing Case T-342/99 *Airtours plc v Commission* [2002] ECR II-2585, para 26.

[72] Meij (n 59), at 20–21.

[73] Guidelines on the method of setting fines imposed pursuant to Article 23(2)(a) of Regulation No 1/2003, OJ 2006, C210/2.

[74] Jaeger (2011) (n 2), at 119–20. See also B. Vesterdorf, 'The Court of Justice and unlimited jurisdiction: what does it mean in practice', *Global Competition Policy* 2 (2009) 139–45.

bound by these guidelines, neither when evaluating the Commission's fines nor when setting a different fine itself. It is in this context that the General Court and the Court of Justice exercise their unlimited jurisdiction regarding fines and the result is a finely balanced system, and yet as EU antitrust fines have increased, so has the debate on this issue.[75]

The end of the new economic approach?

This approach can be said to have started with the Commission's about-turn on the treatment of vertical restraints in 1999. Until then its approach had been characterized by legal formalism (associated with what in shorthand is sometimes dubbed Ordoliberalism)[76] according to which vertical restraints were seen as representing market barriers. Since 1999 vertical restraints were instead welcomed as ancillary to the efficiencies associated with vertical integration.[77] The General Court is considered to have promoted the new economic approach with its 2002 rulings in *Tetra Laval*[78] (the appeal of which was cited earlier), *Schneider*,[79] and *Airtours*,[80] all of which were lost by the Commission. The new economic approach has been much applauded for its market orientation and theoretical underpinnings (not to mention rich pickings for economic consultants and a proliferation of in-house chief economists), but less as source of legal certainty.[81] The zenith of this movement was probably reached with the Commission's 2009 paper on exclusionary abuses under Article 102 TFEU.[82]

On this point, however, the General Court and the Court of Justice have eventually differed in the standard of review to be applied, markedly in the 2009

[75] W.P.J. Wils, 'Optimal Antitrust Fines: Theory and Practice', *World Competition* 29 (2006) 183–208; W.P.J. Wils, 'The Increased Level of EU Antitrust Fines, Judicial Review and the ECHR', *World Competition* 33 (2010) 5–29.

[76] A more subtle contemporary view on *Ordo*liberalism is found in H. Schweitzer and K.K. Patel, 'EU competition law in historical context: continuity and change', in K.K. Patel and H. Schweitzer (eds), *The Historical Foundations of EU Competition Law* (Oxford: Oxford University Press, 2013) 207–30, art 207, fn. 2 and the references cited there.

[77] Commission Regulation (EC) No 2790/1999 of 22 December 1999 on the application of Article 81(3) of the Treaty to categories of vertical agreements and concerted practices, OJ 1999, L336/21; replaced by Commission Regulation (EU) No 330/2010 of 20 April 2010 on the application of Article 101(3) of the Treaty on the Functioning of the European Union to categories of vertical agreements and concerted practices, OJ 2010, L102/1.

[78] Case T-5/02 *Tetra Laval BV v Commission* [2002] ECR II-4071.

[79] Case T-310/01 *Schneider Electric SA v Commission* [2002] ECR II-4071.

[80] Case T-342/99 *Airtours*, above (n 71).

[81] N. Forwood, 'The Commission's "more economic approach"—implications for the role of the EU Courts, the treatment of economic evidence and the scope of judicial review', in C.-D. Ehlermann and M. Marquis (eds), *EUI Competition Law Annual 2009, Evaluation of evidence and its judicial review in competition cases* (Oxford: Hart Publishing, 2011) 191–255; P. Nihoul, 'The ruling of the General Court in Intel: towards the end of an effect-based approach in European competition law?', *Journal of European Competition Law & Policy* 5 (2014) 521–39.

[82] Communication from the Commission: Guidance on its enforcement priorities in applying Article 82 of the EC Treaty to abusive exclusionary conduct by dominant undertakings, OJ 2009, C45/7.

GlaxoSmithKline case.[83] As we have seen in Chapter III on the objectives of EU competition law, the Court of Justice confirmed its view, expressed in a prejudicial reference in *T-Mobile* earlier in the same year, that negative effects on final consumers need not be demonstrated for the proof of a restraint of Article 101(1) TFEU to be met.[84] The General Court had been prepared to follow the Commission's line to the opposite effect, but stood corrected. More recently in the *Intel* judgment of 2014, a case on exclusivity rebates by a dominant undertaking (currently subject of a pending appeal before the Court of Justice), the General Court itself appears to depart decisively from the new economic approach as a whole.[85] Instead, legal standards have come to play a more significant role.

Wouter Wils has argued persuasively against the need to apply an as-efficient-competitor test and in favour of the standard applied in *Intel* by the General Court. He has pointed out that even for a by-object infringement, there is room for an economic justification (efficiency or objective necessity) which, however, the undertaking concerned had not put forward.[86] Richard Whish seeks to distinguish the *Intel* case on the grounds that it concerned rebates as opposed to price abuses in recent cases like *TeliaSonera* (2011)[87] and *Post Denmark* (2012),[88] where the Court had committed itself to an effects-based approach and an as-efficient-competitor test.[89] The jury is still out at least until the ruling of the Court of Justice on the *Intel* appeal.

Judicial review: A coherent approach?

According to one of the most perceptive commentators on this issue, Heike Schweitzer, the CJEU has established a coherent and stringent regime of judicial review of substantive competition law.[90] However, she has also claimed that its coherence with human rights law and national constitutional guarantees may be improved by abandoning the doctrine of the 'margin of appreciation' left to the Commission and by completing the shift from controlling the objective legality of decisions to judicial protection of individual rights.[91] In addition, Schweitzer advocates reconsidering the standard of review for commitment decisions as well as possibly extending some form of judicial control over the soft law rule-making powers of the Commission on the grounds that this would be a more rounded approach without major gaps in legal protection.[92]

[83] Joined cases C-501/06 P, C-513/06 P, C-515/06 P and C-519/06 P *GlaxoSmithKline*, above (n 4).

[84] Case C-8/08 *T-Mobile Netherlands BV, KPN Mobile NV, Orange Nederland NV and Vodafone Libertel NV v Raad van bestuur van de Nederlandse Mededingingsautoriteit* [2009] ECR I-4529.

[85] T-286/09 *Intel Corp. v Commission*, Judgment of 12 June 2014.

[86] W.P.J. Wils, 'The Judgment of the EU General Court in *Intel* and the so-called more economic approach to abuse of dominance', *World Competition* 37 (2014) 405–34.

[87] Case C-52/09 *Konkurrensverket v TeliaSonera Sverige AB* [2011] ECR I-527.

[88] Case C-209/10 *Post Danmark A/S v Konkurrencerådet*, Judgment of 27 March 2012.

[89] R. Whish, '*Intel v Commission*: keep calm and carry on!', *Journal of European Competition Law and Practice*, 5 (2014) 1–2.

[90] Schweitzer (2013) (n 59).

[91] Schweitzer (2011) (n 59).

[92] Schweitzer (2013) (n 59).

A final gloss is that provided by Meij, who states that it is striking that in those cases where the substance of a scientific appraisal is hardly reviewed, the consistency of the reasoning deployed is reviewed all the more thoroughly instead. This statement is set in the broader context of review of administrative discretion and fits well with the internal market case law on coherence, where it forms one of the key tests of the rationality of a public policy, and may be emerging as a principle of EU law in its own right.[93]

6. Conclusion

The picture with regard to the national courts is more complex than that regarding the NCAs as discussed in the previous chapter. I have looked in particular at *amicus curiae* interventions under Article 15(3) of Regulation 1/2003 because these explicitly require the existence of an EU interest as well as an issue that concerns the *coherent* application of Articles 101 and 102 TFEU. The number of these briefs is limited, presumably as a result of self-constraint exercised by the Commission, while not insignificant in terms of their context and results. They have also been issued in cases that led to important preliminary rulings, notably *Belastingdienst v X* (2009), *Pierre Fabre* (2011), and *Schenker* (2013). This suggests the Commission's interpretation alone was not regarded as sufficient guidance in relation to the issues at hand.

Nevertheless, with regard to the national courts too the Commission has trumping powers based on Article 16(1) of Regulation 1/2003, which codified the rule set out in *Masterfoods* (2000).[94] In addition, although by its nature the respect of this rule is largely implicit (the courts' cases are not taken away but they may not rule in conflict with a Commission decision), just as we have seen with regard to NCAs here too there are so far no signs that pre-emption has had to be imposed explicitly.

The main reason why the picture with regard to the courts is nevertheless more complex is because they cannot be said to form part of a network that is coordinated, or in a strict sense part of any hierarchy. Where a hierarchical element exists, it relates to the position of the Court of Justice as the ultimate arbiter of EU law, to whom the national courts have privileged access by means of the preliminary reference procedure. This may be the reason why the practice of requesting Commission opinions cannot be said to have taken off among national courts, and because the CJEU does not hear appeals from national courts, the controls in the system are partially indirect and have to percolate through the system by means of the NCAs and the Commission.

[93] Case C-500/06 *Corporación Dermoestética SA v To Me Group Advertising Media* [2008] ECR I-5785; Case C-169/07 *Hartlauer Handelsgesellschaft mbH v Wiener Landesregierung and Oberösterreichische Landesregierung* [2009] I-1721; Opinion of AG Poiares Maduro, in Joined Cases C-570/07 and C-571/07 *José Manuel Blanco Pérez and María del Pilar Chao Gómez* [2010] I-4629, paras 20ff.

[94] Case C-344/98 *Masterfoods*, above (n 11).

At the same time, there are substantive developments at EUI level such as the marginalization of marginal review and a shift from controlling administrative discretion towards protecting individual rights. Here at national level, the national procedural rules are normally pre-eminent, provided the requirements of effectiveness and equivalence are respected. Early attempts at comparative work on such issues reveal that there is a significant degree of convergence, although it is not always readily explained.[95]

Finally, the post-modernization system of EU competition law can be described as seeking to combine substantive coherence with national procedural autonomy.[96] Yet where the two clash, the tendency is for national procedural autonomy to give way, as in the case of the Damages Directive, even where this corrects the case law of the CJEU which had favoured private damages claims over leniency applications.

As we have seen in previous chapters, in *Schenker*[97] and *VEBIC* (2010)[98] the effectiveness of EU law has called for minimum standards over respect for national procedures that were perceived as falling short. More generally the CJEU has tended to protect the Commission's powers even where they have not yet been used in practice, such as that to take negative decisions under Article 10 of Regulation 1/2003 in *Tele2 Polska* (2011)[99] and again in *Schenker* (with regard to Article 102 and 101 TFEU).[100] Thus the modernization framework is being fleshed out both in the case law and in new legislation.

As regards the general trend of EU competition law, given the standards applied in the recent case law of the CJEU, it may be doubted whether this still reflects the effects based new economic approach and its focus on consumer welfare, but it is not clear what has replaced this approach, which at least had the advantage of being consistent from an economic point of view. The provisional answer appears to be a more rule-based system of competition law enforcement whereby object infringements play a dominant role. It remains an open question whether this approach can provide effective and legitimate guidance leading to a (more) coherent application of EU competition law.

95 Essens *et al.* (n 8).

96 Commission staff working paper accompanying the Communication from the Commission, Report on the functioning of Regulation 1/2003, SEC(2009) 574 at 61.

97 Case C-681/11 *Schenker*, above (n 30).

98 Case C-53/03 *Synetairismos Farmakopoion Aitolias & Akarnanias (Syfait) and Others v GlaxoSmithKline plc and GlaxoSmithKline AEVE* [2005] ECR I-4609; Case C-439/08 *Vlaamse federatie van verenigingen van Brood- en Banketbakkers, Ijsbereiders en Chocoladebewerkers (VEBIC) VZW* [2010] ECR I-12471.

99 Case C-375/09 *Prezes Urzędu Ochrony Konkurencji i Konsumentów v Tele2 Polska sp. z o.o., devenue Netia SA* [2011] I-3055, para 28, with regard to Article 102 TFEU; Case C-681/11 *Bundeswettbewerbsbehörde, Bundeskartellanwalt Schenker & Co et al*, Judgment of 18 June 2013, para 42 with regard to Article 101 TFEU.

100 Case C-681/11 *Schenker*, above (n 30).

VIII

Mergers, State Aid, and Services of General Economic Interest

1. Introduction

I have thus far discussed the different dimensions of EU antitrust law, in particular following its modernization in 2004. In the current chapter I will look at the two remaining instruments of general (as opposed to sectoral) EU competition law, merger control and State aid control. In addition I will briefly examine the rules on services of general economic interest (SGEIs), which are not so much an instrument of EU competition law as a general exception that may be applied against it. The sector-specific competition regimes for energy and electronic communications are the topic of the next chapter.

The approach taken is the same as that in the prior chapters, albeit that their coverage is here compressed into one chapter and with regard to two instruments (and one treaty-based exception). For each, I will first cover the history and objectives, next the main rules and exceptions, and finally the organization of its enforcement and any relevant aspects of decentralization. The main questions addressed are whether the features of mergers, State aid, and SGEIs are similar or different from those in antitrust, whether we can speak of EU competition law as a whole, and whether we can address it as a coherent whole that is larger than the sum of its parts.

2. Mergers

General context

The EU Treaties themselves do not provide a regime for merger control. Instead, this was introduced at EU level in 1989 (and reformed in 2004) based on a Council regulation. It is thus contained in secondary legislation: presently Merger control Regulation 139/2004.[1] This regulation provides a relatively extensive procedural

[1] Council Regulation (EC) No 139/2004 of 20 January 2004 on the control of concentrations between undertakings, OJ 2004, L 24/1.

framework inter alia because merger control must take place within tight deadlines. The objective is to prevent mergers between hitherto independent undertakings that generate a significant lessening of competition in the internal market, in particular, by creating a dominant position. The latter are prohibited as incompatible with the internal market. We will discuss this test in more detail later in this chapter. Today merger control takes place *ex ante*, and is based on prior notification and a clearance system provided certain turnover thresholds are met.

Ex ante control and notification are reminiscent of antitrust procedures prior to modernization, while the criterion of compatibility with the internal market is the same as that used in antitrust as well as in State aid control. The centralized notification of cases to the European Commission that was abolished for antitrust as part of the modernization under Regulation 1/2003 has been maintained for merger control as well as for State aid, including (in both cases) a standstill requirement.[2] The latter means that (with limited exceptions) a merger that meets the thresholds may not be implemented, nor may aid be granted pending a clearance by the European Commission. So far uniquely in EU competition law, merger procedures are characterized by fatal deadlines. This is necessary because mergers are frequently dependent on external financing with a limited window of opportunity. This means that not observing short deadlines would mean killing most mergers, irrespective of their merits.

The turnover thresholds are far above the *de minimis* cut-off for antitrust. Moreover, national competition authorities (NCAs) are not authorized to apply the Merger control Regulation: at national level, merger control is wholly governed by applicable national law, although sometimes based on the EU rules as a result of spontaneous harmonization. There are provisions for delegating mergers with a significant national dimension to the EU and mergers with a significant EU dimension to the national level (if the effects are felt predominantly in the Member State concerned).[3] With these exceptions (and aside from some soft law cooperation based on a Merger Working Group of NCAs)[4] the system of EU merger control is centralized in the hands of the Commission. It is based explicitly on the objective of providing a one-stop-shop, and implicitly on the need for a policy that is relatively neutral with regard to national industrial policy concerns within the EU.

The Commission has on occasion been accused of pursuing EU industrial policy goals itself in other areas of competition law and some of its recent communications explicitly frame certain aspects of competition law in this context: for

[2] Council Regulation (EC) No 1/2003 of 16 December 2002 on the implementation of the rules on competition laid down in Articles 81 and 82 of the Treaty, OJ 2003, L1/1; Commission Regulation (EC) No 773/2004 of 7 April 2004 relating to the conduct of proceedings by the Commission pursuant to Articles 81 and 82 of the EC Treaty, OJ 2004, L123/18.

[3] See Commission Notice on Case Referral in respect of concentrations, OJ 2005 C 56/2, and European Competition Authorities (ECA), Principles on the application, by National Competition Authorities within the ECA, of Articles 4(5) and 22 of the EC Merger Regulation, January 2002.

[4] EU Merger Working Group, Best practices on cooperation between EU National Competition Authorities in merger review, 8 November 2011.

instance the State aid rules in the context of the agenda entitled Europe 2020.[5] However, the Commission clearly signalled that competition would prevail over industrial policy in *Aerospatiale-Alenia/de Havilland*,[6] the first merger it blocked in the 1991, the first year of operation of the original Merger control Regulation.[7] Since then particularly United States' firms have been critical when their mergers were subject to conditions[8] or blocked,[9] but so far no EU industrial policy based on strategic use of its merger control has emerged.

Objectives

Rephrased in general terms, the aim of merger control is to ensure that industrial restructuring takes place in the interest of the internal market without causing substantial damage to competition. The objective can therefore be seen as safeguarding competitive market structures, however Article 2(1) of the 2004 Merger control Regulation does specify that in making its appraisal the Commission shall take into account

> (a) the need to maintain and develop effective competition within the common market in view of, among other things, the structure of all the markets concerned and the actual or potential competition from undertakings located either within or outwith the Community; (b) the market position of the undertakings concerned and their economic and financial power, the alternatives available to suppliers and users, their access to supplies or markets, any legal or other barriers to entry, supply and demand trends for the relevant goods and services, the interests of the intermediate and ultimate consumers, and the development of technical and economic progress provided that it is to consumers' advantage and does not form an obstacle to competition.[10]

In the 2004 Merger control Regulation this is still linked with Articles 3(1)g EC on undistorted competition in the internal market and Article 4(1) EC on the principle of an open market economy with free competition. As we know only the internal market based ground has survived in the Treaty on the Functioning of the European Union (TFEU). Below the more precise wording of the legal standard that is applied will be examined. However, I will first look at the emergence of merger control as an instrument of EU competition policy.

Merger control under Articles 85 and 86 EEC (now Articles 101 and 102 TFEU)

Unlike under the European Coal and Steel Community (ECSC) established by the 1951 ECSC Treaty, merger control was not originally foreseen in the

[5] Commission Communication, Europe 2020: a strategy for smart, sustainable and inclusive growth, COM(2010) 2020, 3 March 2010.

[6] Case M.23 *Aerospatiale-Alenia/de Havilland* [1991] OJ L334/42. G. Monti, *EC competition law* (Cambridge University Press, 2007) at 6ff.

[7] Council Regulation (EEC) No 4064/89 of 21 December 1989 on the control of concentrations between undertakings, OJ 1989, L395/1.

[8] Case M.877 *Boeing/McDonnell Douglas* [1997] OJ L336/16.

[9] Case M.2220 *General Electric/Honeywell* [2004] OJ L48/1.

[10] Council Regulation 139/2004, above (n 1).

European Economic Community context. The main reason for this was national industrial policy. Unlike the rest of the national economies, the coal and steel sectors were governed by a supranational authority and market structure was a key concern. For all other sectors, however, the Member States wished to retain control over the process of industrial mergers, which they saw as a way of promoting the emergence of their own national champions. In addition, national merger control helped to keep unwanted cross-border takeovers at bay, again protecting domestic industry. For international undertakings this was a serious concern because it meant having to submit merger filings under the shadow of national industrial policies in every jurisdiction in the EU that was affected by a particular transaction.

Eventually the Commission began to claim merger vetting powers, albeit initially based on its existing *ex post* competencies, first under Article 86 EEC (now Article 102 TFEU) in the 1973 *Continental Can* case,[11] and next under Article 85 EEC (now Article 101 TFEU) as well in the 1987 *Philip Morris* case.[12] In *Continental Can*, the Court ruled that Article 86 EEC covered not only behavioural abuses by dominant undertakings (such as excessive pricing or refusal to deal) but also structural abuses such as monopolizing the market by merging with a key competitor and thereby compromising the market structure as such.

> Abuse may…occur if an undertaking in a dominant position strengthens such position in such a way that the degree of dominance reached substantially fetters competition, i.e. that only undertakings remain in the market whose behaviour depends on the dominant one.[13]

Although important as a position of principle, it is clear that from a practical perspective, waiting for a merger to have the abovementioned results and then trying to address them is problematic. This is all the more so in the absence of clear-cut powers to impose structural remedies: the power to force the undertakings concerned to undo their merger.

The same objections hold with regard to the approach taken in *Philip Morris*. Here in 1987 the Court confirmed the Commission's finding that taking a minority stake in a competing undertaking could form a restraint on competition (although on the facts this was found not to be the case). Possibly the objections are even stronger here because in this case there was no clear requirement of dominant market power to begin with. In any event, *ex post* control of mergers by definition creates much more uncertainty than *ex ante* controls. Moreover, the remedies involved are so intrusive (divestment under duress, also called 'unscrambling the omelette') that they would be difficult to apply except in the most

[11] Case 6-72 *Europemballage Corporation and Continental Can Company Inc. v Commission* [1973] ECR 215.

[12] Joined cases 142 and 156/84 *British-American Tobacco Company Ltd and R. J. Reynolds Industries Inc. v Commission* [1987] ECR 4487. See K. Banks, 'Mergers and partial mergers under EEC law', *Fordham International Law Journal* 11 (1987) 255–309.

[13] Case 6/72 *Continental Can*, above (n 11), para 26.

extreme cases, even if it were agreed that the Commission implicitly possessed such powers in the first place. There were also fears that this new case law would become a self-fulfilling prophecy: now that the Commission had been handed a hammer, every potential competition problem might start to look like a nail.

These objections were combined with a realization that even national champions must on occasion be able to merge across national borders if they are to compete regionally or even globally. In addition, there was widespread desire among international undertakings for a one-stop-shop for mergers of a certain size in order to reduce both the regulatory burden and the risk of political interference. Together, these factors allowed new proposals for an EU merger regulation to emerge and eventually succeed almost twenty years after *Continental Can* when the idea had first been mooted, but only two years after *Philip Morris*.

The original Merger control Regulation

In 1989, the Council finally adopted a specific EU-level instrument for merger control by the European Commission, the Merger control Regulation.[14] This development fit in with the 1992 internal market drive fuelled by the Single European Act (1986) which streamlined decision-making on harmonization legislation. The idea was that undertakings of a European scale would use the EU as their home market in global competition with (predominantly) US and Asian firms. The idea of national champions (as opposed to EU champions) had become discredited in the area of merger control, as were subsidy races that rendered little practical result in the context of State aid, at least in theory.

The thresholds

The Merger control Regulation was—and remains—based upon one-stop-shop merger vetting for transactions that meet a set of turnover thresholds. These thresholds, which are complex and comprise two relevant alternatives, are as follows.

The first alternative requires:

- a combined worldwide turnover of all the merging firms over €5,000 million, and
- an EU-wide turnover for each of at least two of the firms over €250 million.

The second alternative requires:

- a worldwide turnover of all the merging firms over €2,500 million, and
- a combined turnover of all the merging firms over €100 million in each of at least three Member States,
- a turnover of over €25 million for each of at least two of the firms in each of the three Member States included under (ii), and
- EU-wide turnover of each of at least two firms of more than €100 million.

[14] Council Regulation (EEC) No 4064/89, above (n 7).

In both alternatives, an EU dimension is not reached if all the firms involved achieve more than two-thirds of their EU-wide turnover within one and the same Member State.[15]

The merger review process occurs before the merger can be carried out and, as mentioned earlier, involves a notification requirement (like its equivalent under Article 85(3) EEC at the time) and a standstill requirement (both like its equivalent under State aid clearance under Article 107(3) TFEU even today).

The applicable procedural and substantive rules are mixed: thus mergers of an EU dimension must be notified and may not be carried out prior to receiving clearance from the Commission in either of two stages: a first phase of one month (twenty-five working days) to assess whether there are serious doubts, which is followed in the latter case by a further second phase of three months (ninety working days) to assess whether the objections are serious enough to block the merger or whether it is nevertheless compatible with the internal market. Based on past evidence, only about 5 per cent of mergers tend to go on to second-phase investigation, and only 0.5 per cent (or 1 in 200) are blocked, although larger numbers are approved only subject to conditions or are simply withdrawn by the notifying parties if it looks as though they might be blocked.[16] If these deadlines are not met the merger is cleared by default: the deadlines are fatal.

The substantive test

The relevant substantive rule (which, as we shall see, has been modified since then) was whether, as a result of the merger, there is a significant impediment to effective competition, in the common market or in a substantial part of it, in particular as a result of the creation or strengthening of a dominant position. In principle, market definition is key to determining whether dominance might occur and a great deal of energy is dispensed identifying myriad product and geographical markets that may be involved.[17] However, in the end, in some 70 per cent of merger cases, the markets are left undefined because even the most restrictively defined market would not result in competition concerns.[18]

The test imposed combined the notions of dominance and of effective competition:

> a concentration which creates or strengthens a dominant position as a result of which effective competition would be significantly impeded in the common market or in a substantial part of it shall be declared incompatible with the common market.[19]

[15] Summary provided on <http://ec.europa.eu/competition/mergers/procedures_en.html>.

[16] J. Goyder and A. Albors-Llorens, *Goyder's EC Competition Law*, 5th edn. (Oxford: Oxford University Press, 2009) 407 (figures for 1991–2008).

[17] Commission Notice on the definition of the relevant market for the purposes of Community competition law, OJ 1997, C372/5.

[18] Goyder (n 16), at 416.

[19] Regulation 4064/89, above (n 7), Article 1(3).

The Merger control Regulation was accompanied by a suite of implementation measures and guidance detailing the various aspects of the test and of notification requirements in order to create a process that would be as smooth as possible. The objective was to enforce the newly claimed jurisdiction without creating barriers that would frustrate business initiatives. A dedicated and elite merger taskforce of lawyers and economists working together in case teams was created within DG Competition (then DG IV) to ensure that the Commission met its fatal deadlines. Merger control soon became the Commission's first experience of consistently efficient and (at least initially) successful administration of competition law, to widespread acclaim from the business world. In large part the positive reaction from business may be accounted for by the fact that multiple and unpredictable national notifications were now replaced by the one-stop-shop at EU level which was considered as both more impartial and more professional.

Modern merger review

After almost fifteen years of practical application, merger control was reviewed with a new Merger control Regulation, largely along similar lines but based on a more sound economic approach, which was adopted in 2004.[20] In part, this reform can be explained by three cases where the Commission's had overreached itself with findings of incompatibility with the internal market (a rare event in itself) that were successively overturned by the General Court in 2002 in the *Airtours*, *Schneider*, and *Tetra Laval* cases.[21] As we have already seen in Chapter VII, in particular the *Tetra Laval* case appeared to establish a new and far stricter standard review of the economic evidence presented in merger cases.[22] On final appeal to the Court of Justice, the *Schneider/Legrand* case even resulted in the Commission having to pay compensation for the part of the damages suffered by *Schneider* when its merger was unjustifiably blocked.[23]

The 2004 Merger control Regulation review included a further refinement of the turnover thresholds that determined jurisdiction. In parallel, the merger taskforce was disbanded and merger cases were distributed across sectoral directorates also dealing with antitrust cases. A Chief Economist assisted by a team of specialized academics mostly with a PhD in economics was introduced as well as the vetting of draft decisions by Competition Directorate-General of the Commission (DG COMP) staff who had not been associated with handling the case (called

[20] Council Regulation (EC) No 139/2004, above (n 1).

[21] Case T-342/99 *Airtours plc v Commission* [2002] ECR II-2585; Case T-77/02 *Schneider Electric SA v Commission* [2002] ECR II-4201; Case T-80/02 *Tetra Laval BV v Commission* [2002] ECR II-4519. A negative clearance was overturned by the General Court but upheld by the Court of Justice in Case T-464/04 *Independent Music Publishers and Labels Association (Impala, association internationale) v Commission* [2006] ECR II-2289; Case C-416/06 P *Bertelsmann AG and Sony Corporation of America v Independent Music Publishers and Labels Association (Impala)* [2008] ECR I-4951.

[22] C-12/03 P *Commission v Tetra Laval* [2005] ECR I-987, para 39.

[23] Case C-440/07 P *Commission v Schneider Electric SA* [2009] ECR I-6413.

the fresh pair of eyes and/or devil's advocate procedure). These changes applied to all competition cases, not just mergers, and including antitrust and State aid. In addition, the independent role of the hearing officer was reinforced.[24] Internal controls were thus increased.

A further important structural change was that the standard for blocking a merger was amended. The earlier elements of impeding effective competition and of dominance were in effect reversed in the definition, to now read as follows:

> a concentration which would significantly impede effective competition, in the common market or in a substantial part of it, in particular as a result of the creation or strengthening of a dominant position, shall be declared incompatible with the common market.[25]

The main objective behind this change was to facilitate tackling coordinated and non-coordinated effects that fell short of the creation of dominance, but that did significantly impede effective competition.[26] This would involve coordinated effects, vertical effects, and conglomerate effects. Given how the Commission had previously struggled even with the comparatively straightforward concept of collective dominance (the reason behind one its 2002 defeats before the General Court, *Airtours*),[27] this seems a heroic but unrealistic ambition (falsely suggesting a degree of analytical accuracy that is in fact unattainable), even if it could be justified on technical economic grounds.

The two main categories are as follows; (i) uncoordinated (or unilateral) anticompetitive effects that are generally due to a single firm creating or increasing its dominance are distinguished from (ii) coordinated effects that are generally due to joint (also called collective) dominance.

The former category is straightforward, apart insofar as uncoordinated anticompetitive effects that do not involve the creation or extension of a position of single firm dominance (everything else remaining so far only a theoretical possibility).[28] The main addition in relation to the earlier test is that now mergers between the second and third undertaking active in a particular market, without attaining single dominance, might be blocked. This is so if the result could be anticompetitive, such as price rises due to the small number of parties remaining in the market.[29]

[24] Commission Decision 2001/462/EC, ECSC of 23 May 2001 on the terms of reference of hearing officers in certain competition proceedings; OJ 2001, L162/21; now Decision 2011/695 of the President of the European Commission of 13 October 2011 on the function and terms of reference of the hearing officer in certain competition proceedings, OJ 2011, L 275/29.

[25] Council Regulation 139/2004, above (n 1), Article 2(3).

[26] Guidelines on the assessment of horizontal mergers under the Council Regulation on the control of concentrations between undertakings, OJ 2004, C31/5, at para 24ff.

[27] The terms were eventually clarified by the General Court in Case T-342/99 *Airtours*, above (n 21).

[28] However, the Commission does not exclude such effects arising due to the unilateral reactions of other firms in oligopolistic markets. Guidelines on the assessment of horizontal mergers under the Council Regulation on the control of concentrations between undertakings, OJ 2004, C31/5, para 25.

[29] Goyder (n 16), at 405.

The latter category concerns the creation of collective dominance. Since the General Court's 2002 *Airtours* decision, this requires (a) market transparency, (b) the absence of a threat of market entry, and (c) the existence of an enforcement mechanism.[30] It is clear that these conditions would also be conducive to cartelization.[31] Other categorizations are horizontal mergers versus vertical mergers, which are generally believed to be less problematic and more likely to deliver efficiencies, as well as conglomerate mergers across markets for products that are not directly related. The Commission has issued guidance for both types: horizontal and non-horizontal.[32]

Recent developments

More recently, the Commission has issued a White Paper on merger reform (2014) proposing further review powers, notably with regard to non-controlling minority share holdings.[33] Within the EU, powers to review such cases already exist in Austria, Germany, and the UK. The Commission has two theories of harm with regard to non-controlling minority shareholdings, both of which would in general require that the transaction concerned significantly raises market power. The first is that such transactions can lead to unilateral increases in prices or restrictions in output. A second concern is that a minority shareholding may be used in a coordinated manner by increasing a market participant's ability to coordinate tacitly or explicitly. The new norm proposed in the Commission's 2014 White Paper is that of a 'competitively significant link'. This is based on stakes in a competitor or vertically related undertaking around 20 per cent or between 5 per cent and 20 per cent in the presence of additional factors (such as a de facto blocking majority). This would trigger an obligation to submit an information notice to the Commission. At the same time, a *sui generis* procedure with relatively long lead times (such as four to six months) is proposed for such cases. Needless to say, such a change, if effected by an amendment of the Merger control Regulation, would considerably increase the Commission's reach.

Apart from this major substantive change, the proposals set out in the White Paper also seek to streamline (in general) the referrals of merger cases between the NCAs and the Commission. This process is also intended to involve increased information exchange regarding merger cases between NCAs.

[30] Case T-342/99 *Airtours*, above (n 21). See G. Monti, 'The Scope of Collective Dominance under Articles 82 EC', *Common Market Law Review* 38 (2001) 131–57. Confirmed by the Court of Justice in Case C-413/06 P *Bertelsmann AG and Sony Corporation of America v Independent Music Publishers and Labels Association (Impala)* [2008] ECR I-4951.

[31] Cf. F. Castillo de la Torre, 'Evidence, proof and judicial review in cartel cases', *World Competition* 32 (2009) 505–78.

[32] Guidelines on the assessment of horizontal mergers (n 26); Guidelines on the assessment of non-horizontal mergers under the Council Regulation on the control of concentrations between undertakings, OJ 2008, C265/6.

[33] White Paper, Towards more effective EU merger control, COM(2014) 449.

Exceptions in mergers

Like the rules on antitrust, the rules regarding mergers allow for an efficiency defence. In addition, merger control allows for a failing firm defence. As far as efficiencies are concerned, the guidance on the assessment of horizontal mergers states:

> For the Commission to take account of efficiency claims in its assessment of the merger and be in a position to reach the conclusion that as a consequence of efficiencies, there are no grounds for declaring the merger to be incompatible with the common market, the efficiencies have to benefit consumers, be merger-specific and be verifiable.[34]

Thus, the test for efficiencies is broadly the same as that under antitrust, and unlike the efficiency test for Article 102 TFEU, consumer benefits are required (although a fair share is not mentioned). For vertical mergers the conditions for an efficiency defence are the same because on this point the rules for horizontal mergers apply, but because these mergers in principle take place between non-competing firms, these conditions are more likely to be met. In practice, however, so far there are few examples of a successful efficiency defence under EU merger law.

The criteria for the failing firm defence are as follows:

> First, the allegedly failing firm would in the near future be forced out of the market because of financial difficulties if not taken over by another undertaking. Second, there is no less anti-competitive alternative purchase (sic) than the notified merger. Third, in the absence of a merger, the assets of the failing firm would inevitably exit the market.[35]

The demands of specificity and necessity are similar here to those we have just seen for the efficiency defence. Failing firm defences too are few and far between.

The main common factor between the merger and antitrust exceptions according to the relevant legal provisions and soft law guidance is that they are efficiency based. For Article 101(3) TFEU, but not for Article 102 TFEU, they require a demonstration that benefits accrue to consumers (albeit not at the level of end users, and therefore also including intermediary producers).[36] This demonstrates a difference with the rules on State aid where, as we will see below, the exceptions require a common EU interest and consumer benefits are not explicitly required.

Jointly the use of the efficiency defence across antitrust and merger control suggests a dimension of coherence that is in contrast with what I have observed in Chapter IV with regard to the more disjointed rule of reason, ancillary restraints, and objective justification exceptions. Nevertheless, Article 21(4) Merger control

[34] Guidelines on the assessment of horizontal mergers (n 26), para 78.

[35] Ibid, para 90.

[36] 'The concept of "consumers" encompasses all direct or indirect users of the products covered by the agreement, including producers that use the products as an input, wholesalers, retailers and final consumers, i.e. natural persons who are acting for purposes which can be regarded as outside their trade or profession.' Communication from the Commission Notice: Guidelines on the application of Article 81(3) of the Treaty, OJ 2004, C101/97, para 84.

Regulation contains a safeguard measure with regard to key national interests, as follows:

Member States may take appropriate measures to protect legitimate interests other than those taken into consideration by this Regulation and compatible with the general principles and other provisions of Community law.

Public security, plurality of the media and prudential rules shall be regarded as legitimate interests within the meaning of the first subparagraph.

Any other public interest must be communicated to the Commission by the Member State concerned and shall be recognised by the Commission after an assessment of its compatibility with the general principles and other provisions of Community law before the measures referred to above may be taken.

This rarely used provision can be regarded as a safety valve that was provided to ensure that Member States support the Merger control Regulation in the knowledge that they would have an exit available when necessary. At the same time, the proportionality of its use is guaranteed by the prior requirement that the Commission must agree, based on the compatibility of the national measures concerned with EU law.

Remedies

Voluntary commitments (albeit sometimes achieved with some arm twisting) and mandatory conditions and obligations are jointly know as remedies. In merger control, remedies play an important role because they enable the Commission to clear transactions with problematic features. In contrast to the practice in antitrust, where behavioural commitments are the norm under Article 9 of Regulation 1/2003, in the merger context there is a clear preference for structural (divestiture of assets) rather than behavioural remedies, although there have been some notable exceptions.[37] For antitrust, Article 7(1) of Regulation 1/2003 states:

Structural remedies can only be imposed either where there is no equally effective behavioural remedy or where any equally effective behavioural remedy would be more burdensome for the undertaking concerned than the structural remedy.[38]

The approach prevalent in merger control is in line both with the case law of the General Court[39] and the Commission's own guidance on this topic. Thus the Commission's Remedies Notice states:

According to the case law of the Court, the basic aim of commitments is to ensure competitive market structures. Accordingly, commitments which are structural in nature, such as the commitment to sell a business unit, are, as a rule, preferable from the point of view of the Merger Regulation's objective, inasmuch as such commitments prevent, durably, the competition concerns which would be raised by the merger as notified, and do not, moreover, require medium or long-term monitoring measures. Nevertheless, the

[37] Case No COMP/M.1795 *Vodafone Airtouch/Mannesmann*, 1 April 2000.

[38] See also recital 12 of Regulation 1/2003, above (n 2).

[39] Case T-102/96 *Gencor Ltd v Commission* [1999] ECR II-753.

possibility cannot automatically be ruled out that other types of commitments may also be capable of preventing the significant impediment of effective competition.[40]

This can be explained by the fact that problematic mergers almost by definition raise issues concerning the market structure, which structural remedies are well placed to remedy, aside from the evident additional benefits in terms of effective monitoring and enforcement. Moreover, the alternative, blocking the merger, is likely to be much worse for the undertakings concerned. In antitrust, structural remedies themselves are perceived as comprising a worst-case scenario. In this setting, imposing infrastructure access, such as to energy or communications networks, forms a half-way house between structural and behavioural remedies.

We now move on to the next and final instrument of general EU competition law to be discussed.

3. State Aid

Historical background

State aid was already illegal under the 1951 ECSC Treaty, and State aid policy forms one of the original competition instruments in the 1957 EEC Treaty, now based on Articles 107 and 108 TFEU.[41] However, due to obstruction by the Member States (which long neglected to enact the necessary enabling legislation), it has only been applied actively since the 1990s.[42] State aid review consists of a clearance system that, like merger control, is concentrated in the hands of the Commission and is based on prior notification and standstill requirements. This can lead to the Commission declaring the aid concerned compatible with the internal market based on Article 107(3) TFEU, or a finding of incompatibility and the obligation to repay the aid.

State aid control is now subject to a modernization effort including a measure of decentralization to national courts which can make findings that State aid exists (or that a block exemption applies) but that cannot provide a clearance based on compatibility with the internal market. This is a handicap that resembles that in antitrust prior to modernization. Another important development was the adoption in 2005 and 2012 of a framework for the clearance of compensation for public service obligations, or services of general economic interest (SGEIs), as

[40] Commission Notice on remedies acceptable under the Council Regulation (EC) No 139/2004 and under Commission Regulation (EC) No 802/2004, OJ 2008, C 267/1, para 15. See C. Cook, S. Frisch and V. Novak, 'Recent developments in EU merger remedies', *Journal of European Competition Law & Practice* 5 (2015) 361–64.

[41] See generally K. Bacon (ed.), *European Union Law of State Aid*, 2nd edn. (Oxford: Oxford University Press, 2013).

[42] Notably Council Regulation No 659/1999 of 22 March 1999 laying down detailed rules for the application of Article 93 of the EC Treaty, OJ 1999, L83/1; Council Regulation (EC) No 994/98 of 7 May 1998 on the application of Articles 92 and 93 of the Treaty establishing the European Community to certain categories of horizontal State aid, OJ 1998, L 142/1.

compatible with the internal market based on Article 106(2) TFEU.[43] The latter will be discussed in a separate section.

Objectives

The original objective of adding the State aid provisions to the EEC Treaty was to prevent counterproductive subsidy races between the Member States, and the resultant distortions of the internal market. More recently, the notions of 'bad aid' and 'good aid' have surfaced, although compatibility with the internal market remains the criterion for exemption: this depends on whether the aid is in line with common objectives of EU interest. It is noteworthy that the case law on the objectives of EU antitrust that was mentioned in Chapter II also covers State aid.[44] This means EU State aid law (as is stated there) 'aims to protect not only the interests of competitors or consumers but also the structure of the market and, in so doing, competition as such'. On this point, antitrust and State aid are therefore fully consistent.

The notion of State aid

Here the rule involved is more straightforward than that on the subject of mergers. It is essentially incorporated in the definition of what constitutes an aid, which is in principle illegal unless covered by an exception, or found to be compatible by the Commission. Provided four conditions are met—(i) a state measure conferring (ii) a selective advantage[45] that leads to (iii) a distortion of competition and (iv) an effect on trade—State aid exists. Unless these criteria are met State aid is prohibited, barring certain exceptions that will be discussed in the following, thus the discussion does not revolve around the question whether aid is illegal but rather about whether a measure constitutes an aid and, at a later stage, whether it is compatible. It has been suggested, however, that under the imputability of the measure to the State, the conformity of Member States' action with the EU

[43] Communication from the Commission on the application of the European Union State aid rules to compensation granted for the provision of services of general economic interest, OJ 2012, C8/4; Commission Decision of 20 December on the application of Article 106(2) of the Treaty on the Functioning of the European Union to State aid in the form of public service compensation granted to certain undertakings entrusted with the operation of services of general economic interest, OJ 2012, L7/3; Communication from the Commission, European Union framework for State aid in the form of public service compensation, OJ 2012, C8/15; Commission Regulation on the application of Articles 107 and 108 of the Treaty on the Functioning of the European Union to *de minimis* aid granted to undertakings providing services of general economic interest, OJ 2012, L114/8.

[44] Case T-168/01 *GlaxoSmithKline Services v Commission* [2006] ECR II-2969, para 118; *Case C-8/08 T-Mobile Netherlands BV, KPN Mobile NV, Orange Nederland NV and Vodafone Libertel NV v Raad van bestuur van de Nederlandse Mededingingsautoriteit* [2009] ECR I-4529, paras 38–39.

[45] See P. Nicolaides, 'New limits to the concept of selectivity: the birth of a "general exception"' to the prohibition of State aid in EU competition law', *Journal of European Competition Law & Practice* 6 (2015) 315–23.

interest can play a role in deciding whether there is aid, rather than whether the aid is compatible.[46]

Determining whether these conditions are met is subject to extensive case law, for instance regarding the question whether an advantage has been conferred. The *Altmark* case (2003), where the CJEU decided that compensation for the provision of public services did not constitute advantage but a *quid pro quo* provided that four cumulative conditions had been met, is a well-known example.[47] The Commission has also issued guidance for cases where the *Altmark* conditions are only partly met but where the measures involved constitute compensation for public service obligations that may be found to be compatible with the internal market under Article 106(2) TFEU.[48]

Under the State aid modernization programme, the notion of State aid is being re-examined.[49] An important issue here is whether economic services provided (at least potentially) in competition by undertakings are involved. Since choices regarding the creation of markets can differ according to political and economic criteria there is by definition no fixed list of non-economic services. However, with the liberalization trends concerning various utilities in the 1980s and 1990s (such as electronic communications and energy, in large part under the influence of EU law), and more recently concerning welfare services (such as healthcare), it is clear that the category of economic services has been steadily growing in scope. Most importantly, the notion of aid involves defining the concept of undertaking, for instance in relation to entities active in the exercise of public powers, the provision of social services such as healthcare, social services, and education, as well as in investment in infrastructure. The implications of this categorization are horizontal across other areas of EU competition law which are likewise predicated upon the use of the concept of undertaking.

It is worth noting, however, that no uniform set of criteria applies across these categories (for instance, education and healthcare), but instead each of these more or less privileged sectors has its own set of criteria. Therefore, some sector-specific

[46] A. Biondi, 'State aid is falling down, falling down: an analysis of the case law on the notion of aid', *Common Market Law Review* 50 (2013) 1719–44 at 1732, citing Case T-351/02 *Deutsche Bahn AG v Commission* [2006] ECR II-1047, see paras 101–2.

[47] Case C-280/00 *Altmark Trans GmbH and Regierungspräsidium Magdeburg v Nahverkehrsgesellschaft Altmark GmbH, and Oberbundesanwalt beim Bundesverwaltungsgericht* [2003] ECR I-7747.

[48] Communication from the Commission on the application of the European Union State aid rules to compensation granted for the provision of services of general economic interest, OJ 2012, C8/4; Commission Decision of 20 December on the application of Article 106(2) of the Treaty on the Functioning of the European Union to State aid in the form of public service compensation granted to certain undertakings entrusted with the operation of services of general economic interest, OJ 2012, L7/3; Communication from the Commission, European Union framework for State aid in the form of public service compensation, OJ 2012, C8/15; Commission Regulation on the application of Articles 107 and 108 of the Treaty on the Functioning of the European Union to *de minimis* aid granted to undertakings providing services of general economic interest, OJ 2012, L114/8.

[49] Draft Commission Notice on the notion of State aid pursuant to Article 107(1) TFEU. Available at: <http://ec.europa.eu/competition/consultations/2014_state_aid_notion/index_en.html>.

distinctions should be made and, as such, the sectors concerned should be analysed separately. Apart from noting that the Commission identifies different criteria as relevant for each sector, here I will only briefly look at public policy and social security because they appear to be the most pertinent examples.

Public policy

The first category that is distinguished is that of entities exercising public powers or acting in their capacity as public authorities.[50] The criteria set out in the case law are whether the essential functions of the state are concerned or the activity is connected to those functions by its nature, aim, and the rules by which is governed. In *SAT* (1994), the Court ruled as follows:

> Taken as a whole, Eurocontrol's activities, by their nature, their aim and the rules to which they are subject, are connected with the exercise of powers relating to the control and supervision of air space which are typically those of a public authority. They are not of an economic nature justifying the application of the Treaty rules of competition.[51]

These criteria are to some extent circular and they do not connect with the notion of economic activity, nor is the potential of for-profit performance of these services discussed. Hence, they do not add up to a bright line for distinguishing such entities.

Finally, in its State aid Notice the Commission appears to signal a new trend based on the 2012 *Compass* case, where the Court held the following:

> In so far as a public entity exercises an economic activity which can be separated from the exercise of its public powers, that entity, in relation to that activity, acts as an undertaking, while, if that economic activity cannot be separated from the exercise of its public powers, the activities exercised by that entity as a whole remain activities connected with the exercise of those public powers.[52]

Thus economic activities can be judged separately from public authority functions. The case law on this topic is still relatively scant,[53] however activities connected only loosely with the exercise of public authority are not ruled out of bounds for application of the State aid rules any longer.

Social security

Solidarity is the overarching category here, comprising a number of sub-criteria which are compulsory affiliation,[54] the pursuit of an exclusively social

[50] Cf. W. Sauter and H. Schepel, *State and Market in EU Law* (Cambridge: Cambridge University Press, 2009).

[51] Case C-364/92 *SAT Fluggesellschaft mbH v Eurocontrol* [1994] ECR I-43, para 30.

[52] Case C-138/11 *Compass-Datenbank GmbH v Republik Österreich*, Judgment of 12 July 2012, para 38, with reference to Case C-113/07 P *SELEX Sistemi Integrati v Commission* [2009] ECR I-2207, paras 72ff. Draft Commission Notice on the notion of State aid pursuant to Article 107(1) TFEU, para 19.

[53] Case 107/84 *Commission v Germany* [1985] ECR 2655, paras 14–15.

[54] Joined cases C-159/91 and C-160/91 *Christian Poucet v Assurances Générales de France and Caisse Mutuelle Régionale du Languedoc-Roussillon* [1993] ECR I-637.

purpose,[55] the non-profit nature of a scheme,[56] the award of benefits independent from individual contributions made and not necessarily proportionate to the earnings of the insured person,[57] and supervision by the State.[58] In that respect, in *Cisal* (2002), with regard to a scheme for accidents at work, the Court held:

> it is clear . . . that the amount of benefits and the amount of contributions, which are two essential elements of the scheme managed by the INAIL, are subject to supervision by the State and that the compulsory affiliation which characterises such an insurance scheme is essential for the financial balance of the scheme and for application of the principle of solidarity.[59]

Although not stated outright, this suggests a criterion of universality similar to that found in the SGEI context.[60] It is important to point out that these criteria are not cumulative but largely indicative in nature.

By contrast, in the social security context, schemes that are classified as economic in nature are held to be optional, supplementary,[61] based on market capitalization (that is to say, proportional to individual contributions made),[62] and for profit.[63] In that regard, one should point out that many schemes combine elements from both lists, making it necessary to determine their nature based on the preponderance of the evidence rather than a single clear test or a limited set of criteria. Thus the profitability criterion is not conclusive. In other words, a degree of administrative and judicial discretion is involved: this leads to questions regarding consistency and legal certainty.

[55] Case C-218/00 *Cisal di Battistello Venanzio & C. Sas v Istituto nazionale per l'assicurazione contro gli infortuni sul lavoro* (INAIL) [2002] ECR I-691, para 45.

[56] Joined Cases C-264/01, C-306/01, C-354/01 and C-355/01 *AOK Bundesverband et al. v Ichthyol-Gesellschaft Cordes, Hermani & Co. et al.* [2004] ECR I-2524, paras 47–55.

[57] Case C-218/00 *Cisal di Battistello Venanzio & C. Sas v Istituto nazionale per l'assicurazione contro gli infortuni sul lavoro* (INAIL) [2002] ECR I-691, para 42.

[58] Joined cases C-159/91 and C-160/91 *Christian Poucet v Assurances Générales de France and Caisse Mutuelle Régionale du Languedoc-Roussillon* [1993] ECR I-637, para 14; Joined Cases C-264/01, C-306/01, C-354/01 and C-355/01 *AOK Bundesverband et al. v Ichthyol-Gesellschaft Cordes, Hermani & Co. et al.* [2004] ECR I-2524, paras 51–55.

[59] Case C-218/00 *Cisal di Battistello Venanzio & C. Sas v Istituto nazionale per l'assicurazione contro gli infortuni sul lavoro* (INAIL) [2002] ECR I-691, para 44.

[60] Cf. eg Case T-289/03 *British United Provident Association Ltd (BUPA), BUPA Insurance Ltd and BUPA Ireland Ltd v Commission* [2008] ECR II-81; Case T-79/10 *Colt Télécommunications France v Commission*, Judgment of 16 September 2013.

[61] Case C-350/07 *Kattner Stahlbau GmbH v Maschinenbau- und Metall- Berufsgenossenschaft* [2009] ECR I-1513; Case C-437/09 *AG2R Prévoyance v Beaudout Père et Fils SARL* [2011] ECR I-1003.

[62] Case C-244/94 *Fédération Française des Sociétés d'Assurance, Société Paternelle-Vie et al. v Ministère de l'Agriculture et de la Pêche* [1995] ECR I-4013, paras 17ff.

[63] Case C-67/96 *Albany International BV v Stichting Bedrijfspensioenfonds Textielindustrie* [1999] ECR I-5751, paras 74ff; Joined cases C-115/97 to C-117/97 *Brentjens' Handelsonderneming BV v Stichting Bedrijfspensioenfonds voor de Handel in Bouwmaterialen* [1999] ECR I-6025, paras 74ff; Case C-217/97 *Maatschappij Drijvende Bokken BV v Stichting Pensioenfonds voor de Vervoer- en Havenbedrijven* [1999] ECR I-6121, paras 64ff.

Effect on trade

The guidelines relating to the effect on trade contained in Articles 101 and 102 TFEU do not apply to State aid, where instead a *de minimis* threshold of €200,000 over three fiscal years has been established.[64] A noteworthy State aid case concerning the effect on trade is *Capital allowances for Hospitals* (2002)[65] in Ireland. Because the benefits for investing in hospital-building projects were available only to private individuals with their economic interest (tax liability) based in Ireland, no effect on cross-border trade was found, even though there was an advantage for the hospitals that benefited from the investments. This is a relatively rare finding because for State aid, as for the internal market freedoms, indirect and potential effects may suffice. Normally there is also only a marginal review of the effect on competition.[66] As the Court of Justice stated in *Libert* in 2013:

> for the purpose of categorising a national measure as State aid, it is necessary, not to establish that the aid has a real effect on trade between Member States and that competition is actually being distorted, but only to examine whether that aid is liable to affect such trade and distort competition.[67]

This also appears to be the line set out in the Commission's 2014 draft Notice on the concept on State aid, even although it attempts to exclude purely internal situations that are of minor economic significance.[68]

Procedure

In broad strokes, State aid procedure is as follows. Like mergers (and, prior to modernization, potentially anticompetitive agreements), State aid measures must be notified to the Commission and are subject to a standstill requirement: they may not be granted prior to a Commission verdict on their compatibility with the internal market. Aid that has been granted in violation of these procedural rules is by definition illegal and must be recovered. Notified aid that is found not to be compatible may not be granted. Again, like merger control the State aid rules have a first and second phase procedure. In the first phase the Commission establishes whether or not it has serious doubts about the compatibility of an aid, which is examined in detail in the second phase if such doubts exist. Unlike in the case of merger control, the State aid procedure is not subject to fatal deadlines, and cases may well take several years before they are completed.

[64] Commission Regulation (EC) No 1998/2006 of 15 December 2006 on the application of Articles 87 and 88 of the Treaty to *de minimis* aid [2006] OJ L379/5.

[65] Decision of the Commission of 27 February 2002 with regard to state aid No 543/2001—Ireland, Capital allowances for Hospitals.

[66] The marginal nature of the effect on overall costs and therefore as a restriction on competition of compulsory supplementary pension insurance came up in Joined cases C-180/98 to C-184/98 *Pavel Pavlov et al. v Stichting Pensioenfonds Medische Specialisten* [2000] ECR I-6451, paras 94–95.

[67] Joined Cases C-197/11 and 203/11 *Eric Libert et al. v Gouvernement flamand*, Judgment of 8 May 2013, para 76.

[68] Draft Commission Notice on the notion of State aid pursuant to Article 107(1) TFEU at 48ff. Available at: <http://ec.europa.eu/competition/consultations/2014_state_aid_notion/index_en.html>. (2014)

The rule of reason and State aid

The central test regarding compatibility under the state aid rules under Article 107(3) TFEU can be seen as nothing other than a rule of reason, tallying the overall score on compatibility or non-compatibility with regard to a variety of permissible (EU-based) objectives as part of a balancing exercise. However, it is different from the rule of reason in antitrust because the question is not whether the balance is pro-competitive or anticompetitive.

In addition, the 2003 *Altmark* rule on public service compensation that is discussed in the section on SGEI similarly comes close to the application of a rule of reason in State aid.[69] The issue here was whether a balancing exercise involving public service benefits versus the applicability of the State aid rules was to be preferred over first catching the public service compensation involved as an aid that could then be regarded as compatible with the internal market. *Altmark* can be categorized more accurately, however, as a case revolving around the boundary issue of whether or not an advantage has been conferred. In practice we now have both systems, with cases meeting the four *Altmark* criteria not regarded as aid and the (arguably more numerous) instances where not all *Altmark* criteria are met being examined as aid that may be compatible with the internal market.

State aid exceptions

The State aid rules have various forms of exceptions: (i) those that are specifically set out in the Article 107(2) TFEU,[70] (ii) those that are based on Article 107(3) TFEU, which is ultimately an open-ended category,[71] as are (iii) those that are based on SGEIs in Article 106(2) TFEU. I will focus on the category of Article 107(3) TFEU, where the Commission may declare certain types of aid as being compatible with the internal market.

In the area of State aid, the concerns that can justify an exception are limited to those that are within the scope of a common EU policy. Topical examples are environmental policy and broadband policy.[72] Thus within the framework of the State aid exception, two EU level objectives (the internal market objective and some efficiency or equity objective) are balanced against each other. In practice, this means that thereby national policies in pursuit of the common EU objective are covered by the exemption. As mentioned earlier, although balancing is

[69] Case C-280/00 *Altmark*, above (n 47).

[70] In Article 107(2) this covers aid that is always compatible aid having a social character (granted to individual consumers), disaster relief, and aid to compensate for the territorial division of Germany.

[71] Article 107(3) TFEU sets out (a) aid to promote economic development, (b) aid to promote the execution of an important project of common European interest or to remedy a serious disturbance in the economy of a Member State, (c) aid to facilitate the development of certain economic activities or of certain economic areas, (d) aid to promote culture and heritage conservation, and (e) other categories of aid specified by a decision of the Council on a proposal from the Commission.

[72] EU Guidelines for the application of State aid rules in relation to the rapid deployment of broadband networks OJ 2013, C25/1; Communication from the Commission: Guidelines on State aid for environmental protection and energy 2014–2020, OJ 2014, C200/1.

involved, it is not the type of rule of reason approach that we have seen in antitrust under Article 101(1) TFEU. There the question is whether, on balance, the agreement is procompetitive, not, as in the exception in Article 101(3) TFEU, is a benefit for consumers required. The requirement that a market failure is being addressed, however, may (at least sometimes) involve those dimensions indirectly.

In a 2009 staff working paper on common principles for an economic assessment of the compatibility of State aid under Article 87(3) EC (now Article 107(3) TFEU), the Commission services have sketched the framework for this assessment as follows:

1. Is the aid measure aimed at a well-defined objective of common interest?
2. Is the aid well designed to deliver the objective of common interest i.e. does the proposed aid address the market failure or other objectives?
   i. Is the aid an appropriate policy instrument to address the policy objective concerned?
   ii. Is there an incentive effect, i.e. does the aid change the behaviour of the aid recipient?
   iii. Is the aid measure proportionate to the problem tackled, i.e. could the same change in behaviour not be obtained with less aid?
3. Are the distortions of competition and effect on trade limited, so that the overall balance is positive?[73]

These steps suggest a procedure that is less efficiency-oriented and more geared toward public policy than the exceptions that we have seen in antitrust and merger control law. Like State aid at large, it also does not concern itself with the consumer interest. Finding a restriction need not involve consumer harm nor need an exception show consumer benefits. This is another important indication that there is no coherent approach to the consumer interest in EU competition policy. Increasingly, however, in the context of State aid clearances in general, and SGEI-based ones in particular,[74] proof of a market failure is required.

> Modernised State aid control should facilitate the treatment of aid which is well-designed, targeted at identified market failures and objectives of common interest, and least distortive ('good aid')...Such aid will best contribute to growth when it targets a market failure and thereby complements, not replaces, private spending...State aid which does not target market failures and has no incentive effect is not only a waste of public resources but it acts as a brake to growth by worsening competitive conditions in the internal market.[75]

Apart from the individual decisions that are taken by the Commission on a case-by-case basis, there are several State aid block exemptions based on the same

[73] Common principles for an economic assessment of the compatibility of State aid under Article 87.3, at 3. Available at: <http://ec.europa.eu/competition/state_aid/reform/economic_assessment_en.pdf> (15 May 2009).

[74] Case T-79/10 *Colt*, above (n 60).

[75] Communication from the Commission to the European Parliament, the Council, the European Economic and Social Committee and the Committee of the Regions: EU State Aid Modernisation (SAM), COM(2012) 209, para 12.

principles[76] which have direct effect and can as such be enforced in national courts.[77] Just as was the case for antitrust preceding its modernization, however, national courts cannot apply the individual exemptions found in the State aid regime (regarding the compatibility or otherwise with the internal market), which severely handicaps their effectiveness.

Note, however, that in the context of the application of the rules on State aid, SGEIs, and public service compensation, the focus is largely on the nature of the funding involved such as the existence of parameters set out in advance, and the existence of a recoupment mechanism for overcompensation. The public interest invoked by the Member State is not as such balanced against the Community interest in upholding the State aid rules and/or the internal market.[78] SGEIs are discussed in detail in the next section.

State aid modernization

The State aid policy of the EU has been in constant reform since the groundbreaking developments of the 1990s when the Council adopted the first implementing regulations. An important example is the 2005 State aid action plan (SAAP),[79] which aimed to align State aid policy with the general economic policy objectives of the (relaunched) Lisbon Strategy, to respond to the 2004 enlargement of the EU and to focus on correcting market failures (in addition to the other objectives of promoting social and economic cohesion, sustainable development and cultural cohesion). With the aim of achieving less and better targeted State aid, the Commission aimed to apply a refined economic approach. The market failures it intended to target were externalities, public goods, imperfect information, coordination problems, and market power. For this purpose the rules were streamlined. The proposals included new rules for simplification and recovery.[80]

In 2012 the Commission launched the even more ambitious EU State aid modernization (SAM).[81] Its stated objectives were (i) to foster growth in a competitive

[76] The most important is the General block exemption regulation (GBER): Commission Regulation (EU) No 651/2014 of 17 June 2014 declaring certain categories of aid compatible with the internal market in application of Articles 107 and 108 of the Treaty, OJ 2014, L187/1.

[77] Commission Notice on the enforcement of State aid law by national courts, OJ 2009, C85/1.

[78] See also the block exemption for SGEIs: 2012/21/EU: Commission Decision of 20 December 2011 on the application of Article 106(2) of the Treaty on the Functioning of the European Union to State aid in the form of public service compensation granted to certain undertakings entrusted with the operation of services of general economic interest, OJ 2012, L7/3.

[79] Commission Communication, State aid action plan, Less and better targeted state aid: a roadmap for state aid reform 2005–2009, COM(2005) 107, 7 June 2005.

[80] Commission Notice on a Simplified procedure for the treatment of certain types of State aid, OJ 2009, C136/3; Notice from the Commission: Towards an effective implementation of Commission decisions ordering Member States to recover unlawful and incompatible State aid, OJ 2007, C272/4.

[81] Commission Communication to the European Parliament, the Council, the European Economic and Social Committee and the Committee of the regions, EU State aid modernization (SAM), COM(2012) 209, 8 May 2012; State aid modernization—a major revamp of EU state aid control, Competition policy brief issue 11, November 2014.

internal market, (ii) to focus Commission scrutiny on those cases that have the biggest impact on the internal market, and (iii) to streamline the rules and decision-making.[82] In seeking to realize these ambitions, the State aid modernization programme comprises several notable elements:

- The linking of State aid control with the economic objectives of the EU and indeed with its industrial policy (albeit a sustainable one). This involves linking State aid with the Europe 2020 objectives[83] and so-called flagships such as achieving the digital agenda for Europe, and support for efficient State support to broadband roll-out.[84] It also means that aid is now linked more with the quality and efficiency of public support ('good aid' versus 'bad aid') rather than just seen as nefarious by definition.
- An ambitious legislative programme including ten guidelines on issues such as research and development (R&D) and innovation, broadband connections, energy, and the environment, and so forth; as well as five Commission regulations to enhance the effectiveness of the instruments and procedures of State aid control.[85] This includes a new *de minimis* rule with broader scope (although largely unchanged thresholds).[86] In addition the new General Block Exemption Regulation (GBER) aims to authorize beneficial horizontal aid without prior authorization.[87]
- Third, starting from the title of the programme ('modernization') there are elements mirroring the modernization of antitrust that culminated in Regulation 1/2003. An example is the stress on effective and uniform application of the relevant Treaty provisions. A notable exception to this point is the Commission's exemption monopoly (the finding of compatibility with the internal market in Article 107(3) TFEU) which is not touched, nor are NCAs empowered to apply the State aid rules. Instead, the solution to decentralization is sought in block exemptions (notably the GBER) that may be applied by the national courts—just as the penultimate solution to similar jurisdictional problems and administrative bottlenecks had been with regard to antitrust—which was ultimately replaced by its more radical form of modernization.

[82] EU State aid modernization, above (n 81), at 3.

[83] Commission Communication, Europe 2020, above (n 5).

[84] W. Sauter, 'Squaring EU competition law and industrial policy: the case of broadband', in J.M. Beneyto and J. Maíllo (eds), *Fostering Growth in Europe: Reinforcing the Internal Market* (Madrid: CEU ediciones, 2014) 255–91.

[85] Competition policy brief, (n 81).

[86] Commission Regulation (EC) No 1407/2013 of 18 December 2013 on the application of Articles 107 and 108 of the Treaty on the Functioning of the European Union to *de minimis* aid, OJ 2013, L352/1.

[87] Commission Regulation (EU) No 651/2014 of 17 June 2014 declaring certain categories of aid compatible with the internal market in application of Articles 107 and 108 of the Treaty, OJ 2014, L187/1.

We therefore note a new contextual embeddedness of State aid, a qualitative change in the applicable rules and convergence with the approach that had earlier been adopted with regard to antitrust, albeit with some limitations and exceptions.

Coherence and state aid decentralization

As part of the State Aid modernization programme, Regulation 659/1999 setting out the rules for the application of the State aid provisions has been modified in several respects.[88] Most importantly from our current perspective, the Commission has obtained the power to submit *amicus curiae* briefs before national courts in order to promote coherence. In Article 23a of the amended Regulation 659/1999 on the cooperation with national courts, this power is stated in almost verbatim the same terms as those that are found on the same topic in Article 15(3) of Regulation 1/2003.

In order to promote consistency, under the other clauses of the same Article 23a of the amended Regulation 659/1999, the Commission is to supply national courts with opinions on demand, again in the same terms as Article 15 of Regulation 1/2003. (There is no similar provision for NCAs, which is logical considering they do not play a role in the administration of state aid control.) Needless to say, these are likely to be the same national courts that are already involved in the decentralized application of antitrust. In addition, given their identical provisions (and similar intentions), the case law of the CJEU on cooperation in such cases will apply across both instruments. So far no examples of requests for opinions have been reported, however the Commission has summarized the application of the State aid rules by national courts by a number of Member States, which is an advance over the non-compliance by the Member States with regard to notifying the antitrust rulings by national courts.[89]

Similarly, in the interest of consistency the Commission is empowered to launch inquiries across sectors of the economy or into particular aid instruments across several Member States (sector inquiries). In addition, the updated Regulation provides for various fining powers in relation to obtaining information directly from undertakings, although information can be requested directly from aid beneficiaries if the Member State concerned agrees. The instruments of State aid and antitrust therefore bear an increasingly close resemblance, similarly to the procedural similarities between state aid and mergers, such as the standstill and notification requirements, and the two-phase procedure. At the same time, EU State aid law has a close relationship with the final topic of this chapter, SGEIs.

[88] Council Regulation (EU) No 734/2013 of 22 July 2013 amending Regulation (EC) No 659/1999 laying down detailed rules for the application of Article 93 of the EC Treaty, OJ 2013, L204/15.

[89] Available at: <http://ec.europa.eu/competition/court/state_aid_judgments.html>.

4. Services of General Economic Interest

The role of SGEIs in the context of competition law

In outline, the EU system of State aid law is binary in nature: either an activity is carried out by an undertaking, providing goods and/or services in a market, in principle for profit and at least potentially in competition, or it is not.[90] The formal public or private status of an entity under national law is not relevant for this distinction, which in State aid law (and indeed EU competition law at large) is made on functional grounds. If undertakings are involved then by definition both the competition and State aid rules apply, whereas if undertakings are not involved, these rules are not relevant.

However, reality is not so black and white. It is also generally not static but dynamic: situations tend to change over time. At the same time, Member States wish to combine the provision of public services for reasons of solidarity with market mechanisms for reasons of efficiency and cost control, therefore the EU regime for SGEIs provides a third alternative by introducing an exception in EU (competition) law for services which are caught by the general rule because they are provided by undertakings. These undertakings are exempted from the competition and the State aid rules (as well as, where relevant, the internal market rules) insofar as this is necessary to carry out a legitimate public service obligation. Any restrictions involved are to be proportionate to this task. It is up to the Member State to designate policy objectives and whether to designate SGEIs, although the Commission has claimed the authority to exercise marginal review with regard to the question whether effective provision of the services in question could have been left to market forces.

> The Commission... considers that it would not be appropriate to attach specific public service obligations to an activity which is already provided or can be provided satisfactorily and under conditions, such as price, objective quality characteristics, continuity and access to the service, consistent with the public interest, as defined by the State, by undertakings operating under normal market conditions. As for the question of whether a service can be provided by the market, the Commission's assessment is limited to checking whether the Member State has made a manifest error.[91]

In the realm of State aid, the topic of SGEIs is primarily concerned with the funding of public services.[92] By providing a practical way of matching the reality of

[90] This section is based on my contribution to H. Hofmann and C. Michaux (eds), *EU State Aid Law* (Oxford: Oxford University Press, 2016). See also W. Sauter, 'The Altmark package Mark II: New rules for state aid and the compensation of services of general economic interest', *European Competition Law Review* 33 (2012) 307–13 and W. Sauter, 'Services of general economic interest and universal service in EU law', *European Law Review* 33 (2008) 167–93.

[91] Communication from the Commission on the application of the European Union State aid rules to compensation granted for the provision of services of general economic interest Text with EEA relevance, OJ 2012, C8/4, para 48.

[92] W. Sauter, *Public Services in EU law* (Cambridge: Cambridge University Press, 2015); L. Hancher and W. Sauter, 'Public Services and EU Law', in C. Barnard and S. Peers (eds), *European*

public services with the requirements of EU competition law, SGEIs can be said to play a role in enhancing the coherence of the latter, ensuring the respect of minimum standards. At the same time, from a more theoretical point of view SGEIs can be said to dilute the application of competition law. The significance of SGEIs as an exception to the EU competition rules has increased especially following the *Altmark* judgment on public service compensation.[93]

History of SGEIs and their legal basis

In general, in the founding 1957 Rome Treaty the rules on SGEIs formed part of a compromise between more free trade-oriented (roughly, northern Europe) Member States and those Member States that continued to favour various forms of state involvement in the economy (roughly, southern Europe). Thus the Treaty, in spite of its overall free trade orientation, not least in terms of its State aid rules, made room to accommodate a degree of State involvement as well. This was set out in what is now Article 106 TFEU which deals with SGEIs as well as special and exclusive rights (legal monopolies). Because the effective bite of the EU competition and State aid law has increased, SGEIs have been the subject of increasing interest over the past ten to fifteen years.

More recently, the SGEI concept has been expanded with an additional Treaty provision in what is now Article 14 TFEU (by the 1997 Amsterdam Treaty), which since the 2009 Lisbon Treaty also includes the power for the European Parliament and the Council to legislate on this topic, according to the ordinary legislative procedure. The Lisbon Treaty has also added Protocol 26 on the broader category of services of general interest (SGIs). The latter cover not only SGEIs but also non-economic social services that are not provided by undertakings (for instance, social services, long-term care, and/or public education). Because they are not provided by undertakings, such non-economic SGIs remain wholly outside the scope of the rules on competition and State aid, but they may be covered by the internal market rules.

It is no coincidence that the SGI Protocol 26 is adjacent to Protocol 27 on the internal market and competition. Jointly they reflected a reorientation away from the norm of free competition that was enshrined in EU law. This happened in response to the perceived dominance of competition as an organizing principle and was intended to weaken or at least contain it. Because the principle of competition

Union Law (Oxford: Oxford University Press, 2014) 539–66; J.L. Buendia, *Exclusive Rights and State Monopolies under EC Law: Article 86 (former Article 90) of the EC Treaty* (Oxford: Oxford University Press, 2000); J. Baquero Cruz, *Between Competition and Free Movement: The Economic Constitutional Law of the European Community* (Oxford: Hart Publishing, 2002); M. Krajewski, U. Neergaard, and J.W. van de Gronden, (eds), *The Changing Framework for Services of General Interest in Europe: Between Competition and Solidarity* (The Hague: TMC Asser Press, 2009); E. Szyszczak and J.W. van de Gronden (eds), *Financing Services of General Economic Interest—Reform and Modernization* (The Hague: TMC Asser Press, 2012); L. Hancher, and P. Larouche, 'The coming of age of EU regulation of network industries and services of general economic interest', in P. Craig and G. de Búrca (eds), *The Evolution of EU Law*, 2nd edn. (Oxford: Oxford University Press, 2011) 743–81.

93 Case C-280/00 *Altmark*, above (n 47).

is deeply embedded in EU law this political ambition appears to have been largely frustrated. Here the focus is on Article 106(2) TFEU and SGEIs.

The regime of Article 106 TFEU

The first paragraph of Article 106 TFEU deals with special and exclusive rights, which are only permissible to the extent that they do not infringe the rules of the Treaty. This provision has been invoked in combination with Article 106(2) TFEU, for instance in the 1997 electricity cases, to justify import and export monopolies for gas and electricity (in the absence of EU harmonization).[94] However, it has been overshadowed by Article 106(2) TFEU, which spells out the Treaty regime for SGEI as follows:

> Undertakings entrusted with the operation of services of general economic interest or having the character of a revenue-producing monopoly shall be subject to the rules contained in the Treaties, in particular to the rules on competition, in so far as the application of such rules does not obstruct the performance, in law or in fact, of the particular tasks assigned to them. The development of trade must not be affected to such an extent as would be contrary to the interests of the Union.

It is clear that this exception regards all rules of the Treaty and must be proportionate to the public interest that is pursued.[95] Because Article 106(2) TEU is directly effective it can be invoked in national courts, however in *Banco Exterior* (1994)[96] and elsewhere, the Court has found that this does not apply in the State aid context. This is because the intention of the Treaty requires that the Commission has a monopoly on awarding exemptions for new aid under Article 107(3) TFEU which equally applies in the application of Article 106(2) TFEU.

The third and last paragraph of Article 106 TFEU empowers the Commission to adopt decisions and directives. Such directives have been adopted in the area of electronic communications, as we will see in the next chapter on sector-specific competition law. More pertinent to the State aid context, there is also a directive regarding transparency of the accounts of public undertakings.[97] The Transparency Directive makes it easier to assess whether State aid has been disbursed to such undertakings. Such Article 106 TFEU directives are rare because they are not subject to the normal legislative procedure by the European Parliament and Council but only to non-binding consultation by these bodies, hence they are vulnerable to charges of inadequate democratic accountability.

[94] Case C-157/94 *Commission v Netherlands* [1997] ECR I-5699; Case C-158/94 *Commission v Italy* [1997] ECR I-5789; Case C-159/94 *Commission v France* [1997] ECR I-5815; Case C-160/94 *Commission v Spain* [1997] ECR I-5851.

[95] W. Sauter, 'Proportionality in EU competition law', *European Competition Law Review* 35 (2014) 327–32.

[96] Case C-387/92 *Banco de Crédito Industrial SA, now Banco Exterior de España SA v Ayuntamiento de Valencia* [1994] ECR I-877, para 17.

[97] Commission Directive 2006/111/EC of 16 November 2006 on the transparency of financial relations between Member States and public undertakings as well as on financial transparency within certain undertakings OJ 2006, L318/17. This replaced Commission Directive 80/723/EEC of 25 June 1980 on the transparency of financial relations between Member States and public undertakings as well as on financial transparency within certain undertakings, OJ 1980, L195/35.

The *Altmark* case and *Altmark* package

In its 2003 *Altmark* judgment the Court of Justice established a set of rules regarding the financing of public services in relation to the State aid rules. More particularly, it specified when payment for the provision of public services was to be regarded as a quid pro quo that fell outside the scope of State aid because no unfair advantage was involved.

In order to meet the *Altmark* conditions:

- First, the recipient undertaking is actually required to discharge public service obligations and those obligations have been clearly defined;
- Second, the parameters on the basis of which the compensation is calculated have been established beforehand in an objective and transparent manner;
- Third, the compensation does not exceed what is necessary to cover all or part of the costs incurred in discharging the public service obligations, taking into account the relevant receipts and a reasonable profit for discharging those obligations;
- Fourth, where the undertaking which is to discharge public service obligations is not chosen in a public procurement procedure, the level of compensation needed has been determined on the basis of an analysis of the costs which a typical undertaking, well run and adequately provided with the relevant means so as to be able to meet the necessary public service requirements, would have incurred in discharging those obligations, taking into account the relevant receipts and a reasonable profit for discharging the obligations.[98]

In practice, however, meeting the fourth condition raises difficulties. Thus, building on this judgment the Commission in 2005 adopted legislation to spell out the *Altmark* conditions for those cases where the efficiency criterion could not be met, so there was aid, which might nevertheless be declared compatible.[99] The new *Altmark* package was adopted in December 2011.[100] The core of the new system is a split between, on the one hand, social services that are subject to a decision, which functions as a de facto block exemption, and on the other hand the utilities sectors that are subject to individual exemptions decisions based on a framework. In doing so the Commission has deftly separated the politically most sensitive sectors from the economically most networked ones, saving its energies for the latter.

[98] Case C-280/00 *Altmark*, above (n 47), para 95.

[99] Commission Decision of 28 November 2005 on the application of Article 86(2) of the EC Treaty to State aid in the form of public service compensation granted to certain undertakings entrusted with the operation of services of general economic interest, OJ 2005, L312/67; Community framework for State aid in the form of public service compensation OJ 2005, C297/4; Commission Directive 2005/81/EC of 28 November 2005 amending Directive 80/723/EEC on the transparency of financial relations between Member States and public undertakings as well as on financial transparency within certain undertakings, OJ 2005, L312/47. Now Commission Directive 2006/111/EC, above, (n 97).

[100] Commission Decision of 20 December 2011 on the application of Article 106(2) of the Treaty on the Functioning of the European Union to State aid in the form of public service compensation granted to certain undertakings entrusted with the operation of services of general economic interest,

SGEIs and coherence

As we have seen in the first chapters of this book, there are several filters for removing public interests from scope of Article 101(1) TFEU altogether, like inherent restrictions in *Wouters* and *Mecca-Medina*,[101] and the concept of undertaking as in *Van der Woude*[102] or in *FENIN*.[103] Especially in the State aid context, a comparable role is played by the exception that is provided by SGEIs.[104] Moreover, using SGEIs can promote coherence as it applies across the EU rules (both concerning competition and, in principle, the internal market).

Finally, under SGEIs, the equity or efficiency objective is taken for granted provided there is an act of entrustment and financial parameters are set out in advance (to justify the *Altmark* criteria and/or State aid requirements). These are also guarantees that a bona fide public interest is involved. The eventual result will be NCAs judging whether these SGEI conditions are met because Article 106(2) TFEU is directly effective (with an exception for State aid clearance).[105]

5. Conclusion

In this chapter I have supplemented the detailed coverage of antitrust of the previous chapters with a more concise treatment of the two remaining general instruments of EU competition law, mergers and State aid (alongside a discussion of the notion of SGEIs). This allows me to conclude this chapter not just with some findings on mergers and state aid but also (to some extent) on the parallels with antitrust.

OJ 2012, L7/3; Communication Commission European Union framework for State aid in the form of public service compensation, OJ 2012, C8/15; Communication from the Commission on the application of the European Union State aid rules to compensation granted for the provision of services of general economic interest Brussels, OJ 2012, C8/4. Draft Commission Regulation on the application of Articles 107 and 108 of the Treaty on the Functioning of the European Union to *de minimis* aid granted to undertakings providing services of general economic interest OJ 2012, L114/8. E. Szyszczak and J.W. van de Gronden (eds), *Financing Services of General Economic Interest—Reform and Modernization* (The Hague: TMC Asser Press, 2012); E. Szyszczak, 'Modernising State aid and the financing of SGEI', *Journal of European Competition Law & Practice* 3 (2012) 332–43; W. Sauter, 'The Altmark package Mark II: New rules for State aid and the compensation of services of general economic interest', *European Competition Law Review* 33 (2012) 307–13.

[101] Case C-67/96 *Albany International BV*, above (n 63); Case C-309/99 *J. C. J. Wouters, J. W. Savelbergh and Price Waterhouse Belastingadviseurs BV v Algemene Raad van de Nederlandse Orde van Advocaten* [2002] ECR I-1577; Case C-519/04P, *David Meca-Medina and Igor Majcen v Commission* [2006] ECR I-6991.

[102] Case 222/98 *Hendrik van der Woude v Stichting Beatrixoord* [2000] ECR I-7111; Case C-350/07 *Kattner Stahlbau GmbH v Maschinenbau- und Metall- Berufsgenossenschaft*, Judgment of 5 May 2009 (nyr).

[103] Case C-205/03 P, *Federación Española de Empresas de Tecnología Sanitaria (FENIN) v Commission* [2006] ECR I-6295.

[104] Case T-289/03, *British United Provident Association Ltd (BUPA), BUPA Insurance Ltd and BUPA Ireland Ltd v Commission* [2008] ECR II-81.

[105] It is worth repeating that in a state aid setting Article 106(2) TFEU is not directly effective because only the Commission can make a finding of compatibility.

Taken as a whole across the various instruments, the EU competition rules themselves (and not just their interpretation) are in a constant state of change. This is even more so if they are studied at the level of the case law. While one instrument, or set of rules, may be stable for a number of years, the other instruments, or sets of rules parts are being amended and subsequently the former has to catch up, or even leapfrog the others. At the same time the rules, at least at the centre of the system of EU competition law enforcement, are administered by the same body, DG COMP. To a lesser extent this also holds for national courts and NCAs. It is therefore not surprising that developments with regard to the various instruments of EU competition policy and the relevant institutional arrangements frequently take the same or similar form and take place in the same sequence.

As far as economic rationalization and internal procedural checks and balances are concerned, it has often been merger control that has led the way with respect to antitrust. Antitrust again has led the way for State aid as regards aspects intended to promote consistency and coherence such as more recently applying sector inquiries and acting as *amicus curiae* in relation to national courts. To some extent, the role accorded to national courts in State aid mirrors that in antitrust (minus the power to apply exemptions). In addition, with regard to shared concepts such as (collective) dominance and methods, notably the efficiency defence, convergence appears to be taking place.

There are also persistent differences between the three instruments. Antitrust is the most developed in terms of decentralized enforcement and cooperation with the NCAs and likely to remain so. This is because national merger control remains an exclusively national competence below the EU merger thresholds, although cooperation and information exchange on best practices is evidently possible. In addition, the rule of reason technique has never played a role in merger control or (as we will see in the next chapter) in the sector-specific context due to the explicit and mandatory procedural framework that is provided there.

State aid control is by definition even more difficult to decentralize than merger control because NCAs are so far not considered to be suitable for policing the economic policies of their own national governments. National courts are better placed to apply the State aid rules but lack the power to grant exemptions, as was the case in antitrust before its modernization. Consequently, solutions applied in State aid such as the use of block exemptions (in a next phase consolidating them) mirror those of antitrust prior to its modernization. The exception that is provided by SGEIs is important especially in the area of State aid. Use of SGEIs can promote coherence more generally because it applies across the competition rules as well as in principle concerning the internal market.

IX

The Sectoral Regimes for Electronic Communications and Energy

1. Introduction

This final substantive chapter concerns sectoral competition regimes in relation to the coherence of EU competition law as a whole. At present there is sector-specific secondary guidance and legislation in place within the framework of general competition law, in particular on antitrust and State aid. This spells out the applicability of the general competition rules for agriculture, insurance, motor vehicles, postal services and transport as well as for the two sectors with which this chapter is concerned, electronic communications (antitrust recommendations and guidelines) and energy (State aid guidelines).[1]

I will not go into detail on this type of guidance or on specific block exemptions under the general competition rules but will restrict myself to discussing electronic communications and energy because they have the most extensive wholly specific sectoral competition regimes. These function in parallel to the application of the general competition rules. To complicate matters, these sectors have also been targeted by the application of the antitrust rules in the context of promoting liberalization. This too I will cover here.

Just as the general competition provisions in the Treaty have been elaborated in secondary law provisions on procedure and guidance, the sector-specific rules for electronic communications and energy as set out in secondary harmonization legislation are extensive and complex. Even insofar as these rules regard competition (which in large part they do not) they consist of regulation: that is to say not of black or white prohibitions but of rules designed to modify the behaviour of undertakings in a particular, more modulated fashion that is open to policy choices.[2] The regulatory intervention involved is also more detailed, for instance

[1] European Commission, *EU Competition Law, Rules Applicable to Antitrust Enforcement, Volume 3: Sector Specific rules, situation as at 1st July 2013* (Luxemburg: Publications Office of the EU, 2013). Available at: <http://ec.europa.eu/competition/antitrust/legislation/handbook_vol_3_en.pdf>.

[2] A.I. Ogus, *Regulation: Legal Form and Economic Theory* (Oxford: Hart Publishers, 2004); R. Baldwin, M. Cave, and M. Lodge (eds), *The Oxford Handbook of Regulation* (Oxford: Oxford University Press, 2010).

in terms of the regulation of semi-permanent pricing for access to network bottlenecks rather than relying primarily on one-off fines for an infringement.

There are three main questions that I want to address in this chapter. As in the prior chapter on mergers and State aid, this condenses the approach in the previous chapters on antitrust.

- The first question is why there are sectoral competition rules for electronic communications and energy and what their relationship with the general competition law is. This will be related to the objectives, rules, and exceptions of the two sectoral regimes concerned.
- A second question is how these regimes are organized at EU and at national level, and what the interfaces are with the organizational structure of standard competition law.
- The third question is how developments in these two sectoral regimes can be squared with general competition law with respect to the overall coherence of EU competition law as a whole.[3]

In the conclusion to this chapter I will get back to each of these issues. With that I hope to have collected all the material that is required to move on to the concluding Chapter X and the overall assessment on the coherence of EU competition law.

2. Electronic Communications

Background of electronic communications harmonization

In this sector, natural monopolies backed up by legal monopolies were long considered to be the norm, however, mutually reinforcing technological and regulatory developments have changed the picture fundamentally. Building on a Court of Justice ruling that the state monopolists involved were undertakings subject to the competition rules,[4] the Commission has abolished the special and exclusive (monopoly) rights involved, broadening the scope for competitive provision by incremental steps. Its tools were two directives based on Article 106(3) TFEU (then Article 90 EC),[5] a provision allowing the Commission to legislate unilaterally regarding services of general economic interest (SGEIs), and special and exclusive rights. The legality of these directives (although they were criticized

[3] P. Ibañez Colomo, 'On the application of competition law as regulation: elements for a theory', *Yearbook of European Law* 29 (2010) 261–306; G. Monti, 'Managing the intersection of utilities regulation and EC competition law', *The Competition Law Review* 4 (2008) 123–45.

[4] Case 41/83 *Italy v Commission (British Telecom)* [1985] ECR 873.

[5] Commission Directive 88/301/EEC on competition in the market for telecommunications terminal equipment (Terminal Directive), OJ 1988, L131/72; and Commission Directive 90/388/EEC on competition in the markets for telecommunications services (Services Directive), OJ 1990, L192/10.

as anti-democratic because the European Parliament and the Council were not involved) was likewise confirmed by the Court.[6]

The use of the liberalization directives based on Article 106(3) TFEU played a significant role in abolishing exclusive and special rights, thereby prodding the Member States into adopting more ambitious harmonization rules that were based on the general harmonization clause Article 114 TFEU (then Article 100a EEC). As a consequence, step by step, the EU was equipped with harmonization rules following standard legislative procedures that promoted competition in the sector, by introducing both sectoral competition rules and sectoral competition regulators. The resulting regime regulating the liberalized provision of telecommunications was created in the early and mid-1990s (followed by significant updates in 2002 and 2009), and culminated in full (services and infrastructure) liberalization by 1998. It consists of a number of harmonization directives.[7] In addition, largely for historical reasons, there is still a 106(3) TFEU liberalization Directive in place concerning special and exclusive rights.[8]

In contrast to the general EU competition rules, the electronic communications regime is applied not by the European Commission but directly and exclusively by the national regulatory authorities (NRAs) that were set up by the abovementioned EU directives.[9] The NRAs, however, are coordinated jointly and indirectly by the Body of European Regulators for Electronic Communications (BEREC)[10] and by the European Commission, thus the Commission has a coordination and intellectual leadership function and is responsible for drafting and proposing the relevant EU legislation but cannot adopt or enforce the relevant rules in electronic communications markets itself.

Significant market power

The competition dimension of this regime is based on the concept of significant market power (SMP) which is equivalent to dominance under Article 102 TFEU

[6] Case C-202/88 *France v Commission* [1991] ECR I-1223; Joined cases C-271/90, C-281/90 and C-289/90 *Spain, Belgium and Italy v Commission* [1992] ECR I-5833.

[7] Directive 2009/136/EC of the European Parliament and of the Council of 25 November 2009 amending Directive 2002/22/EC on universal service and users' rights relating to electronic communications networks and services, Directive 2002/58/EC concerning the processing of personal data and the protection of privacy in the electronic communications sector and Regulation (EC) No 2006/2004 on cooperation between national authorities responsible for the enforcement of consumer protection laws, OJ 2009, L337/11; Directive 2009/140/EC of the European Parliament and of the Council of 25 November 2009 amending Directives 2002/21/EC on a common regulatory framework for electronic communications networks and services, 2002/19/EC on access to, and interconnection of, electronic communications networks and associated facilities, and 2002/20/EC on the authorisation of electronic communications networks and services, OJ 2009, L337/37.

[8] Commission Directive 2002/77/EC of 16 September 2002 on competition in the markets for electronic communications networks and services, OJ 2002, L249/21.

[9] P. Nihoul and P. Rodford, *EU Electronic Communications Law: Competition and Regulation in the European Telecommunications Market*, 2nd edn. (Oxford: Oxford University Press, 2011).

[10] Regulation (EC) No 1211/2009 of the European Parliament and of the Council of 25 November 2009 establishing the Body of European Regulators for Electronic Communications (BEREC) and the Office, OJ 2009, L337/1.

but does not require proof of abusive behaviour and is applied *ex ante* to promote market making (not *ex post* to remedy abuse). It also involves a panoply of remedies primarily geared towards promoting third party access.

The approach to effective competition within this framework is remarkable: according to Article 16(4) of the Framework Directive in the absence of effective competition an operator enjoying SMP must be identified.[11] An absence of effective competition is therefore equated with the existence of SMP. The draconian nature of this system is modified by the three conditions that must be met before market definition is carried out: the markets concerned must be characterized by high barriers to entry, must not autonomously tend toward competition in the medium future, and the application of general competition rules would not suffice (for instance because its requirements are not met).

The reason such intervention is needed is that vertically integrated incumbent operators which are former legal monopolists continue to dominate many electronic communications markets even although they have been formally liberalized. Product and services markets are predefined by the Commission, while geographic market definition, dominance assessment, and remedies are in the hands of the NRAs, subject to the coordination mechanisms cited earlier.

Objectives of electronic communications harmonization

Originally at the most general level the broad objectives of electronic communications legislation were twofold: (i) liberalization, or opening markets and moving from monopoly to full competition, and (ii) harmonization, or setting common standards in order to achieve the internal market. This means that achieving effective competition as such is one of the main objectives. More recently a third objective of promoting the interests of European citizens has been added.[12] In the end all these goals are intended to promote the emergence of a true internal market in electronic communications, which is in line with the instruments used, that of directives. These are binding with regard to the results to be achieved but leave scope for the manner in which they are implemented in national law (much as is the case with competition remedies).

Universal service and the consumer interest

A key regulatory device that was introduced by harmonization was the concept of universal service. This enabled the Commission to defuse tensions generated

[11] Directive 2002/21/EC of the European Parliament and of the Council of 7 March 2002 on a common regulatory framework for electronic communications networks and services, OJ 2002, L108/33: 'Where a national regulatory authority determines that a relevant market is not effectively competitive, it shall identify undertakings which individually or jointly have a significant market power on that market.'

[12] Already in the 2002 framework but most clearly by 'Citizens' Rights' Directive 2009/136/EC, above (n 7).

by national claims based on solidarity of telecommunications users by providing a way by which users' rights could be substantiated and realized in a liberalized environment.[13] A minimum set of universal services was defined at EU level which could be extended by the individual Member States provided its financing did not create an unequal playing field, for instance by imposing unbalanced charges on entrants to pay for services provided by the incumbent. In a sense this meant that a new constituency was created for liberalization.

Since then, users' rights more broadly have become a new objective of EU electronic communications law at large [14] as well as for the NRAs in particular,[15] albeit not one with direct implications for competition. This does not make it irrelevant for present purposes; rather, it shows a distinction between the general and sectoral rules as regards the way in which the consumer interest is addressed. The same is true for provisions to protect users against unsolicited messages (Spam), to provide number probability, or to protect against price gouging while roaming on mobile networks abroad. Moreover, the prevalence of such policy goals makes it less likely that the general competition rules will ever replace the sectoral competition rules for electronic communications, rather than complementing them.[16]

Access and unbundling in electronic communications regulation

Mandatory access

The conditions for imposing access are the centrepiece of EU legislation concerning electronic communications. They serve to promote competition and the emergence of effective competitors which are expected to climb a ladder of competition. This starts by entrants providing only services based on third party network access, then building a subscriber base and improving their credit rating in order to eventually roll out proprietary networks ever closer to these subscribers, to engage in network-based competition. For this model to succeed these market entrants rely on regulated access to incumbent networks and mandatory interconnection and interoperability between all those networks that control access to

[13] W. Sauter, 'Universal service obligations and the emergence of citizens' rights in European telecommunications liberalization', in M. Freedland and S. Sciarra (eds), *Public Services and Citizenship in European Law: Public and Labour Law Perspectives* (Oxford: Oxford University Press, 1998) 117–43.

[14] Directive 2002/22/EC of the European Parliament and of the Council of 7 March 2002 on universal service and users' rights relating to electronic communications networks and services (Universal Service Directive) OJ 2002, L108/51, as amended by Directive 2009/136/EC, above (n 7).

[15] Directive 2002/21/EC of the European Parliament and of the Council of 7 March 2002 on a common regulatory framework for electronic communications networks and services (Framework Directive), OJ 2002, L108/33, amended by Directive 2009/140/EC, above (n 11), Article 8(4).

[16] Another regulatory topic that is of increasing importance from a user's perspective but largely absent from competition law is privacy: Directive 2002/58/EC of the European Parliament and of the Council of 12 July 2002 concerning the processing of personal data and the protection of privacy in the electronic communications sector (Directive on privacy and electronic communications) OJ 2002, L201/37.

end-users (so as to be able to allow any-to-any communications). Access obligations can be imposed on undertakings that have SMP. As was mentioned above, this is equivalent to the concept of dominance in antitrust but it is determined by national regulatory authorities in an EU-defined and structured procedure.[17]

Using the dominance standard for SMP ensures that there is no needless proliferation of competition standards and could in theory promote the eventual transition from sector-specific regulation to exclusive reliance on the general competition rules.[18] This also reflects how originally much was expected from the general competition rules, although gradually sector-specific rules have become permanent fixtures.

The SMP rules have several peculiarities that are the result of the fact they deal with different interrelated markets. An example is the need to start with analysing the effects on consumers in retail markets but targeting remedies foremost at wholesale level (which is regarded as less intrusive in the framework of market making). Another example is the balance between infrastructure based competition (which is preferred as fundamentally more effective) and services competition, which as has been discussed above is seen as a stepping stone, or tolerated where there are no viable alternatives.

However, bottlenecks and SMP positions have proven to be persistent in electronic communications networks and services and there is even a migration of SMP positions—and of *ex ante* regulation—to wholly new fibre-optic networks. This does not mean that general competition law is not relevant: it is worth noting that concurrent application of general competition law and sector specific rules means that the main recent examples of price squeeze are precisely in the area of electronic communications.[19]

Unbundled network access

Unbundling is a specific form of network access that must be mentioned in particular because as a concept it is also (and arguably even more so) relevant in the context of energy regulation. Within the framework of electronic communications regulation it refers to providing various forms of access to the fixed connection to the end-user, or local loop ('twisted metallic pair'), which was considered a bottleneck that not even an efficient entrant could hope to replicate. (Even although fibre-based networks are now being rolled out to users throughout the EU to provide high-speed Internet access.)

[17] Commission guidelines on market analysis and the assessment of significant market power under the Community regulatory framework for electronic communications networks and services, OJ 2002, C165/6.

[18] Notice on the application of the competition rules to access agreements in the telecommunications sector—framework, relevant markets and principles, OJ 1998, C265/2.

[19] Case T-336/07 *Telefónica, SA and Telefónica de España, SA v Commission*, Judgment of 29 March 2012; Case C-280/08 P *Deutsche Telekom AG v Commission* [2010] ECR I-9555.

Initially imposed via a specific regulation in 2000,[20] unbundling became a mandatory form of access that would have to be imposed on network operators with SMP for fixed electronic communications networks and services that was coved by Annex II of the Access Directive.[21] This form of network access should be distinguished from a more general obligation to offer unbundled services, which is to counter the risk of tying and imposing joint sales of necessary products with unwanted ones—also a discrete type of dominance abuse in EU competition law.[22]

Access in antitrust cases

A crucial fact in the *Deutsche Telecom* (DT) case (2010) was that the German NRA had set wholesale prices for local loop access at a level where an efficient competitor could not cover its costs while competing at the level of the retail prices set by DT, the vertically integrated incumbent. The Court of Justice did not regard the hapless regulatory intervention as a valid defence for DT

> the appellant cannot... rely on the premise that the wholesale prices for local loop access services set by the national regulatory authorities are excessive in order to demonstrate the inappropriateness of the margin squeeze test.[23]

Nor did the Court accept that an increase in prices to remedy the margin squeeze was excluded because it might harm the interests of end-users: instead it pointed to the reduction of choice and the long-term negative price effects which might follow if the exclusionary conduct based on a price squeeze was successful.[24] Effectively we see the Commission correcting not just a dominant operator but also a ham-fisted NRA—or perhaps just one that was overly sensitive to the political undesirability of rebalancing (and therefore in some instances raising) end-user rates. It did so by using the general competition rules to trump the national application of the EU sectoral regime.

In doing so in this regulated context, the Commission takes as a starting point access standards that are significantly removed from the generally steep barrier for access based on the essential facilities doctrine in *Bronner* (1998)[25] and from the

[20] Regulation (EC) No 2887/2000 of the European Parliament and of the Council of 18 December 2000 on unbundled access to the local loop, OJ 2000, L366/4.

[21] Directive 2002/19/EC of the European Parliament and of the Council of 7 March 2002 on access to, and interconnection of, electronic communications networks and associated facilities (Access Directive), OJ 2002, L108/7, as amended by Directive 2009/136/EC and Directive 2009/140/EC, above (n 7).

[22] J. Langer, *Tying and Bundling as a Leveraging Concern under EC Competition Law* (Deventer: Kluwer Law International, 2007).

[23] Case C-280/08 P *Deutsche Telekom*, above (n 19), para 165.

[24] Ibid, paras 181–183. See Case C-202/07 P *France Télécom SA v Commission* [2009] ECR I-2369, para 103–105.

[25] Case C-7/97 *Oscar Bronner GmbH & Co. KG v Mediaprint Zeitungs- und Zeitschriftenverlag GmbH & Co. KG, Mediaprint Zeitungsvertriebsgesellschaft mbH & Co. KG and Mediaprint Anzeigengesellschaft mbH & Co. KG* [1998] ECR I-7791.

case law on access to intellectual property rights like *Magill TV Guide* (1995),[26] *IMS Health* (2004),[27] and on refusal to supply and authorize the use of interoperability information in *Microsoft* (2007).[28] There are thus parallel access regimes under the general and sectoral competition rules which are bridged by cases such as *DT* where general competition law is used to enforce a standard of access that has effectively been set at sectoral level. In the *O2 Germany* case (2006)[29] the General Court has even held that network sharing between competing mobile operators (the most extreme form of access) should be subject to a rule of reason analysis under Article 101(1) TFEU, instead of being regarded as a per se restriction that required clearance under Article 101(3) TFEU.

The hard correction of an NRA error by means of Commission intervention based on general competition law in the *DT* case is an exception, albeit a notable one.[30] Below we will examine how the system of electronic communications regulation generally seeks to achieve consistency on account of the NRAs by more subtle means of coordination.

The role of NRAs and of BEREC in electronic communications

The independence of NRAs has been stressed from the outset of telecommunications reform in the EU.[31] This is because prior to liberalization the regulatory functions at national level tended to be integrated within ministries that covered both the ownership and the business aspects of providing telecommunications and frequently postal services as well. In order to protect competition and indeed competitors it was therefore necessary to ensure not only that NRAs were established as independent entities but also that they were at arm's length from the incumbent and its owner, which at this stage was generally the national government.[32] Thus, NRAs must be legally distinct and functionally independent from operators, and where Member States retain ownership, the regulatory function must be subject to structural separation.[33] As a result, the NRAs are equipped with guarantees of their independence that well exceed those of NCAs in general

[26] Joined cases C-241/91 P and C-242/91 P *Radio Telefis Eireann (RTE) and Independent Television Publications Ltd (ITP) v Commission* [1995] I-743.

[27] Case C-418/01 *IMS Health GmbH & Co. OHG v NDC Health GmbH & Co. KG* [2004] ECR I-5039.

[28] Case T-201/04 *Microsoft Corp. v Commission* [2007] ECR II-3601.

[29] Case T-328/03 *O2 (Germany) GmbH & Co. OHG v Commission* [2006] ECR II-1231.

[30] However see Case C-295/12 P *Telefónica SA en Telefónica de España SAU v Commission*, Judgment of 10 July 2014, para 133: 'the fact that an undertaking's conduct complies with a regulatory framework does not mean that such conduct complies with Article 102 TFEU'.

[31] L. Hancher and P. Larouche, 'The coming of age of EU regulation of network industries and services of general economic interest', in P. Craig and G. de Búrca (eds), *The Evolution of EU Law*, 2nd edn. (Oxford: Oxford University Press, 2011); S.A.C.M. Lavrijssen and L. Hancher 'Networks of regulatory agencies in Europe', in P. Larouche and P. Cserne (eds), *National Legal Systems and Globalization: New Role, Continuing Relevance* (The Hague: TMC Asser Press/Springer, 2013).

[32] Article 3, Directive 2002/21/EC, above (n 11).

[33] Case C-92/91 *Criminal proceedings against Annick Neny, née Taillandier* [1993] ECR I-5383; Case C-69/91 *Criminal proceedings against Francine Gillon, née Decoster* [1993] ECR I-5335.

competition policy, although they go less far than those in the energy sector, as we will see. However, some NCAs do double duty as NRAs, which complicates the picture.

The NRAs are the authorities that BEREC was created in 2009 to represent, replacing an earlier coordination mechanism, the ERG (European Regulators' Group).[34] According to its own mission statement:

> BEREC contributes to the development and better functioning of the internal market for electronic communications networks and services. It does so, by aiming to ensure a consistent application of the EU regulatory framework and by aiming to promote an effective internal market in telecoms sector, in order to bring even greater benefits to consumers and businesses alike.[35]

The internal market thus takes centre stage, and as regards its promotion so does consistency at national level.[36] The latter is of particular interest here, because it is reflected in an EU-wide coordination process. This starts with (i) the Commission predefining product markets (nominally in line with competition law principles, but somehow without recourse to the Small but significant and non-transitory increase in price (SSNIP) test) and setting SMP standards. This is followed by (ii) the NRAs carrying out a market analysis of these predefined markets (as well as any additional ones that they believe are necessary) according to Commission guidelines,[37] and adopting draft SMP designation measures as well as remedies targeted at specific operators. These measures are then (iii) notified to BEREC and the Commission. This is followed by (iv) a BEREC opinion, which can be either positive or negative. It can be backed up by a (v) Commission veto on market definition and SMP findings, and/or a quasi-veto regarding remedies.

The Commission's Framework Directive veto versus taking over the case in antitrust

Apart from the notification system as such, step (v) is of particular interest here because it involves such a strong power of intervention on the side of the Commission for purposes of consistency. The relevant procedure is set out in Articles 7 and 7a of the Framework Directive under the title 'consolidating the internal market for electronic communications', and the objective is the consistent application at national level of this Directive. Article 7 regards a market definition that differs from the predefined set,[38] and SMP designation, in those cases where

[34] Regulation 1211/2009, above (n 10).

[35] Available at: <http://berec.europa.eu/eng/about_berec/what_is_berec/>.

[36] BEREC also aims to promote competition and investment; as well as the internal market; and empower and protect end-users. Ibid.

[37] Commission guidelines on market analysis and the assessment of significant market power under the Community regulatory framework for electronic communications networks and services, OJ 2002, C165/6.

[38] Commission Recommendation of 9 October 2014 on relevant product and service markets within the electronic communications sector susceptible to ex ante regulation in accordance with

this falls within the scope of the regulatory framework and would affect trade between Member States. Here the Commission, 'taking the utmost account of the opinion of BEREC', may require the draft measure to be withdrawn.

Article 7a was only added in the 2009 revision of the Framework Directive and concerns the consistent application of remedies. The criterion here is whether the draft measure creates a barrier to the internal market or raises serious doubts with regard to its compatibility with EU law. In this case, the NRA (following a process where BEREC and/or the Commission may express serious doubts) is ultimately able to resist a negative opinion by the Commission, but only upon providing a reasoned justification. Of course, doing so in the face of Commission and BEREC resistance is likely to work against the NRA in any judicial proceedings at national level—most contested decisions in this sector are challenged in any event and one undermined in this manner certainly would be.

It is difficult to say whether the system established for antitrust by Regulation 1/2003 or the mechanisms of coordination in electronic communications are more extensive.[39] This is so even if in the end the Commission's power to take cases away from NCAs and to decide them on its own account under Article 11(6) of Regulation 1/2003 is more intrusive: instead of merely blocking an undesirable national decision it takes a decision itself. Like the Article 7 and 7a procedure of the framework Directive, the overriding reason that would legitimize such intervention is consistency: the Commission will normally only apply its Article 11(6) powers under Regulation 1/2003 where there is a danger of conflicting decisions in the same case, or a risk of a conflict with established case law, of undue delay, or where there is a need to develop new policy in the interest of effective enforcement.[40]

The actual vetting of national decisions is similar although the antitrust regime lacks a permanent coordinating body like BEREC that systematically analyses each individual decision. Finally, unlike the competition regime for electronic communications, the antitrust regime does not predefine (under the threat of a veto and a quasi-veto) the areas where action should be taken, nor the nature of this action. There is thus no straightforward way to define one or the other procedure as more intrusive.

Electronic communications law and EU industrial policy

All this seems to suggest that the general and sectoral competition rules are ploughing the same furrow. Meanwhile the plot thickens in this sector that was

Directive 2002/21/EC of the European Parliament and of the Council on a common regulatory framework for electronic communications networks and services, OJ 2014, L 295/79. Case C-410/09 *Polska Telefonia Cyfrowa sp. z o.o. v Prezes Urzędu Komunikacji Elektronicznej* [2011] ECR I-3853.

[39] Council Regulation (EC) No 1/2003 of 16 December 2002 on the implementation of the rules on competition laid down in Articles 81 and 82 of the Treaty, OJ 2003, L1/1.

[40] Commission Notice on cooperation within the Network of Competition Authorities, OJ 2004, C101/43, para 3.2.

once seen as emblematic of the EU approach to liberalization: the Member States have started entering the market again in the form of State aid and even public operations in the field of broadband roll-out (creating high capacity communications networks). The debate on the balance between EU competition law and industrial policy is an inconclusive and lengthy one, however electronic communications has often been used as an example to show that the two are compatible provided the objective is promoting structural adjustment and not preventing it.[41]

The limits of State aid policy are being tested also as a result of the EU's own roll-out ambitions with regard to broadband, access to which is frequently regarded as one of the most important indicators of economic development and competitiveness in the context of the EU's Europe 2020 industrial policy objectives.[42] Permissible public investments in broadband are conditional upon providing third party access that will enable the provision of universal service to end-users.[43] Part of the context is the EU emphasis on infrastructure, and infrastructure-based competition as preferable to services as set out in Article 8(5)c of the Framework Directive.[44] Spectrum assignment is another aspect of infrastructure-based industrial policy essential to mobile broadband where both the Member States and the EU have ambitions.[45]

The balance between sectoral and general rules in electronic communications

The interaction between the general EU antitrust rules and the sectoral framework for electronic communications has been discussed earlier with particular regard to access issues. EU merger policy has also played a major role in the liberalization context. This is especially because in 1996 the Commission made approval of the *Atlas* and *Phoenix* strategic mergers by the French and German incumbent

[41] W. Sauter, *Competition Law and Industrial Policy in the EU* (Oxford: Oxford University Press, 1997).

[42] Communication from the Commission of 3 March 2010, EUROPE 2020 A strategy for smart, sustainable and inclusive growth, COM(2010) 2020. W. Sauter, 'Squaring EU competition law and industrial policy: the case of broadband', in J.M. Beneyto and J. Maíllo (eds), *Fostering Growth in Europe: Reinforcing the Internal Market* (Madrid: CEU ediciones, 2014) 255–91.

[43] European Commission, Guidelines for the application of State aid rules in relation to the rapid deployment of broadband networks, OJ 2013, C25/1 (replacing Community Guidelines for the application of State aid rules in relation to rapid deployment of broadband networks, OJ 2009, C 235/7), para 78(g): 'Third parties' effective wholesale access to a subsidised broadband infrastructure is an indispensable component of any State measure supporting broadband.' In the context of SGEIs: 'the SGEI mission should only cover the deployment of a broadband network providing universal connectivity and the provision of the related wholesale access services, without including retail communication services'. Ibid, para 24.

[44] Directive 2002/21/EC, above (n 11).

[45] D. Gabathuler and W. Sauter, 'The allocation of scarce resources and spectrum assignment in mobile communications: the case of UMTS', in P.A. Buigues and P. Rey (eds), *The Economics of Antitrust and Regulation in Telecommunications: Perspectives from the New Regulatory Framework* (Camberley: Edward Elgar, 2004) 213–38.

operators conditional upon their majority owners, the French and German governments, implementing fixed infrastructure liberalization.[46] Consequently (and in the perceived interest of the newly created undertakings), France and Germany naturally came out in favour of liberalization by the other Member States as well, enabling full liberalization by 1998. Another notable merger was *Vodafone/Mannesmann* in 2000, the (conditional) approval of which provided a green light for the formation of pan-European mobile communications groups.[47]

A critical view on the balance between the general and sectoral competition rules with respect to electronic communications would be that the markets concerned have nevertheless remained largely national in nature. Again, with the exception of mobile communications, infrastructure-based competition generally has not been lively or even largely absent. Incumbents remain clearly dominant in most fixed infrastructure-based markets. Meanwhile, as we have just seen with regard to broadband, the Member States themselves are even making a re-entry into the market by means of State aid in a manner that would not have been believable in the heady days of full liberalization. Thus, the initial view that with the passage of time the application of the general competition rules would gradually take over from harmonization, so the latter could be phased out altogether, appears to be a fallacy not just due to the pursuit of non-competition goals but also in terms of promoting competition. I believe this means that parallel application of the sectoral and general EU competition rules to the electronic communications sector is likely to persist indefinitely.

Oddly enough, from a perspective of coherence this may have beneficial aspects. As we have seen in the section on access conditions, the competition rules are used as a backstop and as a tool to reinforce the direction of sectoral liberalization that the Commission believes is desirable. The use of Articles 101 and 102 TFEU also allows it to intervene directly (albeit in selected cases) where the sectoral rules enable only indirect intervention by means of a veto on market definitions and SMP determinations, and a quasi-veto for remedies. At national level the picture is more complex, depending, for instance, on whether the NCA also combines the functions of the NRA, as is the case in some Member States (as in The Netherlands), or whether they have parallel or even concurrent powers under the general competition rules (as in the UK) in other jurisdictions.

As a consequence there are different incentives for cooperation, which in turn have an effect on the relationship with general EU competition law as interpreted by the Commission at the centre. In general terms, however, the two regimes are mutually reinforcing. The result is likely to be a more coherent whole, albeit not without potential frictions.

[46] Case IV/35.337 Atlas, Commission Decision of 17 July 1996, OJ 1996, L239/23; Case IV/35.617 Phoenix/GolbalOne: Commission Decision of 17 July 1996, OJ 1996, L239/57. P. Larouche, *Competition Law and Regulation in European Telecommunications* (Oxford: Hart Publishing, 2000).

[47] Case COMP/M.1795 Vodafone Airtouch/Mannesmann, Commission Decision of 12 April 2000.

3. Energy

Background: Energy networks

As discussed here, the energy sector exclusively concerns electricity (although this derives from a multitude of sources these will not be examined) and gas.[48] As in electronic communications, the energy sector has a sector-specific framework based on EU directives,[49] and regulations.[50] As is the case with electronic communications, it contains competition rules in the shape of third party access regimes to counteract vertically integrated incumbent operators that are enforced by NRAs and unbundling requirements. The NRAs are coordinated by a network-type regulatory body, the Agency for the Cooperation of Energy Regulators (ACER). This regime has been developed in successive steps, or packages, the first in 1996/98,[51] the second in 2003,[52] and the third and most recent one in 2009 (the third energy package).

The system of energy regulation relies on tariffs set by the NRAs that are (or the underlying methodologies of which are) published and applied objectively and without discrimination.

Objectives of EU energy regulation

Energy is the product of scarce resources that has a (geo)strategic as well as a considerable economic value. In addition, there is a significant environmental dimension (global warming, and pollution more broadly), as well as one of social welfare (energy poverty).[53] The original objectives of EU intervention were the

[48] A. Johnston and G. Block, *EU Energy Law* (Oxford: Oxford University Press, 2012).

[49] Directive 2009/73/EC of the European Parliament and of the Council of 13 July 2009 concerning common rules for the internal market in natural gas and repealing Directive 2003/55/EC, OJ 2009, L211/94; Directive 2009/72/EC of the European Parliament and of the Council of 13 July 2009 concerning common rules for the internal market in electricity and repealing Directive 2003/54/EC, OJ 2009, L211/55.

[50] Regulation (EC) No 715/2009 of the European Parliament and of the Council of 13 July 2009 on conditions for access to the natural gas transmission networks and repealing Regulation (EC) No 1775/2005, OJ 2009, L211/36.Commission Regulation (EU) No 838/2010 of 23 September 2010 on laying down guidelines relating to the inter-transmission system operator compensation mechanism and a common regulatory approach to transmission charging, OJ 2010, L250/5.

[51] Directive 96/92/EC of the European Parliament and of the Council of 19 December 1996 concerning common rules for the internal market in electricity, OJ 1997, L27/20; Directive 98/30/EC of the European Parliament and of the Council of 22 June 1998 concerning common rules for the internal market in natural gas, OJ 1998, L204/1.

[52] Directive 2003/54/EC of the European Parliament and of the Council of 26 June 2003 concerning common rules for the internal market in electricity and repealing Directive 96/92/EC, OJ 2003, L176/37; Directive 2003/55/EC of the European Parliament and of the Council of 26 June 2003 concerning common rules for the internal market in natural gas and repealing Directive 98/30/EC, L176/56.

[53] K. Talus, *EU Energy Law and Policy: A Critical Account* (Oxford: Oxford University Press, 2013).

establishment of competitive markets in electricity and natural gas market as important elements of the completion of the internal (energy) market, however even at this stage they were broadly interpreted. Thus:

> Whereas establishment of the internal market in electricity is particularly important in order to increase efficiency in the production, transmission and distribution of this product, while reinforcing security of supply and the competitiveness of the European economy and respecting environmental protection.[54]

In the third energy package of 2009, the objectives of the NRAs were defined to cover

> promoting, in close cooperation with the Agency, regulatory authorities of other Member States and the Commission, a competitive, secure and environmentally sustainable internal market in electricity within the Community, and effective market opening for all customers and suppliers in the Community and ensuring appropriate conditions for the effective and reliable operation of electricity networks, taking into account long-term objectives.[55]

Here I will not go into the full gamut of objectives listed above, which have also been summarized more succinctly as competitiveness, security of supply, and sustainability.[56] What is clear, however, is that these objectives do not always all pull in the same direction (unlike those in electronic communications that usually do). At the same time the existence of an independent EU competition policy with regard to energy can tip the scales, as we will see.

The role of NRAs in energy and of ACER

By means of its case law on direct effect the Court itself had invested the national courts below it with the power to apply certain treaty provisions, including those on EU competition law, without intermediary. By means of Regulation 1/2003 the Council and European Parliament have effectively repeated this process with regard to the newly created NCAs. The third set of decentralized institutions that are relevant to EU competition law are the NRAs which have also been empowered by means of secondary legislation. With regard to energy, these NRAs were created by Directives 2003/54 EC for electricity and Directive 2003/55/EC concerning natural gas (the second energy package). The energy regimes differ from that for antitrust in that they are also equipped with central coordinating bodies

[54] Directive 96/92/EC, above (n 51).

[55] Article 36(a), Directive 2009/72/EC, above (n 49). An identical provision regarding gas is found in Article 40, Directive 2009/73/EC, above (n 49).

[56] Communication from the Commission of 10 January 2007, Inquiry pursuant to Article 17 of Regulation (EC) No 1/2003 into the European gas and electricity sectors (final report), COM(2006) 851, para 9. This document was accompanied by Communication from the Commission, Prospects for the internal gas and electricity market COM(2006) 841 and Communication from the Commission to the European Council and the European Parliament of 10 January 2007, An energy policy for Europe COM(2007) 1.

(other than the European Commission). In this respect they resemble electronic communications.

These NRAs are responsible for ensuring non-discrimination and effective competition in, as well as the efficient functioning of, energy markets. To guarantee their independence from the gas and electricity industries they are required to be legally distinct and functionally independent from any other public or private entity, their staff and management must act independently from any market interest and may not seek or take direct instructions from any government or other public or private entity when carrying out their regulatory tasks.[57] This emphasis on political independence as opposed to independence from the industry is not found in the electronic communications context (nor in that of the NCAs) and goes a long way in the direction of creating a layer of economic governance that is accountable only at EU level, as well as to national courts. In addition, the Commission has published a comprehensive working paper spelling out the role of NRAs in the energy sector.[58]

The regulatory powers of the NRAs are beefed up by the ability to conduct unannounced on-site inspections ('dawn raids') as well as to fine infringements up to a limit of 10 per cent of turnover, powers also conferred upon the European Commission, but not, in the sphere of competition remedies which remains national, on the NCAs. The sectoral framework on this point is therefore both more intrusive and more EU-oriented than the general regime of EU competition law.

In the energy sector, after an initial period where national experts were consulted by the Commission in a loose framework,[59] the coordination tasks since 2003 were carried out by the European regulators group for electricity and gas (ERGEG).[60] ERGEG focused on what was at the time optimistically phrased as consolidating the internal market in energy. This body was replaced by the agency for cooperation of energy regulators, ACER, which was created in 2009 by the third energy package.[61] ACER inter alia monitors the activities of the transmission network operators for electricity and gas and their respective network organizations: the European network of transmission system operators for electricity (ENTSO-E) and the European network of transmission network operators for gas (ENTSO-G). Importantly it also coordinates the work of the NRAs.

[57] Article 35(4), Directive 2009/72/EC, above (n 49). An identical provision regarding gas is found in Article 39(4), Directive 2009/73/EC, above (n 49).

[58] Commission staff working paper of 22 January 2010, Interpretative note on Directive 2009/72/EC concerning common rules for the internal market in electricity and Directive 2009/73/EC concerning common rules for the internal market in natural gas: the regulatory authorities.

[59] Commission Decision 92/167/EEC of 4 March 1992 setting up a Committee of Experts on the Transit of Electricity between Grids OJ 1992, L74/43; Commission Decision 95/539/EC of 8 December 1995 setting up a committee of experts on the transit of natural gas through grids, OJ 1995, L304/57.

[60] Commission Decision 2003/796/EC of 11 November 2003 on establishing the European Regulators Group for Electricity and Gas, OJ 2003, L296/34.

[61] Regulation (EC) No 713/2009 of the European Parliament and of the Council of 13 July 2009 establishing an Agency for the Cooperation of Energy Regulators, OJ 2009, L211/1.

For these purposes, ACER has the power to issue opinions and recommendations to transmission system operators and to NRAs, as well as the EU institutions. It may take decisions in individual cases regarding cross-border infrastructure access and security issues, including capacity and financial aspects such as access fees. By regulating third party access it therefore has limited supranational competition competencies. There is no exact equivalent to the Commission's (quasi-) veto powers in the Article 7 and 7a procedures found in electronic communications discussed in the previous section, although the Commission may require NRAs to act in accordance with ACER guidelines.[62] The Council of European energy regulators (CEER), which has an overlapping membership with ACER, complements the latter organization on issues where ACER has no competence.[63] Examples are benchmarking, market monitoring, and the promotion of smart metering.

Third party access

The original emphasis of EU sectoral regulation with regard to energy, where unbundling was the core issue and third party access secondary (albeit growing in importance), was arguably the reverse from that in electronic communication, where access (and interconnection between networks) has always been the key issue and unbundling is mainly just one form of access. Nevertheless, under the rules of the third energy package the energy sector is characterized by an extensive system of both unbundling and third party access rules that are now considered to be the cornerstone of liberalization.[64] They are more strict than (but effectively double up with) general EU antitrust law. The standard for access under antitrust was mentioned above in the section on electronic communications.[65] Unbundling for energy will now be discussed.

Third party access was imposed by the broader EU regulatory framework that is applicable for natural gas set out by the Directive.[66] In addition, since 2011, access to natural gas transmission networks as well as liquefied natural gas (LNG) and storage facilities is mandated by directly effective EU law in a regulation.[67] This dual set-up is mirrored by the directly effective rules on access to transmission and distribution systems for electricity that are set out in a European Parliament and Council regulation,[68] as well as for third party access within the

[62] Johnston (n 48), at 140.

[63] Available at: <http://www.ceer.eu/portal/page/portal/EER_HOME/EER_ABOUT>.

[64] Johnston (n 48), at 73.

[65] A. Kotlowski, 'Third-party access rights in the energy sector: a competition law perspective', *Utilities Law Review* 16 (2006/7) 101–9.

[66] Directive 2009/73/EC, above (n 49).

[67] Regulation (EC) No 715/2009 of the European Parliament and of the Council of 13 July 2009 on conditions for access to the natural gas transmission networks and repealing Regulation (EC) No 1775/2005 OJ 2009, L211/36.

[68] Regulation (EC) No 714/2009 of the European Parliament and of the Council of 13 July 2009 on conditions for access to the network for cross-border exchanges in electricity and repealing Regulation (EC) No 1228/2003, OJ 2009, L211/15.

broader regulatory context by means of a directive.[69] The Regulation primarily concerns cross-border flows of electricity, whereas the rules in the Directive are more general and apply at national level.

As is true for electronic communications networks, regulated access to the gas and electricity grids is based on principles of transparent, non-discriminatory, and objective pricing.[70] Such tariffs are set by the NRAs, by means of autonomous and directly binding decisions. This includes the NRAs' authority to establish and/or approve the underlying methodology. Mandatory tariffs apply to (i) transmission and distribution systems as well as access to LNG facilities, (ii) balancing services to balance (or match) demand and supply, and (iii) cross-border infrastructures. It goes beyond the scope of this concise overview to delve deeper into the details of energy access regulation as such. Instead, we will look at a different type of balance: that between antitrust and regulation.

The balance between sectoral and general rules in energy

The energy sector inquiry

As has been the case for electronic communications, the general EU competition rules have been used to back up the sectoral regulatory framework. The Commission carried out a sector inquiry under Regulation 1/2003 in 2005–07.[71] The main findings were that: (i) markets remained national in scope and highly concentrated, (ii) a lack of network unbundling formed an obstacle to entry and security of supply, (iii) inadequate cross-border capacity frustrated market integration, (iv) markets were opaque, (v) price formation was likewise opaque and ineffective, (vi) there was only limited competition at retail level, (vii) balancing markets favoured incumbents and balancing zones (areas where network users are committed to maintaining a specific volume of gas) were too small, and finally, (viii) the potential for LNG to promote less concentrated markets had not been realized.

Essentially, behavioural remedies were found to be insufficient, and structural intervention (especially unbundling) would be required. In response competition law and regulatory remedies were to be applied jointly.

> In order to address the malfunctioning of the market identified in the Sector Inquiry and to significantly improve the scope of competition, it is essential to apply both competition and regulatory-based remedies. Competition law enforcement can make a significant contribution, but cannot by itself open markets and resolve all the shortcomings identified by the Sector Inquiry: a number of regulatory measures are, therefore, also needed.[72]

[69] Directive 2009/72/EC, above (n 49).

[70] Case C-239/07 *Julius Sabatauskas et al.* [2008] I-7523; Case C-439/-06 *citiworks AG v Flughafen Leipzig/Halle GmbH* [2008] ECR I-3913.

[71] Sector inquiry (n 56).

[72] Ibid, para 40.

The main remedy identified by the Commission was tackling vertical integration on the part of the incumbents.[73] This was done in the third internal energy market package of 2009. In the 2009 package, the Member States were given a choice of three alternative regulatory regimes.

Unbundling

Energy regulation goes beyond what we have seen in electronic communications especially with regard to unbundling, although there is unbundling of the local loop for SMP operators of the fixed access network there. This is because the feasibility of duplicating infrastructure has so far been much less with regard to energy networks than electronic communications, where apart from various forms of fixed networks (where copper is in the process of being replaced with optical fibre), there are wireless (such as mobile) and satellite options. Given the lack of scope for infrastructure-based competition the Commission has consistently attempted to break up the chain of the vertically integrated incumbent energy operators.

Under the third energy package there are three options between which the Member States may freely choose. The default position for transmission system operators is that of (i) full unbundling, whereas for distribution system operators legal unbundling is required. Transmission systems operators must also be independent from entities performing functions of generation and/or supply, a rule that applies evenly across the electricity and gas sectors. There are, however, two other options: (ii) having an independent system operator *managing* the transmission network where a vertically integrated entity could continue to exist, or (iii) having an independent transmission operator responsible for *operating* the network even if it remains owned by a vertically integrated entity. In addition, there are derogations for accession states and small isolated systems or markets.[74] In all three cases there are detailed rules regarding the relationship with the (formerly) vertically integrated incumbents.

As mentioned earlier, it is up to the Member States to choose one of these models. Unsurprisingly, however, in the framework of its merger and antitrust control, the Commission has consistently promoted its preferred model of full unbundling, the default listed under (i) above. I will look at energy and antitrust, as well as energy and State aid, in the following, but I will not address the issue of energy mergers in any more detail here.[75]

[73] Competition Commissioner Neelie Kroes, 'More competitive energy markets: building on the findings of the sector inquiry to shape the right policy Solutions', Speech at European Energy Institute, Brussels, 19 September 2007.

[74] Johnston (n 48).

[75] See however Case C-207/07 *Commission v Spain* [2008] ECR I-111 where the Court found that Spanish requirements for prior approval by the national energy regulator of energy mergers formed a breach of EU law (free movement of persons/establishment and of capital).

Energy and antitrust

The introduction of the third energy package coincided with two high-profile Article 102 TFEU cases in the energy sector where the same objective had been pursued as a competition remedy. Under investigation for discrimination in favour of its own affiliated companies and deterring market entry, E.ON committed to divest itself from part of its electricity generation capacity as well as all of its high-voltage transmission systems when the Commission closed case against it with a commitment decision pursuant to Article 9(1) of Regulation 1/2003.[76] In *RWE* (2009), the Commission closed a refusal to supply and margin squeeze investigation when RWE committed to divest its high-pressure gas transmission network.[77] Likewise in 2009, applying Article 101 TFEU the Commission established market sharing agreements between E.ON and GDF and imposed fines of over €500 million on each party.[78]

This was by no means the end of the story, just looking at 2010. In that year E.ON committed to release capacity for entry into its gas transmission grid in order to address a case of refusal to supply (by overbooking capacity).[79] Similarly, in 2010 EDF, prosecuted for foreclosing the supply of electricity to large industrial customers, committed to release at arm's length significant volumes of electricity and to refrain from restricting resale.[80] From a procedural or even from a democratic standpoint it may be questioned whether it is desirable to rely on commitment decisions which are not fully subject to judicial control in order to achieve results that the political process had failed to achieve for lack of support at the level of the governments of the Member States. Antitrust is in such cases a crowbar that may be effective in achieving results but at a cost to (input) legitimacy.[81]

Since then, the heat remains on in the energy sector: inter alia an investigation into Gazprom was launched in 2012 that immediately raised hackles in Moscow. Nevertheless, in April 2015 the Commission sent Gazprom a statement of objections charging this undertaking with market partitioning and applying unfair prices.[82] On the one hand this could be seen as part of an energy policy emphasizing security of supply and the geostrategic dimension. On the other, it could be seen as mirroring EU investigations into leading United States high-technology companies such as *Microsoft* or *Google* to ensure the proper functioning of the internal market even in sensitive areas.[83]

[76] Case COMP/39.402 RWE Gas Foreclosure, Commission Decision of 18 March 2009.

[77] Case COMP/39.388 German Electricity Wholesale market and COMP/39.389: German Electricity Balancing Market, Commission Decision of 26 November 2008.

[78] Summary of Commission Decision of 8 July 2009 relating to a proceeding under Article 81 of the EC Treaty (Case COMP/39.401, E.ON/GDF) (notified under document COM(2009) 5355 final, OJ 2009, C248/5.

[79] Case COMP/39.317 E.ON Gas, Commission Decision of 5 May 2010.

[80] Case COMP/39.386 Long-term contracts France, Commission Decision of 17 March 2010.

[81] Johnston (n 48), at 71.

[82] Antitrust: Commission sends Statement of Objections to Gazprom for alleged abuse of dominance on Central and Eastern European gas supply markets, IP/15/4828, 22 April 2015.

[83] Commission Decision of 24 May 2004 relating to a proceeding pursuant to Article 82 EC against Microsoft Corporation (Case COMP/C-3/37.792, Microsoft) OJ 2007, L 32/23; Case

Finally, as regards state sponsorship of dominance in energy markets, the 2014 *DEI* (Greek lignite) ruling of the Court of Justice on the standard applied to Article 102 TFEU in combination with Article 106(2) TFEU was significant:

> infringement of Article 86(1) EC [now Article 106(2) TFEU] in conjunction with Article 82 EC [now Article 102 TFEU] may be established irrespective of whether any abuse actually exists. All that is necessary is for the Commission to identify a potential or actual anti-competitive consequence liable to result from the State measure at issue. Such an infringement may thus be established where the State measures at issue affect the structure of the market by creating unequal conditions of competition between companies, by allowing the public undertaking or the undertaking which was granted special or exclusive rights to maintain (for example by hindering new entrants to the market), strengthen or extend its dominant position over another market, thereby restricting competition, without it being necessary to prove the existence of actual abuse.[84]

This ruling clearly limits the scope for intervention by the Member States by means of providing or extending monopoly rights to energy producers.

Energy and State aid

In particular following the adoption of renewable energy as a political objective throughout the EU, the energy sector has become a large recipient of State aid. This means that State aid policy gives the Commission additional leverage in the energy sector. In 2014 as part of its State aid modernization programme, the Commission has adopted guidelines on the application of state aid to energy and environmental protection (EEAG).[85] The relevant measures listed there concern: aid for energy from renewable sources; aid for energy efficiency measures, including cogeneration and district heating and district cooling; aid for resource efficiency and, in particular, for waste management; aid in the form of reductions in funding support for electricity from renewable sources; aid for energy infrastructure; and aid for generation adequacy measures. Energy and environmental concerns are also connected in the State aid context by means of the emissions trading system (ETS) which is covered in a separate set of guidelines.[86] A related development is the adoption of a State aid framework for winding up spare capacity in the coal production sector.[87]

T-201/04, *Microsoft Corp. v Commission* [2007] II-3601; Case COMP/39740 Google Search, statement of objections of 15 April 2015.

[84] Case C-553/12 P *Commission v Dimosia Epicheirisi Ilektrismou AE (DEI)*, Judgment of 17 July 2014, para 46.

[85] Communication from the Commission: Guidelines on State aid for environmental protection and energy 2014–2020, OJ 2014, C200/1.

[86] Directive 2009/29 of the European Parliament and of the Council of 23 April 2009 amending Directive 2003/87/EC so as to improve and extend the greenhouse gas emission allowance trading scheme of the Community, OJ 2009, L140/63; and Communication from the Commission: Guidelines on certain State aid measures in the context of the greenhouse gas emission allowance trading scheme post 2012, OJ 2012, C154/4.

[87] Council Decision 2010/787/EU of 10 December 2010 on State aid to facilitate the closure of uncompetitive coal mines, OJ 2010, L336/24.

Under the EEAG, third party access to infrastructure is a factor that the Commission takes into account when assessing the compatibility of State measures with the internal market.[88] Thus, there is a parallel here with third party access to broadband infrastructure and the application of the State aid rules to electronic communications.

Finally, in the recent (2015) *Kernkraftwerke Lippe-Ems* case, the Court of Justice ruled (albeit in Delphic terms) that the German tax on nuclear energy was not selective because it did not aim to discriminate against energy producers of this type as they were not in a comparable situation to other producers. There was thus no aid.

> It must be noted that methods of producing electricity, other than that based on nuclear fuel, are not affected by the rules introduced by KernbrStG and that, in any event, they are not, in the light of the objective pursued by those rules, in a factual and legal situation that is comparable to that of the production method based on nuclear fuel, as only that method generates radioactive waste arising from the use of such fuel.
>
> It follows that KernbrStG is not a selective measure, for the purpose of Article 107(1) TFEU, and it does not therefore constitute State aid prohibited by that provision[89]

This therefore leaves considerable scope for future taxes to direct investment in particular types of energy production. In any event, the debate where State aid and energy are connected is likely to remain lively given the context of global climate control and environmental issues that will require public intervention and agreements across national borders in order to counteract the market failures involved. As a final attempt to contrast sectoral and general competition law, I will now look at the role of NCAs.

4. The Role of NCAs in Electronic Communications and Energy

Thus far I have focused on the Commission and the NRAs, however, beyond (i) EU antitrust law applied by the Commission and (ii) EU sectoral competition rules applied by NRAs in the fields of electronic communications and energy, there are also (iii) NCAs applying both (a) EU antitrust and (b) national competition law in these sectors. The latter follows the familiar distinction of whether there is an EU dimension due to the existence of an appreciable effect on trade.[90] Adding the NCAs further contributes to a rich tapestry of rules, regulators, and competition authorities. It also means that within these sectors the coordination required to find the most appropriate instrument and level at which it is wielded is especially sensitive. The ECN, the network of NCAs, does not, however, have sectoral groups covering electronic communications and energy and it does not

[88] Guidelines on State aid for environmental protection and energy, above (n 85), para 3.8.

[89] Case C-5/14 *Kernkraftwerke Lippe-Ems GmbH v Hauptzollamt Osnabrück*, Judgment of 4 June 2015, paras 79–80.

[90] Commission Notice: Guidelines on the effect on trade concept contained in Articles 81 and 82 of the Treaty, OJ 2004, C101/81.

report separately on the NCAs' activities in these sectors. This makes it difficult to track the relevant events.

In its 2014 Communication on the results of ten years of enforcement of Regulation 1/2003, the Commission indicated that both at EU and at national level under EU law, the liberalized sectors, including electronic communications and energy, were the most important in terms of the numbers of antitrust decisions following the basic manufacturing industries that are the well-established leaders of the pack in terms of cartel infringements.[91] In fact energy was the second most prosecuted sector overall. As the Commission Services document that accompanies the 2014 Communication shows that the majority of these cases taken up by the NCAs involved dominance abuse by vertically integrated incumbents aiming at foreclosure by means of various exclusionary abuses.

However, NCAs have also tried their hand at tackling exploitative abuses. An example in the energy sector was excessive prices charged by electricity providers.[92] In the electronic communications sector we have seen that after a number of successful margin squeeze cases in recent years Commission antitrust action has been relatively limited, nevertheless NCAs have launched a number of excessive pricing cases here as well, although there is no sense of activism comparable to that in energy.[93] Thus the NCAs at a minimum complement the efforts of the Commission to apply the general competition rules—in this case antitrust—in the electronic communications and energy sectors.

This short section on NCAs warrants a caveat. I am aware that the information presented here is sketchy. A separate comparative study at national level to examine what types of cooperation exist between NRAs and NCAs (in those cases where these are not, as they sometimes are, the same bodies) would be required in order to chart the balance and the division of labour between antitrust and sectoral competition law properly. The same holds for the overall balance between the national and EU levels.

More broadly in this context it could also be significant that it is the Commission's Directorate-General (DG) for Competition which coordinates the NCAs and interacts within the ECN whereas the sectoral DGs for energy and electronic communications (ENER and Communications Networks, Content and Technology, CNECT) play a similar (but not identical) role with respect to the NRAs, ACER, and BEREC. Viewing the European Commission as a unified actor at this level is likely to be inaccurate, although in a formal sense its decisions are taken by the Commission as a whole.

[91] Communication from the Commission of 9 July 2014 to the European Parliament and the Council, Ten years of antitrust enforcement under Regulation 1/2003: achievements and future perspectives, COM(2014) 453, paras 15–17.

[92] Decision of the Danish NCA of 20 June 2007 in the Case Elsam A/S; Decision N°B 8-88/05-2 of the German NCA of 26 September 2007 in the Case CO_2 allowances. Commission Staff Working Document SWD (2014) 230: Ten Years of Antitrust Enforcement under Regulation 1/2003, 9 July 2014, para 70.

[93] Decision No S/0248/10 of the Spanish NCA of 19 December 2012; 89 Decision No 09-D-24 of the French NCA of 28 July 2009. Ibid, para 72.

Exploring these two dimensions, worthwhile as it may be, is beyond the scope of this book.

5. Conclusion

The first question posed in the introduction to this chapter was why the EU has sectoral competition frameworks for electronic communications and energy. Broadly speaking, the answer is: in order to promote the internal market in these two areas that were previously dominated by legal monopolies. This requires regulatory intervention because vertically integrated incumbents continue to dominate the markets concerned, such that formal liberalization alone would be ineffective or even counterproductive by creating private instead of public monopolies (although technological development has been a driver for structural change in electronic communications more so than in energy, where structural change has been more regulation-driven—leading to more intrusive rules). At the same time, the complexity and time-consuming nature of the problems concerned mean that reliance on competition law alone would lead to a one-sided overburdening of antitrust resources. Moreover, introducing competition in the networks sectors was not the only goal of liberalization and harmonization.

This is reflected in the objectives of the two regimes, where electronic communications also addresses a range of interests of European citizens and energy not only does the same but adds security of supply and environmental goals. These are objectives that are not easily accommodated by the general competition rules. We have also looked briefly at what the application of these sectoral rules involves and seen the decentralized application by NRAs combined with a network type organization loosely coordinated by the Commission. This is used to prop up the independence of the NRAs from producers on the one hand and from their national governments on the other (interests which are sometimes linked either strategically or based on ownership). At the same time, the sectoral regimes are close cousins of antitrust and the use of common concepts is essential. The antitrust concept of dominance on which the concept of SMP is based is a good example of this.

Second, regarding the question of the interaction between the two sectoral frameworks and general EU competition law, we see a range from competing parallel powers to mutually supporting policies. The Commission uses the general competition rules to exercise influence directly where its opportunities to act under the sectoral frameworks are limited. Antitrust is also used to promote a liberalization agenda. However, there is a difference in timing here: in electronic communications, antitrust powers were used earlier and arguably less extensively than in energy, where their use is both more recent and more widespread. In fact energy is regarded as one of the main sectors where competition law is currently being applied. This may be explained in part by the fact that in electronic communications the NRAs have more competition powers and these are more established. In any event, both sectoral regimes are hybrids and the promotion of competition is just one of their purposes, albeit an important one. Thus, they are not fully integrated into EU competition law because they are only partially concerned with competition.

Comparing the electronic communications and energy frameworks with each other shows that in energy the storage and transmission bottlenecks are even more serious than in electronic communications, and there is a sourcing problem that in electronic communications does not exist where bandwidth and content can be added almost indefinitely, provided adequate funding is available. As I have already written, the objectives in energy are much broader, for instance as regards their interaction with environmental policies, and the Member States are involved much more closely than in electronic communications, for instance in providing all kinds of subsidies. I have also noted how in electronic communications the Member States are entering the scene again with regard to broadband roll-out, and likewise with subsidies. This means that the State aid instrument has become at least as important as antitrust as a general framework for these sectors. Moreover, whereas antitrust is to some extent mirrored in the sectoral regimes, there are no such similar rules for State aid.

The third and final question concerned coherence between this third and outer layer of EU competition law and the other two layers (if we conceptualize antitrust as the first layer or core of EU competition law, and mergers and State aid as its second layer). This is determined by common goals (although these are not exclusive) and concepts, as well as by parallel governance structures based on networks of NRAs/NCAs and network agencies) which are stronger for the sectoral regimes, weak for antitrust, and non-existent for mergers and State aid.

The instruments concerned are applied in a manner that is interlinked and intended as consistent with the common policy goals as well as with the working of EU competition law at large. As regards legitimacy and effectiveness, the jury is still out. Although initially subject to legal and political challenges, it now seems to be generally accepted that liberalization was the appropriate way forward for both the electronic communications and the energy sector. As far as effectiveness goes, it should be noted that in both sectors markets are still largely national, although considerable cross-border entry has occurred. Paradoxically this market partitioning is due at least in part to the fact that under liberalization regulation is still largely national in nature, as are pricing schemes and commercial offers. Moreover, in energy markets disparate national policies on renewables play a market-fragmenting role.

Nevertheless the sectoral rules specifically aim to achieve the internal market in a manner that is even more direct than is the case for general competition law, and as part of a full-feature regime that goes beyond competition. The competition rules embedded within these sectoral frameworks can therefore be regarded as strongly externally coherent in the broader context of EU law. At the same time, for the reasons given earlier, they are more likely to persist rather than to fade away and be replaced by the core (or general) elements of EU competition law. This also means that parallel application of sectoral and general EU competition law is here to stay.

X
Conclusion

1. Introduction and Concepts

Coherence was one of the important themes of the Commission's White Paper on the modernization and decentralization of antitrust enforcement in 1999,[1] just as it was in its ten-year evaluation of modernization and the functioning of the European Competition Network (ECN) in 2014.[2] The main objective of this book is to examine whether EU competition law in fact maintains its coherence while it is subject to centrifugal as well as centripetal forces following modernization and enlargement, and comprises an increasing number of regimes and therefore norms and objectives. If EU competition law does maintain its coherence, I also want to examine by what means this is the case.

Based on an examination of comparable studies in EU law and on the use of the concept in legal philosophy, I have defined coherence as a set of rules that is applied consistently in the interest of achieving a common objective or set of principles. I set out to study coherence at three levels, (i) external, and internally at (ii) systemic and (iii) component level while also using two secondary criteria, effectiveness and legitimacy. The latter are intended to provide a more independent benchmark (as opposed to achieving the systemic objective(s) of competition law) against which to assess what broader effects the degree of coherence achieved by EU competition law may have had.

In this final chapter, I will address the questions that were restated above more directly than I have done previously. I will go over the relevant factors in the same sequence as I have done in the preceding chapters while trying to identify both the main arguments and my conclusions on the relevant points.

2. The Structure of Antitrust

Antitrust, comprising the prohibitions on cartel agreements and dominance abuse, is the traditional core of EU competition law and has been at the heart

[1] European Commission, White Paper on modernization of the rules implementing Articles 85 and 86 of the EC Treaty, Brussels 28 April 1999.

[2] Communication from the Commission, Ten years of antitrust enforcement under Regulation 1/2003: achievements and future perspectives, COM(2014) 453.

of the modernization exercise. It has also been the focus of six of the preceding nine chapters. Here I will first present the thrust of the general findings in these chapters regarding the structure of antitrust.

History and framework

The history of EU competition policy can be seen as a story of coming of age, with the 2004 modernization of antitrust as the major watershed toward a mature and professional policy. As we have also seen, however, competition policy as a whole—including merger and State aid control, and the sector-specific rules on energy and electronic communications—is developing all the time. This is because there is always a new corner being turned on one of its instruments in line with political and economic developments, with the other tools eventually catching up or overtaking it and then being overtaken again in turn.

Thus State aid is now in the midst of reform[3] with changes on merger control in preparation.[4] Nevertheless, there are some pervasive differences: mergers and State aid remain characterized by highly centralized control in the hands of the Commission, and electronic communications and energy are predominantly national affairs. Following modernization, antitrust is perched squarely in the middle.

Objectives and boundaries

Since the entry into force of the Lisbon Treaty in December 2009, achieving the internal market has been confirmed as the overriding objective of EU competition law. This internal market objective includes safeguarding the competitive process and a competitive market structure as well as the consumer interest. In spite of concerted efforts by the Commission supported by case law of the General Court, however, consumer interest has not been recognized as the general or guiding objective of EU competition law by the European Court of Justice.[5] While the underlying dynamics are different (because here national politics in the Member States was decisive) the result is similar to how the principle of competition in free markets has not emerged as an objective of the EU under the Lisbon Treaty.

[3] Following on from Communication from the Commission of 8 May 2012, EU State aid modernisation (SAM), COM(2012) 209.

[4] Commission Communication of 9 July 2014, White paper towards more effective EU merger control, COM(2014) 449.

[5] Joined Cases C-519/06 P, C-501/06 P, C-513/06 P, C-515/06 P, and C-519/06 P *GlaxoSmithKline Services Unlimited v Commission (C-501/06 P) and Commission v GlaxoSmithKline Services Unlimited (C-513/06 P) and European Association of Euro Pharmaceutical Companies (EAEPC) v Commission (C-515/06 P) and Asociación de exportadores españoles de productos farmacéuticos (Aseprofar) v Commission* [2009] ECR I-9291; Case T 168/01 *GlaxoSmithKline Services v Commission* [2006] ECR II-2969; *Case C-8/08 T-Mobile Netherlands BV, KPN Mobile NV, Orange Nederland NV and Vodafone Libertel NV v Raad van bestuur van de Nederlandse Mededingingsautoriteit* [2009] ECR I-4529.

Conceptually, other economic objectives such as promoting efficiency and countering market failures play a role. This is so especially if anticompetitive practices and agreements are counted as market failures, although (beyond State aid) they are rarely mentioned in the case law. Nevertheless, in my view it can be argued that EU competition law does not provide scope for non-economic objectives or half-hearted economic objectives that by some standards could be considered as market failures such as the underprovision of socially desirable goods. Moreover, I see no role whatsoever within EU competition law for non-economic public interest objectives set at national level, which I believe should be addressed under the heading of boundaries or as an exception under the State aid rules to the extent they are coextensive with an EU policy (see below).

The economic objectives can be said to be reasonably clear primarily thanks to their link with the internal market. They represent a relatively limited set even if it is not always evident how they should be achieved in practice. For instance, it has not been established how conflicting objectives should be handled. This could lead to problems regarding coherence, especially if different goals are pursued with different intensity at different levels of administration (by the Commission and by national competition authorities (NCAs)) and in national courts.

In any event, the anchoring of EU competition law in the internal market objective is not only consistent with its earliest beginnings as a complement to the free movement rules but also a solid safeguard against further political encroachment, such as was attempted in the so-called Sarkozy amendments to the Treaty, which led inter alia to the elimination of Article 3(1)(g) EC[6] and the introduction of Protocol 26 on the internal market and competition and Protocol 27 on services of general economic interest (SGEIs). It is difficult to think of a better way to ensure that EU competition law is respected within the overall framework of EU law. It also ensures strong external coherence of EU competition law within EU law as a whole. Yet a further specification of what is meant by the internal market objective in this context (apart from protecting the competitive process and market structure) could make EU competition law more effective. Finally, from the perspective of coherence it is worth noting that in the view of the Court of Justice, the abovementioned objectives apply to EU competition law as a whole—at least covering not only antitrust but also mergers and State aid. This promotes coherence at a systemic level.

A system focused on economic objectives (in shorthand: efficiency) is compatible with the use of boundaries to keep public polices (in shorthand: equity) off limits. This also means that the relevant balancing exercises between equity and efficiency goals will not be made within the exceptions to EU competition law. Boundaries of a legal nature can indeed be found at the most straightforward level (i) in the concepts of undertaking and of economic activity, but also (ii) based on

[6] Which required, to promote the general aims of the Community set out in Article 2 EC, 'a system ensuring that competition in the internal market is not distorted'. Replaced by Article 3(1)b TFEU, an exclusive EU competence in 'the establishing of the competition rules necessary for the functioning of the internal market'.

Article 101(1) TFEU and inherent restrictions as expressed in the *Wouters* rule,[7] or (iii) based on the State action doctrine (in State aid a similar boundary was spelled out in *Altmark*[8]).

Even the most basic boundaries such as the concept of undertaking, however, are currently applied according to different standards across economic sectors. The most important economic boundary is market power: this squares with the new economic approach and its focus on effects, even although the latter may be losing traction.

Rules and exceptions

The various rules of competition policy, without going into detail, appear to cover most imaginable instances of anticompetitive conduct in a comprehensive manner. Because (as we have just seen) they have shared objectives, they would appear to be likely to pull in the same direction, at least potentially. Within the instruments of antitrust the contrast between by object and by effect infringements plays an increasingly significant role, with the by object findings on the rise. This is significant for various reasons: because by object infringements may be both easer to predict and therefore to avoid (promoting legal certainty); as well as to prove and therefore prosecute (promoting deterrence). This also means a diminished role for the more economic approach that pre-dates modernization (but was one of its strands) and one that looks more like establishing simple rules for a complex world. Nevertheless, the boundaries between object and effect infringements may remain fluid for some time, although they may be clarified further in the appeal before the Court of Justice against the (2014) judgment of the General Court in *Intel*.[9]

The various exceptions to the abovementioned rules on the other hand do not complement each other equally well. This is risky because it may well lead to temptations at national level to accommodate national polices under the competition rules especially on non-efficiency grounds. In previous chapters, I have therefore argued against allowing non-competition concerns except efficiency being allowed as valid arguments into the framework of antitrust not just in the form of public policy objectives but also as the basis for applying an exception.

Instead, I believe the pursuit of public policies can provide reasons to keep the agreements concerned outside the boundaries of antitrust in various ways, or find exceptions based on SGEIs. Mergers follow a slightly different logic. Here, the general economic exceptions for efficiencies and failing firms are coupled with a specific public interest escape that is set out in Article 21(4) of the Merger control Regulation, although its application is subject to prior approval by the

[7] Case C-309/99 *J.C.J. Wouters, J.W. Savelbergh and Price Waterhouse Belastingadviseurs BV v Algemene Raad van de Nederlandse Orde van Advocaten* [2002] ECR I-1577.

[8] Case C-280/00 *Altmark Trans GmbH and Regierungspräsidium Magdeburg v Nahverkehrsgesellschaft Altmark GmbH, and Oberbundesanwalt beim Bundesverwaltungsgericht* [2003] ECR I-7747.

[9] Case T-286/09 *Intel Corp. v Commission*, Judgment of 12 June 2014. Appealed in Case C-413/14 P.

Table 10.1 Types of exceptions and beneficiaries

EU framework	Nature of exception		Level of interest promoted			
Antitrust		efficiency		undertaking	consumer	
Mergers	equity	efficiency	national	undertaking	consumer	
State aid	equity	efficiency				EU
SGEI	equity	efficiency	national			

Commission. Fortunately, from the perspective of coherence (as well as in my view, efficiency and legitimacy), all of these routes are rarely used. For State aid however, only EU public interests count, which are to be balanced against the EU interest of achieving the internal market through undistorted competition—although State aids that are coextensive with the relevant EU interest may be found compatible with the internal market.

Within antitrust the fact that the General Court has roundly rejected the rule of reason which calls for balancing the pro-competitive and anticompetitive aspects of a restriction. This has clarified matters, although the possibility of invoking an objective justification reintroduces much the same set of issues.[10] Arguably within each instrument there is an adequate level of consistency, however between the various instruments the differences in the exceptions involved are considerable. In Table 10.1 I have tried to identify the types of exception (again simplified as economic versus non-economic, or efficiency and equity) and the level at which the interest is promoted. That is to say: is it the interest of the consumer, of undertakings, of national policies, of the EU level itself, or of a combination of these?

This simplified overview shows that there are considerable differences between the exceptions to the various instruments. Having a neat and/or comprehensive set of rules matters less if subsequently the exceptions to these rules are haphazard. This leads to a risk of counterproductive divergence, inconsistency, and fragmentation, especially in a context of decentralization. The exceptions thus undermine the coherence of EU competition law.

3. Procedures and Remedies

This is a vast topic in its own right to which it is difficult to do justice here. Each instrument of EU competition law has its own EU level procedural framework. Most importantly, in antitrust we see a shift from Commission-centred procedures to a more decentralized system. At the same time, NCAs operate under national rules because much of competition procedure and remedies remains national law. There is also a tension between centralized enforcement and decentralization,

[10] Case T-65/98 *Van den Bergh Foods Ltd v Commission* [2003] ECR 2003 II-4653.

notably as regards private follow-on actions for damages in national courts. Significantly, the Commission and the EU legislature have both come down in favour of the former (centralized public enforcement) in the very instrument that was designed to promote the latter (decentralized private enforcement), the 2014 Damages Directive.[11] Mergers and State aid remain highly centralized at EU level with notification and standstill requirements, and a Commission monopoly on clearances (styled as a declaration that the transaction involved is compatible with the internal market). In each case, there is a balance to be struck between effectiveness and legitimacy, especially as regard the rights of the defence.

At the level of remedies there is also a tension between the use of behavioural versus structural remedies, and between on the one hand the use of commitments to facilitate effectiveness while foregoing legal certainty and setting precedents—as well as arguably the rights of the defence and equality of arms—and on the other hand formal findings of infringement. The use of commitments may promote far-reaching concrete results at relatively low enforcement costs and thereby increased effectiveness. However, in the process it can undermine legitimacy and thereby support for the policies concerned. Also such negotiated settlements may mean that there is no useful precedent or example to provide guidance for the sector concerned as a whole. The abovementioned unstructured nature of the exceptions available under the different instruments could, at least in theory, be fixed by recasting them, yet the tension between effectiveness and legitimacy with regard to procedures and remedies is likely to be ingrained in the nature of EU competition law enforcement and unlikely to be resolved. This does not mean that a better balance or an equilibrium at a higher level should not be pursued.

4. The Structure of Competition Law except in Antitrust

Having looked at the various findings for antitrust, we will now briefly examine the structure of the second layer of EU competition law, mergers, and State aid, and its third and outer layer, the competition rules for electronic communications and energy.

Mergers and State aid

These two instruments of EU competition law have already come up several times here. They are more recent branches of competition law that share the internal market objective with antitrust, including the process of competition and the structure of the market.

Market and government failure play an enhanced role with regard to State aid, which by definition concerns actions that are purportedly in the national public

[11] Directive 2014/104/EU of the European Parliament and of the Council of 26 November 2014 on certain rules governing actions for damages under national law for infringements of the competition law provisions of the Member States and of the European Union, OJ 2014, L349/1.

interest. At the same time State aid appears to lag behind antitrust while following a broadly similar trajectory. Whether the exemption monopoly for State aid will ever be replaced by a decentralized system, however, is questionable, given the inherent conflict of interests that would exist at national level. Therefore national courts instead of NCAs are playing an increasing role here. Finally, EU State aid policy is developing in contradictory ways, tightening control over national policies while being supportive of EU-level industrial policies (thereby indirectly facilitating national industrial polies again), especially as regards sustainability (such as in energy) and technological development (such as in electronic communications infrastructure). At a minimum this will make it difficult for State aid law to remain consistent.

Economic insights have been important to merger control since its outset and have spilled over into EU competition law at large, fuelling the new economic approach. The improvements made to merger control after the Commission suffered a series of painful defeats before the General Court in 2002 have fanned out across EU antitrust enforcement as well.[12] Since then merger control has been refined and the Commission has extended the economic tests applied to address increasingly subtle forms of unilateral and multilateral effects. Recent proposals would in fact add reviewing non-controlling minority shareholdings as low as 5 per cent to 20 per cent (provided there are additional factors such as blocking rights). As a relative outsider in this field and from a perspective of legal certainly and therefore simple rules, to me it would seem open to question whether these latest proposals are indeed improvements.

Services of general economic interest

Although this is not an instrument of EU competition law per se, SGEIs have been discussed above as potentially the most significant exception to EU competition law. Following the 2003 *Altmark* judgment, this is especially true for State aid.[13] If SGEIs were to be applied more frequently at national level, including regionally and locally, this would form a counterpoint to the State aid modernization that is currently underway, arguably leading to a new balance between the public and private spheres in EU competition law.

Electronic communications and energy

As they are based on harmonization legislation, these two forms of competition policy by definition aim to achieve the internal market. The scope of the internal market objective in this context, however, is much wider than for other instruments of EU competition law and notably includes an important element

[12] Case T-342/99 *Airtours plc v Commission* [2002] ECR II-2585; Case T-77/02 *Schneider Electric SA v Commission* [2002] ECR II-4201; Case T-80/02 *Tetra Laval BV v Commission* [2002] ECR II-4519.

[13] Case C-280/00 *Altmark Trans*, above (n 8).

of consumer protection. Hence the role accorded to the consumer interest is different here. Both the electronic communications and the energy frameworks also have other secondary objectives beyond protecting competition. In the first place this concerns promoting competition by making markets work, such as facilitating market entry by means of third party network access, instead of policing markets that are *a priori* functioning. The national regulatory authorities (NRAs) also have more specific instruments to do so than do the general competition authorities, the Commission and the NCAs. Second, the sectoral frameworks serve sector-specific objectives such as sustainability and security of supply in energy.

Evidently it is precisely these differences from general EU competition law that justify the existence of the sectoral regimes for these sectors. Another rationale is that they are equipped with specialized NRAs which have the requisite technical expertise (for instance to carry out complex cost calculations). The harmonization model leaves some room for differentiation at national level, while at the same time the framework is EU based. The regimes are also *ex ante* instead of *ex post*, and therefore do not shy away from prescribing detailed cost-based access models as opposed to the abuse-based and more general standards of antitrust. However, in the *DT* case regarding access issues, the Commission does not hesitate to correct NRAs (not just using coordination procedures under the harmonized framework) but also does so by using its own antitrust instruments.[14]

Antitrust 'rules'

Thus, we observe that although they are consistent (and coherent) with antitrust at the level of objectives, and complementary as instruments, the second and third layers of EU competition law add new layers of complexity. With the exception of mergers there is also increased decentralization, albeit within limits as regards the State aid exemption monopoly. At the same time, antitrust is used by the Commission as a backstop to ensure its main competition concerns are addressed as it sees fit, even if this means contradicting a national authority. In this context it may be seen as significant that (using its antitrust instruments) the Commission has so far corrected an NRA, but not yet (at least not in public view) an NCA.

5. Organization

Above we have looked mainly at legal categories, but an important practical aspect of coherence is the manner in which enforcement is organized. As we have seen, EU competition law is applied by a variety of organizations with different roles, which interact: this interaction is addressed in some more detail in the following.

[14] Case C-280/08 P *Deutsche Telekom AG v Commission* [2010] ECR I-9555.

The organization of antitrust

In antitrust, the organization of its enforcement is divided between two extremes, the network model based on the NCAs on the one hand and the centralized powers of the Commission on the other. It has been observed that although the network model was added in the interest of decentralization the Commission's powers have on balance not decreased. The result has been a significant net increase in antitrust enforcement under EU law, especially by NCAs.[15] This can be seen as the dominant success story of modernization. National courts also play an increasingly relevant role in enforcing antitrust although less (systematic) data are available here. At the same time, the Commission appears to be focusing on quality control and on pursuing more complex cases while playing a pivotal role within the network. It should be noted that the latter has so far not involved formal use of its pre-emption powers.

The organization of mergers and State aid

The areas of mergers and State aid have in common that they retain a centralized notification system controlled by the Commission. Neither of these two EU regimes is applied by NCAs although national courts play an increasingly significant role in State aid enforcement—albeit handicapped by the Commission monopoly on individual exemptions. Here the challenge seems to be whether both exemption monopolies will persist indefinitely or whether they could conceivably be replaced by an equally effective decentralized system of control as was established in antitrust.

Electronic communications and energy

The lead role in the enforcement of the rules on electronic communications and energy is reserved for the NRAs, while a coordinating role is shared by their network agencies BEREC and ACER, and the Commission. Unlike the area of general EU competition law where national rules still exist (outside the scope of an effect on trade), these areas are fully harmonized and the applicable law is derived from EU directives. National courts mainly play a role in reviewing the decisions of the NRAs (and, unlike in the case of competition law, they are never NRAs themselves). The Commission has (quasi-) veto powers but cannot pre-empt the NRAs by taking the contested decision itself or replacing it. Nevertheless, there is a relatively high level of consistency based on coordination procedures and best practice.

Table 10.2 provides an overview of the different types of organization. Courts here are referred to only where they apply the relevant rules themselves in suits between private parties, not where they hear appeals against decisions of NCAs/NRAs or where they act as NCAs themselves.

[15] W.P.J. Wils, 'Ten years of Regulation 1/2003—a retrospective', *Journal of European Competition Law & Practice* 4 (2014) 293–301.

Table 10.2 An overview of EU competition law enforcement

	Antitrust	Mergers	State aid	Telecom	Energy
EU law at EU level	Commission	Commission	Commission		
EU law at MS level	NCAs Courts		Courts	NRAs	NRAs
National law	NCAs Courts	NCAs			
Coordination	Commission ECN			Commission BEREC	Commission ACER

6. The Role of the Different Bodies in EU Competition Law

We will now look at the different roles of the public authorities that are active in enforcing EU competition law and their mutual interaction.

The role of the Commission

While in the antitrust context the Commission is *primus inter pares* within the ECN, it remains exclusively in control of exemption decisions in mergers and State aid. In the context of the two network sectors we have examined, the Commission mainly coordinates, and attempts to exercise (quasi-) veto power in the interest of consistency. In all these areas it also plays an agenda-setting and intellectual leadership role. It provides opinions on demand and, *ex officio*, *amicus curiae* briefs to national courts. Finally, the Commission also acts in sensitive and high-profile EU competition cases involving undertakings from major trading partners, raising the bar for the aspirations and ambitions of EU antitrust.

The role of the NCAs

The NCAs are the hands and feet of the Commission at national level in the antitrust arena. Jointly they are responsible for the great majority of competition cases under EU law, aside from their enforcement of national competition law. At the same time they may act as NRAs and have other powers such as consumer protection. Thus, they have come to play a key role in national economic regulation which is likely to be strongly influenced by insights from EU competition law. In this sense they are agents for change within their respective Member States which cumulatively add considerably to the transformative force of EU law, and the achievement of the internal market.

The role of the NRAs

We earlier examined the NRAs primarily in their application of competition-type powers but as we have seen they also have broader responsibilities. Nevertheless, applying EU rules in particular to access issues presents an enormous greatest challenge. They derive support from their network organizations (see below) and Commission backing, but can at the same time be undermined by these organizations, for instance where they try to address specifically national issues. The NRAs effectively form bespoke sectoral administrations governing by means of sectoral EU law and largely independently from national policies, however general EU competition law can be used by the Commission or the NCAs to fill any gaps, and/or to correct the NRAs.

The role of the network organizations

ECN, BEREC, and ACER coordinate the NCAs and NRAs and their interaction with the Commission. They form both a venue for information exchange and promoting best practice as an instrument to generate and enforce consensus. They are sometimes seen as fledgling (network) EU agencies,[16] and serve to envelop the NRAs in a distinct EU policy sphere that isolates them from the political concerns and the private interests seeking to influence the politics of their respective Member States.

The role of the national courts

The national courts essentially play three types of role: (i) in some Member States they act as NCAs; (ii) they may apply EU competition law in the context of private lawsuits (such as an appeal to annul an agreement, or an action for damages); and (iii) they may be seised on appeal against decisions of the NCAs and NRAs. The national courts guarantee consistency and the rule of law, including the protection of due process and the rights of the defence. Most procedural law that is relevant to EU competition law enforcement at national level is national law, however on issues of EU law, national courts need not just follow the lead of the European Court of Justice (CJEU) but may actively ask it for guidance by requesting a preliminary ruling.

The role of the CJEU

The General Court is the appellate court for Commission decisions in competition law cases, as well as more broadly across EU law. It rules both on issues of law and of fact and has been instrumental in supporting the more economic approach, which more recently appears to be in retreat. The Court of Justice fulfils a dual role at the apex of the system of EU competition law, and EU law generally. First, it acts as a supreme court on points of law with regard to General Court

[16] S. Lavrijssen and L. Hancher, 'Networks of Regulatory Agencies in Europe', in P. Larouche and P. Cserne (eds), *National Legal Systems and Globalization: New Role, Continuing Relevance* (The Hague: TMC Asser Press/Springer, 2013); S. Lavrijssen and A.T. Ottow, 'Independent supervisory authorities: a fragile concept', *Legal Issues of Economic Integration* 39 (2012) 419–46.

rulings, and second, it provides an authoritative interpretation on questions of EU law submitted by national courts. Both functions have a strong impact on coherence of the system of EU competition law. The relevant standards of review and of proof (from marginal review in economic assessments to comprehensive review of fines) play a significant role in determining on the one hand effective enforcement, and on the other its legitimacy.

With such an array of actors across twenty-eight Member States the ramifications are complex. This is another reason why clear objectives, boundaries, rules, exceptions, procedures, and remedies are important, as well as the application of general principles of EU law, in order to keep EU competition law consistent.

7. Three Types of Coherence

Having briefly recapped the contents and findings of the preceding chapters in general terms, I now want to return to coherence as such. At the outset of this concluding chapter I have identified three levels of coherence, the findings with respect to each of which will now be discussed.

External coherence within EU law and integration

This dimension regards the coherence of EU competition law within EU law as a whole. Starting from its overriding objective, that of achieving the internal market, it is clear that at this level competition law chimes with EU law in toto. This is so even although the latter has other objectives as well including inter alia an area of freedom, security, and justice without internal frontiers, sustainable development based on balanced economic growth and social justice, and a social market economy found in Article 3 TEU. Nevertheless the internal market remains a pillar of European integration and the motherload of EU law.[17]

Similarly, key legal principles including effectiveness and equivalence, preemption, proportionality, and last but not least the rights of the defence, are normally honoured and observed in the context of EU competition law. Because throughout the text I have focused on effectiveness and legitimacy, these will be addressed separately and more fully below. An important role is played by the CJEU which evidently is active across the full range of EU law as a whole. This ensures that EU competition law remains embedded within the latter.

External coherence is also related to the role that EU competition law plays in the context of European integration. This would be a research topic in its own right. However, it appears to me that this role is primarily mediated by the internal market objective, facilitating market entry and economic activity throughout the EU. There is also a certain external defensive aspect involved. This means protecting the internal market from anticompetitive behaviour by

[17] M. Monti, A new strategy for the single market: At the service of Europe's economy and society. Report to the President of the European Commission, José Manuel Barroso, 9 May 2010.

dominant undertakings based outside the EU, such as *Microsoft*[18] and *Gazprom*,[19] to name just two. It appears unlikely that such cases could be pursued successfully at the level of an individual Member State.

Internal coherence of competition law as a system

Naturally, the degree of internal coherence of EU competition law itself depends at least to some extent on how wide the net is cast: just antitrust, just general competition law, or also including the sectoral competition law that was discussed earlier? For each instrument, the centrality of the internal market objectives plays an important role. The same is true for the degree to which the parties (NCAs, national courts) involved are identical, to which degree coordination mechanisms are in place, and whether the Commission has the possibility to overrule the national authorities involved and/or pre-empt their decisions with its own.

On the one hand, we have seen how competition policy emerged incrementally with antitrust being supplemented by merger control and (increasingly effective) State aid, followed by the liberalization of the network sectors by means of a tandem of antitrust enforcement and harmonization legislation. With this we now arguably have a suite of competition policy instruments in place, which are continuously being upgraded to address all competition problems that are likely to arise (as well as arguably some unlikely ones). This notwithstanding, there are still basic inconsistencies within this system, such as the criteria used to establish whether an entity is an undertaking or not.

On the other hand, the impact of public policy is potentially the great dividing force in EU competition law, and especially one that currently separates State aid and sectoral competition policy from the rest. Traditionally this threat was seen as coming from industrial policy in terms of propping up failing industrial sectors (often justified by protecting employment and/or regional cohesion) or promoting national champions. Now it has resurfaced inter alia in an environmentally and consumer-friendly contemporary form, for instance as in the promotion of renewable energy. As regards national policies this problem is multiplied by the decentralization of competition law.

My argument, as stated in the section on rules and exceptions earlier, is that such policies must be regarded and resolved as boundary issues and not as reliant on exceptions at least unless they can be addressed convincingly in terms of efficiency improvements. The same holds for the question to what extent EU policies themselves may justify exceptions in EU competition law. An exception in both cases is EU State aid, where national policies that are consistent with EU policies and objectives (such as environmental protection) may be declared a form of aid

[18] Commission Decision of 24 May 2004 relating to a proceeding pursuant to Article 82 EC against Microsoft Corporation (Case COMP/C-3/37.792 Microsoft) OJ 2007 L 32/23; Case T-201/04, *Microsoft Corp. v Commission* [2007] II-3601.

[19] Case COMP/39816 Upstream gas supplies in Central and Eastern Europe, statement of objections of 22 April 2015.

that is compatible with the internal market. This forms potentially one of the main sources of inconsistency in EU competition law.

If the coherence of the three general EU competition law instruments as a whole is nevertheless increasing, this is because these instruments are based on similar economic theories and given the central role played by the European Commission in their enforcement. Thus, solutions found in one part of EU competition policy will eventually be applied, *mutatis mutandis*, to fix problems found in other parts. However, this occurs primarily at a practical level: there is no overarching grand theory emanating from Brussels that covers antitrust, mergers, and State aid in toto. At best, the components of EU competition law are presented as essential to the internal market, and slightly more suspect (from a competition perspective), as necessary elements in the EU's economic agenda, such as the 2020 strategy for growth.[20]

Since the advent of the Sarkozy amendments to the Treaties, it should be no surprise that the competition rules are not publicly framed as pursuing a coherent agenda in their own right. As we have seen, in itself placing competition policy in the context of completing and policing, the internal market does not threaten its coherence. It is construing competition policy instruments as tools of economic and industrial policies, as we now see in State aid, which may change with the political fashion of the day, that appears to put at risk both their consistency, which is key to legitimacy, and their effectiveness.

Finally, it seems self-evident that EU competition law becomes more coherent if it disposes of a full suite of powers that are tailored to addressing the full range of problems that present themselves. From the perspective of coherence, however, it is remarkable that in addition to competition rules covering anticompetitive agreements, dominance abuse, mergers, and State aid and thereby most imaginable forms of anticompetitive behaviour, there should be sector-specific competition rules. At a minimum this occurrence suggests that the general rules by themselves, even if coherent, are not sufficiently effective to achieve the completion-based objectives in all sectors.

Sector-specific rules exist because *ex ante* controls are deemed necessary, and because the need for third party access is pervasive. This also raises the question whether the specific rules fit in with general EU competition law in terms of its instruments and objectives, and the method of governance. As we have seen, so far the general and sectoral regimes appear compatible and complementary, however a closer examination shows that any expectation that they will be temporary and replaced by *ex post* EU antitrust in the long run seems unfounded, unless we are talking about a very long run indeed. Instead it may be better to regard general EU competition law as providing a context and a basic orientation or stem upon which the sectoral rules can be grafted, each to flower in their own way but grounded in the principles of antitrust.

[20] Commission Communication, Europe 2020: a strategy for smart, sustainable and inclusive growth, COM(2010) 2020, 3 March 2010.

Internal coherence of the components of EU competition law

In essence, internal coherence is the last to be unpacked of a set of Chinese boxes that is concerned with the coherence of the components of EU competition policy at the level of the instruments antitrust, mergers, and State aid, as well as the sectoral rules for electronic communications and energy. At the same time, this section involves what we have already discussed regarding objectives and boundaries, rules and exceptions, procedures and remedies earlier in this concluding chapter, which I will not repeat here.

Each of the instruments is part of a process of constant review and improvement, and has been so since its inception, albeit at a quickening pace. This is in part the result of developing economic insights and an increasing permeability of competition law with respect to these insights. It is also the result of legal developments both within and beyond competition law (and even outside EU competition law with the European Convention of Human Rights). Here, resistance leads to change in a dialectical process in the sense of the clash between two incongruent vectors leading to a third pointing in a different direction. Neither side is likely to be fully satisfied but the result is what in human affairs passes for progress.

8. Effectiveness and Legitimacy

The coherence of a policy can, in principle, be judged on the merits of the degree to which it achieves its own goals or principles and this is to a large extent what we have examined above, however I had set effectiveness and legitimacy as additional independent standards to which I believe competition policy should be held when deciding whether it is coherent or not. This is because EU competition law should also be judged based on the main principles of the overall legal system to which it belongs. Doing so can be seen as a specification of its external coherence (to which I have already referred) based on just these two parameters. At the same time, the demands of effectiveness and legitimacy apply at all levels, not just to that of the legal system of European law, but also to the EU competition law as a whole as well as to its individual instruments.

Effectiveness

Traditionally in EU law, effectiveness is seen as a form of equivalence with the way similar issues are dealt with under national law. This issue arises because national rules tend to govern procedure, as they do in the case of competition law enforcement at national level. This traditional understanding of effectiveness is problematic from the perspective of coherence of EU competition law where a substantive and more uniform degree of effectiveness is desirable. This may mean moving on from divergent national standards to at least a common minimum standard.

The latter is indeed observable in the case law on the guarantees of the effectiveness of the NCAs in *VEBIC*[21] and at the level of secondary legislation on private actions for damages[22]—paradoxically on a topic where the Court of Justice had been prepared to grant considerable leeway to the Member States. This said, both issues remain weak points of EU competition law: (i) the funding and independence of NCAs, and (ii) the fact that public enforcement is favoured over private damages actions, leaving the capacity of national courts to act in the enforcement of EU competition law underutilized. In any event, effectiveness is a dimension where EU competition law is in development.

This can be seen in the (2014) *Kone* case on damages:

> In the absence of EU rules governing the matter, it is for the domestic legal system of each Member State to lay down the detailed rules governing the exercise of the right to claim compensation for the harm resulting from an agreement or practice prohibited under Article 101 TFEU, including those on the application of the concept of 'causal relationship', provided that the principles of equivalence and effectiveness are observed.
>
> Accordingly, the rules applicable to actions for safeguarding rights which individuals derive from the direct effect of EU law must not be less favourable than those governing similar domestic actions (principle of equivalence) and must not make it in practice impossible or excessively difficult to exercise rights conferred by EU law (principle of effectiveness).
>
> In that regard, and specifically in the context of competition law, those rules must not jeopardise the effective application of Articles 101 TFEU and 102 TFEU.[23]

Thus, in the final analysis, in those cases where harmonization is needed to ensure the effective application of EU competition law (in this case antitrust) such harmonization is likely to arise, either based on the case law, or based on new legislation. In my view this norm of the effective application of Articles 101 and 102 TFEU is essentially that which already guides the cooperation between the Commission and national courts under Regulation 1/2003.

Legitimacy

As we have seen earlier, following Fritz Scharpf the norm of legitimacy can be sub-divided between input (or process) legitimacy and output (or results-based) legitimacy.[24] The latter resembles effectiveness.

The input legitimacy of competition policy has surely increased now it is regularly applied by national authorities, both courts and NCAs/NRAs. This means that the process is now more in line with principles of subsidiarity and

[21] Case C-439/08 *Vlaamse federatie van verenigingen van Brood- en Banketbakkers, Ijsbereiders en Chocoladebewerkers (VEBIC) VZW* [2010] ECR I-12471.

[22] Directive 2014/104/EU, above (n 11).

[23] Case C-557/12 *Kone AG, Otis GmbH, Schindler Aufzüge und Fahrtreppen GmbH, Schindler Liegenschaftsverwaltung GmbH, ThyssenKrupp Aufzüge GmbH v ÖBB-Infrastruktur AG*, Judgment of 5 June 2014, paras 24–26 (case reference removed).

[24] F.W. Scharpf, *Community and Autonomy: Institutions, Policies and Legitimacy in Multilevel Europe* (Frankfurt: Campus, 2010).

proportionality, and closer to the EU consumer/citizen. Arguably, judicial review has become more available and pervasive. At the same time the network agencies ECN, BEREC, and ACER provide deliberative fora (*pace* Habermas) that are capable of adding (input) legitimacy to their preferred approach, and a network to support it in terms of independent (vis-à-vis the industry as well as national governments) and fact-based regulatory intervention.

There are no examples of instances where the Commission has forced a NCA to officially surrender a case, hence so far minimum informal coordination processes (albeit in the shadow of pre-emption) seem to be working well. In addition, the strict review by the General Court starting from in particular the *Tetra Laval* case has ensured that the quality of the inputs on which a competition case is based has improved.[25] Other principles of EU law such as the proportionality of the enforcement of EU competition law as well as the limited use of exceptions also form constraints promoting coherence and input legitimacy.

In terms of output legitimacy, since modernization the number of antitrust decisions has multiplied by a factor of five or six almost exclusively as a result of the contribution of the NCAs. This can be seen as the most important result of modernization. The Commission's contribution has remained roughly stable in quantitative terms compared to the period prior to modernization but presumably focuses on producing decisions of higher quality in more complex and more serious cases, as was its ambition.[26] However, how much this has contributed to achieving the internal market (which, like the ever closer Union, is an ever-moving target) is difficult to say with any degree of confidence.

There is little information on the output in terms of the effect on gross domestic product (GDP) although the available evidence suggests that such effects are relatively limited and deterrence, increased quality, and choice may well be significantly more important. In addition, there are beneficial effects on market structure.[27] In any event, since modernization the output of EU competition law has clearly increased both in terms of volume and technical quality of the decisions concerned. This has served legitimacy.

9. Developing the Law of the Land

The approach taken by the Court of Justice does not allow for full economic and hence legal coherence of EU competition law.[28] For instance, it lacks a coherent approach to objectives, notably the consumer interest, and to exceptions, notably those available for public policy, across the various instruments. It does, however,

[25] Case T-5/02 *Tetra Laval BV v Commission* [2002] ECR II-4381.

[26] Wils (n 15).

[27] F. Ilkovitz and A. Dierx, Ex post evaluation of competition policy enforcement: what can we learn from the literature and from the experience of competition authorities? *Competition Policy Brief*, June 2015.

[28] Joined Cases C-519/06 P, C-501/06 P, C-513/06 P, C-515/06 P, and C-519/06 P *GlaxoSmithKline*, above (n 5).

provide an open texture to EU competition law that enables it to take full account of the internal market objective, which, under the Lisbon Treaty, has become its primary justification.

This openness of the legal framework, coupled with its network-type enforcement, coordinated by the Commission, makes for a loosely coherent system of law that is increasingly effective, meets basic standards of legitimacy, and is on a path toward further improvement, or in any event change. Even if not all its aspects have so far been fully tested (or needed to be), such as pre-emption of national courts and NCAs by the Commission, modernization is delivering results in terms of a significantly increased number of decisions as well as, arguably, the quality of these decisions. In fact the absence of the need to apply pre-emption (at least publicly) is in itself a measure of the success of the post-modernization system of EU competition law.

The main challenge now is for the networks involved to formulate and disseminate workable and predictable rules, procedures, and administrative practices in interaction with the courts of the EU, including the national courts. This is needed to shape still further the competition norms as 'law of the land' and, last but not least, to enhance their effective and legitimate enforcement in order to protect the functioning of the internal market.

Bibliography

Alexy, R. *A Theory of Constitutional Rights*, transl. J Rivers (Oxford: Oxford University Press, 2002).

Alexy, R and Peczenik, A. 'The concept of coherence and its significance for discursive rationality', *Ratio Juris* 3 (1990) 130–47.

Atanasiu, I. *Constructing the EU Network of Competition Authorities* (Oxford: Hart Publishing, 2005).

Augenstein, D (ed.). *Integration through Law Revisited: The Making of the European Polity* (Farnham: Ashgate, 2011).

Bacon, K (ed.). *European Union Law of State Aid*, 2nd edn. (Oxford: Oxford University Press, 2013).

Bailey, D. 'Restrictions of competition by object under Article 101 TFEU', *Common Market Law Review* 49 (2012) 559–99.

Bailey, D. 'Scope of judicial review under Article 81 EC', *Common Market Law Review* 41 (2004) 1333–60.

Baldwin, R, Cave, M, and Lodge, M (eds). *The Oxford Handbook of Regulation* (Oxford: Oxford University Press, 2010).

Banks, K. 'Mergers and partial mergers under EEC law', *Fordham International Law Journal* 11 (1987) 255–309.

Baquero Cruz, J. *Between Competition and Free Movement: The Economic Constitutional Law of the European Community* (Oxford: Hart Publishing, 2002).

Barnard, C. *The Substantive Law of the EU: The Four Freedoms*, 4th edn. (Oxford: Oxford University Press, 2013).

Basedow, J. 'The modernization of European competition law: a story of unfinished concepts', *Texas International Law Journal* 42 (2007) 429–39.

Basedow, J and Wurmnest, W (eds). *Structure and Effects in EU Competition Law* (Deventer: Kluwer, 2011).

Bertea, S. 'Does arguing from coherence make sense?', *Argumentation* 19 (2005) 433–46.

Bertea, S. 'The arguments from coherence: analysis and evaluation', *Oxford Journal of Legal Studies* 25 (2005) 369–91.

Bingham, T. *The Rule of Law* (London: Penguin Books, 2011).

Biondi, A. 'State aid is falling down, falling down: an analysis of the case law on the notion of aid', *Common Market Law Review* 50 (2013) 1719–44.

Boer, T, Edmonds, P and Oglialoro, C. 'Economic Aspects of the Single European Market in Pharmaceuticals', *European Competition Law Review* 20 (1999) 256.

Bork, RH. *The Antitrust Paradox: A Policy at War with Itself* (New York, NY: Free Press, 1993).

Botta, M. 'Commission acting as plaintiff in cases of private enforcement of EU competition law: *Otis*', *Common Market Law Review* 50 (2013)) 1105–18.

Bouterse, RB. *Competition and integration: what goals count?: EEC competition law and goals of industrial, monetary, and cultural policy* (Deventer: Kluwer, 1994).

Brammer, S. 'Concurrent jurisdiction under Regulation 1/2003 and the issue of case allocation', *Common Market Law Review* 42 (2005) 1383–424.

Buendia, JL. *Exclusive Rights and State Monopolies under EC Law: Article 86 (former Article 90) of the EC Treaty* (Oxford: Oxford University Press, 2000).

Callaerts, R. 'State Aid for the Production of Electricity from Renewable Energy Resources', *European Energy and Environmental Law Review* 24.1 (2015) 17–26.

Cappelletti, M, Seccombe, M and Weiler, JHH (eds). *Integration through Law: European and the American Federal Experience* (Berlin: De Gruyter, 1986).

Castillo de la Torre, F. 'Evidence, proof and judicial review in cartel cases', *World Competition* 32 (2009) 505–78.

Cengiz, F. 'Multi-level governance in competition policy: the European Competition Network', *European Law Review* 35 (2010) 660–77.

Chirico, F and Larouche, P. 'Divergence, functionalism and the economics of convergence' in S Prechal and B van Roermund, *The Coherence of EU Law: The Search for Unity in Divergent Concepts* (Oxford: Oxford University Press, 2008) 463–94.

Cini, M and McGowan, L. *The Competition Policy in the European Union*, 2nd edn. (London: Palgrave MacMillan, 2008).

Cleynenbreugel, van P. 'Institutional assimilation in the wake of EU competition law decentralisation', *Competition Law Review* 8 (2012) 285–312.

Coen, D and Thatcher, M. 'Network governance and multi-level delegation: European networks of regulatory agencies' *Journal of Public Policy* 28 (2008) 49–71.

Cook, C, Frishc, S, and Novak, V. 'Recent developments in EU merger remedies', *Journal of European Competition Law& Practice* 5 (2015) 361–4.

Craig, P. 'Formal and substantive conceptions of the rule of law: an analytical framework', *Public Law* (1997) 466–81.

Craig, P. *EU Administrative Law*, 2nd edn. (Oxford: Oxford University Press, 2012).

Cremona, M. 'Coherence through law: what difference will the Treaty of Lisbon make?' *Hamburg Review of Social Sciences* 3 (2008) 11–36.

Cseres, K. 'The controversies of the consumer welfare standard', *Competition Law Review* 3 (2007) 121–73.

Cseres, KJ. *Competition Law and Consumer Protection* (The Hague: Kluwer Law International, 2005).

De Margerie, S. '"Pay-for-Delay" Settlements: In Search of the Right Standard', *World Competition* 36 (2013) 85–97.

De Visser, M. *Network-Based Governance in EC Law* (Oxford: Hart Publishing, 2009).

Dekeyser, K and De Smijter, E. 'The exchange of evidence within the ECN and how it contributes to the European cooperation and coordination in cartel cases', *Legal Issues of European Integration* 32 (2005) 161–74.

Dickson, J. 'Interpretation and coherence in legal reasoning', in *Stanford Encyclopedia of Philosophy* (2010), available at: <http://plato.stanford.edu/entries/legal-reas-interpret/>.

Drexl, J, Kerber, W, and Podszun, R. (eds). *Competition Policy and the Economic Approach: Foundations and Limitations* (Cheltenham: Edward Elgar, 2011).

Dworkin, R. *Law's Empire* (London: Fontana, 1984).

Ehlermann, CD. 'Reflections on a European cartel office', *Common Market Law Review* 471 (1995) 471–86.

Ehlermann, CD. 'The modernization of EC antitrust policy: a legal and cultural revolution', *Common Market Law Review* 37 (2000) 537–90.

Ehlermann, CD and Atanasiu, I (eds). *European Competition Law Annual 2000: The Modernisation of EC Antitrust Policy* (Oxford: Hart Publishing, 2001).

Ehlermann, CD and Atanasiu, I (eds). *European Competition Law Annual 2002*. (Oxford: Hart Publishing, 2005).

Emerson, RW. *Self reliance* (1841) respectively Oscar Wilde, 'The Relation of Dress to Art' in the *Pall Mall Gazette* 28 February 1885.

Epstein, RA. *Simple Rules for a Complex World*, rev. edn. (Cambridge MA: Harvard University Press, 1997).

Esposito, F and Montanaro, F. 'A Fistful of Euros: EU Competition Policy and Reverse Payments in the Pharmaceutical Industry', *European Competition Journal* 10 (2014) 499–521.

European Commission. 'State aid modernization—a major revamp of EU state aid control' *Competition policy brief* 11 (2014).

Faull, J and Nikpay, A (eds). *The EU Law of Competition*, 3rd edn. (Oxford: Oxford University Press, 2014).

Fernández, C and Vila Gisbert, C. 'Dual Pricing for Medicines: Is the European Jurisprudence Accepted by National Courts? (Spain)', *Journal of European Competition Law & Practice* (2015) 332–6.

Forwood, N. 'The Commission's "more economic approach"—implications for the role of the EU Courts, the treatment of economic evidence and the scope of judicial review', in CD Ehlermann and M Marquis (eds), *European Competition Law Annual* 2009: *Evaluation of Evidence and its Judicial Review in Competition Cases* (Oxford: Hart Publishing, 2011) 191–255.

Franklin, CMK. 'The burgeoning principle of consistency in EU law', *Yearbook of European Law* 30 (2011) 42–85.

Frese, MJ. 'Decentralised enforcement of EU competition law and the institutional autonomy of the Member States: a Case commentary', *Amsterdam Center for law and Economics Working Paper* 04 (2011).

Gabathuler, D and Sauter, W. 'The allocation of scarce resources and spectrum assignment in mobile communications: the case of UMTS', in PA Buigues and P Rey (eds), *The Economics of Antitrust and Regulation in Telecommunications: Perspectives from the New Regulatory Framework* (Camberley: Edward Elgar, 2004) 213–38.

Gabor, B. *Regulatory Competition in the Internal Market: Comparing Models for Corporate Law, Securities Law and Competition Law* (Cheltenham: Edward Elgar, 2013).

Gemen, van W. 'Towards a Coherent Constitutional System within the European Union', *European Public Law* 2 (1996) 81–101.

Geradin, D and Petit, N. 'Judicial Review in European Union Competition Law: A Quantitative and Qualitative Assessment' TILEC Discussion Paper Series 2011/8.

Geradin, D, Layne-Farrar, A, and Petit, N. *EU Competition Law and Economics* (Oxford: Oxford University Press, 2012).

Gerard, D. 'EU competition policy after Lisbon: time to review the "state action" doctrine?', *Oxford Journal of European Competition Law and Practice* 1 (2010) 202–10.

Gerard, DMB. 'Public enforcement: the ECN—network antitrust enforcement in the European Union', in I Lianos and D Geradin (eds), *Handbook on European Competition Law: Enforcement and Procedure* (Cheltenham: Edward Elgar, 2013) 181–227.

Gerber, D. 'The evolution of a European competition law network', in CD Ehlermann and I Atanasiu (eds), *European Competition Law Annual* 2002: *Constructing the EU Network of Competition Authorities* (Oxford: Hart Publishing, 2004) 43–65.

Gerber, DJ. *Law and Competition in Twentieth Century Europe: Protecting Prometheus* (Oxford: Oxford University Press, 1998).

Gerber, DJ. 'Two forms of modernization in European competition law', *Fordham International Law Journal* 31 (2007) 1235–65.

Gerbrandy, A. 'Procedural convergence in competition law – towards a spontaneous *ius commune*?', *Review of European Administrative Law* 2 (2009) 105–34.

Gerven, van W. 'Coherence of Community and national laws. Is there a legal basis for a European Civil Code?', *European Review of Private Law* 5 (1997) 465–9.

Gerven, van W. 'Rights and remedies in the enforcement of EC law before national court' in Collected courses of the Academy of European Law. 8: Book 1. European Community Law (The Hague: Kluwer Law International, 2001) 241–360.

Gippini-Fournier, E. 'The modernisation of European competition law: first experiences with Regulation 1/2003' Community report to the FIDE Congress (2008), available at SSRN: <http://ssrn.com/abstract=1139776>.

Glynn, D. 'Article 82 and Price Discrimination in Patented Pharmaceuticals: The Economics', *European Competition Law Review* 26 (2005) 135–43.

Goyder, J and Albors-Llorens, A. *Goyder's EC Competition Law*, 5th edn. (Oxford: Oxford University Press, 2009).

Graupner, F. 'The battle over the role of European competition policy: now you see it, now you don't', *Competition Law Journal* 6 (1997) 89–100.

Grigorios Grigoriadis, L. 'The Application of EU Competition Law in the Pharmaceutical Sector: The Case of Parallel Trade', *European Business Law Review* 25 (2014) 144–201.

Gunn, A and Luts, J. 'Tax Rulings, APAs and State Aid: Legal Issues', *EC Tax Review* 2 (2015) 119–25.

Hancher, L and Larouche, P. 'The coming of age of EU regulation of network industries and services of general economic interest', in P Craig and G de Búrca (eds), *The Evolution of EU Law*, 2nd edn. (Oxford: Oxford University Press, 2011) 743–99.

Hancher, L and Sauter, W. 'Public Services and EU Law', in C Barnard and S Peers (eds), *European Union Law* (Oxford: Oxford University Press, 2014) 539–67.

Harlow, C and Rawlings, R. 'Modernisation, cooperation, enforcement: competition', in C Harlow and R Rawlings, *Process and Procedure in EU Administration* (Oxford: Hart Publishing, 2014) 196–219.

Hawk, B. 'System failure: vertical restraints and EC competition law', *Common Market Law Review* 32 (1995) 973–89.

Herlin-Karnell, E and Konstantinides, T. 'The rise and expressions of consistency in EU law: legal and strategic implications for European integration', in C Barnard, A Alboirs-Llorens, MW Gehrin, and R Schütze (eds), *Cambridge Yearbook of European Legal Studies* 15 (2012–13) 139–67.

Hjelmeng, E. 'Competition law remedies: striving for coherence or finding new ways', *Common Market Law Review* 50 (2013) 1107–38.

Ibañez Colomo, P. 'On the application of competition law as regulation: elements for a theory', *Yearbook of European Law* 29 (2010) 261–306.

Ilkovitz, F and Dierx, A. Ex post evaluation of competition policy enforcement: what can we learn from the literature and from the experience of competition authorities? *Competition Policy Brief*, June 2015.

Immenga, U. 'Coherence: a sacrifice of decentralisation', in C-D Ehlermann and I Atanasiu, *European Competition Law Annual 2000: The Modernization of EC Antitrust Policy* (Oxford: Hart Publishing, 2001) 353–9.

Jaeger, M. 'Standard of review in competition cases: can the General Court increase coherence in the European Union judicial system', in T Baumé *et al.* (eds), *Today's Multilayered Legal Order: Current Issues and Perspectives. Liber Amicorum in Honour of Arjen W.H. Meij* (Zutphen: Paris Publishers, 2011).

Jaeger, M. 'The standard of review in competition cases involving complex economic assessments: towards the marginalisation of the marginal review?', *Journal of European Competition Law & Practice* 2 (2011) 295–314.

Jenkins, T and Bushell, G. 'Justice denied or simply delayed? Consequences of excessive delay at the EU's General Court', *Journal of European Competition Law & Practice* 6 (2015) 3–14.

Johnston, A and Block, G. *EU Energy Law* (Oxford: Oxford University Press, 2012).

Kahneman, D. 'Maps of bounded rationality: psychology for behavioral economics', *American Economic Review* 93 (2003) 1449–75.

Kanavos, P and Costa-Font, J. 'Pharmaceutical parallel trade in Europe: stakeholder and competition effects', *Economic Policy* 20 (2005) 751–98.

Khan, N. *EU Antitrust Procedure*, 6th edn. (London: Sweet & Maxwell, 2012).

Kong, Y. 'Competition between brand-name and generics—analysis on pricing of brand-name pharmaceutica', *Health Economics* 18 (2009) 591–606.

Korah, V. *An Introductory Guide to EEC Competition Law and Practice*, 4th edn. (London: Sweet and Maxwell, 1990).

Korah, V. 'From legal form towards economic efficiency—Article 85(1) of the EEC Treaty in contrast to US Antitrust', *Antitrust Bulletin* 35 (1990) 1009.

Korah, V. 'The future of vertical agreements under EC competition law', *European Competition Law Review* 19 (1998) 506–13.

Korah, V and O'Sullivan, D. *Distribution Agreements under the EC Competition Rules* (Oxford: Hart Publishing, 2002).

Kotlowski, A. 'Third-party Access Rights in the Energy Sector: A Competition Law Perspective', *Utilities Law Review* 16 (2006/7) 101–9.

Krajewski, M, Neergaard, U and van de Gronden, JW (eds). *The Changing Framework for Services of General Interest in Europe: Between Competition and Solidarity* (The Hague: TMC Asser Press, 2009).

Kuoppamäki, P and Talus, K. 'Relationship Between General Competition Laws and Sector Specific Energy Regulation', *Oil Gas and Energy Law* (2010).

Langer, J. *Tying and Bundling as a Leveraging Concern under EC Competition Law* (Deventer: Kluwer Law International, 2007).

Larouche, P. *Competition Law and Regulation in European Telecommunications* (Oxford: Hart Publishing, 2000).

Larouche, P. 'Coordination of European and member state regulatory policy. Horizontal, vertical and transversal aspects', *Competition and Regulation in Network Industries* 5 (2004) 277–94.

Larouche, P. 'Coordination of European and Member State regulatory policy: horizontal, vertical and transversal aspects', in D Geradin and N Petit, *Which Regulatory Authorities in Europe?* (Cheltenham: Edward Elgar, 2005) 164–79.

Lavrijssen, S and Hancher, L. 'Networks of Regulatory Agencies in Europe', in P Larouche and P Cserne (eds), *National Legal Systems and Globalization: New Role, Continuing Relevance* (The Hague: TMC Asser Press/Springer, 2013) 183–220.

Lavrijssen, S and Hancher, L. 'Networks on Track, From European Regulatory Networks to European Regulatory "Network Agencies"', *Legal Issues of Economic Integration* 36 (2009) 23–55.

Lavrijssen, S and Ottow, AT. 'Independent supervisory authorities: a fragile concept', *Legal issues of Economic integration* 39 (2012) 419–46.

Lavrijssen, S, Gerbrandy, A, and Essens, O. 'European and national standards of review: differentiation or convergence', in O Essens, A Gerbrandy, and SACM Lavrijssen (eds), *National Courts and the Standard of Review in Competition Law and Economic Regulation* (Groningen: Europa Publishing, 2009) 265–91.

Lavrijssen, SACM. 'The protection of non-competition interests; what role for competition authorities after Lisbon?', *European Law Review* 35 (2010) 634–59.

Lavrijssen, SACM and Hancher, L. 'Networks of regulatory agencies in Europe', in P Larouche and P Cserne (eds), *National Legal Systems and Globalization: New Role, Continuing Relevance* (The Hague: TMC Asser Press/Springer, 2013) 183–220.

Lavrijssen, SACM & Hancher, L. 'Networks on Track, From European Regulatory Networks to European Regulatory "Network Agencies"', *Legal Issues of Economic Integration* 1 (2009) 23–55.

Lenaerts, K. 'Effective judicial protection judicial protection in the EU', available at <http://ec.europa.eu/justice/events/assises-justice-2013/files/interventions/koenlenarts.pdf>.

Lenaerts, K. 'The unity of European law and the overload of the ECJ—The system of preliminary rulings revisited', in I Pernice, J Kokott, and C Saunders (eds), *The future of the European judicial system in a comparative perspective: 6th International ECLN-Colloquium/IACL Round Table Berlin, 2–4 November 2005* (Baden-Baden: Nomos, 2006) 211–39.

Lenaerts, K, Maselis, I, Gutman, K, *et al.* (eds). *EU Procedural Law* (Oxford: Oxford University Press, 2014).

Lianos, I. 'Is the availability of appropriate remedies a limit to competition law liability under Article 102 TFEU? The mischiefs of "discretionary remedialism" in competition law', in F Etro and I Kokkoris (eds), *Competition Law and the Enforcement of Article 102* (Oxford: Oxford University Press, 2010) 165–202.

Lianos, I. *Some reflections on the question of the goals of EU competition law*, CLES Working Paper Series 3/2013.

Lianos, I. 'Competition law remedies in Europe', in I Lianos and D Geradin (eds), *Handbook on European Competition Law: Enforcement and Procedure* (Cheltenham: Edward Elgar, 2013) 362–455.

Lianos, I. Some reflections on the question of the goals of EU competition law, CLES Working Paper Series 3/2013, January 2013.

Loozen, E. 'The Requisite Legal Standard for Economic Assessments in EU Competition Cases Unravelled through the Economic Approach', *European Law Review* 1 (2014) 91–110.

MacCormick, N. 'Argumentation and interpretation in law', *Ratio Juris* 3 (1993) 16–29.

MacCormick, N. 'Coherence in legal justification', in W Kravietz *et al.* (eds), *Theorie der Normen* (Berlin: Duncker & Humblot, 1984) 37–53.

MacCormick, N. *Rhetoric and the Rule of Law: A Theory of Legal Reasoning* (Oxford: Oxford University Press, 2009).

Maher, I. 'Functional and normative delegation to non-majoritarian institutions: the case of the European Competition Network', *Comparative European Politics* 7 (2009) 414–34.

Maier-Rigaud, F. 'On the Normative Foundations of Competition Law – Efficiency, Political Freedom and the Freedom to Compete', in D Zimmer (ed.), *The Goals of Competition Law* (Cheltenham: Edward Elgar, 2012) 132–68.

Marsden, P. 'Checks and balances: EU competition law and the rule of law', *Competition Law International* 5 (2009) 24–8.

Meij, A. 'Judicial Review in the EC Courts: Tetra Laval and Beyond', in O Essens, A Gerbrandy, and SACM Lavrijssen (eds), *National Courts and the Standard of Review in Competition Law and Economic Regulation* (Groningen: Europa Publishing, 2009) 7–22.

Milward, AS. *The European Rescue of the Nation-State*, 2nd edn. (London: Routledge, 1999).

Milward, AS. *The Reconstruction of Western Europe 1945–1951* (London: Routledge, 1982).

Monti, G. 'A plea for "extraterritorial" antitrust enforcement by national competition authorities' EUI Law Department Research paper (2014).

Monti, G. *EC Competition Law* (Cambridge: Cambridge University Press, 2007).

Monti, G. 'Independence, interdependence and legitimacy: the EU Commission, national competition authorities and the European Competition Network' EUI Law Department Research paper 2014/01.

Monti, G. 'Managing decentralised antitrust enforcement: Toshiba', *Common Market Law Review* 51 (2014) 261–80.

Monti, G. 'Managing the intersection of utilities regulation and EC competition law', *The Competition Law Review* 4 (2008) 123–45.

Monti, G. 'The Scope of Collective Dominance under Articles 82 EC', *Common Market Law Review* 38 (2001) 131–57.

Monti, M. A new strategy for the single market: At the service of Europe's economy and society. Report to the President of the European Commission, José Manuel Barroso, 9 May 2010, available at: <http://ec.europa.eu/internal_market/strategy/docs/monti_report_final_10_05_2010_en.pdf>.

Moral Soriano, L. 'A modest notion of coherence in legal reasoning: a model for the European Court of Justice', *Ratio Juris* 16 (2003) 296–323.

Motta, M. *Competition Policy: Theory and Practice* (Cambridge: Cambridge University Press, 2004).

Nagy, CI. 'The distinction between anti-competitive object and effect after Allianz: the end of coherence in competition analysis', *World Competition* 36 (2013) 541–64.

Nic Shuibhne, N. *The Coherence of EU Free Movement Law: Constitutional Responsibility and the Court of Justice* (Oxford: Oxford University Press, 2013).

Nicolaides, P. 'New limits to the concept of selectivity: the birth of a "general exception" to the prohibition of State aid in EU competition law', *Journal of European Competition Law & Practice* 6 (2015) 315–23.

Nihoul, P. 'Freedom of choice: the emergence of a powerful concept in European competition law' available at SSRN: <http://papers.ssrn.com/sol3/papers.cfm?abstract_id=2077694>.

Nihoul, P. 'The ruling of the General Court in Intel: towards the end of an effect-based approach in European competition law?', *Journal of European Competition Law & Practice* 5 (2014) 521–39.

Nihoul, P and Rodford, P. *EU Electronic Communications Law: Competition and Regulation in the European Telecommunications Market*, 2nd edn. (Oxford: Oxford University Press, 2011).

O'Donohue, R and Padilla, J. *The Law and Economics of Article 102 TFEU* (Oxford: Hart Publishing, 2013).

Odudu, O. 'Economic activity as a limit to Community law', in C Barnard and O Odudu (eds), *The Outer Limits of European Union Law* (Oxford: Hart Publishing, 2009) 225–43.

Odudu, O. *The Boundaries of EC Competition Law: The Scope of Article 81* (Oxford: Oxford University Press, 2006).

Odudu, O. 'The meaning of undertaking within 81 EC', *Cambridge Yearbook of European Legal Studies* 7 (2005) 209–39.

OECD and OCDE. 'Competition and Regulation Issues in the Pharmaceutical Industry', *OECD Journal: Competition Law and Policy* (2002).

Ogus, AI. *Regulation: Legal Form and Economic Theory* (Oxford: Hart Publishers, 2004).

Ortiz Blanco, L (ed.). *EU Competition Procedure*, 3rd edn. (Oxford: Oxford University Press, 2013).

Ortiz Blanco, L. *Market Power in EU Antitrust Law* (Oxford: Hart Publishing, 2011).

Pace, LF and Seidel, K. 'The drafting and the role of Regulation 17: a hard-fought compromise', in KK Patel and H Schweitzer (eds), *The Historical Foundations of EU Competition Law* (Oxford: Oxford University Press, 2013) 54–88.

Parret, L. *Side Effects of the Modernisation of EU Competition Law. Modernisation as a Challenge to the Enforcement System of EU Competition Law and EU Law in General* (Nijmegen: Wolf Legal Publishers, 2011).

Patel, KK and Schweitzer, H (eds). *The Historical Foundations of EU Competition Law* (Oxford: Oxford University Press, 2013).

Pielow, JC, Brunekreeft, G and Ehlers, E. 'Legal and economic aspects of ownership unbundling in the EU', *J World Energy Law Bus* 2 (2009) 96–116.

Poiares Maduro, M. *We the Court: The European Court of Justice and the European Economic Constitution* (Oxford: Hart Publishing, 1998).

Posner, R. *Antitrust Law*, 2nd edn. (Chicago, IL: Chicago University Press, 2001).

Prechal, S and van Roermund, B. *The Coherence of EU Law: The Search for Unity in Divergent Concepts* (Oxford: Oxford University Press, 2008).

Prosser, T. *The Limits of Competition Law: Markets and Public Services* (Oxford: Oxford University Press, 2005).

Ramírez Pérez, SM and van de Scheur, S. 'The evolution of the law on Article 85 and 86 EEC (Articles 101 and 102 TFEU): Ordoliberalism and its Keynesian challenge', in KK Patel and H Schweitzer (eds), *The Historical Foundations of EU Competition Law* (Oxford: Oxford University Press, 2013) 19–54.

Reichelt, D. 'To what extent does co-operation within the European competition network protect the rights of undertakings?', *Common Market Law Review* 42 (2005) 745–82.

Riley, A. 'EC Antitrust modernization: the Commission does very nicely – thank you! Part 1: Regulation 1 and the notification burden', *European Competition Law Review* 24 (2003) 604–15.

Riley, A. 'EC Antitrust modernization: the Commission does very nicely – thank you! Part 2: Between the idea and the reality: Decentralisation under Regulation 1', *European Competition Law Review* 24 (2003) 657–72.

Riley, A. 'The EU reform Treaty and the competition protocol: undermining EC competition law', *European Competition Law Review* 28 (2007) 703–7.

Rose, V and Bailey, D (eds). *Bellamy and Child: European Union Law of Competition*, 2013 edn (Oxford: Oxford University Press, 2013).

Sauter, W. *Competition Law and Industrial Policy in the EU* (Oxford: Oxford University Press, 1997).

Sauter, W. 'Proportionality in EU competition law', *European Competition Law Review* 35 (2014) 327–32.

Sauter, W. *Public services in EU Law* (Cambridge: Cambridge University Press, 2015).

Sauter, W. 'Services of general economic interest and universal service in EU law', *European Law Review* 33 (2008) 167–93.

Sauter, W. *Squaring EU competition Law and industrial Policy: the case of broadband*, TILEC Discussion Paper 17/2013.

Sauter, W. 'Squaring EU competition law and industrial policy: The case of broadband' in JM Beneyto and J Maíllo (eds), *Fostering Growth in Europe: Reinforcing the Internal Market* (Madrid: CEU Ediciones, 2014).

Sauter, W. 'The Altmark package Mark II: New rules for State aid and the compensation of services of general economic interest', *European Competition Law Review* 33 (2012) 307–13.

Sauter, W. 'The economic constitution of the EU', *Columbia Journal of European Law* 27 (1998) 27–68.

Sauter, W. 'The impact of EU competition law on national healthcare systems', *European Law Review* 38 (2013) 457–78.

Sauter, W. 'The notion of Undertaking' (forthcoming) in H Hofmann and C Micheau, *State Aid Law of the EU* (Oxford: Oxford University Press, 2016).

Sauter, W and Schepel, H. *State and Market in European Union Law: The Public and Private Spheres of the Internal Market before the EU Courts* (Cambridge: Cambridge University Press, 2009).

Scharpf, FW. *Community and Autonomy: Institutions, Policies and Legitimacy in Multilevel Europe* (Berlin: Campus, 2010).

Schwarze, J. 'Judicial review of European administrative procedure', *Law and Contemporary Problems* 68 (2004) 85–106.

Schweitzer, H. 'Judicial review in EU competition law', in I Lianos and D Geradin (eds), *Handbook on European Competition Law: Enforcement and Procedure* (Cheltenham: Edward Elgar, 2013) 539–83.

Schweitzer, H. 'The European competition law enforcement system and the evolution of judicial review', in CD Ehlermann and M Marquis (eds), *EUI Competition Law Annual 2009, Evaluation of Evidence and its Judicial Review in Competition Cases* (Oxford: Hart Publishing, 2011) 79–146.

Schweitzer, H and Patel, KK. 'EU competition law in historical context: continuity and change, in KK Patel and H Schweitzer (eds), *The Historical Foundations of EU Competition Law* (Oxford: Oxford University Press, 2013) 207–30.

Simonsson, L. *The Legitimacy of EU Cartel Control* (Oxford: Hart Publishing, 2010).

Siragusa, M. 'A critical review of the White Paper on the reform of the EC competition law enforcement rules', *Fordham International Law Journal* 23 (1999) 1089–127.

Smits, R. 'The European Competition Network: Selected Aspects', *Legal Issues of Economic Integration* 32 (2005) 175–92.

Snyder, F. 'The effectiveness of European Community law: institutions, processes, tools and techniques', *Modern Law Review* 56 (1993) 19–54.

Stevens, S. 'Tax aid and non-profit organizations', *EC Tax Review* 4 (2010) 156–69.

Subiotto, R, Little, DR and Lepetska, R. 'The application of Article 102 TFEU by the European Commission and the European Courts', *Journal of European Competition Law & Practice* 6 (2015) 175–81.

Subiotto, R, Little, DR and Lepetska, R. 'The application of Article 102 TFEU by the European Commission and the European Courts', *Journal of European Competition Law & Practice* 6 (2015) 277–86.

Svetiev, Y. 'Networked competition governance in the EU: centralization, decentralization, or experimentalist architecture?', in C Sabel and J Zeitlin (eds), *Experimentalist Governance in the European Union: Towards a New Architecture* (Oxford: Oxford University Press, 2010) 79–120.

Svetiev, Y. 'Scaling experimentalism: from convergence to informed divergence in transnational competition policy', in J Zeitlin (ed.), *Extending Experimentalist Governance?: The European Union and Transnational Regulation* (Oxford: Oxford University Press, 2015) 169–95.

Szyszczak, E. 'Modernising State aid and the financing of SGEI', *Journal of European Competition Law & Practice* 3 (2012) 332–43.

Szyszczak, E and van de Gronden, JW (eds). *Financing Services of General Economic Interest—Reform and Modernization* (The Hague: TMC Asser Press, 2012).

Talus, K. *EU Energy Law and Policy: A Critical Account* (Oxford: Oxford University Press, 2013).

Talus, K. 'Long-term natural gas contracts and antitrust law in the European Union and the United States', *J World Energy Law Bus* 4 (2011) 260–315.

Talus, K. 'Role of the European Court of Justice in the Opening of Energy Markets', *ERA Forum* 8 (2007) 435–48.

Thaler, RH and Sunstein, CR. *Nudge: Improving Decisions about Health Wealth and Happiness* (London, CT: Yale University Press, 2008).

Tosato, GL and Bellodi, L (eds). *EU Competition Law: Volume I, Procedure: Antitrust—Merger—State Aid*, 2nd edn. (Deventer: Claeys and Casteels, 2014).

Townley, C. 'Co-ordinated diversity: revolutionary suggestions for EU competition law (and for EU law too)', *Yearbook of European Law* 33 (2014) 1–51.

Townley, C. *Article 81 EC and Public Policy* (Oxford: Hart Publishers, Oxford, 2009).

Tridimas, T. *The General Principles of EU Law*, 2nd edn. (Oxford: Oxford University Press, 2006).

Van Bael and Bellis, *Competition Law of the European Community*, 5th edn. (The Hague: Kluwer Law International, 2010).

Vandenborre, I and Goetz, T. 'EU competition law procedural issues', *Journal of European Competition Law and Practice* 5 (2014) 648–55.

Vedder, HHB. 'Of jurisdiction and justification: why competition is good for "non-economic" goals, but may need to be restricted', *The Competition Law Review* 6 (2009) 51–75.

Veljanovski, C. 'Margin squeeze: an overview of EU and national case law' (2012) *e-Competitions: Competition Laws Bulletin* No. 46442, available at: SSRN: <http://ssrn.com/abstract=2079117>.

Venit, J. 'Brave new world: the modernization and centralization of enforcement under Articles 81 and 82 of the EC Treaty', *Common Market Law Review* 40 (2003) 545–80.

Vesterdorf, B. 'Judicial review in EC competition law: reflections on the role of the Community Courts in the EC system of competition law enforcement', *Global Competition Policy* 1 (2005) 3–27.

Vesterdorf, B. 'The Court of Justice and unlimited jurisdiction. What does it mean in practice', *Global Competition Policy* 2 (2009) 139–45.

Viros, D. '*Si.mobil Telekomunikacijske*: the rejection of complaints as tool to manage decentralized enforcement within the ECN', *Journal of European Competition Law & Practice* 6 (2015) 415–17.

Völcker, SB. '*Ignorantia lex non excusat* and the demise of national procedural autonomy in the application of EU competition rules: *Schenker*', *Common Market Law Review* 51 (2014) 1497–520.

Volpin, C. 'The ball is in your court: Evidential burden of proof and the proof-proximity principle in EU competition law', *Common Market Law Review* 51 (2014) 1159–85.

Warlouzet, L. The rise of European competition policy, 1950–1991: A cross-disciplinary survey of a contested policy sphere, EUI Working papers RSCAS 2010/80, available at: <http://cadmus.eui.eu//handle/1814/14694>.

Weiler, JHH. *The Constitution of Europe: 'Do the New Clothes Have an Emperor?' And Other Essays on European Integration* (Cambridge: Cambridge University Press, 1999).

Wesseling, R. 'The Commission's Notices on decentralisation of EC antitrust law: in for a penny, not for a pound', *European Competition Law Review* 18 (1997) 94–7.

Wesseling, R. 'The draft regulation modernizing the competition rules: the Commission is married to one idea', *European Law Review* 26 (2001) 357–78.

Wesseling, R. *The Modernisation of EC Antitrust Law* (Oxford: Hart Publishing, 2000).
Whish, R. 'Editorial. Motorola and Samsung: an effective use of Article 7 and Article 9 of regulation 1/2003', *Journal of European Competition Law and Practice* 8 (2014) 603–4.
Whish, R. '*Intel v Commission*: keep calm and carry on!', *Journal of European Competition Law and Practice* 5 (2014) 1–2.
Wilks, S. 'Agencies, networks, discourses and the trajectory of European competition enforcement', *European Competition Journal* 3 (2007) 437–64.
Wilks, S. 'Agency escape: decentralization or dominance of the European Commission in the modernization of competition policy?', *Governance* 18 (2005) 431–52.
Wilks, S and McGowan, L. 'Disarming the Commission: the debate over a European cartel office', *Journal of Common Market Studies* 33 (1995) 259–73.
Wils, W. *Efficiency and justice in European antitrust enforcement* (Oxford: Hart Publishing, 2008).
Wils, W. 'Ten years of Regulation 1/2003—A Retrospective', *Journal of European Competition Law & Practice* 4 (2013) 293–301.
Wils, WPJ. 'Optimal Antitrust Fines: Theory and Practice', *World Competition* 29 (2006) 183–208.
Wils, WPJ. 'The Increased Level of EU Antitrust Fines, Judicial Review and the ECHR', *World Competition* 33 (2010) 15–29.
Wils, WPJ. 'The Judgment of the EU General Court in Intel and the So-Called More Economic Approach to Abuse of Dominance', *World Competition* 37 (2014) 405–34.
Zimmer, D (ed.). *The Goals of Competition Law*, papers of the 5th ASCOLA conference (Cheltenham: Edward Elgar, 2012).

Index

The manufacturer's authorised representative in the EU for product safety is Oxford University Press España S.A. of el Parque Empresarial San Fernando de Henares, Avenida de Castilla, 2 – 28830 Madrid (www.oup.es/en or product.safety@oup.com). OUP España S.A. also acts as importer into Spain of products made by the manufacturer.

www.ingramcontent.com/pod-product-compliance
Lightning Source LLC
LaVergne TN
LVHW011914200926
848484LV00002B/621
* 9 7 8 0 1 9 8 7 4 9 1 5 8 *